ALEXANDRE DUMAS

ALEXANDRE DUMAS

Genius of Life

———◆•◆•◆———

CLAUDE SCHOPP

Translated by A. J. Koch

FRANKLIN WATTS
New York • Toronto
1988

To Julien

First published in France in 1986 by Editions Mazarine
Translation copyright © 1988 by Franklin Watts, Inc.
All rights reserved
PRINTED IN THE UNITED STATES OF AMERICA

6 5 4 3 2 1

Design by Tere LoPrete

Library of Congress Cataloging-in-Publication Data

Schopp, Claude.
  [Alexandre Dumas, le génie de la vie. English]
  Alexandre Dumas / by Claude Schopp ; translated by J.M. Koch.
    p. cm.
  Translation of: Alexandre Dumas, le génie de la vie.
  Includes index.
  ISBN 0-531-15093-3
    1. Dumas, Alexandre, 1802–1870—Biography. 2. Authors,
French—19th century—Biography. I. Title.
PQ2230.S3613 1988
843'.7—dc19   88-26136
                                                        CIP

Contents

PART
I

O Youth, Spring
of Life

I

Portrait of His Father

Villers-Cotterêts was a small town in Valois, "whose white houses, grouped in the curve of a horseshoe formed by its immense forest, resembled a bird's nest that the church, with its long-necked spire, dominated and watched like a mother."

During the evening of July 23, 1802, unusual comings and goings were noticed along the Rue de Lormet: Viton had been seen walking rapidly up the street, then returning with Jean-Joseph Lécosse, the young physician, while Mère Petitfie, the pastry seller, had gone to fetch Mère Crescence, the midwife.

Nothing was kept secret in the small town: Marie-Louise, the daughter of Claude Labouret, ex-owner of the Hôtel de l'Epée, was in labor. She had married that big mulatto general of the Republic, who returned in such bad shape after his capture by the King of Naples.

The labor lasted until dawn. The new-born, with much turning and twisting, caught his neck in his umbilical cord. When he appeared, purple and half-strangled, he was only capable of expelling a kind of growl, but a few tricks of Dr. Lécosse's magic hands exorcised the diabolic apparition; it was only a healthy, chubby baby.

The same day, the infant's grandfather, Claude Labouret, registered the birth at the town hall of Villers-Cotterêts:

On the fifth day of the month of Thermidor, in the tenth year of the French Republic [July 24, 1802]. Certificate of birth for Alexandre Dumas, born today at five-thirty in the morning, son of Alexandre Davy-Dumas, Division General, born at Jérémie, on the coast of San Domingo, and of Marie-Louise Labouret, his spouse, born at the said Villers-Cotterêts. The sex of the child has been certified as masculine. . . .

The birth of a boy cheered a family seemingly destined to have only girls. Marie-Louise, the only daughter of Claude Labouret, had borne thus far two daughters: Marie-Alexandrine-Aimée on September 18, 1793 and Louise-Alexandrine (who died after a year) on February 14, 1796. In the war-torn France of 1802, to bear only daughters was almost dishonorable.

It is easy, therefore, to understand the pride of the General when he announced Alexandre's birth to the future Maréchal Brune, his old companion in arms:

I hasten to announce to you, my dear Brune, my wife's happy delivery of a big boy who weighs 10.5 pounds and is nearly 20 inches long. You see, I hope, that unless this child has an accident, he won't be a pigmy when he is twenty-five. This is not all, my friend, you must prove to me that you are enough of a friend to accept being his godfather along with my daughter. There is no hurry, since the child is in good health and my daughter will be here in a month's time when she takes her vacation. Adieu . . . you have no better friend than A. Dumas. My wife sends a thousand sincere thoughts to yours. Assure her, please, of my respect. If it is not asking too much of Madame Brune, she would give us great pleasure by accompanying you.

In a re-writing of this letter in *Mes Mémoires*, Dumas embellished it with a phallic boast. "The fellow has just peed way over his head. It is a good omen, I'd say!" which, though apocryphal, was nonetheless prophetic.

Ten-and-a-half pounds, nearly twenty inches long. His son's birth was a rebirth for the General who felt his own life ebbing. The child, who bore his first name, could grow as tall as the six-and-a-half feet recorded on the General's enlistment papers.

Général Brune, who had seen five of his own little daughters die, refused the role of godfather and so Claude Labouret became godfather to his grandson who was christened on August 12. Brune, however, remained the preferred godfather. Dumas even forged a procuration which made Brune godfather in spite of his refusal to accept the role.

The General's wife was proud of her son: the little quadroon had elegantly curling blond hair which would not frizzle until very much later, and he had her superb sapphire-blue eyes. The little boy's first playmate was Charmante, his grandfather's dog. Every moonless night Charmante trotted to the café tended by Mademoiselle Waffart and Monsieur Camberlin to carry a lantern to her master, a fanatic dominos player. Thus, the old man could safely return to the Rue de Lormet.

The boy attracted the admiration of neighboring women and brought joy to his Deviolaine cousins, Léontine, Quartidi (called Eléonore), Cécile and Augustine. The older ones were ten and fourteen and were in a boarding school at Soissons, but the younger ones, two and five, handled the big baby like a doll, much to the alarm of Madame Dumas.

When he wrote *Mes Mémoires* and tried to shed some light on the first shadowy days of his life, Dumas highlighted only the days spent at the small château Les Fossés that his ailing father had rented in 1803 or 1804. At the end of a path coming from the village of Haramont, surrounded by moat and forest, the château retained a tower from the fifteenth century. The main floor kitchen was the child's favorite place. He would clutch the skirts of Marie, the kitchen maid, to beg for sweets. Next to the fireplace, three steps led to the dining room with its pine floor and wooden wainscoting painted gray.

In this solitude of trees and water, Alexandre's world was populated with Truffle, a big, black dog that he often used to ride (and which caused him grief only when it died in 1805)....the General's black valet who, when asked to bring pots of flowers inside, emptied them first so that they would occupy less space, and who opened the door of the bird cage under the logical assumption that the cage smelled of stale air ... Pierre, the gardener, who pleased Alexandre by catching frogs and garden snakes in the moat and the wet grass . . . and Mocquet, the guard, an inexhaustible teller of fantastic stories, who suspected that Mère Durand of Haramont was causing him nightmares. And then there was the snake that Pierre split in two with a shovel and out of which came a frog, barely stunned; and there was Hippolyte who, aided by the General, saved from drowning three young men of Villers-Cotterêts who had come to swim in the moat of the château to cool off in the summer heat. Madame Dumas delivered to them all a short sermon on the danger of water—but her son had eyes only for his father and his marvelously sculptured physique, "cast, it seemed, from a composite mold of the statues of Hercules and Antinouis." The image of the General, "naked, dripping with water and smiling benevolently, like a man who had just accomplished a feat that made him an equal to God— he had just saved the life of another man," was imprinted never to be retouched.

In Paris another "god" created himself. Between the child's birth and his baptism in 1802, Napoléon Bonaparte had made himself Lifetime Consul. In 1804 he proclaimed himself Emperor of the French at a coronation ceremony worthy of grand opera. Général Dumas sensed that Bonaparte's glory rang a death knell on his illusions for payment of his pension arrears. Napoléon, Commander-in-Chief of the Egyptian Campaign (1798–99), never would forget that Général Dumas had once doubted his Commander's destiny. The General's desperate letters of appeal to Napoléon remained unanswered. The First Consul had not forgotten the resentment of the General in Chief.

Général Dumas, eligible for his retirement pension on Fructidor 26, year X, was no longer listed on the roster of the Division Generals of the Republic. Bonaparte assigned him a military death long before the illness caught in Neapolitan jails caused his natural end. The family left the paradise of Les Fossés for a much more modest house located at Antilly, near Betz. The General saw his income diminished; it was not yet poverty, but it was already penury.

In the ensuing months, the General's health faltered. In September of 1805 he went to Senlis to consult Dr. Duval. Like a daguerreotype badly developed, this trip left only vague shadows in the memory of the child. The illness was so grave that Dr. Duval referred the General to higher authority for a second opinion: Jean-Nicolas Corvisart, first physician of Napoléon. The family left for Paris on September 18 and stayed with Michel-Séraphin Dollez, ex-surgeon of the Army of the North, whose wife Manette had probably not been indifferent to the General's athletic figure when he served in the same army as her husband.

The family's first visit was to Aimée, the eldest daughter, who was nine years old and had been accepted in the excellent boarding pension of Madame de Mauclerc and Mademoiselle Ryan. The Abbé Jacques Conseil, another cousin of Madame Dumas and ex-governor of the pages of Louis XVI, had been influential in the acceptance. The little savage of the château Les Fossés reluctantly accepted the pettings of the young boarders; he dealt them countless blows with feet and fists which hit, among others, the future Comtesse Houdetot and the future Duchesse d'Osmond.

The trip to Paris left such a vivid impression in the memory of the three-year-old child that one can only wonder at the authenticity of these recollections: those small gold circlets, then so much in fashion, which Alexandre allowed to be hung from his ears in exchange for a big apricot; the visit to the venerable Marquise de Montesson, widow of the Duc d'Orléans; the evening at the Opéra-Comique.

The next day, Maréchaux Brune and Murat, whose epaulettes within a few weeks would shine with the sun of the decisive French victory at Austerlitz, were invited to the Corvisart house for lunch. During the meal, the child stared out the window at an immense kite that floated gracefully above the windmills of Montmartre. Suddenly, his father called him, thrust Maréchal Brune's sword between his legs and pulled down the two-cornered hat of Murat on his head: a grotesque and touching ritual of knighting. Did the warrior, who felt himself dying, want thus to pledge his son to war and glory?

In spite of the reassuring words of Corvisart, Général Dumas knew that death, which he had so often defied on the battlefield, awaited him. He had invited Brune and Murat to lunch in order to trust to them the soon-to-be widow and orphan. "With death both in his soul and his body," Général Dumas returned to Villers-Cotterêts on September 26.

Winter came and death was on the prowl. The Dumas family had retired to Haramont, a small hamlet near Villers. The General kept to his bed more often and brooded over the prospect of eternal rest. After Napoléon's December 2 victory, he requested that his bones be mingled with those of his old companions-in-arms who had fallen on the battlefield of Austerlitz. In death he would participate in the glory that Bonaparte had refused him during life. On February 16, 1806, Général Dumas left Haramont for good and settled at the Hôtel de l'Epée, located on Grande-Rue de Soissons, managed by a friend of the family—Charles-François-Eléonor Picot, called Picot de l'Epée. Pain riveted him to his bed—he was dying of stomach cancer, the same ailment to claim Bonaparte fifteen years later.

On the 25th, to help him forget his pains, he attempted a horseback-ride but soon had to admit defeat. He returned to his bed and did not rise again. Most probably the servants of the hotel spread straw in the courtyard so that the loud noise of the carriages would not disturb the dying man. While Madame Dumas ran to fetch Dr. Lécosse, a neighbor, Julie-Eléonore Darcourt, watched over the General and listened to him complain of dying in his bed like a coward. His mind wandered: he asked that someone go to Duguet, the jeweler who had a shop across from the hotel. He wanted the golden knob of his cane melted down immediately.

At ten o'clock he asked for a priest. Jean-Chrysostome Grégoire, curate of Villers, heard his confession. For what could he reproach himself, except a remnant of hatred for Berthier and for Bonaparte, who had driven him to almost complete poverty? He wanted to see his son once more but he changed his mind. "No, poor child! He is sleeping, do not wake him up." Moments after his confession, he died in his wife's arms.

Midnight had just rung—it was February 26, 1806.

But where was the child during this tragic commotion? Marie-Françoise-Pétronille Fortier, a cousin whom Alexandre called "Maman Zine," had taken him with her to the house of her father, François, the locksmith. The cousins added a bed to the bedroom where a large bed with baldaquin of green baize already stood like a throne.

At eight o'clock, cousin Marianne came to fetch the child to put him to bed. At midnight a loud blow on the door awoke both Marianne and Alexandre. Frightened, Marianne saw Alexandre get out of his bed.

"Where are you going, Alexandre?" she cried. "Where are you going?"

"As you can see very well," he answered quietly, "I am going to open the door for Papa who has come to tell us goodbye."

Marianne, bewildered, succeeded in putting back to bed the child who struggled and cried: "Adieu, Papa! Adieu, Papa!"

The next day someone told him, "My poor child, your father who loved you so much is dead."—He died at midnight when the loud knock struck at the door.

Alexandre did not cry. He asked: "What does that mean?"

—It means that you won't see him any more . . .
—And why should I not see him any more?
—Because God has taken him back . . .
—And where does God live?
—He lives in heaven.

Unwatched for a moment, the child escaped from his uncle's house. He ran to the Hôtel de l'Epée, took a gun belonging to his father, and climbed to the first floor. There he met his mother, in tears, on the landing of the dead man's room.

"Where are you going?" she asked, surprised to see him there.

—I am going to heaven!
—What, you are going to heaven?
—Yes, let me pass.
—And what are you going to do in heaven, my poor child?
—I am going to kill God who has killed Papa.

Madame Dumas' tears doubled. She hugged her son, almost smothering him:

"Oh, do not say those things, my child, we are unhappy enough now." Later, Alexandre would write:

I adored my father. Perhaps, at that age, this feeling that I call love today [1850] was only a naive awe for the Herculean physique and gigantic strength that I had seen him display on several occasions; perhaps, again, it was only a childish and proud admiration for his embroidered clothes, for his tricolor egret feathers and for his huge sword that I could hardly lift.

But, regardless, even today the remembrance of my father, each curve of his body and each feature of his face, is as present for me as if I had lost him yesterday; so much so, that today I love him still, I love him with a love as tender, as profound and as real as if he had watched over my youth, and as if I had had the happiness to pass from youth to adolescence leaning on his powerful arm.

The General rests in the cemetery of Villers-Cotterêts. His image was magnified in the remembrance of his widow, and Alexandre was confronted incessantly with this ideal. His father would be his first and his most permanent model of conduct. The son ardently desired glory so he could share it with the elder Alexandre Dumas, the hero of the battles of camp de Maulde and the Pyramids.

II

The Gospel of Childhood

The death of the General accelerated the family's financial distress. In vain, Madame Dumas multiplied her pleading letters. The answer came that no pension would be paid since the General was not on active duty at the time of his death. As for Napoléon, he would not receive petitioners. The General carried to his grave his miserable four thousand francs of retirement pension.

On May 10, 1806, a guardian was named for the orphans. He was Jacques Collard, lord of the manor of Villers-Hellon who, it was said, had married the bastard daughter of Philippe-Egalité and Madame de Genlis. The next year he entered the *Corps Législatif*. This protection was not negligible. However, the Dumas family had to leave Antilly and the house in the Rue de Lormet to take refuge near Claude Labouret, Alexandre's grandfather, who had rented the quarters in which the General died at the Hôtel de l'Epée. There the family lived, surrounded by the souvenirs of the deceased. The family had increased, too, for the oldest sister, Aimée, had been recalled to Villers-Cotterêts. The fee of twelve hundred francs at her boarding school was far beyond the means of the widow.

The orphaned Alexandre became everybody's pet—friends and neighbors, the Darcourts, the Deviolaines, the Collards. Madame Darcourt's daughter, Claude-Eléonore, at twenty decided to remain celibate and she soon took the place of Maman Zine, whom death carried off on May 2, 1807. While Madame Dumas went on her daily pilgrimage to the cemetery, Eléonore gave Alexandre a big book by Buffon. He immersed himself in the marvelous illustrations, fascinated, in spite of his fear, by the toads and snakes. Perhaps it was from Buffon that the child learned to read. He wanted to discover the habits and instincts of the animals portrayed. One evening, he learned from the *Journal de l'Empire* that a snake had devoured a prisoner in the jails of Amiens. From then on the pictures in Buffon became animated and threatening to the child; terror overtook him, a primeval fear became confused with reality.

The tenderness of women surrounded the child at the house of the Darcourts . In contrast, a masculine authority reigned at the house of Jean-Michel Deviolaine. The master of the house, over six feet tall, with small eyes shadowed by enormous eyebrows and thin, long lips, was about as sociable as the boars that he oversaw as forest inspector. Although he was rude and strict, his house was gracious, with waterfalls and weeping willows in its English garden, and with pear, peach, and plum trees in the orchard. Beyond were the triumphal oaks and centenary beech trees in the park of the château built by François I. Against the horizon were the endless green waves of the forest.

It was a paradise regained for the child who used to run in the parks of Les Fossés and Antilly. The older cousins, Victor, Léontine and Eléonore, looked down with the condescension of adults on the little Alexandre but the younger ones, Cécile and Félix, were his playmates in games that were continued during the summer at the old abbey of Saint-Rémy which Deviolaine had repurchased in 1804.

How many childhood remembrances of the townhouse and of the house in the fields stayed with Alexandre! It was Monsieur Deviolaine who succeeded in coaxing away a swarm of bees which had unluckily fallen into the boy's half-open shirt, by talking to the bees with honeyed sweetness and smiling graciously on them—a unique event, this smile on the surly face of the Inspector. It was again Deviolaine who, with a pole, cut the Gordian knot of two long garden snakes entwined near the ruins of the turret of Saint-Rémy. The hero of these feats inspired affection and dread. "He is the man . . . I loved the most after my father," wrote Dumas. *After* meant intensity, but also indicated the succession. Deprived of a father, Alexandre thrust his need for protection upon another Hercules, one who tamed and charmed the animals. The substitution seemed natural since all the children around him called Monsieur Deviolaine "Papa."

Nine miles from Villers-Cotterêts, his guardian's château also welcomed the child. Jacques Collard, a smiling fifty-year-old, was a vivid contrast to his intimate friend Deviolaine. Villers-Hellon was a nest of swans: Herminie, alleged daughter of Philippe-Egalité, had given three girls to Jacques Collard. In 1807, Edmée-Caroline-Fortunée-Alexis was ten years old; Hermine-Emma was eight; Louise-Félicie-Jacqueline was five. Their brother, Paul-Maurice, was six.

But the distance between Villers-Hellon and Villers-Cotterêts was much more than nine miles: it was the difference between wealth and poverty. For Jacques Collard was rich, a Deputy, and through alliance, related to royalty, albeit illegitimately. He allowed his ward, however, to play with his children and he lent Alexandre the magnificent Bible from which Alexandre learned sacred history.

The houses of the Darcourts, the Deviolaines and the Collards formed the three points of Alexandre's enchanted childhood triangle. No remembrance they evoked could be dated; it was as though time stood still while the child rooted himself in a primordial landscape from which he would later draw the essence of his vitality.

Although only a poor relative to the Deviolaines and the Collards, Alexandre astonished the neighborhood with the extent of his knowledge. High as a squire's boot, dressed with a jacket of Indian cotton that he wore till he was fifteen, he expressed his opinions on everything with a strength gained from his reading of the Bible, Buffon, *Robinson Crusoe*, and above all, the *Lettres à Émilie sur la mythologie* by Demoustier who had died only a short distance away. So much knowledge did not go without conceit, however. One day when he presumed to advise Monsieur Deviolaine not to read the gazette in which there was "nothing important, only a session of the Corps Législatif," the Inspector's boot brought him back to a bit more humility.

Alexandre's erudition received a much warmer welcome from some older devout women, particularly Jeanne-Catherine Pivert. Mademoiselle Pivert, who never tired of listening to him tell sacred or profane stories, died on September 16, 1825 at the Villers-Cotterêts hospital. Over eighty, she died too soon to know that she had been the first audience of a famous dramatic author. Admiringly, she asked to have access to the library of the young savant who loaned her a volume of *Mille et une nuits*, the one that contained the tale of *La lampe merveilleuse*. After reading it, she demanded the next volume, but as it was one of an incomplete set, Alexandre had no other alternative than to loan her again the first volume about the lamp. This transaction was renewed each week, punctually for one year. When Alexandre finally decided to ask her whether the *Mille et une nuits* still amused her, the old lady naively answered:

"Prodigiously, my little friend, but you, who are so smart, could perhaps tell me something . . . , why are they all called Aladdin?"

Madame Dumas realized that, in spite of the compliments she received from her neighbors, the education of Alexandre needed to be more complete. He would become a violinist. The choice of a master was quickly made for there was only one in Villers-Cotterêts: Antoine-Nicolas Hiraux, a Hoffmanesque figure, scraggy and grimacing, topped with a black silk cap that he pulled down over his ears when his pupil exceeded the acceptable limits of squeaking. In the three years during which he endeavored to initiate Alexandre to the rudiments of violin, he had innumerable opportunities to pull down his silk cap. He honestly told Madame Dumas that Alexandre's aversion was too great to cherish hope—after three years of relentless fighting, the pupil still did not know how to tune his violin.

The child grew up in the gentleness of provincial life. The reports from the Grande Armée which filled the *Journal de l'Empire* built up a heroic fable which was no more nor less marvelous than biblical stories or mythological legends. Alexandre was five at the victory of Friedland, six at the meeting of Erfurt, seven at the victory of Wagram, eight for the marriage of Napoléon and Marie-Louise, nine at the birth of the king of Rome. All mothers brought up their sons while praying that soon the wars would end.

Claude Labouret died September 30, 1809. He had complained of violent pains in his side and had taken to his bed. Just as three years before, Alexandre was taken away and entrusted to the Lepages, the glazier. Claude Labouret died the very day of his sixty-sixth birthday, leaving Marie-Louise nearly destitute and in utter solitude. In fact, Marie-Louise's father, the once thriving owner of the Hôtel de l'Écu de France, and a major in the National Guard of his native town, had been unable to overcome a slump in business.

He had to sell his hotel after having dispersed the furniture by auction. What was left to his daughter? Forty-five acres of land and a house purchased from an artillery ex-major, Nicolas Harlet, against the payment of an annuity. Obstinately, the major lived until 1820.

In this little town in Valois, where everybody knew his neighbor's social position, the widow and two orphans remained in uncertain social status: "Composed of both aristocratic and commoner elements . . . aristocratic from my father, commoner from my mother," Alexandre wrote much later in his diary *Le mois* (1849). By simplifying, Dumas stretched the truth in calling his father aristocratic. No doubt, he was the son of Alexandre-Antoine Dumas Davy de La Pailleterie, an impoverished Normand squire in search of adventure, but he was also the son of Marie-Césette Dumas, a black slave of Saint-Domingo. Eventually recognized by his father, the mulatto Thomas-Alexandre Dumas Davy de La Pailleterie belonged as much to slavery as to nobility. On the eve of the Revolution, he was nothing more than the legitimized scion of a salacious and cynical adventurer, who unhesitatingly had sold three of his children—the brothers and sisters of Thomas-Alexandre—in order to return to France and claim his inheritance. It was the Revolution that had given Dumas his letters of nobility, raising him to the rank of General of Division. The aristocracy of the Dumas', or rather of the Davy de La Pailleteries, was not pure fiction. The family had its arms, its château at Bielleville-en-Caux and its proof of nobility registered in 1710 and 1712. But Alexandre-Antoine had none of the qualities of the eighteenth-century gentleman that his grandson depicted in *Mes mémoires*. He was an adventurer who had broken with the class of his birth; himself fallen, he fathered a racial and social bastard, the Général Dumas.

Was Marie-Louise Labouret, Dumas' mother, a commoner? Again, desirous of antithesis, Dumas betrayed reality. Claude Labouret, former majordomo of the Ducs d'Orléans in their Villers-Cotterêts château, belonged to the better class of servants but his marriage with Marie Prévôt introduced him into the petite bourgeoisie of trade. On the eve of the Revolution, he belonged to the ascending class who had called for reforms. By 1790, he was the Commandant of the Villers-Cotterêts National Guard. Only business failures interrupted the ascent of those like Deviolaine, the son of a candle-merchant, who knew how to get to the top. Where should the young Alexandre be placed in this great shake-up of society? The death of the General dissolved any imaginary attachment to the displaced nobility and the glory of arms. The child had ancestors worth a mention in the chronicles of the past and a legendary father, but he was condemned to a slow impoverishment imposed on him by his maternal family. Alexandre was a child with no expectations. In the little town, impoverishment and its parade of humiliations could not be concealed. To lose his social status while surrounded by equals who steadily climbed the social ladder inspired Alexandre with a secret desire for future revenge.

Soon, Alexandre was merely the son of Marie-Louise Labouret. The destitution, the tears, and the confusion of his mother imprinted a shade of melancholy on that spring in Villers-Cotterêts. After the grandfather's death they had to leave the Hôtel de l'Epée for a small house in the Rue de Lormet, a few steps from his birthplace; even small provincial boroughs had a geography of status. Madame Dumas had not enough money to put on their grave the stone of which she dreamed. Seeing only the past, she survived to bring up her children. She provided a master of arms for her son. A kindly drunkard, Père Mounier gave lessons in the old château, now a shelter for beggars from the city of Paris, where he was a boarder. Alexandre handled épées and swords much better than a violin bow. He would always panic from fear of heights but he promised to be brave.

He was ten now, and it was necessary to arrange for his intellectual education. The preceding year, 1811, Jean-Chrysostome Grégoire, the curate who attended the dying General, had opened a school which in Villers-Cotterêts was, by courtesy, called a college.

When young Alexandre Dumas presented himself on the threshold of the small college, he was rather a pretty child. He still had his long, blond, curly hair falling on his shoulders, large sapphire eyes, a straight, small and rather well-molded nose, thick lips, pink and attractive, teeth rather badly aligned but glittering and lastly, a dazzling-white complexion which Madame Dumas claimed was an effect of the brandy the General had made her drink during her pregnancy. His character, however, did not correspond to his physical features. He was spoiled, vain, roguish, insolent, and self-confident.

One morning in October, Madame Dumas outfitted his long frame, skinny as a bean-pole, with a light-brown suit cut from an ancient frock coat of Claude Labouret. When he reached the college in the Rue de Soissons in the premises of the Hostellerie du Lion d'Argent, its court seemed empty. He had hardly passed through the archway when a cascade poured down upon him from the bladders of college pranksters who, perched on barrels, showered their future comrade. Naturally inclined to whimper, Alexandre added his tears to the offering. He was streaming wet when the Abbé Grégoire, returning from mass, discovered him. The Abbé, who had a strong hand, gave the culprits forty whacks and assigned them three hundred verses to copy for the next morning.

A squealer has much to fear, and, indeed, the frustrated pupils had chosen their champion. It was François-Hippolite Bligny, son of the clothier on the Place de la Fontaine. After class, he waited for Alexandre. His coat was off, his sleeves were rolled up. Greeted with hoots, the General's son conquered his fear by exhorting himself to fight like a Homeric hero. He fought with determination. Bligny retreated. The victorious boy, now applauded, picked up his own book and one of those of his vanquished opponent which had slipped from the latter's vest, and returned, head high, to the Rue de Lormet.

No doubt, Madame Dumas did not glance at the book that her son had filched from Bligny; she would have been horrified. It was *L'Onanisme, ou dissertation sur les maladies produites par la masturbation* by Tissot. An old book from 1760, it was not yet timely for young Alexandre, but read two years later, would be "providential,"—then giving through veiled words, information about his sexual awakening.

College life, save for pranks, impositions and punishments, had hardly any advantages, except to point the child toward adolescence. He knew little when he entered the college, he would know little more when he left, except some rudiments of Latin.

Napoléon had entered Moscow. How many of his soldiers were buried on the battlefield of the Moskowa? So many distant deaths were only counted as statistics. But the death of one adolescent dismayed all the inhabitants of Villers-Cotterêts. Eléonor-Stanislas Picot, son of the farmer of Noue, returning from hunting, forgot to unload his gun; his dog put his paw on the trigger. The shot hit Stanislas in the leg. Alexandre was present when the surgeon attended to the horrible wound. Three days later a tetanus infection caused the adolescent's death. Madame Dumas wept with Marie-Anne Picot; life had taught her how to weep. She never again saw her own son go hunting without exhortations to be careful.

Madame Dumas' apprehensions were useless: Alexandre dreamed only of hecatombs of wild game. Circumstances were in his favor, however. A new character joined the family. He was called Joseph-Marie-Victor Letellier and was twenty-six years old. He belonged, as did his father, to the Administration des Droits Réunis. He was in love with Aimée Dumas. To court her, he offered her younger brother a pocket-pistol, the first firearm for Dumas who would later on furnish Devisme, the firearms seller, with a steady income. Alexandre got hold of a powder-horn and, in the park of the château, let go a volley of shots which ended only with his last grain of powder. Informed of this firing exercise, her mind still impressed by Stanislas Picot's accident, Madame Dumas called the authorities. Tournemolle, the gamekeeper, came to disarm Alexandre—not without a fight—but authority remained with the law.

In *Mes mémoires* Dumas placed this episode at the eve of Malet and Lahorie's unsuccessful "coup d'état" against Napoléon on October 23, 1812. The parallel between the situations (disarmament of Alexandre; disarmament of the conspirators) tied private history with actual history and corresponded perhaps more to the necessities of Dumas' narration than to strict chronology. Alexandre's firing the shots in the middle of an admiring circle of children from Villers-Cotterêts seemed a parody of the military epic that unfolded in the snows of Russia. Napoléon had left Moscow on October 14, leaving remains of his Grande Armée at each stone marker on the interminable road that brought him back to Paris.

In this disaster, Alexandre was born again—at least his name was. On July 24, 1802 Alexandre Dumas was born; on April 27, 1813, a judgment of the *Tribunal Civil de Première Instance* in Soissons certified he was Alexandre Dumas Davy de La Pailleterie, son of Thomas-Alexandre Dumas Davy de La Pailleterie. On May 7, the rectification was posted on the register of civil certificates of Villers-Cotterêts. It was not only a certificate that was rectified, it was an attempt to give a direction to a life. With this certificate, the boy with the pistol entered the nobility that Napoléon had reorganized on May 1, 1808.

Although Marie-Louise Dumas clutched at such relics of former splendor, this could not hide the family's true misery. She had to see her daughter married without a dowry. Moreover, the *Contrôleur principal des droits Réunis* of Soissons, Antoine-Marie-Pierre Letellier and his wife, Barbe Capitan, opposed the marriage of their son Victor to Aimée Dumas, even if she, too, were a Davy de la Pailleterie. But Victor was very much in love, and after fulfilling the legal forms required to proceed without his parents' consent, he married Aimée on June 3, 1813. On the register, after the signature of the family's friends, there trailed the humble name of her young brother, who signed simply Alex Dumas—first appearance of a signature which would later appear throughout the world on the covers of thousands of volumes.

Once his sister married, Alexandre remained his mother's only concern. Abbé Grégoire had abandoned teaching and closed the "petit collège." But, for the modest sum of six francs a month, he continued to force Alexandre to learn what little Latin he could. An elementary school teacher, Jean-Baptiste-Honoré Oblet, was in charge of arithmetic and calligraphy. Though Alexandre would never be good with figures, and was satisfied with knowing how to subtract, he was eager to emulate his teacher's magnificent handwriting, and traced freehand not only letters but ornaments, hearts, rosettes and decorative swirls. Alexandre sharpened three or four pens, with large, medium, and fine points, and on a beautiful sheet of white paper, he fashioned the thick, bold and thin strokes. It took hardly three months to equal, even to surpass, the good Papa Oblet.

Madame Dumas was not indifferent to this talent, but she would have preferred that he make more progress in arithmetic. "Writing, writing!" she muttered. "What is the merit in writing well! All imbeciles write well."

She used Bonaparte as an example, for his letters to the General had been illegible. Oblet, the sophist, retorted that if Bonaparte had better handwriting, his marshals would have better understood and carried out his orders. How many failures would have then been avoided!

At that time, the Imperial Eagle's wings were already clipped: the accord between Napoléon and France was deteriorating. The Corsican had been defeated at Leipzig (October 16–19, 1813) and in January 1814, Napoléon's allies deserted him and, joining the opposition, crossed borders that had been secure since the battle of

Valmy. Victory no longer acted as a soporific that made one forget the horrors of war, although a few unexpected battles were won again at Montmirail and at Champauvert.

The cannons had not yet been heard at Villers-Cotterêts but everybody knew that they were approaching. The inhabitants were getting ready for the invasion. Soissons surrendered on February 13. Madame Dumas put linen, furniture, and mattresses down in the cellar. In her garden, she buried thirty old gold coins and threw herself into concocting an enormous mutton stew which, she hoped, would soften the ferocious Cossacks of the Don, Volga, and Borysthene whose horrifying image propaganda posters had spread all over the country. As an added precaution, she had even reserved a place in a quarry that opened its labyrinth six hundred feet from the farm of Noue.

Anxiously, they waited for the Cossacks, but it was Maréchal Mortier, Duc de Trévise—an exhausted commander-in-chief—with his army corps of beardless young soldiers nicknamed "Marie-Louises" after Napoléon's wife that arrived instead. In the evening, the Duke dined at Deviolaine's who, that afternoon, had accompanied the commander to reconnoiter the forest, his tricolor cockade on his hat and blunderbuss in his saddle holster. The Marshal, who had known Général Dumas in better times, took Alexandre on his lap and patted him. At midnight the enemy reached the park of the Château and captured the French artillery. At dawn the Marshal abandoned Villers-Cotterêts.

The French army had gulped down the mutton stew and the wine from Soissons intended for the Cossacks so Madame Dumas bought from Nicolas-Louis Mauprivez enough mutton to prepare a second propitiatory stew. She let it simmer on low heat, but the Cossacks did not arrive and the Dumases ate mutton stew morning and night.

On the third day of March 1814, while she prepared her third stew, horsemen erupted at full gallop through Rue de Soissons. Shots resounded; Alexandre ran into the street. At the entrance of a shop, a woman wrung her hands. A man's head rested on her daughter's lap. Blood poured from his throat, his back was broken. The Cossacks had shot Jean Ducoudray, the haberdasher, who out of curiosity had opened, then closed his door. "The Cossacks!" cried Madame Dumas, half-crazed with terror, as she swept her son along to the quarry.

All of the people of Villers buried themselves for twenty-four hours, not daring to get near the quarry opening. When they risked poking their heads above the surface again, the Cossacks had disappeared.

Madame Dumas chose to run away. The Dumas family began their exodus in the company of an old hunchback, Mademoiselle Adélaïde, and her valet, Crétet. Should they go to Paris? The thirty gold coins would not be enough money. They spent that first night, March 21, in an inn at Nanteuil-le-Hardouin; very early the next day they took to the road. In some places they heard the cannon. Contradictory rumors circulated: the Comte d'Artois was at Nancy, the Emperor of Austria was at Nogent! Exhausted, the fugitives decided to go no further than Mesnil-Amelot. They had covered twelve miles and were even closer to the theater of action.

The insatiable Adélaïde, who in her later years had known love in the arms of her valet, burned with the desire to discover Paris, where a great parade of the national guard was expected. Madame Dumas no longer had any curiosity, and put herself and Alexandre in the hands of her companions who, on March 26, took them on to Paris. The next day, with fanfares of brass instruments and flags clapping in the wind, fifty thousand national guards swarmed in the court of the Tuileries. The unfortunate and frightened son of Napoléon and Marie-Louise of Austria was brought forth and raised above the guards' heads; a gigantic cry burst from their chests: "Long live the Roi de Rome! Long live the Regency!" They swore loyalty, they promised to die to keep him in Paris.

When the roar died down, a cannon was heard, thundering two miles farther away; and in the Courts of the Tuileries the carriages were ready for flight. So many men assembled together excited the whores who, from the windows of their mezzanines, called to prospective clients with lecherous voices and licentious gestures. Alexandre was surprised, Madame Adélaïde and Crétet laughed lewdly.

Paris was preparing to undergo a siege. As Le Mesnil-Amelot would be included in the radius of attack, a reverse flight began for Alexandre and his mother. Their companions were forgotten by the time they left Le Mesnil. At Nanteuil the travelers heard that the Cossacks had violated the shelter of the quarry of Noue, perpetrating unspeakable abominations in the abetting darkness. Where should they fly? Only the road to Crépy-en-Valois remained open. There they knew Madame de Longpré, widow of a former valet de chambre of Louis XV, who was selling piece by piece a collection of magnificent Chinese porcelain dishes in order to get drunk on brandy. To escape the cramped lodging and the disgusting sight of her perpetual drunkenness, Madame Dumas rented a furnished apartment from Madame Millet. The Millet family were not without their own worries, for their son, a military surgeon, was lost in the general debacle.

Crépy was surrounded by enemy troops, but a small corps of French soldiers camped on the square, guns stacked, horses saddled and bridled. They expected the enemy, who appeared before long. Glued to the garret window that he refused to leave even at the worst part of the skirmish, Alexandre gorged himself on this magnificent and terrible sight, while his mother, who had chosen to die of fear rather than leave her son, huddled in a corner. The Prussian cavalry returned in a whirl of smoke and explosions, bullets ricochetted against the Millet house. The Prussians faced about and hurled themselves into a man-to-man fight. A dozen soldiers fell. Overcome, the Prussian hurricane retreated, pursued by the French, but a few minutes later the retreating hussars reappeared, chased into the midst of a new tempest of men who rushed into the town. Silence followed the squall. The Millets' eldest son, also a surgeon, attended to the wounded with Alexandre clutching the skirt of his coat. He opened the door and a Prussian petty officer who was leaning against it fell into the house. He had received a sword wound in the chest. His name was Farina, a perfumer at Cologne (fourteen years later Dumas would visit him). The wounded piled up in the drawing room which was turned into an infirmary. The women comforted and nursed them while the servants prepared bandages; Millet washed and dressed the wounds and even Alexandre assisted by bringing him basins full of water.

"What's the good of these battles?" declared one of the wounded. "Paris surrendered yesterday."

"It is not true, Paris would not surrender that way," claimed a voice coming from the door. Everyone looked in the direction of the voice. An officer leaned against the threshold. His handsome, martial head showed a hole above the left eyelid, a rivulet of blood ran from it—he died during the night.

A great heroic epic was ending, they believed. Betrayed by Marmont, Napoléon abdicated unconditionally and the Senate recalled the future Louis XVIII, Stanislas-Xavier de Bourbon, Duc d'Artois and surviving brother of Louis XVI. On April 21, he entered Paris triumphantly. On the 17th, at Fontainebleau, Napoléon bade adieux to the Vieille Garde and took the road to Elba.

On April 17, Alexandre and his mother returned to Villers-Cotterêts and the house in the Rue de Lormet. Deviolaine, the firm pillar of the Empire, was getting ready to submit to Louis XVIII. On the church steeples, weather vanes creaked; as they turned, the wind was resolutely royalist.

Alexandre was now twelve. He had seen the collapse of an empire and the underside of the imperial mantle: the sobs of unfortunate mothers whose sons drew the wrong number at conscription and had to leave the workbench or the plow to find faraway deaths that were called heroic; the panic and fright of the populations threatened by the war, who hid or wandered in disorder on the roads; the fury of battles in peaceful small towns; the blood that flowed, the life that fled.

In two months the horrors of war had ravaged the quiet landscape of childhood. Alexandre could not yet write but his eyes had recorded everything. The little garret window of Crépy-en-Valois was the first observatory for the writer. The noise and the furor of the world rose up to him; he opened his ears and eyes widely. Would he not perceive among the hussars, taller than all of them, their Général, a black Hercules who showed a small mole on his right cheek and a raised mark at the left of his forehead? A hero who would throw back the enemy and uphold the falling genius of Bonaparte? But, his father was dead and the world was a bloody melee in which the weak were vanquished.

III
White, Blue, White, Red

France turned to the white flag of the Bourbons; Deviolaine remained the host that he had always been, but Russian officers sat on the chairs formerly reserved for the officers of Maréchal Mortier. Jacques Collard rushed to Paris to see if he could claim an alliance as the Duc d'Orléans' brother-in-law, even if it were the wrong side of the bed. He took all the hopes of the Dumas family to Paris. He brought back the government's concession to run a tobacco shop for the General's widow, but nothing for the young orphan.

On November 18, Abbé Jacques Conseil died at seventy-three years of age. Abbé Conseil was, or rather used to be, rich: former assistant governor of the pages of His Highness Monseigneur le Duc d'Orléans, dean of the members of the Conseil Général of the department of Aisne. From the beginning of the Révolution, he was Mayor of Largny-sur-Automne where he owned the small château of La Muette. He also had a house at Villers-Cotterêts, in the Rue de Lormet. Jacques Conseil was a remote cousin of Madame Dumas, his only heir: he was the widow's last hope. Thus, twice a year, on the first of January and on the feast of Saint-Jacques, she insisted that young Alexandre go to see the irritable old man. Only once was the child rewarded with a small coin.

The opening of the will brought a bitter disappointment: the Abbé left, as expected, some ten thousand pounds income, but six thousand francs were bequested to the hospice of Villers-Cotterêts "in favor of sick inhabitants of Largny." Pensions and properties went to Mademoiselle de Ryan, native of Cork, in Ireland, the very person who managed the boarding school where Aimée Dumas had been educated. Madame Dumas had to be content, all in all, with fifteen hundred francs, a pittance compared with her expectations.

Alexandre was not forgotten: he was given a scholarship at the seminary of Soissons. Alexandre, a seminarian? Why not, thought Madame Dumas who had only one desire: to give the best possible education to her son. But Alexandre rebelled against a fate that his cousin Cécile Deviolaine had promised him a thousand times, the priesthood. He fought for three months, but finally gave up. He gathered together all his small possessions while his mother tried, heroically, to hide her tears. He needed only an inkstand, a beautiful inkstand, made of horn with a hollowed out space for the pens. He ran to the grocer Joseph-Albert Devaux who had promised to give him the inkstand that night. But fate reversed itself that very evening, for his cousin Cécile was in the grocery, and mocked her poor cousin, wishing him a thousand successes in the vocation he embraced and promising him that as soon as he was ordained he would become her confessor. This was too much for Alexandre who threw the inkstand at her head and ran from the grocery, screaming that he would not be a seminarian.

Alexandre bought some bread and salami and ran off to Boudoux. Boudoux was the "Gargantua" of Villers-Cotterêts who, it was rumored, was capable of devouring a whole calf, even its crushed bones, of making twenty-four mouthfuls of twenty-four chickens, of depriving forty dogs of their shares of tripe and bread.

The ogre gave shelter to Alexandre in his hut, near the pond on the road to Compiègne, the ideal site for the kind of bird hunting which was his preferred activity. Alexandre and Boudoux spread glue on small birch branches. Boudoux then mimicked the cries of jays and owls and soon flights of birds landed near the pond where they became stuck on the branches. For three days Alexandre lived as a trapper, his conscience free since he had warned his mother: "Do not worry about me, bonne mère, I am running away because I do not want to be a priest. . . ."

Madame Dumas had obtained her tobacco concession thanks to the influence of Jacques Collard. She opened her shop on the Place de la Fontaine, the main square of Villers, in a space rented from

Lafarge, the kettlemaker. Tobacco was sold at one counter, salt at another one. Alexandre and his mother lived above the shop. In *Mes mémoires*, Dumas had only contempt for the insignificance of this privilege granted to the widow of a hero of the Republic. Madame Dumas had, however, recovered her serenity. With the dazzling days of glory and love now passed, she rediscovered her ancestors' tradesman's traits.

An insistent rumor grew that Napoléon had landed at Golfe Juan on the first of March. "The Dumas' will put their flags out," whispered some busybodies of Villers who, under the first Restoration, accused the widow and her son of Bonapartism, to the mortification of the shopkeeper who feared for her privilege. On March 7, *Le moniteur* confirmed that a well-armed Napoléon had broken through into the department of Var. Everyone in Villers-Cotterêts descended into the streets, forming a rather hostile crowd. Madame Corny, the wife of the hatter, uttered imprecations against the "Corsican bandit." Alexandre and his mother felt threatened and hid. Ten times in the evening gangs of urchins opened the door of the shop with shouts of "Long live the King!"

The people of Villers took their positions in the streets, waiting for carriages, stage coaches, and couriers. On March 15, they saw the Généraux Frédéric and Henri Lallemand pass through. They were being taken to Soissons where they were to be tried: in the name of Napoléon, they had attempted to seize La Fère. Insults were spit at them. In a kindly effort, Madame Dumas succeeded in sneaking her son into the jail of Soissons with two pistols and a roll of fifty gold coins for the brothers Lallemand. The Généraux refused them, saying: "The Emperor will be in Paris before our trial is ended." Alexandre was given the two magnificent pistols as a reward.

Napoléon reentered the Tuileries that Louis XVIII had left in haste.

It was probably in the spring of this unsettled year that Alexandre was called to renew his baptismal vows. Alexandre's piety was anything but edifying. He knew only three prayers: the Pater, the Hail Mary, and the Credo, only in French, and not exactly to the letter. Abbé Grégoire, however, arranged that his pupil obtain the supreme honor of renewing his baptismal vows. Alexandre prepared himself for his solemn communion by devouring the *Lettres d'Héloise à Abélard*.

The night before his communion, Alexandre tossed and turned in his bed, trying to sleep. The idea of communicating with the body of Jesus Christ bothered him: he suddenly felt suffocated and had a continuous desire to cry. "Non dignus sum," he repeated to himself. He was worried, too, by an event the previous afternoon when a child who had not received the sacrament before had been baptized in haste. He was called Maêl, and there were suspicions that he was Jewish. A conditional baptism, of course. Alexandre had been godfather.

On the solemn day, Alexandre was lost in dazed contemplation beside a two-pound candle. When the host touched his lips, he became dizzy, burst into sobs, and fainted. It took him three days to recover from this shattering experience. Abbé Grégoire, suspicious of this excessive ecstasy, would have preferred that it had been less extreme and that it might have lasted.

The vague and bubbling religion of the adolescent would never disappear completely, and would continue in the form of changing moods. Dumas would never again approach the communion table, except at the hour of his death.

The flowers in the vases on the altar had barely faded when the troops began to pass through Villers-Cotterêts. Napoléon's enemies had promised each other not to abandon their arms until the Cossack had been completely crushed. For three weeks the town was transformed into a military camp. Trumpets or drums resounded everyday around four o'clock. The children never tired of the performance and ran toward the clamor to follow these regiments of the *Vieille Garde* they believed had been buried forever: the infantry men wearing their tall fur bonnets and carrying streamers; the dragoons with splendid uniforms; the gunmen, pulling their cannons on their carriages. Alexandre saw all of them pass, right up to the last fragments of the consular guard, the two hundred Mameluks with their baggy red pants, their turbans and their scimitars. Bands played the old republican tunes, but mostly *Veillons au salut de l'Empire*. Seized by patriotic frenzy, Alexandre ran along streets and roads, drunk with glory, himself becoming part of the marching legend.

On June 12, *Le moniteur* announced that Napoléon would take the road the next day. At dawn the townspeople gathered at the edge of the Paris road. With some children of his own age, Alexandre went farther, to a hill from which they could see three miles ahead. The wait lasted until three o'clock in the afternoon when there appeared on the horizon two carriages drawn by six galloping horses. The children pulled back toward the town, crying until they were hoarse: "The Emperor! the Emperor!" Panting, Alexandre had hardly perched himself on the edge of the relay post when the sweating horses stopped to be changed. Postillions with beribboned, white powdered wigs bustled about. Alexandre hardly noticed them: he saw the Emperor, or rather his head and shoulders, framed by the square of his coach door. The head, waxen-pale, was bowed on the chest, the eyes alone held a glimmer of life. He wore a green coat, with small epaulets embroidered with green frogs, and the plaque of the Légion d'Honneur. "Where are we?" he asked his brother Jérôme, seated to his left. "Villers-Cotterêts, six miles from Soissons," answered a voice in the pressing crowd. "Be swift. . . ." The whips snapped, the horses neighed, the apparition faded: it had dazzled the adolescent's eyes for only five minutes. The Emperor was in a hurry. He had an appointment at Waterloo.

Torpor took hold of the town again, until June 20, when three horsemen, their uniforms in rags, arrived. The population surrounded them, pushed them into the court of the City Hall. Were they Westphalians? Polish? They stammered only a few words of French. Pressed, they admitted that they had left Waterloo when the battle was lost. Their news was met with disbelief. They were spies from Prussia. They would be arrested, put in jail, shot. But in fact they were merely the first men to flee a defeated army in confusion. All day other deserters, pale, wounded, disbanded, drifted through Soissons' streets to confirm the June 18th disaster.

Madame Dumas and her son settled in at the post-house where all the news converged. Alexandre looked on a map for the name of Waterloo, and could not find it, as if all the stories he heard were born from the imagination of insane soldiers. At seven o'clock in the evening, however, a mud-covered courier ordered four horses for a carriage to follow. The horses were taken out of the stable and harnessed. At ten o'clock a carriage stopped. With a torch in his hand, the post-house master rushed to the coach door. Then he stepped back: "The Emperor!" Alexandre climbed on a stone bench to look over his mother's shoulder. It was the same waxen-pale face he had seen a week before, a little more bowed to the chest, perhaps. It was the same voice, brief and strident, which asked, "Where are we? . . ." The Emperor spent that night at the Elysée Palace.

What remained of the beautiful and smart regiments whose bands played "Veillons au Salut de l'Empire" again passed through Villers in successive waves: first the able-bodied or slightly wounded soldiers, in disorder, without drums and almost without arms; then the wounded who could still walk or straddle a horse; finally, those who had been loaded into wagons, arms blown away, broken legs, bodies full of holes, badly bandaged. Some of them still had the strength to raise themselves up, to move their bloody stumps and cry, "Long live the Emperor!" The hideous vision of this dismal procession lasted three days, from June 22nd to the 25th.

It remained now only to await the enemy, and for Madame Dumas to put another mutton stew on the fire. On June 18, the Prussians appeared briefly in the park and in the streets but withdrew after a skirmish with the French. Finally their bugles resounded: five or six thousand soldiers from Baden, dressed in parade uniforms, emerged into the square of the town; a British regiment marched with them. Two English officers were billeted at the tobacconist's. One tried to speak Latin to communicate with Alexandre, but Abbé Grégoire's pupil persisted in believing that the foreigner was obstinately speaking the language of Shakespeare. The great flood of foreigners hardly touched Villers. The château was already full of Parisian beggars; no garrison could settle there.

Louis XVIII returned to the Tuileries on July 8. On July 15, Napoléon, destined for exile at St. Helena in the southern Atlantic, boarded the British ship *Bellérophon*. History ended and legend began.

Everything in the small town went back to its normal routine. During the debacle Aimée Dumas had joined her mother; her husband had been named Contrôleur Ambulant at Villers-Cotterêts. Monsieur Deviolaine had sent a letter proclaiming his unfailing fidelity to legitimate kings. When, on July 24, the rights of appanage for the forest were granted to the Duc d'Orléans, Monsieur Deviolaine was named its Conservator-in-Chief.

IV

Hunting and Love

‹◊›━━‹◊›

The legitimists declared open season on the revolutionary and Napoléonic regimes. Général Brune, who had been asked to be Alexandre's godfather, was slaughtered in Avignon, and across France the White Terror avenged the Royalists' fear.

In the fields and forests which surrounded Villers, it was open season, too, but it was lark, partridge, hare or wild boar that were hunted. Alexandre dreamed of joining the hunters. He succeeded in persuading the lawyer Picot to take him hunting if Madame Dumas gave her permission. The widow, frightened by firearms accidents, grew very pale, sighed a little but did not know how to resist. Picot told her that Alexandre was a chip off the old block, and the remembrance of the General softened her resistance.

Alexandre had his initiation in arms. Very soon he was accepted as a cohort of the foresters managed by Deviolaine. Forest guards were reserved, dreamy and religious; they could walk side by side with their best friends, for eight or ten miles across the great woods, without exchanging a word, without seeming to hear, without appearing to see anything. Yet, their ears picked up every passing sound and their eyes appraised every motion in the thickets.

In the evenings, around the forest bivouac, they talked of their hunting. In nature and solitude, they had forsaken the language of men to speak that of the winds and the trees. They kept themselves distant from the town, visiting only once a week to take orders from the inspector while their wives went to church.

Alexandre had left the hands of women to join the fraternity of men. As an adolescent, he was striving to imitate his dead father. Who could not see in hunting a lesser form of war? Only animals were killed, but with the same gestures and arms that asserted a warrior's courage.

In the primeval forest, in the middle of the archaic population of foresters, Alexandre almost forgot that he had reached fourteen and it was time for him to choose a career. He did not have the twenty-thousand-franc income that would have permitted him to forget that time marched on. Instead, Madame Dumas chose for him. She crossed the Place de la Fontaine and convinced her attorney, Armand-Julien Maximilian Mennesson, to hire Alexandre as an errand clerk in his office.

The apprenticeship was easy and despite the humiliating title of errand clerk it turned out to be a pleasant job. Alexandre would go to the neighborhood peasants' homes to get their signatures on the documents Maître Mennesson had drawn for them. He never forgot to take his gun or to watch for birds along his way. He returned with the signed documents, but also with his bag filled with hares, rabbits, thrushes, or jays. Legal functions were how he earned his living; still, they were only an extension of hunting.

Alexandre now knew how to rough out the copy for a document, to prepare a contract, and to process a payment of account. Eventually, the errand clerk became a legal clerk. His hair darkened and began to frizzle, downy hair appeared on his chin. He grew tall and began to resemble his father more and more. One day, through the dirty windowpanes of the law office, he saw a young man of twenty-six or twenty-seven wearing the uniform of an officer of hussars, whose slightly feminine face owed its male character to a magnificent sabre slash which began at his forehead and ended at the upper lip. He had taken part in the battle of Leipzig, in the campaign of France, had passed through Villers-Cotterêts on the road to Waterloo and had met Alexandrine-Louise-Marguerite Waubert. War had led the elegant hussar to Villers-Cotterêts; love would keep him there. Put on inactive duty, he preferred to resign rather than remain a dependent of the state. He rejoined Louise.

His name was Amedée de la Ponce. He was a son of a former Secretaire Général de Guerre and had an income of five or six thousand francs. Above all he was well educated and spoke Italian and German as well as his native tongue. He felt friendly toward Alexandre (Louise was a friend of Aimée Dumas) and offered to teach him the foreign languages he knew. The improvised pedagogue and the pupil began with Italian, but more than Italian, Amedée taught Alexandre the virtue of work.

During the spring of 1818, the Paris coach dropped off two young strangers: Laurence, niece of Abbé Grégoire, and her friend, Victoria Aunis. Abbé Grégoire, not knowing what to do with these two young girls, sought an escort for them and chose Alexandre.

In his search for clothes worthy of this event, Alexandre climbed to the attic where, in a large chest, Madame Dumas had stored the frock-coats, breeches and trousers of the General and Claude Labouret. Among the vests of satin brocade and the breeches made of rep, he discovered the small, paper-covered volumes that Victor Leteillier had left at Villers when he had been named Controleur des Contributions in Paris. Alexandre opened one of the volumes. It was *La vie du Chevalier de Faublas*. He hid the first four volumes under his vest, and in one of the furthest corners of the park he devoured this manual of seduction. It was far superior to some slightly obscene books his adolescent curiosity had prompted him to buy from the itinerant peddler who passed through Villers three times a year. Alexandre discovered in himself an avocation: he would be another Faublas.

On May 10, Pentecost Sunday, Alexandre, in a gray-blue suit and the nankeen breeches from his first communion, was introduced to the indolent and taunting Laurence, who was tall, thin, and blond with a clear, fresh complexion, and to Victoria, a chubby girl with dull skin lightly touched by small-pox, an hourglass figure, an arrogant bosom, and burning eyes.

Alexandre chose the gentler of the two, offering Laurence his arm for the walk in the park. He felt ridiculous in his breeches which were now worn only by obstinate hangers-on to the past century who insisted on wearing knee-length trousers. He felt all the more absurd because a crowd of admirers surrounded the two beautiful girls from Paris. Among them was Miaud, a clerk at the beggars' shelter—blond, pink, plump, a real fop dressed in tight pants of coffee-and-milk color, a buff vest with chased-gold buttons, and a brown coat with a high collar. When this squeaking dandy made fun of Dumas' clothes, Alexandre wanted to make him swallow his gold pince-nez with its fine steel chain and his trinkets hanging from his pocket. To make up for the disastrous impression his clothes gave, Alexandre decided to amaze the young girls by crossing the sunken fence with one gigantic, wolf-like leap. He jumped, accompanied by a sinister ripping sound. The bottom of the nankeen pants had split. Alexandre ran a frantic race to the house where Madame Dumas' needle mended the damage caused by her son's vainglorious leap. Alexandre swallowed a tall glass of cider and resumed his race to the Parterre.

The ball had begun and the dreadful Miaud had taken hold of Laurence. Once the contredance ended, Alexandre took his turn to invite the young girl to dance. He was not a beginner; he had taken lessons from an ex-corporal of the light infantry named Brezette, but his friend Fourcade who opened the contredance dazzled the audience with his entrechats and his flip-flops. He wriggled his ankles admirably, crossed and uncrossed his legs gracefully. Alexandre absorbed these intricate steps in a few minutes, and when his turn came, he was welcomed with a flattering murmur. A frenetic dancer was born.

The fiddler began a waltz and Alexandre drew the ardent Victoria in a whirlwind. He had practiced at length with a chair as a partner and found it much more pleasant to waltz with Victoria. He smelled her perfumed breath—felt her hair pass over his face. His eyes lingered on her bare shoulders, his arm clasped her plump and undulating waist. He shivered with joy. When the music stopped the two dancers remained immobile, he with knitted eyebrows, teeth bared, a fixed look; she supple, panting, yielding. Later, he would say this waltz had "made him a man in a few minutes."

Alexandre had sworn to himself that he would seduce the niece of Abbé Grégoire. He needed a pair of boots, such as Miaud's. Landereau, the bootmaker, would make them. They would be paid for on credit. The first communion suit would be fitted according to the dictates of fashion. Madame Dumas sighed a little, not so much at the expense as at seeing her son grow up.

When, after having amazed all Villers with his elegance, he arrived at Abbé Grégoire's house, he found only a letter that Laurence had left for him. Gently, she prayed him to go back with his young comrades who were expecting him to play tag and quoits. He was thunderstruck and re-read the letter with despair and rage. Immediately, he challenged Miaud to a duel. By way of reply, Alexandre received the next morning a handful of twigs, accompanied by Miaud's card. Alexandre was seized with shivers and Madame Dumas put him in a well-warmed bed. Dr. Lécosse diagnosed a cerebral fever. Alexandre prolonged his convalescence until the departure of the two young Parisian girls.

He was sixteen. Hunting had crowned him a man among men, but women, laughingly, had refused to recognize him. All was not lost. He learned the first rule women had to teach: pay careful attention to one's appearance. Moreover, he came away with a magnificent pair of boots that stirred the envy and admiration of his companions.

V

The Lover of Aglaé, the Friend of Adolphe

The eyes of women are the best mirrors. Alexandre had discovered he had beautiful hands, well-formed nails, white teeth, singularly small feet for his tall, gangly stature—undeniable signs of aristocracy.

Alexandre glanced at the young girls of nobility who dwelled in a neighboring château. He stared at the young girls of the bourgeoisie who flocked around the Deviolaine cousins: Cécile, whimsical and fickle, a real tomboy at twenty; Augustine, sixteen, as serene and beautiful as a Raphael painting; Louise, the youngest, who did not belong yet to any definite age.

Alexandre's desire hovered over young girls who belonged neither to the bourgeoisie nor to the common folks: milliners, seamstresses and shopkeepers who, on Sundays, played in the park, ran and walked two or three together, their bare arms linked like a chain. They wore white dresses, pink or blue belts, and bonnets that they had fashioned themselves.

When he left the law office, the young man passed back and forth before the small house where large hats, collars, bonnets, embroideries, and gloves were displayed. A sign creaked in the wind: "Mesdemoiselles Rigolot, Merchant of Fashion." Alexandre was in love. Was it with Marie-Louise Rigolot or with her younger sister, Adelaide-Victoire? Marie-Louise was fifty; Adelaide-Victoire was forty-one: fruit rather too ripe for his juvenile taste. Or was it with Aline Hardi, the seamstress, with her darker and duller complexion, her large, velvety, black eyes, who looked like a queen, who was so beautiful that nobody dared to love her. No, Alexandre had eyes only for Aglaé, the other seamstress with blushing cheeks and golden hair. Her smile was charming. Rather gay, rather small, rather plump, she was the daughter of two good and simple people, farmers at Villers-Cotterêts. She was born May 2, 1798 and was twenty, four years older than her swain, who exchanged enamored looks with her through the half-open curtain. Alexandre stood on tiptoes to stretch his sixteenth year, and never admitted being less than seventeen. Alexandre attacked and Aglaé defended herself, bestowing only very small favors which were the young man's delight.

Life was quiet at Villers, its rhythm changing only with the succession of seasons. In the morning, he woke up to his mother's kiss, from nine to four he mechanically recopied deeds with a free mind and a full heart; at four, he went back to his mother's for dinner and, at eight in summer and six in winter, he flew to his loves and his friends. Fourcade was director of the training school. Louis-Alexis Saulnier was Alexandre's clerical colleague and had only two passions: Manette Thierry and the clarinet. Louis Chollet, a Parisian living in Villers in order to study forest management, was a handsome but slightly vulgar man who, to Alexandre's amazement, sometimes carelessly left two or three gold coins on the mantlepiece of his fireplace. The three friends hurried to the rendezvous where their lovers awaited them. The women offered a forehead, a cheek or a hand, according to the stage of intimacy. In summer, they walked in the park, forming couples, holding hands, billing and cooing and exchanging longing glances.

In winter, they met at the home of Louise Moreau. The mother and the aunt, seamstresses by profession, withdrew, taking the lamp to work on their embroidery or to read the *Imitation de Jésus-Christ*, leaving the young people in darkness. They pressed close against one another, two on the same chair, murmuring and whispering sweet nothings.

At ten, they scattered. Each young man took his love to her parents' threshold where they lingered, in spite of the maternal scolding.

On June 27, 1819, Alexandre, Aglaé and their friends danced

at the feast of Courcy, a neighboring village nestled in the forest. Alexandre left the ball to visit Pierre-André Leroy, Mayor of the village and an old friend of the General. Following a path bordered with double hawthorn hedges, he met Caroline Collard and her little Marie, who was only three. A young man accompanied them— tall, brown, and gaunt, with black, military-cut hair, admirable eyes and strongly accentuated nose. He was Alexandre's age and looked like a German student, with his gray coat, his buff vest and his oil-cloth cap. Caroline introduced the stranger to Alexandre as a possible future friend; his name was Adolphe Ribbing de Leuven. To become better acquainted, they all agreed that Alexandre would come for a lunch in the forest with them the next day and that later he would spend two or three days at the Collards' château at Villers-Hellon.

The next day, when he arrived at Mr. Leroy's farm, the first person he saw was Adolphe, pencil in hand, gesticulating like a master of arms. He was struggling with the verse he was writing, a quatrain which he hoped would prevent Louise Collard from marrying a Russian suitor.

Alexandre's admiration for Adolphe and his verses was great but it knew no bounds once Adolphe had unwound the thread of his life. His father, one of the plotters who had conspired to kill Sweden's King Gustave III during a masked ball, had left for exile when he was twenty-one years old, his possessions confiscated. On route through Switzerland, he met Germaine de Staël who had not been unattracted to the "handsome regicide." After the Terror in France, he bought châteaus and abbeys at low prices. He sold back one of them, Villers-Hellon, to Jacques Collard. He lived quite peacefully during the Empire but the White Terror of Restoration had caused the regicide to flee to Bruxelles where he had founded a refugee periodical. Following one of his articles, Prussia demanded that Leuven be extradited unless he chose to take refuge in France. For three days he had been staying at Jacques Collard's home where he had sought refuge. Alexandre of Villers-Cotterêts was awestruck by a man who was so important that he was mixed up with the Bourbons, the King of Prussia, and William of the Netherlands.

However, a new friendship had not made love disappear. Aglaé began to receive Alexandre in a small, isolated pavilion that she was allowed to use, but they had to pass below the bedroom windows of her mother who watched all their comings and goings.

At the end of the year of care, attentions and love, of small favors granted, refused, taken by force, the door that had closed inexorably at eleven o'clock, pushing Alexandre out, opened again quietly one night at eleven-thirty. Alexandre then felt trembling lips, two caressing arms, a heart beating against his heart, sighs and tears. Virtuous Aglaé gave herself. Amidst the sighs and sobbing, they could not know what share each one contributed to this passion. Once their bodies had embraced, the adolescent who had overcome his awkwardness, who had obtained what he had desired for so long, naively triumphed; Aglaé was sobbing. Older, more mature, she knew that in a small town the gift she had made of herself could bring her the scorn that accompanied a woman's loss of her virginity. Alexandre was filled with the wonder of being a man; Aglaé was afraid of becoming known as a loose girl.

At three o'clock, Alexandre ran away like a thief in the night. To avert any suspicion, he carefully took a diversionary path from lane to field, from field to park, that permitted him to reach the tobacco shop. Madame Dumas waited for him. She had had time to prepare a short moral sermon and when Alexandre crept home, she scolded him a little on principle.

Having to pass under the window of Aglaé's mother gave the lovers pangs of apprehension. So Alexandre arranged for another route that led to the pavilion where he now spent two or three nights each week.

Once Alexandre left Aglaé's at three in the morning. A shadow, armed with a gnarled stick, waited near the ditch in the park. A hand-to-hand fight began. The assailant fell and his head struck a stone. He pulled a knife. Alexandre twisted the man's fist and seized the knife. The man picked up the stone on which he had hurt his head, but a blow from a stick left the attacker sprawled on the ground.

The next day, to protect himself against such encounters, Alexandre told Amedée his misadventure and borrowed his pocket pistols. To avoid compromising Aglaé, he settled her in another house. Nearby was the home of Attorney Pierre-Alexandre Lebaigue whose wife, Eléonore, the daughter of Jean-Michel Deviolaine, was pretty, witty, and a bit of a coquette. She liked to be seen, to be admired, to have her aristocratic, pretty hand kissed. Her husband was a fat man, pockmarked, and rather vulgar looking.

Thus when Alexandre had told the story of his attack to others, besides Amedée, the gossip spread fast. Soon Alexandre heard, via the grapevine, that he was Eléonore Lebaigue's lover. He was proud of such a glorious conquest attributed to him. He denied it weakly and that denial was considered an admission.

The Lebaigue house, so welcoming before, was now closed to Alexandre and his mother. Doubtlessly, too, Jean-Michel Deviolaine did not easily forgive the smear on his daughter's virtue.

In autumn, Antoine-Vincent Arnault, the famous dramatist, came to visit his companion in exile, Comte de Leuven. His two sons were with him. While rabbit hunting, Alexandre was side by side with the prominent literary figure and got acquainted with his two sons. The Arnaults then took Adolphe de Leuven away with them to spend the season in Paris.

On All Saints' Day, thanks to the munificience of a client, Maître Mennesson's three clerks enjoyed the delights of a visit to Soissons, the subprefecture of Aisne. There a poster attracted the attention of the young men: "This evening, through extraordinary circumstances, *Hamlet*, tragedy in five acts of M. Ducis, by the students of the Conservatoire." Alexandre, who was bored to death by the reading from Corneille and Racine that Madame Dumas imposed on him, was afraid of the word tragedy. He did not know what *Hamlet* was. Ducis and Shakespeare did not mean anything to the hunter. But the performance was the best entertainment Soissons offered that evening. There was a line of people waiting but the young men succeeded in getting seats in the pit. The house lights dimmed and Hamlet appeared played by the actor Cudot, a tall, pale fellow. Alexandre was captivated by his powerful voice.

From then on, Alexandre dreamed only of the theater; he had no peace until he obtained a copy of *Hamlet*. The masterpiece made a prodigious impression on him. At the end of three months, he knew Hamlet's role by heart. He then gathered around him a troop of young men and women of Villers. An attic, makeshift but well-covered at the end of a court near the Hôtel de l'Epée, sheltered the theater decorated with flowers and shrub picked in the nearby forest.

Alexandre chose the play, studied its effects, made his actors give readings, suggesting intonation, gestures, entrances and exits. When the applause was thin, he was rough with the actors. From

Paris, Leuven supplied him with dramatic texts, but Alexandre's girl friends yawned a bit when he forced them to suffer the reading of the tragedy then in fashion.

In spring, Adolphe came back; at the Arnaults he had rubbed elbows with the literary world. He had read a play at the Gymnase theater; he had gone backstage. Dazzled, he now dazzled Alexandre who, during interminable walks, questioned him feverishly about the stars of the day: "And Talma? and Mademoiselle Mars? and Mademoiselle George?"

Adolphe condescended to advise the amateurs of Villers and to mix with the budding actors. The pretty young girls were excited by the action on stage and the fiery feelings that were expressed. Flirtations began in spite of the presence of disapproving mothers. Now and then Alexandre betrayed Aglaé with another blonde, Julie Dambrun, who was just barely fifteen.

Alexandre's company of amateurs competed with the Robbas, Villers-Cotterêts' residing company of actors whose melodramatic repertory was at the end of its tether. To stay afloat, they organized a benefit performance and asked a few amateur actors to join with them. Alexandre was given the part of Dom Ramire; the others had declined. Madame Dumas' needle moved quickly to make a tunic. She sewed together two shawls of red cashmere with large gold flowers brought back from Egypt by the General. For the lower part of the costume, she attached long silk stockings to a pair of drawers. The Mayor loaned Alexandre a Louis XV sword. The whole town, the surrounding villages, and even some eccentrics from Soissons attended Alexandre's debut.

Perhaps dizzy with Alexandre's success in Don Ramire, Adolphe proposed to Alexandre that they collaborate on writing a play. Alexandre's horizon, until then limited to a provincial tax-collector's office and a fifteen-hundred-franc salary, was now unveiled: the theater!

Alexandre, having known only the worst of Voltaire's writing, now doted on Pigault-Lebrun and knew by heart Bertin, Parny, Legouvé, and Demoustier. He had never before opened a book of Walter Scott, or Byron, or James Fenimore Cooper who were to be his next inspirations. As for Shakespeare, he considered him a barbarian who owned his renown solely to the adaptations made by Voltaire or Ducis: the accepted idea of his time.

Adolphe, however, did not give up on Alexandre. They put together the scenario for a one-act farce, *Le Major de Strasbourg*. The title described the inspiration. The hero belonged to the family of brave officers now retired after Waterloo and Leipzig, whose patriotism, expressed in rhymed couplets, continued to defeat the enemy.

These beginnings intoxicated Alexandre. With the prospect of Adolphe's return to Paris, he increased the pace of the collaboration's writing. He was certain that works of such distinction would receive the success they deserved and that Paris, capital of European taste and genius, would open a path for them, a way strewn with wreaths and gold coins. For him, there would be glory! Money! Glory to raise again the General's forgotten name, money to raise the still decreasing fortune of the General's widow.

Adolphe and Alexandre concocted a second farce: *Le Dîner d'amis*, and then wrote their first drama, *Les Abencérages*.

While the two friends sang the Empire's glory on paper, on Saint-Helena, Napoléon pronounced his last words. A more modest death, that of Nicolas Harlet, permitted Madame Dumas to take possession of the house her father had bought from the ex-major. This Knight of the Royal Order of Saint Louis died on July 19, 1820, at the age of ninety-three. Claude Labouret and his daughter had paid an annuity for forty years. Madame Dumas, however, had borrowed so much on this house that she foresaw, with dread, that her resources had reached an end.

As for Alexandre, he expected a miracle from Paris, where Adolphe had taken their masterpieces. He watched anxiously for the post-woman, Mère Colombe; letters came after long intervals, each time crushing Alexandre's hopes a little more. One after the other, the theaters refused the drama and the farces. *Le Dîner d'amis* did not show sufficient intrigue, *Le Major de Strasbourg* was too much like *Soldat laboureur* that had just been played again, they said; as for *Abencérages*, melodramas on the same subject were offered in every Paris theater.

His worried mother wondered what to do with Alexandre. Jean-Michel Deviolaine, who had just been named Conservator of the Duc d'Orléans' forest, would probably leave Villers to undertake the direction of the forestry administration in Paris. Could he take Alexandre among his baggage? Unfortunately, since Alexandre had compromised the honor of his daughter, Deviolaine considered Alexandre a scoundrel and a sluggard who was not above creating scandal in the small town.

Madame Dumas was crestfallen. Either she had to remove her son from Maître Menneson's law office, or the attorney, exasperated by his clerk's lack of interest in drawing up deeds, would dismiss him.

She entrusted her son to Victor Letellier who had been nominated to a post in Dreux. She hoped that with his brother-in-law's help, her nitwit of a son would get a start in the administration of indirect taxes. In the letter Alexandre wrote from Dreux on March 1, 1821, to his friend Boussin, there is much about women but little about professional projects. This letter threw doubt upon the alleged abundant tears that Dumas swore he had shed when he was separated from Aglaé, who was now twenty-three and must have dreamed of finding a mate before her reputation was completely compromised.

In Dreux, Alexandre versified, courted Lucie, and no doubt learned the arcana of indirect taxation from his brother-in-law. He stayed long enough to be there for the September 1 opening of the hunting season, during which he was "acclaimed as a hero" for having slaughtered a three-legged hare. Upon his return to Villers, he was met with the hypocritical commiseration behind the question: "Do you know that Aglaé is getting married?" To whom was she getting married? To Nicolas-Louis Sébastian Hanniquet, a pastry cook and caterer. The betrothed was some thirteen years older than Aglaé but he was a well-off tradesman. Aglaé was making not only a marriage of convenience, but also a very handsome one.

In the evening, Alexandre crept to the old pavilion, but the room was unoccupied, the bed empty. Aglaé had chosen social convention instead of the love of this mad-dog, Alexandre. He spent his chagrin by spitefully batting a hand ball so vigorously that he just missed hitting the police-corporal's son.

Aglaé's wedding was planned for October first. On that day, Alexandre ran away. He had arranged a bird-catching party with the harness-maker's son in the thickets near Haramont. That evening, in the hut made of leaves, while the hunters counted the birds they had snared, a joyous uproar dominated by the shrill sound of a violin drew them out of their shelter. Along a cross-path, a fiddler led a parade of young girls in white dresses and young men in blue or black coats, carrying big bouquets and long ribbons: it was Aglaé's wedding party. The young bride was leaning on the shoulder of Hanniquet, who clasped her in his arm. As night fell, Alexandre's eyes followed for a long time the figure of Aglaé, who walked away with her white veil and her orange-flower bouquet.

Thirty years later, Alexandre remembered. "My first dream had just vanished, my first illusion had just died!"

VI
Farewell to Villers-Cotterêts

Marie-Louise Dumas worried about her son's future. She pulled strings with an old hunting friend of the General, and with Aimée's mother-in-law who both recommended Alexandre to the attorney, Pierre-Nicolas Lefèvre, in whose office at Crépy-en-Valois a position of second or third clerk was available.

With his bundle of belongings on his back, Alexandre kissed his weeping mother and walked toward Crépy, three and a half miles away. Crépy was a small village, not quite a town. Of the three attorneys practicing there, Pierre-Nicolas Lefèvre was the one who had the best manners. It was easy to see that he had lived for a time in Paris. Periodically he revisited it for the pleasures that his pallid complexion and his worn-out body betrayed in glimpses. Actually, he was rather a good man, cold and demanding, but fair.

He gave Alexandre a comfortable room, overlooking a garden full of flowers, but Alexandre was bored with drawing up interminable deeds that a thick coat of dust would eventually cover in the archives of Maître Lefèvre's successors. He was so deeply bored that almost each Saturday he took his gun and, hunting on the way, returned to sleep under the maternal roof. It also happened that at Villers Joséphine-Thérèse-Louise Leroy, called Brézette, was waiting for him, and in her arms he tried to forget Aglaé. He returned on Monday mornings in time for the opening of the law office.

For his introduction into the society of Crépy, he had a coat, a vest and pants made by Bamps, a Parisian tailor. He paid twenty francs down on a bill of one hundred fifty francs and would pay the balance monthly, twenty francs at a time. A law clerk, Alexandre nevertheless wanted to be a poet: he posed a little in the houses he frequented, he sighed around young girls among whom he had singled out Athénaïs Lecornier. He used his evenings of boredom to write—half in verse, half in prose—a very bad pastiche of Demoustier, titled "Pélerinage à Erménonville." The title was stale, the verses mediocre, the prose pale, but Alexandre was proud enough of it to send it to Adolphe. Not a single review or collection accepted it.

How many months did this ennui at Crépy last? Dumas' chronology here is very imprecise. He put back a year his stay at Dreux and Aglaé's marriage, but it is probable that he began at Maître Lefèvre's law office in October of 1821. He walked along the gloomy, small streets of Crépy for almost a year, dreaming during his chores of the glory that, without fail, would be his in Paris.

Providence did not make Alexandre wait too long. On November 2, 1822, it sent Pierre-Hippolyte Paillet to Crépy. Maître Mennesson's former first clerk invited Alexandre to spend three days with him in Paris. Maître Lefèvre had also planned his monthly visit to the capital and would not notice his clerk's absence. Paillet probably had no more than twenty-eight francs in his pocket and Alexandre, seven, but Paillet owned a horse and each had a gun. One would hunt while the other distracted the gamekeeper, and the game they killed would pay for the inns. They left the same evening and lodged at the Hôtel de la Croix at Erménonville. There they used six of their thirty-five francs but the grounds at Erménonville abounded in game; the next morning Alexandre killed two hares and three partridges and they galloped off on Paillet's horse when the warrener appeared. With the help of a twenty-sou coin, Paillet established his innocence, then went hunting in his turn. In Dammartin the same trick put three hares and eight partridges in the bag. The meal cost a hare and three partridges, but in the afternoon the capital was regained and increased. When the two friends arrived at ten in the evening at the Hôtel des Vieux-Augustins, they had four hares, twelve partridges and two quails which they exchanged for two nights of lodging, plus a pâté and a bottle of wine for the return trip. They claimed they had bet with an Englishman, eccentric as all Englishmen were, that they could go to Paris and back without spending a sou.

In Paris, on Monday morning, Alexandre got up at dawn and hurried to Rue Pigalle to see Adolphe Leuven. He strayed a bit and stumbled on a large poster at the entrance of the Comédie-Française: "Tomorrow, Monday, *Sylla*, a verse tragedy in five acts by M. de Jouy. M. Talma will play the part of Sylla." Alexandre swore to himself that he would not leave Paris before he had seen *Sylla*, and especially Talma, the actor who epitomized the French theater in 1822. He dragged Adolphe from his bed to Rue de la Tour-des-Dames where the tragedian lived. Talma was dressing. In spite of the almost reverent trembling that seized him, Dumas noticed Talma's head was almost completely shaved. How, he wondered, could his hair stand on end when, in *Hamlet*, the father's ghost appeared? No matter, when he wrapped his naked chest in his dressing gown the tragedian regained all his majesty. With a kind of antique stylus, he signed two tickets for Adolphe and Alexandre and held his hand to the young provincial who felt a great desire to kiss it.

With long strides, Alexandre paced the sidewalks of Paris, visited the Museum, followed the quays, discovered Notre Dame. Paris did not belong to him yet, but he recognized it as the only stage where destiny played.

Adolphe had asked him to meet at the Café du Roi, at the corner of Rue Richelieu, the center of the literary bohemia. There Alexandre stumbled on Auguste Lafarge, once a frisky law clerk in Villers, now a wreck who nursed a stomach ruined by too many small shots of alcohol. Literature is not only a road to glory, it can also lead to ruin. The Café du Roi was a kind of literary club where clients wrote more than they drank. Alexandre felt that he was definitely at the center of the world. It was here that one must be.

Adolphe was late, but thanks to the diligent usher, the two friends succeeded in slipping into orchestra seats. The curtain rose. When Talma entered the stage, Alexandre let escape a cry of surprise: the tragedian had made for himself a mask of Napoléon at the eve of his abdication. Slowly, with irony on his lips, Talma crossed the distance that separated him from his accuser:

I do not question if your emboldened hate
Pursues in Claudius Valérie's mate . . .

The voice was incisive and sonorous. Alexandre was stunned, dazed, fascinated. The curtain fell to the roar of immense bravos. Hardly recovered, he followed Adolphe through the inextricable labyrinth of the Comédie-Française which opened into the inner sanctum: Talma's dressing room. The elite of those who wrote and played tragedy in Paris had come to pay homage to the master!

Alexandre did not force his way through this illustrious flow but remained at the door, humble and blushing. On a word from Adolphe, Talma asked Alexandre to come closer. Questioned, he confessed with sighs his mediocre position as provincial clerk. No matter! Was not Corneille a clerk to a prosecutor? Then Talma, in the name of Shakespeare, of Corneille, and of Schiller, baptized Alexandre a poet by laying his hand on Alexandre's head.

On that evening of November 4, 1822, Alexandre's aspirations were suddenly solidified. He had recognized the two literatures: that by which one lived (and sometimes, died) at the Café du Roi, and that, in Talma's dressing room, which gave glory. He held the cards and now it was up to him to try and take the hand.

When at seven o'clock the next day he took the road back to Crépy, he had only twelve francs left in his pocket, but his hand had touched Talma's hand; he had laid eyes on the glorious dramatist whose world he must now try to join. On his return to the law office on Wednesday, he heard that Maître Lefèvre had returned the preceding night and had asked for him. The interview between the attorney and the clerk was short. The attorney explained: "For a machine to function well, none of the cogs must stop." The warning might have been provisional but the clerk chose to take it as definitive and decided to do everything possible to leave the provinces and conquer Paris. He spent a part of the night dreaming up his plan of assault.

At Villers Madame Dumas, informed by the postman, awaited Alexandre on the doorstep of the tobacco shop. She was all tenderness, beaming to have her son back. Business was slow, he declared, and he had obtained a few days of vacation. But days followed days, and Alexandre did not mention going back to Crépy. Madame Dumas understood but didn't say a word.

Alexandre resolved to put into practice the project he had formed: to choose from his father's papers a dozen letters from Maréchal Jordan, Maréchal Victor, and Général Sébastiani, gather a small sum of money, leave for Paris, call on these old friends of his father and find a position at twelve hundred francs a year.

While he tried to find the necessary sum of money, the worried tailor Bamps arrived to claim three months' overdue payment. Alexandre received Bamps, made him visit his property—the decrepit house that Harlet had finally abandoned—and offered him dinner. But Bamps did not give up his claim and persisted in asking for the overdue forty francs. This embarrassing situation was saved by the unexpected arrival of a servant from the Boule-d'Or: an Englishman was clamoring for Alexandre, an obese Englishman who weighed some three hundred fifty pounds, an Englishman who had been charmed by Pyrame, Alexandre's greedy dog, and wanted to buy it at any cost. Alexandre, who was desirous of getting rid of this hunting companion given to stealing tripe and meat from the butcher's stall, would have given it for nothing. But the Englishman insisted so much that he finally accepted five "napoléons" for having fed the dog.

It was not without a mocking pride that Alexandre gave two of the "napoléons" to Bamps, making them ring with the three others in the palm of his hand, three handsome gold coins which would very soon be engulfed by Madame Dumas' debts.

Indeed, the General's widow had borrowed so much that she had to resign herself to selling her meager assets, the Harlet's house, and her forty-five acres of property. All debts canceled, there remained only two hundred and fifty-three francs to her name. She fell into deep despondency. Since the General's death she had fought against the exhaustion of her resources; at last, she had to admit defeat. As for Alexandre, he had never felt so joyous and confident.

On March 8, 1823, Alexandre decided to cross the Rubicon that separated him from Paris. He sold some etchings of Piranese that the Général had brought back from Italy. They were worth four hundred francs; he let them go for fifty. Then, with Modeste Cartier, owner of the Boule-d'Or, he engaged in a billiard game with high stakes. He won six hundred small glasses of absinthe which, once exchanged for money, brought him ninety francs, or twelve trips to Paris since the coach stopped at the Boule-d'Or.

Again he ran to the farm of Vouty at Faverolles, whose owner, Jean-Chrysostome Danré, friend of Alexandre's father, had helped influence the election of Général Foy as a Deputy of the Départment of Aisne. Danré agreed to write a letter recommending Alexandre to Général Foy. Even better, he proposed to convince Madame Dumas of the necessity of Alexandre's departure on the following Thursday, market day. Madame Dumas resisted a little, cried a lot, and sighed with resignation, remembering that a fortune teller had predicted that the then five-year-old Alexandre would belong to the class of men she called dominators. Alexandre was now twenty-one, and to fulfill the prophecy he would have to leave Villers, much too small a stage for his talent.

The departure was fixed for Saturday evening, March 19, 1822. He would leave Villers on the ten o'clock coach. Alexandre consoled the poor Louise, deserted by her new lover, as she had been by the previous one, Louis Chollet. He visited Maître Mennesson, who advised him to distrust priests, to detest the Bourbons and to support the Republic. The good Abbé Grégoire gave him the Gospel's maxim: "Do not do to others what you would not want others to do to you." There was a last pilgrimage to the cemetery in the company of his mother to pray at the General's grave. In the court of the Boule-d'Or the horses of the coach were already pawing the ground. Alexandre and his mother parted, Madame Dumas with doubt, Alexandre with hope. The coach rolled away and Villers faded as if submerging into the forest that encircled it. At the end of the night, he arrived in Paris.

Under the austerity of the Bourbons, Paris was sad on Sunday. The stores were closed, the streets empty. Alexandre surprised the sleeping Adolphe. He made certain that Victor, Maréchal de France, was still Ministre de la Guerre and with his best handwriting, he drew up a petition asking for an audience with the Minister. Adolphe was dubious about the success of his friend, but Alexandre was certain that the letters addressed to his father, letters that were proof of services previously rendered, would be "sesames" that would open the door to the Ministre de la Guerre, or at least the doors of Maréchal Jourdan and Général Sébastiani.

The next day, Jean-Baptiste, Comte Jourdan, remembered well there once existed a Général Dumas, but refused to be convinced that this General had a son. Slightly discouraged, Alexandre entered Comte Sébastiani's office. Napoléon's cousin was dictating to four secretaries posted at the four corners of the room. Each time he stopped in front of one of his scribes, the latter had to hand him a gold snuff-box into which the General plunged his delicate fingers. Alexandre did not feel the least avocation for becoming a snuff-box handler.

Alexandre immersed himself in the *Almanach des 25,000 adresses*, looking for other potential patrons. Jean-Antoine, Comte Verdier, Rue du Faubourg-Montmartre, he read by chance. Verdier had been under the orders of Général Dumas in Egypt. Alexandre flew to Faubourg-Montmartre, climbed to the fourth floor as advised by the concierge, and rang at the small door on the left. A fifty-year-old man opened the door. He wore a cap bordered with Persian lamb, a jacket trimmed with frogs, trousers, and white flannel socks. In his hand he carried a palette full of paints and held a paint brush with his thumb. The would-be-artist—who handled the brush more awkwardly than he formerly handled the sword—was Général Verdier, who had fallen from grace. What could he possibly offer to the son of his old companion in arms? Some lessons from a bad painter and two gold coins that he had still in his purse. Alexandre took leave of the Général with a light heart: his kindness had reconciled Alexandre with humankind. They dined together the same evening, and thanks to the intervention of Adolphe, attended Talma's performance of *Regulus* by Arnault. Talma, whom Alexandre had seen before in the role of a somber Sylla with flattened hair, head crowned and forehead creased by worry, now entered the stage with quick steps, his head high, clothed in a simple tunic tightened with an iron belt. The general of a free people had succeeded the fierce dictator. Alexandre was wonderstruck. He confessed to Verdier that he had come to Paris mostly to write literature.

At ten o'clock the next day, Alexandre was introduced to Maximilian-Sébastian Foy, his last hope. The champion of liberty was a small, thin man with sparse and graying hair, a Roman nose and a bilious complexion. He was quite ready to help a protégé of Danré, but the questions to which he subjected Alexandre left little hope. Alexandre had no notion of mathematics, algebra, geometry, physics, or law; he knew little Latin and did not understand book-keeping. Alexandre blushed with shame at his completely deficient education. He confessed that he was ignorant and lazy. Moved by the admission, the General asked him to leave his address and in doing so, Alexandre displayed his one talent. The ignoramus had handsome handwriting! He could therefore be a copying clerk. As it happened, the General would be dining that same day at the Palais Royal. He could ask the Duc d'Orléans for a position for the republican General's son. Alexandre drew up another petition, carefully emphasizing his handwriting, his only strong point.

When he greeted Alexandre the next day, Général Foy's face showed good news. The matter was settled. If he wanted, Alexandre could enter the secretarial staff of the Duc d'Orléans as a supernumerary—paid twelve hundred francs per year—that very next Monday. In his joy, Alexandre jumped to the General's neck and kissed him. A second table setting was added. In the course of the lunch, the young man disclosed his literary project, his dreams of glory, to Foy. The General smiled benevolently.

Alexandre boarded the coach for Villers at four-thirty. At one in the morning he was at the Boule-d'Or. The streets were dark, everybody was in bed. Madame Dumas had recognized it was her son by his special way of opening the door. All disheveled, she sat up in her bed. Alexandre kissed her, running around the room and crying: "Victory!"

The next day, Alexandre drew a conscription number. He did not worry about it because as the son of a widow, he could not be enlisted. Without apprehension, he took a bad number, numero 9. "Why," asked the greedy Boudoux whom he had just paid for a large loaf of bread, "why not put thirty centimes on numero 9 at the lottery office?" Boudoux would take charge of this transaction himself while Alexandre and his mother attended to the preparation of the great trip. Madame Dumas would have packed everything in the house for him to take with him. Didn't he need money while waiting for his first wages? She was ready to give him one hundred francs, half of all she had left. But her generosity was unnecessary: "Numero 9 has been drawn," Boudoux triumphantly announced. One hundred fifty francs were paid to Alexandre, in handsome écus worth six francs each. It was enough to live on for a month and to pay the carter for the move.

At ten o'clock Saturday evening, in the court of the Boule-d'Or, most of Villers gathered for a last farewell, as if a navigator were departing for unknown seas. Some of them in the crowd later would well remember this day, April 5, 1822. Arms were extended, kisses smacked on cheeks. The departure of the preceding Saturday was only a rehearsal. This time, the actors had more conviction. When the coach passed the first curve on the road to Paris, it was not just a small town that disappeared—a whole part of his life had sunk into the past.

PART
II

The Fall of the Bastille

I

The Supernumerary

On Sunday, April 6, 1823, Alexandre traveled up and down stairs, looking for lodging. He ended by choosing a small room on the fourth floor of No. 1, Pâté des Italiens. Wallpapered in yellow and opening onto the court, it offered the luxury of an alcove. Then he strolled along the boulevards, feverishly reading the newspapers. All were preoccupied with the expedition of the French against the Spanish. The next day, the French army under the leadership of the Bourbon heir, the Duc d'Angoulême, would cross the Bidassoa. The minister of foreign affairs, Monsieur de Chateaubriand, was delighted: this expedition lent a bit of glamour to the rather deflated Louis XVIII, who had sunken into a chair fitted to ease his gout. Alexandre looked in vain for programs of shows; they had disappeared in the heroic excitement.

Alexandre examined himself carefully in the mirror of the Hôtel des Vieux Augustins where he had temporarily settled. With his too-long hair, he resembled one of those pomade merchants who used their own hair as their main promotion. His morning coat fell down to his ankles and would have to be shortened by a few inches if he wanted to appear fashionable. Alexandre gave orders to a barber who smoothed down his frizzy hair to such an extent that he looked like a seal. The tailor needed a whole day to remove all anachronisms from the cut of his clothes. Alexandre would have to present himself in the office of the Duc d'Orléans in morning dress.

At the Palais-Royal his heart beat violently as he went up the staircase that lead to the secretariat. On the third floor, nobody except the service boys had yet arrived. At last, a lively young man, tall, handsome and blond, came and took down the office key hooked to a nail. Alexandre got up. The service men introduced him to Monsieur Ernest who expected him and took Alexandre to a small room lighted by only one window. Alexandre entered the office where he would work in the company of the handsome Antoine-Eléonor, called Ernest Basset, the clerk in command who had a salary of eighteen hundred francs per year, and the assistant-chief, Espèrance-Hippolyte Lassagne, a young man twenty-eight to thirty years of age, who held out the warm and trembling hand of a future friend.

But Alexandre's fate was in the hands of Jacques-Parfait Oudard, manager of the office, secretaire du cabinet of the Duchesse d'Orléans. Oudard received him standing in front of his office fireplace. He was still young, with a face that was immobile, sweet and firm. His teeth were beautiful, but his smile was scarce. His hard and fixed look focused on Alexandre to take his measure. He was dressed formally in black pants and a vest of white piqué, black tie and suit; stockings of very fine cotton outlined his calves. At any time the Prince or the Princess might call.

To his surprise, Alexandre learned that he owed his position not only to Général Foy's recommendation, but also to that of Jean-Michel Deviolaine, that diamond in the rough, who, as Director of the Administration of the Duke's woodlands, worked five minutes from this office. Alexandre hastened to go and thank him. Grumbling, Deviolaine again threatened to use his foot on some part of Alexandre's anatomy if he were guilty of writing filthy plays or rag-bag verses, as he did at Villers-Cotterêts, but Alexandre left the meeting with the comforting impression that he was not completely alone in Paris.

Once the presentations were made, Alexandre had two free days for settling into his new home. In his poet's garret, he was happy: he was twenty, he was in Paris. He hurried to Rue Pigalle to give Adolphe his first impressions of his new job. The Leuvens asked him to choose an evening to come for dinner. On that day, his place would be set at their table. In the meantime, they invited him for the next day to get acquainted with the Arnault family. To dine at the same table with the author of so many masterpieces! To sit near his son, Lucien-Émile Arnault, whose play *Regulus* had recently been a hit at the Comédie-Française! When he was introduced to them, these demi-gods showed themselves mere mortals. Antoine-Vincent Arnault did not lack wit; his plump, brunette wife was charming; his second son, Telleville, was a good looking captain, very brave and very loyal; his younger son was a handsome boy, brimming with admiration for his father. Alexandre was most attracted to Lucien, the author of *Regulus*, whose face showed traces of well-controlled physical suffering. Two or three times a week, for five years, Alexandre would see this friend whom he chose for his gentleness and his serene sadness. For the moment, he contented himself with his office colleagues' impressed reaction when he announced: "Last evening, I dined with the Arnaults." That was what gave a man status!

On April 10, at precisely 10:30, Alexandre made his official entrance to the Duc d'Orléans' offices. His table was back to back with that of Lassagne who very graciously gave him the necessary instructions: he had to copy, with the most elegant handwriting possible, the greatest number of letters which, according to their importance, Monsieur Oudard, or Monsieur Manche de Broval, secretary to the Duke, or the Duc d'Orléans himself would sign.

Hardly had he begun his first letter when he heard the door opening. It was the Chevalier de Broval himself who had come to visit the newcomer. Monsieur Manche de Broval was a small man of sixty-three, slightly hunched, a little tilted to the left, with a close hair-cut, a very big red nose that said a lot, and small gray eyes that did not say anything. As he hadn't abandoned the Duc d'Orléans during his exile, he had been rewarded with the management of the household, estates, forests and finances of His Highness. This allowed him to tyrannize his inferiors, except the handsome Ernest whom he addressed tenderly in the familiar "tu"!

A stickler for small details, he waited until Alexandre had finished his letter. The clerk had the impression that all the weight of his superior bore down on his shoulder; his hand shook a little. He passed his letter to Broval, who signed it and dried the ink with sand. But did Monsieur Dumas know there were ten ways to fold a letter? Monsieur Dumas knew only the square one which was reserved, as everybody should know, to princes and kings. Monsieur Dumas used scissors to cut the paper, when paper should not be cut, but torn. Monsieur Dumas was of extreme awkwardness in applying the ducal seal. Ernest, the favorite, was charged with giving the provincial a bit of polish.

When Manche de Broval at last turned his back, Alexandre could say the words he had held down all the morning: "I dined with the Arnaults." The effect was mediocre. Lassagne did not think much of their Bonapartist politics or their literary work. Their tragedies, he suggested, would have been booed if Talma did not play them. In his gentle voice, Lassagne gave to Alexandre his first lesson in romanticism. If one wanted to become a man of letters, one should read, reread, learn by heart the essential writers first. For the theater there were Aeschylus, Shakespeare and Molière, then the writers "related" to these three luminaries. Euripides, Seneca, Racine and Voltaire after Aeschylus; Schiller after Shakespeare; Terence, Plautus and Aristophanes after Molière. Corneille must be dealt with separately. For the novel one should study Goethe for poetry, Walter Scott for character development, James Fenimore Cooper for the evocation of the mystery and grandeur of the prairie, forest and oceans. France was waiting for a historical novel. She already had memoirists. She pined for a novelist. As for poetry, Alexandre should forget Voltaire as quickly as possible as well as the others he had read. He should nourish his talent on the central works of Homer, Vergil and Dante, then move toward such modern writers as Ronsard, Mathurin Régnier, Milton, Goethe, Uhland, Byron, Lamartine, Victor Hugo and especially toward that small volume of André Chénier's poems soon to be published.

Alexandre was crushed by his ignorance, frightened by the reading program that he must undertake. Would two or three years be long enough? He would read. He would study all night.

On his first free Sunday, Alexandre confessed his impression to a friend:

> For four days now I've been settled in my office which keeps me busy from ten-thirty until five o'clock in the evening and which brings me twelve to fifteen hundred francs a year and a ticket for one of the first boxes at the Théâtre-Français every week. I get along perfectly with my bosses, who are more my friends than my superiors.

This letter was addressed to everyone in Villers-Cotterêts. The once poor, young boy was now only a memory. He hurried rapidly toward glory. Already he had access to the Comédie-Française. The evenings he did not spend with Manette Thierry, a young seamstress from Villers-Cotterêts who had come to the capital to perfect her skill, Alexandre devoted to the theater. Once he stood in line to see *Vampire*, a three-act melodrama. He finally found an orchestra seat next to a gentleman about forty-five years old who was absorbed in an expensive seventeenth-century reprint published by Elzévir. Curious, Alexandre succeeded in reading the title in old French: *Le pastissier françois où est enseignée la manière de faire toute sorte de pastisserie*. Perhaps this gentleman with a kind and benevolent face was a gourmet? No, he was a bibliophile who learnedly extolled for Alexandre the respective merits of these Elzévir editions whose value was determined by the width of the margin: the larger the margin, the more valuable was the book. But the bell was ringing: the overture began, murmurs of "hush!" ran along the audience and the curtain rose. The gentleman again lost himself in *Le pastissier françois*.

On stage in the Staffa grotto, Malvina, in the middle of a storm, slept on a grave. Lord Buthwen on another grave, this one comfortable, prepared his terrifying apparition, while the angel of marriage and the angel of the moon set the stage with a narrative exposition. Alexandre's neighbor gave a start and, to the great scandal of the spectators, loudly corrected the grammatical mistakes of the angel Ithuriel. "My God, what writing!" he murmured. When Ithuriel crossed the theater in a cloud, the neighbor complained of the absurdity of the situation. But Alexandre found the decoration magnificent, and the intervention of ethereal beings in human destiny pleased his imagination.

Mixed with applause at the end, a formidable catcall resounded in the loges. The public growled; the stupefied actors stopped short. A policeman grabbed the whistler and evicted him. Alexandre just had time to recognize his gracious neighbor who had created the disturbance.

The next day, Alexandre enthusiastically narrated his evening to Lassagne, who was reading the newspaper. *Vampire* was indeed mentioned: "A scene which reminds me of the first performance of La Fontaine's *Florentin* took place last evening at the third perfor-

mance of the revival of *Vampire*. Our learned bibliophile, Charles
Nodier, was expelled from the theater of the Porte-Saint-Martin
because he disturbed the performance by whistling. Charles Nodier
is one of the anonymous authors of *Vampire*," read Lassagne aloud.

Summer came. Alexandre had progressed greatly in the art of
copying without reading what he copied. Thus he was able to think
of other things: of the verses that he obstinately roughed out and
Manette, of whom he was tiring. Several times on his landing, he
had run across a young woman, blonde, pink and plump like Aglaé.
Little by little, as the landing encounters multiplied, he learned
that she came from Rouen, where she had abandoned a half-mad
husband. She had opened a small dressmaking studio in Paris.
Biographers have called her Catherine Labay, but she signed her
name as Laure Labay. Laure was almost thirty. She was born in
1794 at Eterbec in the suburbs of Bruxelles to French parents who
most probably had followed the revolutionary armies. What attracted her to this young supernumerary, who was eight years
younger than she? His impetuosity, his energy. After a few sentimental walks in the woods of Meudon, the employee and the dress-
maker shared their loneliness. To settle in with his new mistress,
Alexandre carried his chairs and his chest of drawers across the
landing. Thrift gained what morality lost. Laure represented all
that Alexandre had left: Aglaé and Madame Dumas, a mistress and
a mother who attended to his material needs, who forgave his young
man's eccentricities, who understood that Alexandre was running
from pillar to post to secure his future, who accepted his evenings
at the theater or with the Leuvens.

Housekeeping with Laure did not mean settling for half a loaf.
The poetic image of the seamstress and the poet, like two pigeons
in a garret, was not for Alexandre. He slept with a working-class
woman but he frequented socially prominent Bonapartist salons
whose opinions, little by little, he adopted as his own. Thus he
received the news of the capture of the Trocadero with anger, for
the liberating French army had stifled liberty in Spain. Thus, too,
he avidly read *Le mémorial de Sainte-Hélène* which Las Cases had
begun to publish. To the generation of 1826, it was almost a holy
book. Napoléon crucified at Saint Helena became the universal
model to imitate. All budding Bonapartists fervently dipped their
pens in the inkwell of fame. The time of the sword had passed, the
next battles would be poetic. Power was promised to those who

knew how to spot their fingers with ink. Would this power go to Casimir Delavigne? His *L'école des vieillards* at the Comédie-Française, with Talma's role simultaneously gentle, noble and charming, was an immense success. But the play belonged to the past. This, Lassagne pouted, was not the literary revolution he had wished. One would have to be satisfied with Lamartine's *Nouvelles méditations poétiques*, but in spite of its new sound, it was also too reminiscent of older forms.

Alexandre was now familiar with Parisian society. Thanks to Adolphe, he knew some second class dramatists. He hung around Lucien Arnault and was sometimes allowed backstage at the Comédie-Française. In 1823 he succeeded in placing two puny poems, "Blanche et Rose" and "Romance," in a souvenir-album entitled *Almanach dédié aux demoiselles*. The twenty-year-old philosophe's eyes shone to see his name printed there beside others more illustrious. In Laure's arms he dreamt of elusive glory, but it was still too early. Laure frowned at his ambitious efforts: she guessed that she had rivals but knew that the most formidable was this thirst for glory that never left her young lover.

On February 14, 1834, Jacques-Parfait Oudard sent a request to Manche de Broval:

> Since April 10, 1823, M. Dumas has worked as a supernumerary in the office of the secretaire des commandements. I am very satisfied with his zeal and foresee that he will become a distinguished employee. . . . It seems fair to me, in the meantime, to increase to 125 francs per month the salary granted to him (100 francs per month). It is an incentive he deserves to receive. . . .

Manche de Broval approved. With fifteen hundred francs per year, Alexandre's situation was almost flourishing. He immediately wrote to his mother, asking that she come to Paris. Madame Dumas so missed her son that she sold the right to her tobacco shop and put a part of her miserable furniture up for sale, a transaction that brought one hundred francs. She arrived in Paris about February 10, 1824 with the rest: her bed, a chest of drawers, a table, two armchairs and four chairs. Alexandre had found a second-floor apartment at No. 53 Rue du Faubourg-Saint-Denis, in the house next to the Lion d'Argent. It looked onto the street, had two bedrooms, a dining room, and a kitchen and cost three hundred fifty francs per year.

His mother was immensely happy, while Laure, increasingly conscious of unexpected kicks from her swelling belly, shed a tear on the handkerchief she was embroidering. Since his mother had come to settle in Paris, she understood that Alexandre would have to leave her. Already she regretted their too-brief happiness that now left her distraught. Alexandre would come only for fleeting visits. He would not be around anymore, reading voraciously while she readied their meals; he would not have time to tell her his life, in detail, day by day. The celebration of spring had ended, the fruits of pleasure had been gathered. Only the unborn child would remain to her . . . and to her alone.

Alexandre assured his mother that he was a model employee, appreciated by his superiors. While he could not help showing her the verses he had succeeded in having printed, he did it with a hypocritical indifference, as though it were of little importance. He did not mention Laure, nor the child she carried. Madame Dumas must be kept unaware that she was to be a grandmother. Only a lie could avoid the kind of dramatic scene Alexandre hated.

II

Ode and Farce

Every morning, about half past ten, Alexandre arrived at his office in the Palais Royal, from which he emerged at five. But when the Duc d'Orléans resided at Neuilly, Alexandre had to come back from eight to ten in the evening to prepare the "portfolio," which involved sending the evening newspapers and the day's mail and receiving in return the orders for the next day. Monseigneur adored the country, the extra work of the "portfolio" multiplied, and Alexandre had very little time to study and dedicate to his literary projects. There were, of course, tickets for the Théâtre-Français, but Oudard distributed them parsimoniously and reserved the poorest shows for his subordinates. That's how Alexandre learned what should not be written for the theater.

At five, Alexandre hurried to 53 Rue du Faubourg-Saint-Denis where his dinner, prepared by his mother, waited for him. Alexandre's attentiveness helped her become accustomed to her new surroundings. After a week Madame Dumas had settled to her own corner. She had never really left her son. The only worry was the rent. It was so high their small savings could be compromised. When their neighbor across the landing died from a chest ailment at his brother's (April 26, 1824) the Dumas' carried their belongings over to his now empty apartment. One hundred twenty francs were saved by crossing the landing.

Once he had gulped down his dinner, Alexandre lost himself in a recent book, the *Nouvelles odes* by Victor Hugo. Then, if it was Ernest Basset's week to do the "portfolio," Alexandre ran to the theater. After the theater he met some friends in a café, or he visited Laure whose waist line was growing thicker every day. Alexandre moved quickly throughout Paris, trying to make up for lost time.

One morning Oudard called in Alexandre. In a solemn tone he explained to his employee that the Duke needed someone to copy rapidly and accurately a secret document. Alexandre had been chosen. He waited, not without trembling, the arrival of the Prince. He was quite a handsome man, though heavy, even corpulent, with an open face, sharp witty eyes and a pleasant voice.

With emotion, Alexandre applied himself to copying some fifty pages of the Duke's elongated handwriting.

At eleven o'clock in the evening, Alexandre put a final period at the end of his work. He was still a nobody, but he kept company with the great, those people who make history, or whose ancestors had made it. He did not possess glory, but he gathered its scraps. He was the grandson of Claude Labouret, majordomo of the Duc d'Orléans, grandfather of the present Duke.

Alexandre had begun to read Byron, who had recently died in Greece, which he had wanted to deliver from Turkish oppression. It was a long way from Missolonghi to Paris and it was not until May 18 that the news reached Paris. Young men took to mourning, for Byron's revolt against society, against worldly obligations, against God himself, was their cause as well. Byron's cries of grief were those they did not dare to shout themselves. In Byron's death, as in that of Napoléon earlier, were flashes of heroism and greatness. The modest employee remembered that at his own age, his father the General had been slashing the enemy. On such days, Alexandre would dip his pen in the inkwell with rage.

However, the poet's death only momentarily revived the tarnished glamor of "romanticism." In Paris, Shakespeare, the god, received the homage he deserved. Only two years before, English actors had been greeted with cabbage stumps. This barbarian literature, so far from French traditions and customs, had provoked universal disapproval. On Lassagne's advice, Alexandre read Shakespeare, Scott and Schiller, but the circles he frequented, the liberal Bonapartist salons, rejected with horror the foreign monstrosities.

Still too weak to show his individuality, Alexandre joined the general clamor.

On Tuesday July 27, 1824, Madame Dumas worried: Alexandre had not returned home. He was with Laure Labay and the small red creature on whom they imposed a life that began with a birth certificate that read: "Born of an unknown father. Surname, Alexandre."

The joy and pride of begetting life are not without mixed feelings. Could a fifteen hundred-franc-a-year employee, with a dependent mother, afford the luxury of paternity without giving up all his ambitions? He was twenty-two and had a great love for life. Now he would succeed for his son, too.

While the child of a poor couple was born in a garret, old King Louis XVIII agonized at the Louvre. From his window Alexandre saw the lugubrious procession pass, carrying to Saint-Denis the remains of the last king to be buried there.

This winter of 1824, Alexandre scraped his funds together to buy a large overcoat, fashionably called the "Quiroga," after the Spanish general who headed the constitutional troops. The purchase was a political protest. On January 3, 1825, majestically draped in this liberal overcoat, Alexandre was dragged by his office colleagues, Betz and Tallancourt, to the Dutch Tavern. As they entered, laughter burst out, winks were exchanged. The hot-tempered Alexandre caromed the billiard balls of the sneering players who had been peacefully busy with their game. The insults escalated and a rendezvous for a duel was set for the next day. The hopeful Alexandre initially felt the exhilaration at his first duel. Betz and Tallancourt, ex-military men, were worried. How would the young provincial handle arms? They experimented with a pistol at the Gosset shooting range and were both amazed. But the adversary, Charles B., chose swords. The exaltation lessened as they waited. Alexandre thought of his mother and of his son whom he would leave without protection; he repented for having left himself thus exposed for such a pecadillo. The next day he cooled his heels in vain: his adversary had caught a cold the evening before while skating on the canal. The encounter was postponed to the following day.

Alexandre returned to his office. Now and then he felt a slight anxiety, then yawned. It was the feast of the Three Kings. Alexandre showed more tenderness toward his mother who had discovered the bean hidden in her piece of the traditional brioche and thus was crowned queen of the feast day. He slept badly. In the morning, it was cold and it began to snow as they left Paris through the Rochechouart gate.

The group looked for a place suitable for the duel. A circle of curious onlookers formed. Alexandre had chosen the shortest épée, because it was his father's—he preferred a disadvantage of five inches of blade rather than having the General's sword turned against him. He took off his coat but on Charles B.'s insistance he had to take off his shirt and jacket, too, and he shivered on the first break. To his great surprise, Charles B. was off guard. A simple maneuver threw him on the snow. The épée had entered his shoulder; the wounded man had never handled an épée before.

During the duel Alexandre was attended by André Thibault, a physician without a regular practice whom Alexandre had consulted in the past. Weak lungs were as fashionable as "la Quiroga"-style coats. It was considered smart to spit some blood at the least emotion, especially when one wanted to pass for a poet, and to die, if possible, before reaching thirty. Tall and skinny Alexandre seemed to have all the necessary tendencies. He consulted with Thibault who had become a friend. He often accompanied him to the anatomy demonstrations at the Hôpital de la Charité; in the evening he attended experiments in physics and chemistry that Thibault practiced in his small room in the Rue du Pélican, under the eyes of his beautiful neighbor, Mademoiselle Walker, a milliner who was clever enough to satisfy the two friends without setting them against each other. From his studies with Thibault, the future novelist retained a certain smattering of medicine that would become useful to describe Madeleine's and Amaury's consumption in *Amaury* or the poisoning symptoms in Monte-Cristo.

Tuberculosis, however, does not make a poet: in 1824 the reviews had not accepted Alexandre's verses, and theater directors had hardly looked at the unhappy tentative scenarios that Adolphe and Alexandre had submitted to them. The Dumas' savings became exhausted. They had to take care of the most pressing matters first: making money.

Alexandre and Adolphe decided to take on a collaborator who already had a foothold in the theaters. Their choice was James Rousseau, who would add the finishing touches. They visited him in his lodging, and after buying him a good lunch at the Café des Variétés, the meeting place of actors and artists, they all went to Leuven's to start work. Adolphe first insisted on reading the two friends' dramatic efforts. At the second scene, Rousseau lay down on Adolphe's bed; at the fourth, he snored. When he woke up, drowsily, he chose to take the precious manuscript home with him.

The following Thursday (March 17, 1825), Rousseau eagerly responded to the invitation that promised him two bottles of champagne. But he spread desolation: nothing pleased him, neither the farces nor the melodrama, none of which he probably read. A hunting story that Alexandre told over dessert captured his enthusiasm; why not turn it into a farce called *La chasse et l'amour*? The second champagne bottle had delivered up its last drop. A third one was promised, once the plan of the play was in the works. The dishes, silver, table cloth were taken away, replaced at once with pens, ink and paper. While the bottle was drunk in fifteen minutes, the plan took an hour. The play would have twenty-one scenes (twenty-two in the final version) that the collaborators would share in thirds: the seven exposition scenes for Alexandre, the seven central scenes for Adolphe, the seven final scenes for Rousseau. They made an appointment for eight days hence to read the play while dining (a hook was necessary to catch Rousseau). The next day Alexandre had already taken care of his scenes. On the following Thursday, Adolphe was ready, too, but Rousseau had not written a single line. They had to be content with reading Alexandre's and Adolphe's contributions. Alexandre's bawdy verses about the Parisian hunter who boasted of his self-merits were an unqualified success that spurred Rousseau's admiration. He held his glass to be filled again. The next day, between ten and one o'clock in the morning, while Alexandre was on "portfolio" duty at his office, Rousseau's share was written. *La chasse et l'amour* could face the footlights. To which theater would they give this masterpiece? Adolphe and Rousseau were inclined toward the Gymnase where Rousseau's play had been given and he rapidly obtained a reading. However, they had to wait three weeks. It was decided that only two of the authors would be named. Alexandre willingly accorded the honor to Adolphe. To debut with *La chasse et l'amour* seemed to him rather unworthy of his hopes as well as his pride.

On the great day of the reading, after a lunch with his collaborators at the Café du Roi, Alexandre returned to his office. He was in a trance. At three o'clock Adolphe and Rousseau crept through the half-opened door, desolate: *La chasse et l'amour* was unanimously turned down. The readers had been scandalized by Alexandre's double entendres.

Alexandre appeared so dazed, so beaten down, that the gentle Lassagne proposed they collaborate on another farce. In spite of this ray of hope, the dinner the rejected authors shared was melancholy indeed. The disastrous reception at the Gymnase had crushed their confidence. Nevertheless, they decided to ask for another reading at the Ambigu theater, whose manager was one of Rousseau's friends.

The next day a reading was granted for the following Saturday. Again, Alexandre waited anxiously at his office. This time the double door was opened widely to let the victors enter. The play was accepted, by acclamation. This time the offending lines were a hit.

La chasse et l'amour had no pretension other than to make money. Alexandre immediately inquired about the royalties and what could be expected from a farce performed at the Ambigu: twelve francs in copyright and six author seats in the theater. He made a rapid division; he would receive four francs and two 40-centime seats, or six francs per evening. It was modest, but it was one and a half times the salary he received from the Duc d'Orléans.

A play accepted was not a play performed. How long would they have to wait for the premiere? Not very long, since the play would be read to the actors during the first days of May. If Alexandre were in a hurry, he could sell his author's seats and royalties in advance to a good man, Jean-Baptiste Porcher who, after having owned a barber shop, had turned himself into a chief of claques, then a ticket seller. Rousseau had strongly recommended Alexandre to Porcher, who at once agreed to give a fifty-franc advance for the tickets to *La chasse et l'amour*. What a delightful feeling to hold this first money earned with his pen! From now on Alexandre would have his name in Porcher's big record book, alongside other prosperous playwrights.

All along the way to Faubourg Saint-Denis, Alexandre jingled the fifty francs in his pocket. He displayed his modest treasure to his amazed mother. Hope that had begun to fade, miraculously bloomed again.

While Porcher consecrated Alexandre as a writer, under a radiant sun that followed the rain, Charles X, the last anointed King of France, solemnly received crown and sceptre on May 29, 1825.

The Duchesse d'Orléans related the incident of the coronation in her diary. She was a Neapolitan Princess and wrote in Italian. She asked for a translation from Oudard who unloaded the chore on Alexandre and granted him two free days to complete the project. Alexandre conscientiously translated the passage, then indiscreetly read the entire album in which the Duchess had noted her most secret actions and thoughts. In the cloud of angelic thoughts, Alexandre focused on the account of the death of the father of the Duchess, the odious Ferdinand the First of Naples whom, he suspected, had poisoned Alexandre's father while he was a prisoner in Taranto. The tyrant had coughed several times, then given up the ghost. Assassins have a sweeter death than their victims.

Oudard was complimented for his translation. Alexandre received two tickets for a performance at the Comédie-Française.

The Duke's office was abuzz over the project of Jean Vatout, one of His Royal Highness's librarians. He had begun to make available his first issue of the *Galerie lithographiée des tableaux de S.A.R. Mgr. le Duc d'Orléans*, a magnificent work containing reproductions and an accompanying text in prose and verse. Vatout did not hesitate to include young poets, and Alexandre was eager to impress him with his talent. For the eighth issue, the librarian had singled out Frédéric Soulié, who then owed his modest reputation to a single booklet of poems. Soulié was correcting his contribution to the Galerie (*La folle de Waterloo*) when Adolphe introduced Alexandre to him in the luxurious mezzanine he occupied in the rue de Provence. Soulié lived on his private income and even owned a piano on which he played the two or three tunes he knew. Alexandre was amazed by this aristocrat who offered tea, cakes and sandwiches to his friends. They talked of literature and of overrated reputations. And to the shamefaced authors of *La chasse et l'amour*, Soulié professed profound disdain for second-class writings.

They also discussed the nomination of Isidore-Severin-Justin Taylor as the head of the Comédie-Française. Young and passionately devoted to the arts and literature, he would surely get rid of the old fashioned conventions constraining the theater company founded by Molière and dedicate the new reign to the same healthy revolution in the theater that Lamartine and Hugo had begun in poetry. The friends drank a counter toast: a plague on all merchants of antiquated fashions . . . including Antoine Arnault. Alexandre hung his head, but Soulié didn't notice the young clerk who smelled of the provinces.

During the summer of 1825, Alexandre worked with Lassagne and Vulpian, a man of great wit whom they had chosen as a collaborator on a farce whose subject was borrowed from the *Mille et une nuits*. It was titled *Le nouveau Simbad ou la noce et l'enterrement*. A poor widower, contrary to the tradition of the time, refused to be buried with the spouse he had just lost. Alexandre had concocted the scenario, they split the work, then put together their various segments. Lassagne varnished the whole play. The new masterpiece was offered to the Vaudeville. Its success was almost as brilliant as the initial failure of *La chasse et l'amour* whose production was postponed to the next season. Alexandre had already mortgaged the future profits of his second play to Porcher who loaned him three hundred francs. He had to feed his mother and son and his obligations exceeded his income. This would be a constant preoccupation for the rest of his life. He would never have the money to match his appetites.

The harvest began—*La chasse et l'amour* was announced for September 22 at the Ambigu-Comique. The play was right on target, for the opening of the hunting season was very close. Although the actors were duly applauded, the shopgirls of the Faubourg-Saint-Denis only had eyes for the young leading man, appropriately named Chéri. It was a near triumph. Adolphe and Alexandre congratulated themselves; Rousseau was more blasé, he had had several such triumphs. The play continued to be performed: five times in September, five times in October, four times in November, twice in December. Sixteen performances meant ninety-six francs in Alexandre's purse with which he could begin to refund Porcher. Even better, though Alexandre had not been mentioned as one of the authors at the first performance, his name did figure on the printed version of the play, not as Dumas but simply as Davy. Perhaps he did not want the General's glorious name, de la Pailleterie, to be mixed up with a vulgar farce. Perhaps, too, he wanted to avoid letting his superiors know of his detours into commercial theater. But Alexandre was so proud of his current and forthcoming plays that he talked too much. Bureaucrats do not like diversity. Jacques-

Parfait Oudard knew already, soon Manche de Broval would know too. The storm gathered.

Lassagne warned Alexandre. Oudard had expressly recommended that Alexandre should not be encouraged in his literary ambitions. Such advice from a superior is an order. All of Alexandre's dreams collapsed, and with them the hope of quadrupling his salary with literary work. With tears in his eyes, he rushed into Oudard's office. How could he dare condemn three persons to live on one hundred and twenty-five francs per month? Did his office work suffer from his literary activities? Was he more guilty when writing *L'amour et la chasse* and *Le mariage et l'enterrement* than when taking on outside work copying other's plays to relieve his near destitution? Oudard fell back on Manche de Broval's lack of taste for literature. "If you wrote like Casimir Delavigne, instead of criticizing you we would encourage you," Oudard finally blurted out. Casimir Delavigne enjoyed the sinecure of a librarian with the Duc d'Orléans. Alexandre lost his temper: "Sir, I'm not yet as old as Monsieur Casimir Delavigne who became poet laureate in 1811; I have not received the education of Monsieur Casimir Delavigne, who was brought up in one of the best colleges of Paris. No, I am twenty-two (twenty-three, in fact); I teach myself everyday. I do it perhaps at the expense of my health. For all that I learn—and I swear to you I learn many things—I learn while others amuse themselves or sleep.... Finally, Monsieur Oudard, listen attentively to what I am going to say, even if what I am going to say will seem very strange to you: If I believed I would never write any better than Monsieur Casimir Delavigne, well, Monsieur, I would go along with your wishes and those of Monsieur de Broval and, at this very moment, I would offer you my sacred promise, my solemn oath, to never again write another word."

Out of breath, Alexandre stopped at last. Oudard was thunderstruck by such arrogance. How could anyone claim to surpass Casimir Delavigne? He went down to Deviolaine to report the atrocities that his cousin had just uttered. That evening, Madame Dumas wept when Deviolaine notified her of her son's scandalous conduct. Alexandre consoled her and promised all she wanted, knowing very well that he wouldn't keep his promise. Madame Dumas felt that a position at fifteen hundred francs per year was already good enough.

The next day, the sixty-three employees of His Royal Highness greeted each other with "Do you know what Dumas said yesterday to Monsieur Oudard?" The story, once told, was corrected, embellished, added to. Everyone sneered and laughed out loud. Everyone, save an employee who had begun the day before in the bookkeeping department: his name was Amédée de la Ponce. As office opinion divided, Alexandre could count on only two allies, Lassagne and Amédée.

The political panegyrics Alexandre had criticized in Casimir's writing would ironically be his next genre. Coming out of his office on November 23, 1825, he learned from passersby that Général Foy had died. The protector who had first helped him to escape misery was dead. Alexandre went back to the Rue du Faubourg-Saint-Denis in despair. He took paper, pen and ink and wrote a title: "Élégie sur la Mort du Général Foy." When he put down his pen in the early morning hours, he was thrilled to find himself a poet.

On the 30th, under a slashing rain, thirty thousand people followed the funeral train of General Foy from his mansion to Notre Dame de Lorette. Thousands of spectators clogged the sidewalks. Soaking wet, Alexandre took note of every detail to include in his poem that evening: the hundreds of arms that were held up to take the coffin, so that he was carried on the backs of men; the Général's two young sons, who stumbled, fearful of the crushing crowd, and were held back from the open grave; the carriage with the Duc d'Orléans' livery among the mourning carriages. With this tactful allusion to the Duc's liberal sympathy, the poet deliberately enlisted himself in the current of the Orleanist party. He needed a patron, and he took the one closest at hand.

Alexandre borrowed three hundred francs which he took to the printer and bookseller Setier: the "Hommage à Foy," born from a first move of gratitude, must be published. If the protectors did not turn a deaf ear, the poetic career of the clerk was assured.

Barely printed, the ode was immediately distributed by its author. He gave away more than he sold. Général Foy's widow, to whom it was dedicated, received a copy with "homage of respect, sorrow and gratitude" from Alexandre himself. The Arnaults received copies, too.

Congratulations poured in—the birth of a liberal bard was nothing to disdain in the emerging ideologic fight against the ultras whose beardless romantics sang themselves hoarse in praise of the throne and the altar. The hope of a coterie, Alexandre was to be smiled upon, encouraged, and received a little better than a poor relative. Among the first to receive the budding liberal poet was Guillaume Guillon, known as Léthière or Letiers, a painter of historical subjects who had recently been selected a member of the Institut. Remembering his friendship with the Général, he received Dumas' son and widow each Thursday in his drawing room. There Alexandre paid court to the spirit of the house, Mélanie d'Hervilly, a tall, thin, blonde young woman with a dry heart and a cold mind. Once a pupil of old Léthière, she had become his mistress. Alexandre had no great chance with her. Mélanie liked only older men; after the painter's death, she married the inventor of homeopathy, Hahnemann, who was near eighty. But at this series of Thursday gatherings, Alexandre met the illustrious and aging figures of the Empire who were amused by his ambitions and desires. Though self-satisfied, their patronage was not negligible for a clerk. Alexandre felt himself very much alive.

Alexandre's verses began to be noticed. Publishers of memorial volumes in honor of the glory of Général Foy requested permission to include his poetry. It was not yet glory, but it was the beginning of Alexandre's reputation. The recently-founded *Le Figaro* published a long and laudatory article February 24, 1826 about the "Élégie."

Dumas was twenty-three. He knew what he wanted: "a career strewn with roses and banknotes"—glory and money. The young men of his generation did not put their stake on the red or on the black. Dumas gambled on ink. His aspirations remained, the instruments of ambition had changed. It was literature that now led to glory and money, which meant social status. But writings were only means to his ends: farces for money, elegies for glory. Alexandre would lend his talent to Grub Street; he gave himself to the glory of Literature.

The "Élégie" confirmed the arrival of a poet. Though poor, he was not alone. His strategy was to utilize the influence of the salons of the Leuvens, the Arnaults, the Léthières, as many Bonapartist circles as opened their doors for him. By a strange irony of history, the son expected aid and protection from the sycophants or incense-bearers of Napoléon whom he considered the executioner of his father. But by then Bonapartism was only a current of the liberal movement, and Dumas, Orléanist by conviction and by necessity, shared in the same ideology.

The farce gave him a small pittance, the ode gave him a ray of glory.

III

A Newborn Reputation

Alexandre passed by 7 Cour des Fontaines, address of Louis-Paschal Setier, *his* publisher. It was half-way between his office and the room of Thibault. Alexandre only had eyes for the beautiful Madame Setier, Abigail Samuda, whom Setier had brought back from London. She was twenty-eight, Jewish, and beautiful with long hair as black as the wing of a crow, and aristocratic manners. She offered to translate for Alexandre English plays that he could adapt for the theater. Their intellectual exchange was accompanied with an amorous friendship. It was probably in the course of one of these conversations that it was decided to found a review of poetry. Adolphe was a partner in the project.

Alexandre volunteered to recruit the writers he knew: the Arnaults, father and son, as well as the poetic beehive of the Duc d'Orléans' office: Casimir Delavigne, of course, Jean Vatout and Lassagne. Each one offered his verses. As founders, Leuven's and Alexandre's names were on the masthead. It was, Alexandre recalled, "an admirable means . . . of publishing what I would henceforth write, in prose or verse, without having to pay the expense of printing."

The first issue came out in March 1826. Alexandre composed two poems for it: "L'adolescent Malade," which was dedicated to another contributor, Marceline Desbordes-Valmore, and "La Néréide," an elegy in the antique style appropriate for a journal called *La Psyché*. Antoine Arnault should have been pleased. Alexandre adopted his attitude by setting up the antique as the standard of beauty—a taste epitomized in the pseudo-Athenian mask of such contemporary nineteenth-century Parisian temples as the Church of the Madeleine and the Stock Exchange.

What did it matter! A review was merely a means to his end. For Manche de Broval, Alexandre was only an employee. But for Delavigne and Vatout, the Duke's librarians, and Lassagne, chief-assistant, he had the power (albeit very modest) to decide on the publication of one's work. Before, Alexandre could only be refused, now he could refuse. He had known how to take advantage of the opportunity he recognized in Madame Setier's smile.

Alexandre was a writer as long as he had a printer. He had momentarily abandoned commercial literature to throw himself entirely into poetry. He followed in the steps of Lamartine and Hugo. But the fashion was for small pieces—a short novel or novella. Why not write short stories? wondered Alexandre, who had no doubt about his talent, even if he still hesitated as to which genre he should apply it. He threw himself into prose with the same certainty as he had thrown himself into verse. Three women heroines gave their names to the short stories entitled "Blanche de Beaulieu, ou la vendéene," "Laurette" and "Marie." The prose writer was better than the versifier. Put together, the three stories formed the *Nouvelles Contemporaines*, dedicated "to my mother, with love, respect and gratitude." As with his elegy, Alexandre remembered his debts.

Madame Setier found these stories charming. She asked her husband to publish them for fifty percent of the profit. Why endure rejection after rejection from publishers, when he had within his reach a publisher-printer, and above all, the latter's wife? The printing of a thousand copies of the stories cost six hundred francs. Alexandre wrung three hundred francs out of Porcher. The presses went to work. Alexandre corrected his proofs with joy. The ink had hardly dried when the words were transformed into the pages of his book. At first, he took great pride in the task which later would become an awful chore.

Every day Alexandre visited his publisher. But the *Nouvelles* did not sell, the pile of books remained untouched. Only four copies were sold. Was it necessary, as a bookseller had once told him, to make a name for oneself before being printed?

The results of the foray into prose would have been very bitter if there hadn't been a delightful article in the *Figaro*, on June first:

After the homage rendered to the memory of Général Foy, M. Alex Dumas has left the language of the gods for vile prose, as Voltaire said. The muses have not punished him for his infidelity, and the *Nouvelles Contemporaines* from the young prose-writer's pen could not harm the reputation of a rising poet. Son of a distinguished warrior, M. Dumas has chosen his heroes from the ranks of the army. His remembrance of our misfortune and of our former glory give life to his stories. . . . Although they recount similar misfortunes, all three prepare their many readers for different feelings, in turn sweet, sad and heart-rending.

The writer responsible for *La Psyché* pursued his poetic work. In April he presented "L'aigle blessé" to the review. The metaphor was transparent: the eagle was Napoléon who disdained the saccharine happiness of the doves. The poet's imagination was still tuned to heroism. When Paris failed to provide inspiring examples, he looked farther afield.

On April 23, despite the determined resistance of Greek insurgents, Missolonghi was taken. The battle in faraway Greece awakened Parisians to Philhellenism. Alexandre celebrated Kanaris who four years earlier, in the company of Pipinos, had dared attack the Turkish admiral's command with a fireship.

"Canaris" was the fruit of the Léthière's salon. Mélanie d' Hervilly had watched over the work in progress, as indicated in the dedication with which Alexandre decorated the copy he gave her: "To Mlle d'Hervilly. Homage and proof that I have benefited from her advice." Inserted in the third issue of *La psyché*, "Canaris" was immediately reprinted in a brochure and sold for the Greeks' benefit. It was dedicated to Casimir Delavigne. Leaning on Alexandre's vigorous arm, Mademoiselle d'Hervilly could be recognized among the visitors of the great exhibit at the Le Brun Gallery that was entirely dedicated to the Hellenic cause. They could admire the *Massacre de Chio* by Eugène Delacroix. The Muses, however, did not stop the cannons from thundering—on August 26, 1826, Ibrahim-Pacha besieged Athens.

Would *La Psyché* mix romanticism with classicism? In its later issues, the names of Chateaubriand and Victor Hugo were noticed. One by one the young royalists lost their hopes for the Bourbons while the young classicists lost theirs to the literary status quo.

Romanticism in literature already embodied liberalism. Despite the ideological divisions inherited from the past, the generation born with the century was little by little coalescing. Royalist? Classic? Romantic? Liberal? The era of the literary cliques was over, the world was wide open to an ambitious twenty-five-year-old author. Alexandre became slightly less interested in the review; he published only two new poems: "Souvenirs" (July) and "Le Poète" (October).

Vatout, who had published in *La Psyché*, returned the compliment. He asked the young employee of His Royal Highness for a poem for *La galerie lithographiée*. Alexandre could write accompanying verses below one of two or three lithographs. He chose a painting by Monvoisin, *Jeune pâtre romain endormi* and, in the style of Vergil, he sang of the "golden poverty" of the shepherd who sleeps happy on the ruin of the ancient mistress of the world. But what was the good of sighing on graves? Life was to be simple and tranquil.

By the time Alexandre's child was two and had learned to say "Papa" his father began to get in the way in Laure Labay's small lodging. He was too big, too agitated; he bumped into all the furniture, spoke too loudly, kissed too hard. Papa was a disturbance in the modest home. Thus, though Alexandre occasionally let himself be caught in domestic happiness, he soon tore himself away to pursue literary glory.

Vatout's request for verses seemed to confirm his place in contemporary literature. Moreover, he boasted, women led him to believe he was irresistible. To an old comrade from Villers-Cotterêts he exclaimed, "I'm not presumptuous enough to call myself a miracle worker but I shouldn't be surprised if in the future a curly-haired baby appeared here below to confirm my powers."

After having languished a long time in the files of the Vaudeville, *La noce et l'enterrement* was at last put in rehearsal at the Porte-Saint-Martin. Alexandre excused himself from the office. He was the author and that gave him a right to be backstage and close to young actresses who had more beauty than talent. Second-class theaters were a nursery for courtesans. The Porte-Saint-Martin theater was more generous than the Ambigu: eight francs for copyright plus tickets for every performance were promised. For the premiere on November 31, 1826, Alexandre had reserved an orchestra seat for his mother. She was proud of her son, the author, and unconcerned about what she saw. She laughed happily. The play succeeded perfectly. Once the curtain came down, the person on the next seat might well have said, "Well, well, this isn't the Great New Hope of the theater." But by the end of 1826, Alexandre could count with satisfaction sixteen performances of *La chasse et l'amour* at the Ambigu (ninety-six francs) and twenty-five performances of *La noce et l'enterrement* (two hundred francs). He would have to reimburse Porcher for his advances, but the generous ticket seller was content with half the royalty to help replenish his funds. Alexandre and his mother spent the winter of 1826–1827 quite peacefully. Once again, Alexandre had hidden himself behind the pseudonym of Davy. Davy wanted the money, Dumas the glory.

To conciliate glory and money Alexandre now proposed an oeuvre, be it drama or tragedy, which he could dare sign Dumas. He considered a partnership with Frédéric Soulié, who dazzled Alexandre with his luxurious life and wealth. They began their collaboration with an attempt to adapt *The Scottish Puritans* by the then fashionable Sir Walter Scott. In spite of all their efforts, neither this idea nor any of the various projects that followed satisfied the two collaborators. In the middle of these disappointments, Alexandre could now give more time to literature during office hours, for a revolution had shaken the Palais-Royal. Betz had received a promotion, leaving open his two-thousand-franc position. Ernest Basset, Manche de Broval's protégé, had taken Betz' position and Alexandre, in turn, became a candidate for Ernest's eighteen-hundred-franc position. Oudard could hardly refuse but, perhaps to show his disapproval, he made Alexandre transfer from the Secretariat to the Office of Assistance, the bureaucratic administration of traditional princely philanthrophy. Alexandre now walked all over Paris, sometimes for entire days, to obtain information on the unfortunate who had applied for help. He climbed filthy stairs in buildings that smelled of cabbage, entered freezing hovels heated with two blocks of peat, and tearfullly commiserated with starving women and pale orphans. He had known poverty; now he discovered wretchedness.

Alexandre's ambition to succeed was spurred by these painful sights. August Lafarge, the bright and handsome law clerk he had first known at Villers-Cotterêts, had fallen on hard times in Paris and recently died a pauper. His death was connected in Madame Dumas' mind with literature, and gave her nightmares. She feared that her son's raise in salary was actually a disguised form of exile. As the Deviolaines pointed out to the alarmed mother, to be far from the Secretariat meant to be far from the Duke and his favors.

Talma was in his grave, his costumes sold at auction on April 17, 1827. The Comédie-Française struggled to survive his loss under the firm direction of the Baron Taylor. Talma's would-be-successors fought to don his mantle but it would take several tragedians to be worth one Talma. Taylor, however, believed in a new theater. He personally saw to the accuracy of the costumes, the details of the decoration, the precision of the production of *Louis XI à Péronne*, the historical play based on Scott's novel *Quentin Durward*, which opened at the Comédie on February 15, 1827. Alexandre was not able to get a free ticket and was not rich enough to buy one, but the ostentatious Soulié had attended the play. At the end of the evening, he shared his enthusiasm with his collaborator at the Café des Varietes. *Les Puritains d'Écosse* was taken off the back burner and revived. Alexandre and Frédéric felt that a new theater must be born, a theater of national history, whose plays would be inspired by the chronicles and whose dramatic technique would be based on Shakespeare, Schiller and Scott.

Paris was illuminated. On April 18, printing press workers walked along the boulevards, crying "Long live the King!" Facing the thundering opposition, the government had been obliged to withdraw its projected legislation for the regulation of the press, mockingly dubbed the "law of justice and love." The government had become so unpopular that when reviewing the National Guard on the Champ de Mars in April 29, Charles X was greeted with the piercing and obstinate cries of "Down with the ministers!— Down with the Jesuits!" The young Alexandre had been among the marchers that day. He was in his new clothes as were six thousand new Guardsmen. He also cried, "Down with the ministers!" The next day, the National Guard was disbanded. The revolution that was brewing would be more than literary.

The last two poems Alexandre published in 1827, "Leipzig" and "Le Siècle et la poésie," signaled his return to Bonapartism. He more willingly accepted a vanquished Napoléon who was more tragic than heroic. Ultimately, however, he sang the glory of the hero in the hope that this glory would reflect on himself. *La Psyché* had to stop publication at the beginning of the year for Jean-Paschal Setier reckoned that his spouse's poets cost him too much. It was annoying, but for Alexandre who had several pies in the oven (the drama with Soulié, the poems for *La galerie lithographiée*, his farces which still had a decent run), *La Psyché* was no longer necessary. From now on, he was someone—not great yet, but someone.

In a later novel (*Les Mohicans de Paris, 1854*) Alexandre assessed the situation in Paris in 1827:

> Charles X had reigned two years; he was fainthearted but honorable, yet he let two parties grow up who, believing they strengthened him, would topple him—reactionary "Ultras" and the conservative "party of the priests." Aristocracy was worried and divided. . . . The bourgeoisie was as always: the friend of order and champion of peace; it wanted a change and trembled that this change would take place. . . . The people openly espoused the opposition, not knowing very clearly if it were Bonapartist or Republican. . . .

It was this divided Paris that he had to embrace and conquer. Alexandre did not feel he belonged to any social class. Aristocrat on his grandfather's side, bourgeois on his mother's, plebeian by necessity, he was nowhere and he wanted to be everywhere.

IV
Melalex

On June 3, 1827, at eight in the evening, Alexandre was leaning against the door frame of the auditorium in the Théâtre de l'Athénée, in Rue de Valois. The hall was full. The lecturer was very widely known in society and had distributed tickets to his acquaintances and to his close friends—tickets that they coudn't refuse. Mathieu-Guillaume-Thérèse Villenave had a certain fame. He taught a course in the literary history of France. Alexandre did not listen to the lecturer, but tried to discover in the audience some prominent literary luminaries who considered it a duty to suffer through Villenave's discourse and whose acquaintance could be useful. His eyes fastened on a woman, about thirty, very thin, with a dull complexion and dark eyes, sitting in the first row. His insistent glance bore like a weight on the woman who returned his steady look. But Alexandre had to run off soon: the "portfolio," back from Neuilly, was waiting for him at the Palais-Royal.

What did he remember besides this burning look? A podium, lighted by two candelabras and the standing lecturer, a glass of sweetened water near his hand. A handsome old man, Villenave was sixty-five, with fiery southern eyes and a magnificent mane of white hair, rolled coquettishly at his temples. Slightly bent, his body had elegance and distinction. It was impossible to imagine that this same old man had really participated in the great revolutionary tragedy.

He was the son of a physician and, to preserve within the family an ecclesiastical benefice, had prepared for the holy orders at an early age. He had been brought up in a convent by his godmother, then had pursued his studies at a college before obtaining a scholarship for the seminary of Toulouse. He had received "tonsure," but, more attracted by profane poetry than theology, had left the southwest of France for Paris where he had been trusted with the education of the Duc d'Aumont's son. In this intellectural milieu, frequented by the "blue-stocking" Germaine Necker, the Abbé de Villenave, as he then was called, first joined the poetic fray. When the Revolution broke out, he discarded the cassock to rally with the new cause. He founded *Le Rodeur français*, and for the love of Jeanne-Marie-Anne Tasset, settled at Nantes in 1792. There, in the middle of the antirevolutionary Vendée region, Villenave became an influential member of revolutionary associations. He was even named assistant to the Public Prosecutor at the criminal tribunal of the Loire-Inférieure jurisdiction. Suspected of moderatism, he was arrested on September 9, 1793. With one hundred and thirty-two citizens of Nantes, he was driven to Paris to be judged for the crime of conspiracy against the unity of the Republic. Saved by the overthrow of Robespierre's radical Committee of Public Safety in the month of Thermidor (July 27, 1794), he returned to Nantes and divided his time between his function as a professor at the Institut National, an unofficial public defender and a writer of many anti-Jacobin pamphlets.

A publicist and a versatile author, he settled in Paris at the end of 1803 and managed *Le journal des curés* from 1806 to 1809. He adopted the career of a man of letters, writing more than three hundred articles for Michaud's *Biographie universelle*, translating Ovid, proofreading the *Oeuvres complètes* of eighteenth-century writers, collecting rare books and autographs, and, since 1824, teaching at the Athénée in the Rue de Valois. By tireless work he gained enough of a reputation to challenge the traditional preserve of aristocratic literati—the former Public Prosecutor to a revolutionary tribunal had opened a literary salon. For the most part, the habitués belonged to the Philotechnic Society and the Society of Christian Morals, an assortment of rather rationalist savants, men of letters and artists. They were not opposed to a prudent innovation in matters esthetic, but continued to be deeply rooted in classicism. Villenave was a secondary star of the Parisian constellation.

Cordelier-Delanoue invited Alexandre to meet Villenave for tea after the lecture. Villenave received their congratulations and introduced his family to Alexandre: his spouse, a small, very gracious old lady, was witty and knowledgeable; his son, Théodore, was a tall and vigorous twenty-nine-year-old youth who flattered himself in claiming to be a dramatist; and finally his daughter, Madame Mélanie Waldor. It was she whom Alexandre had noticed in the front row. As they walked to the Villenaves' residence at No. 84 Rue de Vaugirard near the Luxembourg, Alexandre took Mélanie's arm.

The small house of the erudite lecturer was severe and gloomy. A high wall of gray stone surrounded a battered, flowerless garden. The main floor was dark, humid and musty. The guests were introduced in the first floor drawing room. In the shadows, against the indescribable wallpaper, Alexandre could make out four large paintings, a landscape by Claude Lorrain and three portraits. The guests sat on large sofas with thin white arms, on chairs and armchairs, all covered with Utrecht velvet. At the end of the room, enthroned on a marble table, was a funeral urn: it contained the heart of Bayard, Alexandre was told. After tea and biscuits it was agreed that from now on 84 Rue de Vaugirard would always be open to Alexandre, whose eyes had not left Mélanie. She was more than a woman—she was a salon of literary and social opportunity.

Every Friday Alexandre set out for the Luxembourg. Villenave greatly appreciated him. By July 14, he was writing to his old friend, the Princesse de Salm: "He is a young man with a real talent, son of Général Alexandre Dumas. He is a facile and brilliant poet who believes himself a romantic—which he is not—he never recites or reads in public; his memory is prodigious: he has memorized thirty or forty thousand verses." Alexandre had begun an encircling maneuver: first he would conquer the family before he threw himself on Mélanie. He offered candy to Mélanie's daughter, Elisa. Alexandre listened to the interminable reminiscences of Villenave, fraternized with Théodore and ingratiated himself with the intimate friends of the family.

It was certainly a gloomy and boring salon. But Mélanie was there. She had solemnly accepted a declaration of friendship and allowed a few confidences to escape. She regretted what she had left at Nantes, which was part of childhood: the house Cloître-Notre-Dame and above all the estate of La Jarrie where she spent her adolescence. She spoke little of her five-year marriage to the Lieutenant François-Joseph Waldor, but Alexandre could sense the unhappily married woman behind those veiled avowals. In February, Waldor had returned to his post as a quartermaster at the Thionville garrison. Mélanie had preferred to stay in Paris with her father. In the evening, before the fire, Mélanie tried to stifle her sighs and felt a bit old for this young man who squeezed her hand at every opportunity—she was thirty, though she only confessed to twenty-eight. She had to lower her eyes under his insistent stares and breathed deeply in an attempt to forget that she was desired.

Since June 20, 1827, almost every evening Alexandre had slipped a dreaded but expected letter into her hand. She trembled like a moth before a flame and energetically rejected the idea that their friendship could become anything more, but she had promised the token of a curl of her hair. She hardly knew how to resist so much love, each day reaffirmed.

You saw yesterday how you had the power to fan my emotions—to set them aflame and to extinguish them. I am speaking only of emotions, not the affection they surround. The very first time you spoke in favor of our friendship you said: "One must have friends to share one's suffering". . . . Do you remember this and what you told me yesterday, "that your life was upset for some time." Aren't emotions only the complement of shared suffering . . . ? I do not dare to ask you this question. You may still find again an answer, a mention of revery and of the passage of time. . . . No, you are mistaken, my love does not become more demanding, it becomes more timid. (September 7, 1827)

Mélanie kept her principles in separate compartments. She didn't forbid her soul the rapture of an ideal love. Although her body belonged only to the father of her child, François-Joseph Waldor, she also adored the dance that swept away the heart and the principles with it. There was a ball on September 12. A waltz entwined Mélanie in Alexandre's arms. Panting, out of breath, she removed a half-faded corsage of geraniums from her breast and allowed Alexandre to kiss it. It was more than a promise, it was a symbol. Alexandre exulted.

For eleven days Mélanie held back, eleven days of suffocation and palpitations, ardent kisses and forbidden caresses. The morals of the small, intellectual bourgeoisie of Nantes, from which she came, taught her that an adulterous woman was cursed. She fought eleven days, then on September 23 . . . the door of a cab opened, a woman, face concealed under an opaque veil, entered it rapidly. Two vigorous arms snatched her. The cab started, the coachman knew the way. A hand fumbled with her blouse and under her skirts: the chest was meager, the thighs birdlike, but the explorer was not discouraged. The woman murmured some stifled "no's." The cab jolted and shook, the ribald coachman smiled. For him, the loss of virtue meant a substantial tip.

Mélanie had given herself. Alexandre, his head buried in her underclothing, made a pretense of consoling her. Only tears could express the measure of the sacrifice. It was a beautiful Sunday at the beginning of autumn. Near the end of the Restoration, a Sunday tryst in a closed carriage was the only liaison available to an unhappily married woman and an office clerk who worked six days a week. Their time together was stingily allotted and Alexandre rushed through his work from ten-thirty in the morning to five in the evening. He had to take his meals with his mother and to visit his son and his son's mother. Mélanie had her obligations, too, as a mother and as a daughter. Villenave expected his daughter to grace his soirées. Nocturnal rendezvous were out of the question. How much time was there left? In the morning, between breakfast and the office; in the evening, between the closing of the office and the beginning of the salon; Sunday, and a few delightful moments "stolen from the angels"—or rather, stolen from society and its laws which banished sexuality into dingy rented rooms and cabs. Neither work, nor familial life, nor social life could be interrupted. Mélanie adjusted her clothes and welcomed Alexandre in the evening salon, still sensing his musky maleness. With a furtive blush she hardly betrayed the remembrance of her pleasure and her suffering. Once again, she closed her eyes, for she was his every time he looked at her.

Everything meant danger: the despotic father, the insidious brother, the perfidious friends, and her faraway husband, whose furlough loomed. But François-Joseph Waldor did not leave Thionville. Alexandre rented a small room with soiled wallpaper. Mélanie readjusted her clothes in front of a tarnished mirror. Lovemaking made them hungry, so they filled the larder with butter, jams and potatoes. They sometimes drank sweet wine from Lunel. But the small room was too far from 84 Rue de Vaugirard. It was also too exposed. Alexandre soon discovered another haven above a furniture merchant. If she were unexpectedly seen there, Mélanie could pretend that she had come to do some shopping. In a room decorated with wallpaper of large blue daisies, Alexandre and Mélanie made love on a slightly squeaking sofa.

The lovers met each evening, free to let their passion flow in the small room. However, they felt it necessary to continue the first rites. At each encounter they exchanged letters. One such letter reads:

I wanted to try to write to you yesterday when I came back, dear love, I was so disheartened that I could not, I woke up after having slept seven hours . . . but it was seven hours without living, for how can I live without thinking of you? Nonetheless, during my sleep, as deep as it is, there is a permanent thought that is you . . . I cannot account for it, but each time this sleep becomes lighter (you know, it happens often and yet one does not wake up), you become more visible, until I open my eyes and I see you completely. Have you forgiven me, my angel . . . I'll offer no more arguments to convince you. I will clasp you in my arms, or I will kneel before you. Looking at you, I will entreat you to love me, and you will forget everything for me, yes, all, won't you? And you will come back calm, and you will not suddenly shiver in my arms, or if you do, it will be with pleasure and love. (September 27, 1827)

The letters repeated the feverish words clandestinely exchanged. Because they were redundant they may appear useless, but they affirmed more than love—they affirmed literature. The lover disappeared behind the poet. Love must be subsumed by writing, it existed only to be expressed, even printed. Alexandre no longer saw himself as a simple employee at the Office of the Assistance (how many pretended visits to indigent people were, in fact, lovers' rendezvous!).

He was Lord Byron's Childe Harold who, from his fatal love, discovered the petrified forms of morality, who attempted to draw his lover toward social disintegration, who denied God, the guardian of prevailing ethic, and who rejected religion as an invention of imbecilic schemers. She was split between her passion and her respect for the social code of her milieu. He preached revolt against that world, against her father, against the society of puppets, prejudices and concession. Heaven was empty; all was permissible— above all, there stands passion. Alexandre wallowed in blasphemy and anathema. He believed himself a romantic, said Villenave. Who was he, really? A writer who rebelled against his own times to achieve recognition. All was allowed to the genius, but society was stingy and slow to certify talent. Yet the glittering prizes were worth the winding course. Chateaubriand circulated among ministries, embassies and the peerage; Victor Hugo received an income from the Monarchy. Through Mélanie, Alexandre already possessed a salon, albeit a modest one, but one salon opened into others when they espoused the same quarrels. He loved Mélanie—who was not very beautiful, who was not very young—more for what she represented than for what she was. For an impecunious young man, seducing a society woman was a social promotion from the seamstresses whose beds he had known. Bed sheets became a social ladder.

The predator, Alexandre, feared that his prey could be taken away. The enemy was the husband, poor François-Joseph Waldor whose superiors judged him in different lights. Either they recognized his solid education, great uprightness and probity, or they found that he lacked breeding and energy. Alexandre was jealous of the absent husband who languished in his Thionville garrison:

> . . . you were capable of jealousy! How happy I am! at last you have understood me, you know what it is to love since you knew the physical suffering of jealousy. . . . Don't you know it is the equivalent of the hell invented by religious maniacs who are expert in torture! It is pitiful, a hell where I could see you continually in another's arms. Dammit, this thought could give birth to a crime. Mélanie, my Mélanie, I love you insanely, more than one loves life, for though I understand death, I could not understand indifference to you. (end of September-beginning of October 1827)

One is tempted to judge Alexandre's sentiments by the overblown and pompous conventions of the period. Alexandre learned to compose love letters as he learned to make up alexandrines. He restricted himself to the laws of the genre: all that was not excessive was insignificant. He did not want so much to prove to Mélanie that he loved her, as to offer his writing talent for admiration. Secrecy dictated that the letters were never signed—they could be from the hand of any would-be writer of the year 1827 who had read a lot of Byron.

Led by Mélanie, Alexandre introduced himself into the salons she frequented. The great maneuvers had begun. Each evening was a skirmish. The avowed objective was to allow the lovers to meet in society, but Alexandre's real goal was to reconnoiter the Parisian scene and to search for allies among the lords of public opinion who made and unmade reputations. One must first make one's name in the salons before succeeding in the theater or in publishing. Who was this tall, skinny young man with frizzy hair and such beautiful, fiery eyes? He was the son of Général Dumas, and a promising poet. "He has African blood." That was indeed portentous, thought the social crowd, shivering a little. Mélanie had reason to be jealous. Lovers love, but poets must also sing "like two swans." Why shouldn't Mélanie also provide verses for the *Galerie lithographiée du Duc d'Orléans*? Vatour did not resist Alexandre. Mélanie and Alexandre, entwined on the sofa in the little room, gave themselves up to poetry. Mélanie would sign *La Bergère d'Italie*, though she found it too "masculine." In the pairing of swans, she would have only a minor voice.

In salons Alexandre did not confess that he was the author of such masterpieces played at the Ambigu or the Porte-Saint-Martin, which bore the names *La chasse et l'amour* and *La noce et l'enterrement*. Gravely, he said he was working on an adaptation of *Fiesque de Lavagna* by Schiller and had asked Baron Taylor for a reading. It would be a historic drama in five acts.

It was Gustave Drouineau who first read *Fiesque*, which was returned for corrections on October 1, 1827. When Alexandre set to work again on his historic drama, it was without enthusiasm or illusion. One needed very powerful patronage when one was an almost unknown author.

Mélanie's conquest, recognition in the salons and the undertaking of an ambitious work all belonged to the same social and literary strategy. But in spite of Casimir Delavigne's modest success, the theaters still needed to fill their empty stages. Alexandre set his sights on the Comédie-Française, the now-wavering fortress of classicism.

Though this may have been a calculated move, machiavellianism was not Alexandre's forte. He progressed, knowing intuitively which direction to take and pursuing it with formidable and singleminded energy. Mélanie lavished encouragement. She could not be wrong: if she allowed herself to be seduced, her excuse was to have surrendered to the impetuosity of genius. For her, Alexandre's every success was a justification. She had known how to divine the great man beneath the guise of an employee of the Duc d'Orléans' Office of Assistance. She demanded verses, fragments, outlines of scenes. She was his first and perhaps too tolerant reader. Apparently, Alexandre still only wrote for her; she was, however, the starting point of the huge public he dreamed about.

Alexandre had begun to write his tragedy while Mélanie composed fleeting poems into which she poured her worshipping heart. She could see only love; he saw only glory.

V

Checkmate to the Queen

Paris was a festival: love led off the ball. Paris no more resisted romanticism than Mélanie resisted Alexandre. The first Salon of 1824 had presaged the brilliant Salon of 1827, which opened on September 4th. On the 9th, Alexandre had eyes only for *La Naissance d'Henri IV* by Eugène Davéria. He thought it would be difficult, after this masterpiece, to paint as before. He also admired the dramatic *Mazeppa* by Boulanger and *Édith cherchant le corps d'Harold* by Horace Vernet. He stood a long time before a small bas-relief by Félicité de Vauveau, representing the assassination of Monaldeschi on Queen Christine's orders. Certainly the chisel had been handled with sensitivity and energy, but the subject, especially as it digressed utterly from history, intrigued him. It could possibly make a magnificent drama. Coming out of the museum he went to spend the evening with Frédéric Soulié who managed a woodworking shop. A great wood fire burned in the fireplace, the kettle bubbled for tea, and the conversation ran to present events: the English actors who had just begun their performances at the Odéon (September 6). The two friends' comments were punctuated by frequent exclamation marks. The future of the theater was in expressing the real passion of men and women made of flesh and bone; it was no longer to be a set of conventions that killed the emotions. It might be necessary to the conventions of the English stage, but essential inspiration could come from it as a model for the creation of a new theater. Alexandre said he might abandon his *Fiesque* and Frédéric his *Roméo et Juliette* to throw themselves into this exciting work. But what about a subject? Alexandre got hold of a *Biographie universelle* by Michaud, read the article on Christine, then read it again to Frédéric. Monaldeschi's assassination by the exiled queen made an ideal subject. Frédéric agreed, but as he expected to be officially decorated with the Croix d'Honneur for his first solo effort, he declined the offer of collaboration. Alexandre and Frédéric would compete against each other and each one would write a *Christine*. Alexandre's rivalry was of little concern to Frédéric.

In spite of the dark September night and rain, Alexandre dreamed of success as he walked along the boulevard. At the Porte Saint-Denis, screams pierced the night—two thieves were attacking a strolling couple. Alexandre ran forward chivalrously and had soon pinned down one thief under his knee while the other flew away as fast as his legs could carry him. When the police arrived, Alexandre thought he recognized a voice which stammered indistinct thanks. Then he recognized the face: it was Aglaé Tellier, in the company of her husband. They had come to Paris to see a performance of *La noce et l'enterrement*.

She had heard that the play was written by her ex-lover. Did the irreproachable spouse, the mother of a family (she had already given birth to four children, two of whom survived), still think often of Alexandre? The policeman did not want to distinguish between robbers and robbed. Because "all cats are gray in the dark," all of them were taken to jail. Aglaé and her husband settled on a cot. Alexandre looked sadly at this woman who had been his lover but was now gradually falling asleep on another man's shoulder, whom she addressed in the familiar "tu," and with whom she seemed perfectly happy. The young dramatist already felt the melancholy of remembrances. Once or twice in the following days he saw Aglaé again, but he realized that the ambitious author of *Christine* and the merchant of fashion accessories now had little in common.

Alexandre shook off these stale remembrances. He saw his future on the Odéon stage, where a company of English actors including Kemble, Kean, and Miss Smithson, presented Shakespeare as it should be played. Bouquets of flowers had succeeded the cabbage stumps of 1822. Alexandre borrowed from Porcher to buy a ticket and enjoy the beauty of *Hamlet*, the translation of which he had learned by heart. On September 11, he left his office at four o'clock to take his place in the queue which snaked before the Odéon. The performance was a revelation: Kemble was a marvelous Hamlet, Miss Smithson an adorable Ophelia. Alexandre, deeply moved, experienced Shakespeare with new eyes and ears. Suddenly the drama reached the greatness it had lost through the interpretation given by the Comédie-Française. A new dramatic tradition must be built and Alexandre would be its premier architect. About the 15th of September, he cried at the farewell scene on the balcony in *Roméo et Juliette*, shivered at the poisoning in the tomb. By the 18th or so of September, he understood Othello's jealousy, he for whom Mélanie risked at any moment the return of her husband. And he pitied the gentle Desdemona, suffocated by her small pillow:

Let's imagine a man born blind to whom sight is then given, who discovers a whole world of which he had no idea; imagine Adam awakening after his creation and finding under his feet the enamelled earth, over his head the flaming sky, around him trees bearing fruits of gold, and far away a river, a beautiful and large river, on its edge a woman, young, chaste and naked, and you will have an idea of the enchanted Eden to which this perfomance opened the door for me.

Between Mélanie and the theater, life during that autumn was an endless excitement in which imagination played a larger part than the heart. *Fiesque* was abandoned. He worked at *Christine* because, he said to Mélanie, "our future depends in part on my work; perhaps you will love me more and longer if I have successes." Success to be loved or loved to have successes? Mélanie corrected his lame alexandrines and he kept her informed each day of the progress of his oeuvre.

France had declared war on the Bey of Algiers; the Chambre des Deputés had been dissolved. Alexandre had almost finished *Christine*; he was up to Scene IV of the last act. He connived to interest Imbert Galloix, a poet from Geneva, in his tragedy. Gallois, like Dumas, had come to Paris to win glory. Of Gallois, Alexandre wrote:

He is a man as precious as his illusions: strangers willingly let themselves be taken in by him, as he is a charlatan—but an honest charlatan. It is to him that I will probably owe an introduction to Hugo, who could be useful to me at the Thé-âtre-Français; you know how much Taylor admires him. (December 7 or 8)

It was important to gain access to the steps that led to critics such as Taylor. As supreme judge, he alone could decide to whom the public would award the laurels of victory.

At 6:15 Galloix arrived unexpectedly at the Duc d'Orléans office. The manuscript of *Christine à Fontainebleau* was on the table. In a letter to Mélanie, Alexandre had described the essence of his play: the invincible force of love. Nonetheless, he understood very well the man from Geneva and his predilection for glory. Galloix was his double. He reflected Alexandre's own image, a double already veiled in mourning. Death would come before glory for Galloix, who died on October 27, 1828.

Even before the play was finished, Galloix had written to a friend that it had been accepted by the Théâtre-Français. Mélanie believed it; Adolphe was convinced of it; Méry—whom Alexandre hardly knew—assured him that the play would be accepted. However, Jacques-Parfait Oudard did not share this enthusiasm. He probably understood that Alexandre's visits were not only to the homes of the needy. He had possibly imagined the ecstasies above the furniture store, the delights of the jams and wine from Lunel. Alexandre was transferred and moved up to the Secretariat of Archives where he was welcomed by a kind, small eighty-year-old man dressed in the fashion of 1788, with satin culottes, dappled stockings, silk jacket, embroidered with designs of flowers, cuffs and jabot. Once his work was done, Père Bichet did not object to his subordinate's time spent on writing tragedies. He was even quite proud to have a poet among his employees. Thus, he hastened to gather his friends for the purpose of introducing, in his unique style, "this child of the muses." Alexandre appeared in front of a group of sages, whose youngest member was seventy. He had the cleverness to read an ode that he had just composed: *La Peyrouse*.

Senility somewhat tempered the vigor of the applause, but the audience's heart was in it. The young man would certainly soon gather his laurels from Melpomene. With becoming modesty, Alexandre was pink with pleasure.

The bureaucracy did not disdain the use of a sinecure as long as it was not too obvious. It was quite evident that Alexandre had no other activity at the Archives than his literary work, which advanced with great steps. He was transferred to the Office of Forestry under the protection of the grumbling Deviolaine.

The immense office rustled with the sound of private conversations as the employees tried to kill time. Alexandre had his eyes on a storeroom where empty ink bottles were discarded, and asked it for his own use. Upheld by his superiors the manager let it be known that Alexandre's demands were much too exorbitant. One clerk, quite pleased to humiliate a pretentious greenhorn, decided to continue to deposit his empty bottles in the cubicle. Furious, Alexandre, with the back of his hand, sent the poor devil's hat waltzing around the room. Boiling with anger, he withdrew to his tent, or more prosaically, his lodging in the Faubourg Saint-Denis.

Monsieur Deviolaine was then absent. For three days Alexandre refused to go to the office, to the great despair of his terrorized mother who feared that once more her son would be fired. She tried to appeal to Deviolaine's wife for pity, but the latter did not understand how a clerk could have any other ambition than to become a principal clerk, then a chief-assistant, and finally, a chief.

When Alexandre received a call from Deviolaine, he trembled as he always did when he had to face this redoubtable cousin, whom he had vested with a paternal power. Jean-Michel did not spare his usual interjections of *bougre!* and *jean-foutre!* but he finally conceded the only thing Alexandre desired: a quiet place where, once his office work was done, he could finish writing his *Christine*. And that was what Alexandre did, watched by the chief of the department, whose unpleasant face appeared regularly at the door of Alexandre's retreat.

The creation had taken over its creator. *Christine* reigned tyrannically over Alexandre. At the office, he hurried to expedite his reports to devote himself entirely to her. At home, he asked to be awakened at midnight, after only three hours of sleep, so he could go back to his manuscript. At Laure Labay's he also worked. Sometimes his little son, Alexandre, woke up howling; one night his father, furious at being disturbed, took hold of him and threw him violently onto his bed, thereby terrifying Laure. She scolded Alexandre who was already sheepish, and the next day, to obtain forgiveness, he brought her a superb melon. When with Mélanie in their tiny room, he took her quickly to get the gesture over with, so he could read the verses or some improvements in a scene he had written the night before. Mélanie, a mediocre lover who was afraid of a second pregnancy and the scandal it would involve, enjoyed these quiet interludes during which her lover opened himself to her and accepted her suggestions. At the salons of Villenave, Lethière, or Arnault, he never needed to be coaxed to recite his most impressive tirades.

When the work was finished, Dumas looked for a protector—or at least pretended he was looking, as he already had the support of Arnault and his family. Yet, Dumas feared they would not read more than ten verses of *Christine* before rejecting it. But that had to be seen. Actually, *Christine á Fontainebleau* was a good classical tragedy that respected the unities of time, place and action, which never lacked credibility and which did not offend decency or good taste. Perhaps, as if in spite of herself, *Christine* breathed an air of irepressible youth, a vigor of tone and action, a fresh violence.

Still that might not be enough to spur a romanticist! Antoine Arnault, or his son Lucien, had no doubt pushed *Christine*, as had Vatout, Athalin and Casimir Delavigne (who, like Alexandre, were employees of the Duc d'Orléans), even though Jacques Oudard had declared that he would not use his influence for *that*. But Alexandre was impatient, he suspected his supporters were lukewarm. On the advice of Garnier, the prompter at the Comédie-Française who came each month to bring ninety tickets reserved for the Duc d'Orléans, Alexandre wrote to Charles Nodier, who was known to be very friendly with the Baron Taylor. Nodier's helpfulness as well as his paternal kindness to young people were common knowledge. The Baron Taylor himself replied on March 10, 1828: he granted an audition, eight days hence at seven in the morning and excused himself for this outlandish hour. The Baron Taylor was a man very much in demand.

On the agreed day (probably Monday, March 17) Aleaxandre, who had not slept during the night, entered the antechamber full of busts and books. He had to ring three times before the door opened; his emotion was so great that he had rung too timidly. He knew that his future depended on the Baron's good or bad disposition. He felt drained of courage and strength.

After a long wait, Taylor—surprised in his bath by an author who had come to inflict on him the reading of a tragedy—came in shivering and lamenting his miserable condition. When Alexandre pulled his *Christine* out of his pocket, Taylor, confronted by the considerable volume of the manuscript, suppressed a gesture of fear. Alexandre's voice quavered, but Taylor seemed to take some interest in the first act and actual pleasure with the next four. He put up with the two thousand twenty alexandrines of *Christine á Fontainebleau* without giving the least sign of impatience. Once the reading was finished, he jumped down from his bed to accompany Alexandre to the Comédie-Française: the young author must immediately take his turn for a reading.

On March 20, 1828, the reading committee of the Théâtre-Français met, although far from its full complement of members, as Dumas would claim. Alexandre, probably too filled with emotion or enthusiasm, read indistinctly. He had to repeat the monologue of Sentinelli (Act III, scene IV) and the scene of Monaldeschi (Act III, Scene V) three times. Alexandre did not doubt that it was received with definite enthusiasm; he was intoxicated with his own words. The result of the following debate may have disappointed him: the play was accepted only on condition of possible "corrections." But accepted, anyway! Exultant, Alexandre ran toward the Faubourg Saint-Denis, measuring each passerby with a great air of superiority, so much that in his joyful agitation, he fell flat in the middle of a gutter, creating a gridlock of carriages and horses. The manuscript disappeared, but Alexandre did not care. He knew it by heart.

He swept up his bewildered mother in a mad sarabande; he had not told her he was going to read his play. For Madame Dumas literature was something vaguely disreputable. She appreciated only administrative work. She pushed Alexandre out to his office in the Rue de Valois where a heap of reports to copy were waiting for him. But that day, even this chore seemed light to Alexandre. The very same evening he rewrote the manuscript, finishing by dawn.

The next day all the services of the Duc d'Orléans were in an uproar: the newspaper had announced that, "strongly protected by the House of Orléans, a young employee, named M. Alexandre Dumas, had persuaded the Théâtre-Français to accept a five-act play, in verses, entitled *Christine*." This news had circulated from corridor to corridor, from floor to floor. People rushed into Alexandre's office to overwhelm him with compliments of doubtful sincerity. But he also received a quadruple assignment from his superior. Alexandre knew what persecution from mediocre people was; they did not forgive him his semblance of glory. The employees' modest salaries permitted them just to survive, therefore many of them had supplementary activities. One could marry a seamstress and keep a boutique; one could have some interest in an enterprise of carriages; one could be owner of a cheap eating place. Nobody would hold this kind of industry against them as a crime, while poor Alexandre was persecuted. He was confined to his cubbyhole as a soldier under arrest and was constantly checked to see whether he was at work. Alexandre had insults ready in his mouth but hope in his heart.

Christine was offered to Picard, an academician and author of light plays. Picard liked little comedies and detested the great dramatic contraptions. When he gave back the manuscript, he asked Alexandre whether he had some means of subsistence and, on an affirmative answer, advised him to return to his office. Alexandre gave the edited manuscript to Taylor. It was stuffed with crosses, brackets, exclamation and question marks, intended as marks of stupefaction: "Instead of a man, one found praise" (!!!) "And one would say that I have the favor of the throne" (!) "Ah! I have pity on him, my father. . . . Let him end" (Impossible!). Taylor forwarded the manuscript to the good Nodier who, sensitive to everything new, assured that, "on (his) soul and conscience," *Christine* was one of the most remarkable works he had read in twenty years. Not quite reassured, however, Alexandre asked the actor Samson's help with the necessary corrections. He also courted Mademoiselle Mars by offering her the part of Christine. Corrections came quickly. Alexandre immediately wrote to the reading committee that he was ready.

Samson, the corrector, had done the work well and rallied his comrades. Alexandre was overpowered by all these actresses, their hats and their flowers, tragic and comic theater queens. On Wednesday, April 30, *Christine* did not meet with any opposition but received general acclaim. It was unanimously accepted. Alexandre looked with gratitude and envy on all the beautifully displayed actresses' shoulders. The heady perfume of amber heightened the joy of his triumph. Actresses are more than women, they are all the women they know how to portray.

The play was accepted. When would it be performed? Probably tired of being harrassed by dramatic authors, Taylor had embarked for the Orient on May 10. *Christine* underwent the fastidious scrutiny of the censors who gave a first report on May 30.

One censor accepted the performance "on the condition that the author submit himself to changes and corrections" which were specified on June 7. Alexandre feared opposition from the powers that insisted in looking for political allusion in dramatic plays. He asked Manche de Broval, the director, to intervene, then sent a petition to Jean-Baptiste-Sylvère Gray, Comte de Martignac, Ministre de l'Intérieur:

Sir,

Allow me to add some information on my position regarding the request that M. le Chevalier de Broval had agreed to address to you in my favor; they perhaps will add a special interest to the general interest that Your Excellency shows for men of letters.

I am the son of Général Alex. Dumas. I am twenty-five, the play that is now in your hands is the first that I could have performed at the Théâtre-Français. My mother was without fortune and without pension when the Duc d'Orléans granted me a position; from that time, my salary was split between my mother and myself. A success would bring me the title of librarian for the Duc de Chartres, and consequently, would insure the positive side of my future. A success is, therefore, doubly important. If Your Excellency will take the trouble to read my drama, *Christine*, you will see that nowhere have I used political illusions to assure the success of my play. Such tactics seem to me false and provide only ephemeral results. On the contrary, I have drawn my action from the root of the subject which never diverges from History . . . (about June 10, 1828)

Alexandre did not bluff: he was considering literature, above all, as a means for social climbing, not as an ideological weapon. If he was ready to let a censor cut some verses that could be interpreted as allusions to the present political situation, he would fight for the integrity of a scene crucial to the dramatic success of his play. Alexandre had his political opinions but kept his sights directed on the artistic realm. Martignac did not turn a deaf ear to Alexandre's petition: the play received its visa on June 13 and was, after casting, put in rehearsal.

Alexandre was harrassed by actors who honored him with visits in his cubicle at 216 Rue Saint-Honoré. Mlle. Mars wished (Mlle. Mars' wishes were orders) that some verses were modified; Alexandre resisted her. She refused to recite the controversial verses, did not come to rehearsal, then took her leave until September 8. The ill will of actors, the pestering of censors which required suppression of the Père Lebel's part (August 20, 1828) and the acceptance of another *Christine* by the Comédie-Française (August 4) killed Alexandre's hope. What could a debutant do against those powers?

Queen Christine descended into the vaults of the Comèdie-Française. How many tragedies, although accepted, never saw the footlights? Of course, it was promised to Alexandre that once the first *Christine* was performed, his would be considered for the next production, but this was not enough to keep his illusions alive. Failure or success, *Christine de Suède* devalued *Christine á Fontainebleau.* To make matters worse, Frederic Soulié also had a *Christine* accepted at the Odéon, taken over by Harel after a short closing for "disorder." Soulié triumphed in this strange and friendly duel, based on the challenge accepted the previous December. His adaptation of *Roméo et Juliette* had received a benign success at the Odéon (June 10, 1828). Alexandre had been there, suffering from the coldness and the slowness of the first acts, applauding the fifth act which seemed to have stolen its sparkle from Shakespeare.

But on the whole, *Christine* was not really the flop that it appeared to be. When necessary, Mélanie could console Alexandre. Of course, the play might not be performed, but the Comédie-Française had an obligation toward him. Alexandre was no longer an unknown.

The failure of *Christine* could very well be a sure success for Alexandre.

VI
The Kingdom of this World

$\mathbf{F}$or Alexandre the alternative was clear: either become famous before he reached thirty or vegetate like the bureaucrats with whom he worked every day, the administrative wood lice. Alexandre was in a hurry. He had not waited for another avatar of *Christine*. A new subject came to him by chance. One day when he needed some paper, he went up to the accounting office to borrow some sheets from his friend Amédée de la Ponce. On a table, Alexandre saw an open book, *L'Histoire de France*, by Anquetil. Instinctively, Alexandre read some of its lines:

> Although devoted to the King and through his position an enemy of the Duc de Guise, Saint-Mégrin felt attracted to the Duchess, Catherine de Clèves; it was said that she returned his love. . . . Her husband, indifferent about the real or alleged infidelity of his wife . . . punished the indiscretion or crime of the Duchess with a cruel joke. One early morning, he entered her room holding a potion in one hand and a dagger in the other. After a brusk awakening followed by a few reproaches, he told her, with appropriate anger: "Decide, Madame, to die either by the dagger or by poison!" Vainly she asked for mercy, but he forced her to choose: She swallowed the beverage and fell on her knees, praying to God, but expecting only death.

One hour passed in this frightening state: The Duke then came back, his face serene, and he told her that what she had swallowed as poison was only an excellent consommé.

Alexandre's imagination worked on this scene which belonged to modern history. It mixed the tragic and the comic, as Victor Hugo recommended in the preface of his *Cromwell* which had just come out and was much discussed. From the providential *Biographie Universelle*, the article on Saint-Mégrin led Alexandre to read the *Mémoires de l'Estoile* which related the tragic death of King Henry III's favorite, ambushed as he left the Louvre and killed with an épée and pistols by twenty or thirty men. Henry III did not inquire into the death. He knew very well that his cousin, who took badly to the favorite's courting of his wife, was behind the crime. A few pages further another short story gave a complete idea of amorous customs in the sixteenth century. The handsome and unhappy Bussy d'Amboise was assassinated by the Seigneur de Monsoreau with whom he had a long standing affair. It was said that the Dame de Monsoreau herself had enticed Bussy into the ambush.

Alexandre asked Monsieur de Villenave, who had loaned him the *Journal de l'Estoile*, for advice on useful reading. He skimmed over *La Confession de Sancy* by d'Aubigné and *L'Ile des Hermaphrodites*, an anonymous pamphlet against the court of Henry III; he remembered, too, the narcotic potion in *Romeo et Juliet*, the handkerchief in *Othello*, the page in Schiller's *Don Carlos* and the hand of iron in *L'Abbé* by Sir Walter Scott.

When, at the beginning of September, he returned to Villers-Cotterêts for the opening of the hunting season, Alexandre could talk of his planned work to friends while they accompanied him to Vauciennes. The outline was done and the play was ready quickly, since Alexandre had chosen to write in prose, which was easier for him than verse.

Mélanie was not content impersonating Marie de Clèves, martyr of a husband she did not love. With all her strength she backed Alexandre's *Saint-Mégrin* and organized a reading of the play in the grand, musty drawingroom at Rue Vaugirard. Young literary buffs were fired up by it but Villenave raised his arms, imploring heaven—he considered these essays aberrations of Alexandre's mind. The latter knew well that a success with Villenave would not mean much in Paris. He contacted journalists who defended the ideal of romanticism and gathered them in the room of Nestor Roqueplan, Director in Chief of *Le Figaro*.

They all piled into a room on the fifth floor. A wash basin was enthroned on the mantel instead of a clock. The men lay on mattresses rolled out on the floor; a kettle was placed in front of the fireplace and they drank tea between each act. Alexandre had invited the actor Firmin, who agreed to report the reading to his fellow actors of the Théâtre-Français. The audience had one opinion: *Christine* should be stored in a drawer and *Henri III* should be launched. Firmin was already enchanted with his role as Saint-Mégrin and offered to arrange a meeting with other actors for a read-through that would precede the official reading and hurry it along.

When this meeting took place, Firmin had composed his audience carefully: Berger, who actually wrote odes when he believed he composed songs, Mlle. Mars, Michelot, Samson, Mlle. Leverd. Alexandre, having no doubt about the quality of his drama, had persuaded his mother to accompany him to this meeting. She sat toward the rear of the room, timid, surprised that her Alexandre could be a center of such interest in the midst of these beautiful, bejewelled women and these men whose names were mentioned in newspapers. Emboldened from the result of two previous readings, Alexandre thrilled the audience. Béranger predicted a great success for the play. The actors, already grabbing at parts in the play, begged him to hurry the official reading.

On Wednesday, October 17, 1828, the play was accepted with acclamations at the Théâtre-Français. Alexandre was immediately called into the office of the director, occupied by Albertin during Taylor's absence. Alexandre did not want to be deceived as he had been for *Christine*. But at once the distribution of parts was adopted and signed. The committee of the theatre immediately began to get the play ready for the stage. Mlle. Mars and Alexandre had differences about the cast. Mlle. Mars would have liked Armand as Henry III and Madame Menjaud for the page. Alexandre did not want Armand, who resembled Henry III too much and had, allegedly, the same special inclinations. He wanted the pretty Louise Despréaux, a student of Firmin, for the page—the costumes brought out the best features of her slender body. Louise Despréaux would know how to show her gratitude!

The *Courrier des Théâtres* on October 19 scoffed at the welcome of such theatrical fare and asked for "censure of these 'mignons' who would create a scandal, certain to stir up the crowds." This was an invitation to the censors to sharpen their knives. Alexandre took hold of his own figurative stick and obtained from the *Courrier* a "droit de résponse," which was printed on October 26. He claimed that *Henri III et sa Cour* had not for its subject a portrayal of amorality, but the rivalry between the Duc de Guise and the last of the Valois kings. It was a serious dramatic essay. The censors approved of the drama without mutilating it too much.

Alexandre's office in the Rue Saint-Honoré was very close to the Comédie-Française. There were always problems to solve, which gave him a good excuse for being absent from work as well as time for his amorous escapades. The administration protested: Alexandre was called before the General Director, Manche de Broval, who received him with a stern face, forerunner of a storm. Alexandre, however, was calm. Two acceptances by the Comédie-Française gave him great self-assurance. Manche de Broval explained that literature and office life were incompatible. He had to choose. Alexandre took this reprimand with arrogance. If this was so, he would leave and thus permit the Duc d'Orléans to save one hundred and twenty-five francs a month, but he would wait for the Duc d'Orléans himself to give him notice. For the time being, his salary was stopped and Alexandre could use his days as he desired.

Needing to find a means to survive, Alexandre thought of Jacques Laffite, a banker who had loaned money to authors. Alexandre laid plans: Béranger would introduce him to the banker. Lafitte did not show much enthusiasm but still loaned three thousand francs that Alexandre swore on his honor he would refund with the money earned by the manuscript that he would deposit with one of the bank tellers. Madame Dumas, who had been in despair, revived after the reading at Firmin's. She began to believe in literature now that she had three thousand francs in hand.

The casting of *Henri III et sa Cour* stopped because of discussions, recriminations and quarrels. Furious that his wife had not been chosen for the part of the page, Menjaud refused the role of Joyeuse. Samson accepted it as a favor to the author. Mlle. Mars did not accept Louise Despréaux who, she pretended, was knock-kneed but was in fact too young and too pretty; Mlle. Mars was close to fifty. Alexandre had intimate proof that Mlle. Despréaux's legs were without flaws. On November 7, a reading for the actors at last took place. Free from his office, Alexandre sat in on all the rehearsals. The truth was, he had noticed in the role of Marie, attendant to the Duchess de Guise, a very pretty actress, Virginie Bourbier. A novice, she could only aspire to the love affairs bestowed on supporting players. For her, Alexandre was almost a god. All Paris talked of him. But the young god had to accommodate other powers: the actors. He had to accept the corrections and demanded deletions. He humbled himself before Mlle. Mars. For now all he wanted was for his plays to be performed. Later, the actors would become his servants.

He was unperturbed by his final squabbles with the administration. The Duc d'Orléans wrote in his own hand, in the margin of the bonus roll for the past year, "Suppress all bonuses to M. Alexandre Dumas who is busy with literature." Alexandre worried more about the costumes and the sets of his play. He passed by the office sometimes to visit the few friends who believed in him but, more often, he rushed around Paris to prepare his first performance. He had to charm the journalists, rally his friends and acquaintances, forget nobody in the distribution of tickets that he tried to get from the committee of the Théâtre-Français.

He had sent tickets to Vigny, to Victor Hugo, to Louis Boulanger. The costumes of Mlle. Mars, Michelot (Henry III) and Firmin (Saint-Mégrin) were dazzling with silk, moire and jewels. The stage manager's three knocks raising the curtain would be the summons of destiny; but fate arrived in advance. As Alexandre worked on a last adjustment, one of Monsieur Deviolaine's servants burst in, very upset. Madame Dumas had fainted on the stairs as she was leaving the Deviolaines and had not yet regained consciousness. Hastily, Alexandre left the theater to attend to the domestic tragedy. He found his mother lying in a large armchair; the left side of her body was numb and immobile. She had had a stroke, preceded by a violent dizziness. The Comédie-Française's physician had followed Alexandre. He tried bloodletting, and Madame Dumas rallied to say a few words. Alexandre and his sister, who had come from Chartres to see the première of *Henri III*, rented an empty apartment on the third floor of the Deviolaines' house at the corner of Rue Saint-Honoré and Rue Richelieu. A bed was carried down for the sick woman; mattresses brought from Rue Faubourg Saint-Denis served for her children, who decided to stay with their mother constantly. Cazal, physician and friend, spent the whole night near

Madame Dumas. In the morning he would reassure them that if there were no relapse she would live.

As death approached, Alexandre wanted his dying mother to be filled with hope for her son's future. Casting caution aside, he skirted the guards of the Palais-Royal and penetrated the private apartments of Louis-Philippe who was quite surprised at the audacity of the employee who had recently upset the routine of his administration. Alexandre asked him to attend the premiere of *Henri III et sa Cour*. The Duke was not free, he had some thirty princes and princesses for dinner the same evening. But why not! The dinner could be served one hour earlier and the opening of the show could be postponed one hour; all the first gallery would be reserved for Monseigneur's guests to attend the premiere. The Duke claimed he was very pleased with this idea, and Alexandre was wild with joy. When he met the Duchess after his visit with Louis-Philippe, he almost kissed her hand.

The day so full of expectation almost arrived too soon. Alexandre remained with his half-conscious mother. Hours passed slowly. At a quarter to eight, he left his mother to go to the theater, a few steps away. He moved like a sleepwalker. He welcomed Hugo and Vigny who had found seats in Aimée's loge and almost hid himself in a small loge large enough for two persons. Mélanie was near him; she held Alexandre's hand with her own dry and nervous one. "How is my collar?" he asked. That morning he had cut it from a piece of paper, a sign of poverty in this glittering theater, sold out eight days before. People had nearly fought over tickets; the price for a loge seat had climbed to the exorbitant amount of twenty francs. Every time he raised his eyes, Alexandre believed he was dreaming. The first gallery packed with princes, the front of their uniforms or frock coats breastplated with decorations, ribbons of Orders from five or six nations; the first and second loges filled with the nobility of the Faubourg, women covered with diamonds; the nervous roar of expectation—Alexandre was the originator of all this! His forehead dripped with sweat, and Mélanie loaned him a fine batiste handkerchief.

When the curtain rose, a strong draft brought a delightful coolness. Alexandre's heart was nearly bursting. On the stage, in Ruggieri's study Catherine was setting her trap: she needed to compromise Saint-Mégrin, the minion who had too much influence

with the King. Mégrin must confess his love to the Duchesse de
Guise. The Duke was a redoubtable adversary of the Duchess, as
had become clear by the end of the first act. As he discovered the
handkerchief of the Duchess, he cried: "Saint Paul! Bring me the
men who have assassinated Duguast."

In the audience, women shivered in expectation of the implied
violence; spectators and actors were warming up. The prelude had
been long, cold and tedious. The audience primarily applauded the
pleasure it had expected. During the intermission, Alexandre ran
to his mother. The nurse reassured him that all was well. On his
return into the corridor of the theater, Alexandre saw Deviolaine
entering the men's room. Emotion had also taken hold of this rigid
man.

The next scene took place at Henry III's court. The minion's
fluttering about amused the audience. Saint-Mégrin blew a *dragée*
from a blowpipe and hit the chest of the Duke, who was wearing
a bulky armor. The audience laughed. The Duc de Guise asked
that a chief be named as head of the league which could accept no
other chief than the Duke himself. The historical drama was also
a political play.

The success or the failure of the play hung upon the third act.
To the beautiful and trembling Duchess, the young page Arthur
praised the qualities of Saint-Mégrin who had once risked his life
to catch a bouquet she had let fall in a lion's cage, and had pressed
the flowers on his lips with passion. Suddenly the Duchess quivered
with terror, and the Duke burst into her room. Clutching her with
his iron gauntlet, he forced her to write to Saint-Mégrin requesting
a rendezvous. Such dramatic brutality shown for the first time on
a stage brought cries of terror from the spectators. The curtain fell,
amid thunderous applause, leaving the audience with the promise
of a finely set trap.

Alexandre felt that the evening had swung in his favor; it was a
great success. He wanted to share it with his mother, at least symbolically, since she was home sleeping peacefully. As the fifth act
continued, the reaction became a delirium. De Guise was a pawn
in the hand of the King, who named himself head of the league.
But de Guise took his revenge, hiring a private assassin. Saint-
Mégrin fell in the trap and was choked with the Duchess' handkerchief. "Death will be sweeter for him; the handkerchief is marked

with the Duchess' coat of arms," sneered the Duke who, having finished with the valet, was getting ready to deal with the master: King Henry III.

Even the women's delicate hands applauded. The actress Marie Malibran leaned from the third gallery, hugging a column to avoid falling. The curtain was lowered, and a beaming Alexandre went backstage. Firmin had stepped on the proscenium and silenced the applause. He named the author. The audience stood, voices become hoarse from shouting. Alexandre noticed that the Duc d'Orléans took off his hat when Alexandre was named. Literature bestowed royalty, too. The première of *Henri III* was more than a success, it was a coronation.

It was said that during the next days young romantics, excited by the endless ovation, danced around the bust of Racine, singing: "Racine has fallen," and, "Finally, Racine is a mere scoundrel." An academician tragically claimed that he had seen, with his own eyes, young dissidents dance, screaming: "Racine has fallen! Voltaire has fallen," and attempt to throw the busts of famous men out the windows. Not quite a literary riot, but certainly a revolution, a breach in the stronghold of the Théâtre-Français, through which the troops of romanticism would storm.

Dumas took refuge near his mother. He lay down on a mattress and savored a letter from his General Director who congratulated him on his success.

The next day flowers filled Madame Dumas' room. Alexandre arranged bouquets on the sick woman's bedcover. He had to honor his author's duty and give tickets to his many friends who begged for seats. But he was called in by the managers of the theater whose faces showed dismay. The Minister of Interior had suspended the performances. Alexandre obtained an audience with M. de Martignac for the next day.

The Minister was kindly, witty and polite. He made Alexandre understand that certain religious words that had shocked the first Aide de Camp of the King and some courtiers had to be suppressed. The manuscript, slightly revised, was saved once more.

The Duc d'Orléans attended the second performance. He called Alexandre to his loge. Louis-Philippe was delighted to repeat to the young victor the details of the quarrel that had almost caused the King's opposition to *Henri III*. Charles X had said: "I am told that there is a young man in your offices who wrote a play in which

we act, both of us: I play Henri III and you play the Duc de Guise."
The Duc d'Orléans said he had answered: "Sire, you have been
misled for three reasons: the first one is that I do not beat my wife;
the second one is that Madame la Duchesse d'Orléans does not
cuckold me; the third one is that your Majesty has no subject more
faithful than I." Alexandre smiled. How witty his Majesty was!
However, he would be as disloyal as the Duchesse de Guise.

The press became excited and divided—each day presenting a
crop of divergent criticisms that Alexandre read feverishly. He accepted almost everything: they talked of him, they talked only of
him. But he could not accept that an obscure tabloid dare to affirm
that his success was not surprising "for those who know how all
the literary and the political dealings are made in the House of
Orléans. The author is only a small employee in the service of His
Royal Highness."

Alexandre would not stand for this insult. He sent Amédée de
la Ponce as his second to the man who insulted him, who, it was
said, had already been challenged by Armand Carrel. During the
duel which had priority, the pistol of Carrel had blown off the small
and the fourth fingers of the unfortunate journalist. Alexandre visited him and found that the offender almost regretted his unwar-
ranted insult as much as the loss of his two fingers.

The cash register of the Comédie-Française rang full! Alexandre's
pockets became used to a swelling flood of banknotes. He had sold
his manuscript for six thousand francs on February 17. Alexandre
could refund Laffitte and offer a few trinkets to Virginie Bourbier.
When he balanced his books he had 3,617 francs in February and
4,326 francs in March. Alexandre moved from the proletarian Faubourg to the Quartier Latin and rented for his mother an apartment
with a garden on the main floor of No. 7 Rue Madame. Now
convalescing, Madame Dumas could take short walks accompanied
by Mélanie and Madame Villenave, who had deserted the paternal
and conjugal roof of the Rue de Vaugirard to settle nearby at No.
11 of Rue Madame. Alexandre lived in his own apartment, decorated with some elegance, on a fourth floor at the corner of the Rue
du Bac and the Rue de l'Université.

His tall figure and "physiognomy eminently romantic" was recognized when he walked on the Boulevards. He kept Paris society
talking, and salons fought for his company. Almost an unknown
on February 9, 1827, he had become famous the next day. Nobody

was indifferent toward him. Without even knowing him, some hated him for the tumult he caused and because he had become the bearer of the romantic flag. Some loved him, sometimes unreasonably. He was known simply as "Dumas," the writer who eclipsed the real man. His popular lithographed portrait by Achille Deveria personified the legend he was becoming: nonchalantly posing on a sofa, the legs of his pants slightly raised to show his fine ankle and his small foot, Alexandre Dumas looked languorously toward heaven; a gold chain crossed his vest. His right hand, fingers buried in the frizzy forest of his hair, held his head which seemed too heavy. That head contained a world of fiction, of drama and of ambition.

PART
III

The Revolutionists

I

Slave of Caprice

The boat was leaving the bank of the Loire river, its wheel churning the lazy water. A young man stood at the prow. The captain mentioned to some women passengers, intrigued by the lone figure, that this young man had created a sensation in Paris. To himself the young man was still Alexandre, but to the public he was Dumas.

> No physical change had occurred; nonetheless he was not the same man; he no longer belonged to himself; for the price of applause and honors he had sold himself to the public. He was now a slave of caprice, fashion, even of cabals. He could feel his name torn from him as a fruit from its branch. Publicity, with its thousands of voices, would break him into pieces, scatter him over the world and now, even if he wanted to, it was no longer in his power to reverse the process and go back to a private life. (A. *Dumas, Un Succès, Revue et Gazette Musicale de Paris*)

He had left Paris on May 5, 1829 to run away from the insults of small newspapers, the demands of new, avid friends, and from sentimental storms. Once a child of the forest, he now wanted to find a sense of solitude on the ocean shore. He also wanted to work, so he had stayed with his sister in Chartres. Aimée was so proud of her younger brother that she had forced him to walk with her along the rough cobblestone streets of Chartres and to attend the solemn military funeral of a general who had just died. The military music with its trumpets and drums undoubtedly caused Alexandre to shed some tears, not for the corpse lying in the middle of a sumptuous catafalque, but in remembrance of his father, that forgotten hero. The next day he left for Angers.

Now, at the railing of the riverboat, Alexandre wrote in a notebook the names of the landing piers. As the boat gently swung in the current, he jotted down in alexandrines the dialogue of his next drama, *Le Roi Robert et la Belle Édith*. He had dreamed for a long time of Horace Vernet's painting hung at the Salon of 1827, *Édith Cherchant le Corps d'Harold*, with its image of Edith with her long hair. Borrowing from Shakespeare and August Lafontaine, he had built for this poetically named heroine a drama in which history yielded to imagination. When inspiration faltered, he sketched a beautiful three-masted ship or he rhymed his impressions of the moment.

At Nantes he was welcomed by François-Aimé Panneton, a shipowner and a successful merchant, who was very friendly with the Villenaves. Eulalie Panneton, the mistress of the house, was rather intimidated by this illustrious Parisian, but her five-year-old son, nicknamed Fifi, was amused by this tall, bean-pole of a man, who had such strange hair and was so gentle. Alexandre petted and caressed the child who was the same age as his own son. Dumas wanted to continue down the estuary of the Loire to the Atlantic. It was simply done: the *Pauline*, a lovely three-masted merchant ship which was unofficially used for slave trading, was just then anchored between Nantes and Paimboeuf. It was going to set sail the next day. Paimboeuf stretched its long, melancholy ribbon of houses along the Loire. There, at the inn, while he was dining, Alexandre befriended a young woman who refused to eat and held back heavy sobs.

She was a newlywed whose husband was carrying her far away from the old European frontiers to a business in Guadeloupe. There were very few amusements in Paimboeuf; Dumas killed the time and a few gulls that flew within reach of his gun; he fired, as a native advised, only when he could distinctly see the bird's eye.

Dumas, dressed in nankeen pants, vest of white piqué and velvet coat, inspected the rigging of the *Pauline* as the small boat carrying the young woman, who now cried openly, approached. Alexandre gallantly helped her pass from the gangplank to the deck. Her name was also Pauline. The sailors were busy and the pilot and the captain gave orders: "Hoist the anchor"; "Let out the top-sail, the lower sails and the jibs." Dumas had arranged to leave the ship at the Piliers with the pilot boat. The wind from the open sea already filled the passengers' lungs.

Dumas asked that the dinner table be set on deck so that Pauline could get a last sight of the France she was leaving: the gloomy Saint-Nazaire in its landscape of heather and sand. Soon the yellowish water took greenish tints and foamed with the first waves. Then they reached the sea, the endless horizon under a sky darkened with clouds in which the sun was sinking. It was his first sight of the sea. But it was also time for him to leave the ship. He pressed Pauline tenderly to his chest and promised to give her name to the heroine of one of his next books. He then regretfully left the young woman he had met only the day before. Dumas hung tightly to the cord ladder that had been thrown over the rounded side of the ship; he masked his dizziness and fear under a brave front as long as Pauline watched. He finally reached the bottom and the smaller, pilot's boat. In the process he had lost his hat, but he could have lost his head. The fully rigged large ship sailed on until Pauline's waving handkerchief disappeared, while Dumas' small craft was shaken and rocked, its pilot forced to lower sail and use the oars. The sea spray whipped at Dumas who had flattened himself onto the bottom of the craft. Water poured through his shirt collar and into his stockings, until a strong undertow carried the boat into a cove between Saint-Nazaire and Le Croisic. Dumas quickly trotted to his inn. It was eleven o'clock in the evening. To get the door open, he had to throw a five-franc coin through the window until at last the grumpy innkeeper's head appeared. While he ate some biscuits he had his bed warmed and his clothes put into a lukewarm oven. The next day his clothes were dry and he could return to Nantes, fetch his luggage left at the Pannetons' and find a seat in the coach to Paris. According to a misdated chapter of *Mes mémoires*, he completed an errand for Pauline, then went to L'orient, Quimper and Brest. He had read in *Le Pilote* by James Fenimore Cooper that the famous sailor John Paul Jones had called three times at L'orient. Alexandre consulted the maritime archives of that city in vain, but he did hear a strange and mysterious tale from an old clerk involving John Paul Jones. From that one incident, Dumas got all the elements for one of his future dramas, *Le Capitaine Paul Jones*. If he continued on his way to Quimper and Brest, it was only to soak up the local atmosphere, to get intoxicated with the sea wind and the rage of the ocean.

During those fifteen days of wandering, Dumas had been driven only by his fancy. Now he had to go back to the whims of Paris, to his surly critics, to the small, insolent tabloids and to his possessive mistresses. At this point he was the author of only one successful drama. Could he live with this single, ephemeral success? He had to buttress and expand his legend. He showed up at every premiere in the theaters. Mélanie Waldor, proud of her lover and creation, gathered a small coterie devoted to Alexandre at 5 Rue de l'Ouest. Victor Hugo and Alfred de Vigny appeared there briefly. Dumas had narrowed his focus to two goals: the Duc d'Orléans and the Comédie-Française.

On June 17, 1829, he applied to His Highness for the position of librarian at the Château d'Eu. Dumas was now more than a simple entity: he was a power whose name attracted the public, especially young people who were his future. The Duc d'Orléans, artfully maneuvering his way toward political power, had no intention of refusing Dumas' request; after all, it cost him only twelve hundred francs per year. The employee himself was more valuable to him than filling the position. Dumas' denial that he had dedicated *Henri III et sa cour* to the Duc d'Orléans in order to obtain this position may or may not have been true. On July 20, 1829, three days after having officially asked, Dumas was named librarian attached to the Duke, not at the Château d'Eu, but at the Palais-Royal. There he rejoined his colleagues: the kind Vatout who had taken him under his protection a long time ago, and Casimir Delavigne, who was reticent to accept this young rival whose amazing success had slightly tarnished his own glory as a tragic liberal.

With his administrative career reassured, Dumas could now devote himself entirely to his second masterpiece. Would it be *Christine á Fontainebleau* which could follow the rival *Christine*, already in rehearsal? Dumas threatened to sue if his wishes were not accepted. The management of the Comédie-Française gave up, but Dumas realized that these twin Christines had little chance of success. He asked to have *Édith*, the play he had begun while navigating the Loire, take precedence.

The young man now spoke arrogantly; he almost disdained what he had desired in the past and retreated to his sister's at Chartres to work quietly at his next tragedy, far from the Parisian brouhaha. Dumas did not mince his words in a letter to the Baron Taylor. (postmarked July 7, 1829)

I received at Chartres the letter from the Committee who asks me to come and discuss my affairs. First, I have nothing to discuss with the Committee. I stated my demand; the Committee now must reply yes or no, and shouldn't have waited so long in any case. I will be ready for the first reading between the 15th and the 30th of July, but I will read only after having a yes or no response.

Make way for the young! This shout of each generation resounded even louder because it was addressed not to the fathers but to the grandfathers. The generation in between was buried in Spanish sierras, in the Egyptian deserts, in the Russian ice; it had been burned in the path of Napoléon's meteoric career. The geriatric crowd resisted. The young Dumas, who paraded himself at the Opéra, whose work was played at the Théâtre-Français, and who stirred with his frizzy hair—was the manifest sign of the barbarian—provoked homicidal desires in these old men who had long lost any other. He was tracked down to be assaulted with quarrels. On the evening of May 28, 1829 at the premiere of *Pertinax*, a tragedy in five deadly acts, he sat quietly in the orchestra, between the classic Jouy and the romantic Hugo, when a confrontation flared. Some spectators called for Antoine-Vincent Arnault, the author, to take a bow; others hooted at the idea. In the middle of the uproar, a friend of Arnault stood up and vindictively pointed to Dumas who had remained seated and speechless: "No wonder people in the orchestra boo when M. Dumas is there; aren't you ashamed, sir, to be the head of a cabal?" Dumas protested that he had not said a word. And his accuser replied: "What does it matter! It is you who direct the whole clique." Outwardly annoyed to be the target of the classicists, Dumas was nonetheless flattered to be recognized as the head of a faction.

But the fortifications of the senile had little chance against the young guard who attacked them in waves. On July 9, 1829, Victor Hugo, who had finished *Marion Delorme* in twenty-six days, invited to his home in the rue Notre-Dame-des-Champs all the fiery young assault troops: Honoré de Balzac, Louis Boulanger, Prosper Mer-imée, Alfred de Musset, Sainte-Beuve, Frédéric Soulié, Alfred de Vigny, the Baron Taylor and, of course, Alexandre Dumas. Pale of face, looking almost demented, Hugo began the reading. He read very well. The others went wild with enthusiasm; they jumped up and down, they shivered. Shouted interjections were quickly interrupted. The reading was hardly finished when Dumas, who had been waving his gigantic arms about, put them around Victor Hugo whom he lifted up, proclaiming, "We will carry you to glory!" When refreshments were served, Alexandre stuffed himself with cakes, continuing to repeat, with a full mouth, "Admirable! Admirable!" As he took Mélanie back home to 5 Rue de l'Ouest at two in the morning, he knew very well that it would be Victor Hugo who would first enter the breach that he, Alexandre, had opened. He arrived home at dawn.

However, the victory that they believed to have won was slipping away. On July 15, Dumas read his *Édith* for the committee of the Comédie-Française. It was a masterpiece, he did not doubt it, but he felt that little by little his audience was freezing. In spite of his benevolent disposition, the outstanding points fell flat. He wanted to roll up his manuscript and bow out, but he had to continue his reading to the last hemistich. Mlle. Mars was appointed by the committee to hand the verdict to the author. She had made up her face to suit the lugubrious circumstances. She floundered about with circumlocutions, and Alexandre understood that his play was not good enough to be performed. When he was asked to take back his manuscript, he answered, "Throw it in the fire!"

He fled from Paris boarding the first coach he found ready to leave, settling into its empty carriage; the horseman whipped the horses and they rolled along to Le Hâvre. Wherever it was, he wanted only to take hold of himself and recapture his inspiration. The landscape unfolded during those twenty hours of travel. In his inspiration he was in Stockholm, at Fontainebleau, in Rome. He envisioned reshaping his *Christine á Fontainebleau*, but it was in much too classic a mold to be compatible with his newly made reputation as an innovator. At Le Hâvre, he hardly saw the ocean before returning to Paris. He took time, however, to eat some dozens of oysters and to buy two porcelain vases. He decided to continue his trip to Cherbourg, then up to Dieppe. These repeated escapes were a confession of distress.

Once again calm, Alexandre went back to the Parisian furnace and found there only signs of defeat and oppression. Indeed, Vigny's *Le More de Venise*, adapted from *Othello*, was received at the Co-médie-Française, but the regime watched and its heavy censorship fell on journalists and their pamphlets. Did the King hate drama?

Marion Delorme was accepted at the Comédie-Française on July 11, but on August 1 the censor notified Hugo that his play was forbidden. "It is not only an ancestor of the King who is ridiculed, it is the King himself. Everybody could see in Louis XIII, a hunter overly influenced by a priest, an allusion to Charles X," explained Martignac, who was His Majesty's minister. His Majesty did not like the portrait drawn of him. Hugo obtained an audience in the Château of Saint-Cloud on August 7. The King, kind and gracious, worried about these tremors which announced revolutions. "But, Sire, can one stop and tame the people who rise up or the ocean which swells?" Although the injunction remained, the poet's pension was raised to six thousand francs. With dignity, Hugo refused the increase. During this trying time friends closed ranks. In *La Revue de Paris* Sainte-Beuve wrote that these disagreements were less frivolous than one would think "even from a political point of view." Alexandre had chosen to make his voice heard with a pro-testation in verse, published in *Le Sylphe* on August 20, 1829:

TO MY FRIEND VICTOR HUGO

They said "The work of a genius
Is for the world a blazing torch;
Let its light be banished
And all will return into night."
Then with their funereal breath
They thickened the darkness;
But all their efforts were powerless
Against the flickering flame
That God put, weightless and bright,
On the forehead of the newborn poet!

Adversity fused unity. All for one; one for all. The young men, now twenty to thirty years old, coming from various orientations—

royalists, Bonapartists, Orléanists, republicans—had re-grouped together under a vague, aesthetic banner. What did they have in
common? Nothing, except their youth and the rejection of ancient
art; nothing, except common literary heroes: Shakespeare, Schiller,
Goethe, Byron, Scott, Cooper, Lamartine, Chateaubriand; nothing,
except a place to rally, the Arsenal. Later in 1846 Dumas would
recall to Marie Nodier:

> This place . . . was much more than a palace, much more than
> a kingdom, it was this good and excellent home, the Arsenal
> at the peak of its joy and its happiness, when our beloved
> Charles (Nodier) did the honor of it with all the openness of
> old-fashioned hospitality, and you, Madame, with all the gra-
> ciousness of modern hospitality . . . Do you remember my son
> dressed as a stevedore and myself as a postilion? Do you re-
> member that alcove in the drawing room where the piano was,
> where you sang "Lazzara," marvelous melody . . . Dear mem-
> ories that time carries on its silent wings, through the grayish
> mist of the past.

In 1829, the Arsenal was not yet the symbol of all this incurable
nostalgia. Still, even then it was not merely the large dark and
gloomy building above the Seine on the Quai des Grands-Augustins. The Arsenal was Charles Nodier, who knew nearly all that a
man could know and who, when he did not know, knew how to
invent; who loved for the happiness of loving, who sympathized
with all that was good, all that was beautiful, all that was great. A
"lover," Dumas would call him.

If we must choose from those garlands of Sundays full of gaiety
and happiness that they called "soirées" at the Arsenal, let us pick
a Sunday in the month of August 1829; Sunday the 30th, for
example. At six o'clock in the evening the dinner table was set.
The guests who had originated these regular Sunday suppers came
first, one by one or in groups: Francisque Vey, the Baron Taylor
with Cailleux, Alfred and Tony Johannot, Louis Boulanger. Soon
more space was needed. When a thirteenth guest arrived, he was
exiled to a small table with the hope that a fourteenth friend would
come. When the big Alexandre entered noisily, the place between
Madame Nodier and Marie was at once freed for him: habit had
already created a right. Nodier savored his brown bread and gravy

in pewter dishes (he hated white bread and silver). The guests forgot what they were eating; Nodier was speaking.

Not only was Nodier pleasant to hear, Nodier was charming to look at. His long, lanky body, his long, skinny arms, his long, pale hands; his long face expressing melancholic kindness, all this harmonized with his slight drawl, his modulation of certain tones that came back periodically, with a Franc-Comtois accent that Nodier had really never lost. The stories were inexhaustible, always new, never repeated. Time, space, history, nature were for Nodier a purse of Fortunatus from which Pierre Schlemill's hands could always come out full.

He told of his perpetually renewed pleasure at the fiftieth performance of the *Boeuf Enragé* by the mime Deburau and of his miraculous quests as a bibliophile. Madame Nodier frowned, thinking of the unlikely dowry of her daughter Marie, diminished three hundred francs by a rare book's purchase. One day Nodier told of his encounters with the wandering Jew whose name was not Ashasverus but Isaac Laquedem. Three times Nodier crossed his interminable path, the first time in Rome at the time of Gregory VII, the second time in Paris on the eve of the Saint Bartholomew's Day massacre, and the last time in Vienna, in the Dauphiné. "I have most precious documents regarding him," he claimed. Or he talked of the sinister *"guillotineur,"* Euloge Schneider, who terrified his childhood.

Coffee was served on the dining table. Madame Nodier led Alexandre, who was not fond of this modern stimulant, into the drawing room. He was tall enough to light the chandelier without climbing on a chair. The drawing room, when lighted, showed white wainscoting, Louis XV moldings, spare furnishings, sofas covered in red, a bust of Hugo, a statue of Henry IV, a portrait of Nodier and a landscape. The guests came in, Nodier last, leaning on the arm of Dauzats. He stretched out in a large armchair, fell into a kind of beatific silence before resuming his interrupted tale. A little later, Marie sat at the piano and sang melodies that she had composed from the poems of Lamartine and Hugo. Some young men with feverish eyes listened amorously. Some tried to stop the coughing that harassed them even during this beautiful month of August. Suddenly, Marie played a contredanse. The dancers paired.

Alexandre took Mélanie in his arms and they waltzed until they were out of breath. Mélanie was a fanatic waltzer, the flowers in her hair lost most of their petals.

That special evening, Lamartine consented to recite his poetry, standing in front of the fireplace. Victor Hugo listened, smiling as an equal, while Adèle Huge, half-lying on a sofa, fussed with her admirable hair. Victor squeezed Alexandre's hand more warmly than usual to thank him for his poem in *Le Sylphe*.

The dancing resumed: *traverse, chaîne des dames, chassé-croisé*. Nodier disappeared, he continued the life he had not left all day long and lost himself again in his dream world. As dawn rose the guests found themselves on the Quai des Grands-Augustins. They embraced, they hugged, they walked one another home. It had been a Sunday, like all those Sundays between 1829 and 1833, before the mediocre hatred, or worse, indifference, broke up their allegiance, before death brought them down in full flight.

II

Victories and Conquests

The direction of contemporary literature depends upon *Christine* and on *Hernani*. If these two dramas succeed, the reform, for the most part, will be achieved; if they fail, the situation will stagnate.

(*Le Sylphe*, December 1829)

Victor Hugo and Alexandre Dumas, like two generals on the eve of a battle, reviewed their troops. In Paris, theater conditions were changing. New directors were named at the Porte-Saint-Martin and at the Odéon, which was reopening with *Catherine de Médicis aux États de Blois* by Dumas' melancholic friend, Lucien Arnault. The sets and costumes were sumptuous but the play was considered mediocre. The director understood that he had to abandon this play and drum up enthusiasm for the next drama, *Christine á Fontainebleau*, which Frédéric Soulié had refused to write in collaboration. Newspaper columns, fillers and announcements stirred up some interest. In the meantime Dumas had offered to the Théâtre Porte-Saint-Martin his *Édith* which had been shamefully refused by the Comédie-Française. The play was accepted but on the condition that Dumas, talented but inexperienced, would work with an old theatrical battlehorse, Victor Ducange, who had already added a few verses to the drama. Dumas raged with indignation:

I am furious with Ducange. I grant you that he is of good faith; we know that as a fact. Moreover, it is not everybody who is that honest, but I want to talk with you of the changes he made to my play. Of the verses he substituted for mine, every one of the thirty would dishonor Corneille. If I had a jockey and he wrote one of the verses that Mr. Ducange put into my play, I would throw him out at once. (Dumas to Froissard)

Alexandre did not realize the strength of the connection at the moment. M. Ducange was worth *more*, even if he was no *better* than M. Dumas. The play that was due for rehearsals the following Friday was postponed *sine die*. It was a last barrage deployed by the ill-matched rear guard, which could still hurt even if it no longer had the power to destroy. The young army suffered wounds but it did not break ranks. On September 29, Victor Hugo gave his reading of *Hernani*, composed in twenty-five days. There was an almost frightening appetite for living and writing among those young men. They applauded, they exchanged congratulations, yet Alexandre missed the poetic beauties of *Marion Delorme* in the new work. The Baron Taylor took the manuscript away under his arm and five days later made the reading committee of the Comédie-Française accept the play. Perhaps Hugo was deceived by the enthusiastic welcome. The fifty-year-olds of the Comédie-Française, Mlle. Mars, Michelot, Armand, politely did the honors for their theater but they reserved their opinions. Their attitude was to give a break to the barbarians since they brought money. But they were "sociétaires" above all; their traditions, their acting routines, their established tastes, rejected this novel form of art imposed on them. Only the old Joanny felt a real sympathy for the romantic literature.

In the romantic's camp, enthusiasm was sustained through emulation. Battles that followed bear the names *Othello*, *Hernani*, and *Christine*. However, even the renegade queen did not bring luck to the dramatic authors. Soulié's *Christine* closed forever on October 13 and was forgotten despite one character. An Italian bandit, placed in the thick of the forest of Fontainebleau, added a most picturesque effect. Dumas, uninvited to the premiere, seized the opportunity, and called on the Comédie-Française to put his work into rehearsal. The committee feigned astonishment: the present *Christine* had nothing to do with the one previously accepted! It told Dumas he needed a new acceptance for the altered play.

With rage in his heart, Dumas gave his drama to the poor director Harel at the Odéon, who lamented the expense of Soulié's *Christine*.

Such expensive costumes! Such magnificent decorations! Why throw them into the fire when they could be used to great effect in Dumas' drama? Dumas knew having this play performed at the dull Odéon, lost on the left bank of the Seine, was a meager honor for an author. Only the Théâtre-Français would bring him recognition. Meeting in haste, the reading committee of the Odéon had reservations: Would Dumas accept some advice? More advice! Would he always be kept on a leash? He contemptuously refused. *Christine* was received on December 4 and read to the actors, who did not hold back their applause . . . good, noble actors who put a brake on the doubts that had begun to creep in. Being continually rebuffed, one finally believes the objectors are right. Harel, however, was still worried. Burned by the previous *Christine*, he proposed that Alexandre put his *Christine* into prose! Alexandre only laughed.

Othello opened October 24, 1829. It was a simple adaptation, even if it was of Shakespeare. The play provoked an unexpectedly hostile critical reaction which came, sometimes, from unexpected directions. In *La Revue de Paris* Henri de Latouche opined about the new school of writing:

A congregation of bizarre rhymesters has become a mutual admiration society, the conspiracy of a few school boys against the illustrious elite. If you are not highly gifted with a faculty to applaud, to reach exaltation in your enthusiasm, to raise your intoxication to the point it produces ecstasy, we would never advise you to approach this group who have told themselves that the "century belongs to them," who call themselves, modestly, a cénacle, and find among themselves their own martyrs and divinities. Among them, as divinities and martyrs, everyone wants words that smack of transfiguration, yet the suppliant posture implores, at the door of every gazette, a favorable mention, even if it is a lie. Among them, they have made praise a duty, a constant obligation. It is, in their small, ultraromantic chapel, the morning and the evening prayer; it is a tithe levied on all contributors at any reading, at the revelation of any new project on the disclosure of a hemistich on which one is working. Any time one postulant meets another, they exchange a look which means, "Brothers, we must praise each other!" (*De la camaraderie littéraire*, October 1829)

Latouche was a republican; the publications that harassed the romantics were liberal newspapers that preached the romantic movement and progress in politics, while those that gave support belonged to the reactionary opinion. How could this paradox make sense? The editors of those liberal newspapers had heretofore probably supported the Théâtre-Français and wanted to keep their hold upon it. But Victor Hugo, the prestigious leader of the feared invasion, had once given his pledge to the legitimate party, celebrating in turn the virgins of Verdun, the death of Louis XVIII, the birth of the Duc de Bordeaux, and the coronation of Charles X. Little by little the literary question infringed on the political field. Many adjustments would be necessary to affirm clearly that romanticism was liberalism in literature.

As winter weighed down upon Paris, the Seine froze and everything seemed to darken. Latouche had betrayed the romantics; Janin followed in his steps. As Mlle. George's lover he was allpowerful at the Odéon and had recommended that the Director postpone *Christine* and give precedence to Soumet's *Une Fête de Néron.*

Alexandre wanted to step free from the trap of the Odéon and return to the bosom of the Comédie-Française. "Break the contract that ties you to Harel, since he has not respected it," advised the Baron Taylor on December 18. At 5 Rue de l'Ouest, Mélanie Waldor entertained. The guests drank tea, they warmed and comforted each other before the fireplace. A new name flew from lip to lip: Alfred de Musset, a very young man with a budding moustache, blond, thin, with long curled hair thrown in a bunch on one side of his head, seemingly detached probably because he was timid. He had read his *Contes d'Espagne et d'Italie* the previous evening at the Arsenal. Lamartine, Hugo, Vigny, Dumas and Taylor welcomed this youth into the group's heart.

Frozen Paris seemed a slippery mirror. Victor Hugo wore his wool houseshoes to prevent falling as he crossed the bridges on his way to the rehearsals of his *Hernani.* The Comédie-Française, too, was full of traps. Mlle. Mars suffered when she had to recite certain verses that hurt her mouth: " 'My lion, superb and generous'—do you really like that, Monsieur Hugo? Why not say, rather, 'You are, my lord, superb, etc.'?" The great tragedienne with the strength of her past behind her and the great poet who wrote for the future confronted each other politely; the barbarians were, thank God, people with good manners!

Mlle. Mars picked over *Hernani* with distaste. The censors nit-picked *Christine*: they wanted no ecclesiastical costumes. When, in the play, Descartes asked: "Do they not say that I was an atheist?" "Suppressed," answered the censor. Then Christine: "(The crown) was a royal rattle that I found in my cradle." "Suppressed." The censor, more royalist than the King, more papist than the Pope, looked for the mere shadow of allusions to the throne or the altar. On January 8, 1830, the suppressed lines were indicated to Dumas. He tried to coax the censor, who insisted on the heresies that studded poor *Christine*. "You attack altogether the legitimacy, the law, and the succession! The scene of Christine sending her crown to Cromwell is dangerous. Is it historic? To remind mankind of it was incendiary." Dumas made an appeal to the chief of censors, Monsieur de Lourdoneix. The interview, arranged by a lady subscriber to the Académie's prize-winning works, was short: "Finally, monsieur," Lourdoneix said curtly, "all you might add would be useless for as long as the oldest royal branch is on the throne and as long as I am a censor, your work will be suppressed."

"Very well, monsieur, I will wait," and Dumas bowed out coldly.

Christine was put on hold but, despite what he had said, the author did not want to wait—he could not wait with a mother and a son who lived from his pen. He worked some new innocence into the censored verses and with magnanimity the censor accepted the scene of the crown. Out of the hands of the censors, the play remained in those of Harel. Dumas had brought a suit against him to reclaim possession of *Christine*. The suit was dismissed in February 1838. *Christine* could not be played at the Comédie-Française.

But few people were interested in those obscure disputes. All energies were deployed for the expected battle at the Comédie-Française. *Hernani* was the object of all conversations: people quoted its verses and were already ecstatic. The "long hairs" bristled, the "billiard balls" shined, excess was the only fashion. Hugo refused a claque; he distributed his author's tickets made of a red square of paper stamped with the signature "Hierro," meaning "iron" in Spanish and which began with an "H" and ended with an "O" as in HUGO. A duel to the death was ready; the red paper passed from hand to hand, proudly exhibited by the young men who, for the most part, wore extravagant rags and assumed names with heraldic connotations. Theophile Gautier challenged the drab winter day with a red satin vest. On February 25, 1830, the crowd piled up on the Rue de Valois, in front of the still-closed king's entrance. The gaudy, riotous assemblage spoke loudly to get warm, attracting the neighborhood to its windows. People pointed to the bushy hair styles, the carnival-like clothes. First there were jeers followed by rotten vegetables which fell thickly on the crowd. The gang stoically resisted the vulgar provocations. At three o'clock the theatre doors opened and swallowed the throng. The curtain was due to rise at seven. The chandelier was not down nor was the stage lighted. In the semi-obscurity, the young rebels whiled away the time. They pulled bread, salami and onions out of their pockets; they looked for dark corners in which to urinate. The smell of a bivouac invaded the theater.

The classicists pinched their noses and cleared their throats. Dumas observed the position of the troops on his side; he felt himself invested with the power bestowed upon authors. He encouraged them but there was no need for it. French actors, stiffened by their methods, do not pass very well from the tragic to the comic. But what did it matter? People had come to applaud or to boo. So they applauded or booed from the moment the curtain went up to the time it fell. The battle raged mostly around the exact use of words.

On the stage Charles V asked for the time. It was midnight. The classicists shouted. The crowd was like an unbridled sea that shook with convulsive gestures; sometimes the actors' voices rose above the tumult, mostly Mlle. Mars' voice, who was respected by the audience. They fought about everything and about nothing.

The play swung between success and failure until the fifth act when Mlle. Mars, with her usual acting dignity, made herself heard and won the battle. It was a victory. Exhausted and hoarse, wrapped in their sumptuous tatters, the romantic youths escorted the victorious author into the cold night. Dumas, who had refused all other invitations so he could uphold his brothers-in-arms, was on the scene and among the noisiest. He did not realize then that *Hernani* had already erased *Henri III et sa Cour* in everyone's mind, then and for all posterity.

There was a slight feeling of intoxication the day after such a victory, but the literary battle continued. Yesterday Hugo; today Dumas. He had re-written *Christine*'s epilogue and read it March

6. On the 12th, the censor approved it. On the 15th he gave his visa to the play. The rehearsals began. The literary war moved to the other bank of the Seine and inflamed the Latin Quarter. Alexandre became acquainted with the household of Mlle. George, at 12 Rue Madame, in which the official lover, Harel of the Odéon, lived on the second floor and the "amant de coeur," Jules Janin, lived in the garret, in addition to Mlle. George's younger sister, called Maman Bébelle, and her two children: Tom, who for six or seven years kept his age as ten to further his theatrical career (which he detested) and Popaul, enormous and bulimic. Mlle. George lived like an oriental queen; she liked to show off her magnificent hands, her arms, her shoulder, her neck—which swept Alexandre away. She was forty, but Dumas courted her when she received him, voluptuously lying on a large sofa, dressed in velvet, furs and Indian cashmere. Dumas could admire through a half-opened negligee the miraculous whiteness of her throat. He was following two emperors and three or four kings; the company was most honorable! They loved more than a woman, they loved a legend. Dumas would sit near her zinc bathtub in which she was submerged and indicate to her each point he wanted emphasized, with such and such an intonation for such and such a line. The beautiful white arms came out of the foaming water to secure a gold pin that had let escape waves of hair. The greyhounds raised their necks at her slightest gesture. The steaming room was a sensual invitation during that timid spring which burst out slowly.

In spite of the rehearsals, Alexandre went frequently to the library of the Palais-Royal where he was assistant librarian. There he studied, worked and often met Ferdinand, Duc de Chartres, eldest son of Louis-Philippe d'Orléans, a charming seventeen-year-old adolescent who was attracted by the perfume of the amorous freedom backstage at the theater. Had he not been told that Alexandre had "African passions"?

The young prince had his own erotic curiosity and was more interested in the enticements of actresses than in the merit of new literary work. He whispered, vaguely ashamed, when he was called or when he heard his father's falsetto voice singing the mass, and ran away through some secret door. This friendship, born clandestinely between the adolescent and the young man, lived to survive the pomp of later power. Ferdinand wanted to attend the premiere of *Christine* with his two younger brothers. He begged

Dumas to plead for him with his father before whom he trembled. Louis-Philippe was not too keen on a play that had had difficulties with the censor. Dumas did his best to reassure him, and with two or three doubtful "Hum, hums" the authorization was given. Ferdinand was exultant.

Harel was preparing the presentation of *Christine, ou Stockholm, Fontainebleau et Rome* admirably, with multiple notices released to the press and also any number of news snippets. On March 29, the general rehearsal gathered all the romantics, still a cohesive group; Soulié, who had recovered from his pique, had joined again. He had asked Alexandre for a pass. After the fifth act, which had been received enthusiastically, Dumas came out of the orchestra and ran into Soulié. The two ex-collaborators embraced with deep, overflowing emotion: "Admirable thing! The performance is still a trifle deficient but this can be improved," said Soulié, and he asked Alexandre for fifty seats in the pit to distribute to the workmen of the woodshop he managed, so they could form a claque. Those old, fraternal feelings would not last, but Alexandre's eyes, just then, were misty.

Hardly a month after *Hernani*, the "longhairs" and the "billiard balls" met again for *Christine*—some with grotesque wigs—but with their hatred or enthusiasm intact. At seven in the evening, Dumas settled into a loge from which he could feel the impatience of the rabble rousers rise from below. The prologue was played in the midst of such a brouhaha that it had to be started again. Invectives flowed around: "Canailles! Imbeciles! Wigmakers! Wigs! They do not understand anything." "Send the blue-stockings back to the House of Rambouillet!" someone screamed. Boos were rarely interrupted. The play continued in the midst of great turmoil; the actors stayed firmly anchored on stage. By Act IV, the play had already lasted more than four long hours when Sentinelli's monologue began.

The hooting increased. Was it for the author or for the character? Or was it simply mechanical reaction? When Monaldeschi tried to reconquer the queen, Lockroy threw himself upon Mlle. George with such passion that Delphine Grey exclaimed: "Well, now, Lockroy!" At last Christine cried to the Pére Lebel a final provocation: "I pity him, father . . . let's finish with him." The audience was moved. It seemed a victory.

It could have been a victory if, as in the first *Christine*, the drama finished there. But there was an epilogue during which Christine and Sentinelli, now sinners with white hair and cold hearts, meet again in Rome after thirty years, one without hatred, the other without love. The audience was tired. When Christine asked her physician, "How long before I die?" an exasperated spectator answered her, "If you're not finished by one o'clock I am leaving."

Failure? Success? When the curtain fell the tumult did not permit a conclusion. The combatants of that doubtful encounter regrouped on the peristyle of the Odéon. They walked to 25 Rue de l'Université where a very late supper had been spread by Mélanie, who acted as hostess. Fatigue struck some but spurred others on to an artificial gaiety. They drank and ate, or rather they devoured food to fill bellies emptied by emotion. Alexandre was worried; he understood that he should cut the action taking place in Rome. He should patch up the "poignant" verses that had made the audience howl and were likely to sink the play at each performance. "Let us help," offered Hugo and Vigny. "Stay with your guests; we will take care of it." They withdrew into a small room and settled down to the work they had assumed while bacchic songs resounded in the next room. Alexandre forgot all about them. The next day, when he awoke very late in the morning, he found his manuscript, trimmed and polished, on the mantel. All for one!

In spite of curses and clamoring from the press great and small, the play enjoyed an honorable success as proved by the bookseller, Barba, who the next day bought the manuscript for twelve thousand francs. Some reviews, however, hurt. Was the play "an inconceivable chaos"? (Ph. Charles, *Revue de Paris*, April 4). Was Mlle. George "an immense pumpkin in the shape of a woman"? (*Courrier des Théâtres*, March 31). Was Mlle. Noblet "blue and green in the reflection of a lamp"? Was the success of the play due to an "infamous claque"? (*Courrier des Théâtres*, April 2).

At one o'clock in the morning, after the second performance, Alexandre came out from the light of the theater into the obscurity of the Place de l'Odéon. He dreamed of his next drama. From the door of a passing cab, a woman's voice called him by name. When the cab stopped, Dumas opened the door. "Well, come up and kiss me . . . Ah, you have a rare talent and you know how to create women rather well."

Alexandre laughed and kissed; he was already in love. He had recognized this woman who had more than talent. She was Marie

Dorval, the famous actress. After this and the homage of his brothers and sisters in art, it did not matter that the head of an office of the Maison du Roi opposed his obtaining the Légion d'Honneur that had been asked for him by the Duc d'Orléans himself. He saw Dorval again, describing how his head burned and his heart beat each time he saw her. Marie rebuked this love given too quickly. Alexandre was desperate. On April 30, 1830, he wrote from Paris:

> Ah, this letter, cold and mocking! . . . What did I ask you in mine? Nothing. I mentioned myself perhaps more than you; I tried to explain my thoughts more than I tried to read yours. Would it not be possible for a friend, when his head burns, to lay it on your shoulder, when his hand shakes, to place it on your hand, and to find himself happy, without asking more? No. If your letters, without tiring you, could give me back your conversation, I would ask only for your letters . . . but where would be the expression of your eyes which double the value of a word; where would be the vibration of your voice which colors your thoughts; where would be, *finally*, *the soul* which fills you so completely and which, in other women, one finds nowhere?

Alexandre enjoyed neither her ardent soul nor her yielding body, but only the position of friend and accomplice which he had to accept, despite all his desires.

Spring had come back at last and legitimists treated themselves to a last feast: the King of Naples, the ignoble François, arrived at Saint-Cloud on May 8. It was a family visit (François was the brother of the Duchesse de Berry) but still protocol had to be observed. They tried to hide a very unpopular king. The Duc d'Orléans, who protected his own new-born popularity, dared what Charles X judged impolitic; the Duke organized a great ball to which he invited all the illustrious literati and artists of France. Alexandre was forgotten, but the young Duc de Chartres insisted so much that he was granted the pleasure of sending an invitation to the man who initiated him in the ways of the theater.

The once young savage of Villers-Cotterêts was radiant this May 30, 1830, when he climbed the Palais-Royal's stairs of honor. Louis-Philippe welcomed him in person, a sign of honor that the courtiers noticed. The prince gave only one tip on etiquette:

Monsieur Dumas, if by chance the king does you the honor of speaking to you, you know that, when answering him, you must not say either 'sire' or 'majesty' but simply 'king.'

When the brass band played the salute, the Orléans family rushed forward, bunched together behind a double row of guards. The King appeared—after long and laborious dealings he had consented to honor his subject, the Duc d'Orléans, with his visit. The last King of France was an elderly man of seventy-six, tall, thin, whose head bent slightly under beautiful white hair. He still had bright and smiling eyes, a most Bourbonian nose, an ungraceful mouth whose upper lip hung on the chin. Suppressing his dislike for the Bourbons, Alexandre would have liked to have the King notice him, to honor him by a glance. But the old monarch passed through without so much as a look on one of the kings of the day. Uneasy, Alexandre went to the terrace when a loud clamor suddenly came from the gardens of the Palais-Royal and bright flashes of light broke upon the night. Groups of young people had pushed through the barriers, started a round dance and were singing the revolutionary "Ça ira," while others built a pyramid with chairs and Chinese lanterns. Soon the makeshift pyre caught fire. Women ran away to the stone arcade. The Duc d'Orléans gesticulated from a window; on his shoulder Alexandre felt the hand of the Duc de Chartres who wanted to know what these illuminations were about. For his prince, Alexandre rushed toward the bonfire; it was only a childish prank whose architect was a writer by the name of Alphonse Signol who had, in staging the event, created his best drama. He wanted to challenge the whole army to a duel. Alexandre attempted to calm him. The gardens were evacuated but the feast continued into the morning. It was remembered by a witticism of Monsieur de Salvandy to Louis-Philippe:

Monseigneur, this is a true Neapolitan feast, because we are dancing on a volcano.

To these few lines Monsieur de Salvandy owed his political good fortune and the essence of his glory.

Alexandre indulged in dreams of gold and blood: he had seen the King, he had seen the Prince, he had seen the sparks of revolution. It was Signol who woke him up the next morning, Signol who was preparing himself to die and trusted Dumas with a melodrama he had written that needed retouching. He made Dumas promise that even the impossible would be done; he thought of his mother whom his death would leave without resources. The same evening at the Théâtre-Italien, Signol provoked an officer who by chance sat in the same row. The next day the blood poured. Alexandre heard of the young man's death at the Café des Variétés. He had been looking for Signol after receiving a letter from him, notifying Alexandre of the duel and asking him to be his second. The letter had arrived too late.

Mélanie Waldor wore herself out trying to hold Alexandre, who sometimes found that love was just a dull repetition. She knew he was unfaithful and prowled about him as if she were afraid of losing him completely.

She knew that he wanted to publish their own story in a play: a man who, surprised by his mistress' husband, kills her, claiming that it was because she resisted him. He dies on the scaffold for this murder, thereby protecting the woman's honor and atoning for his crime. The man, Antony, was Alexandre; the mistress, Adéle d'Hervey, was Mélanie Waldor, and the husband was Commandant Waldor. The assassination and the scaffold were only romantic adornments to a very bourgeois adultery—the fictional characters extended from the real persons and became literary prototypes. They were children of reality as well as of previous fictions. Antony was also the Didier of *Marion Delorme*, the Werner or the Lara of Byron. Dumas had put aside a vague project for a play on Charles de Bourgogne so he could throw himself entirely into this new drama which would represent passion in modern costume. But was it possible to write about love that still lived or could words describe only dead passion? Did Mélanie see in this project the end or the apotheosis of love?

In any case she left on June 3, 1830, in the coach for Nantes heading toward the family property, La Jarrie, where she had lived during her childhood and adolescence. She was pregnant and was running away from scandal. The child she had so much dreaded at the beginning of her liaison with Alexandre she now ardently desired as a last tie which could hold her lover. Alexandre had accompanied her and at the door of the coach the two lovers whispered together: she would take good care of the little Antony she carried; yes, yes, he would rejoin her very soon when his drama was finished and accepted. Certainly he loved her, he loved only her. Then the postilion whipped the horses. The coach left rapidly and disappeared.

Paris was calm. The Chambre des Députés had been dissolved on May 9 because two hundred twenty deputies had dared to reply to one of the King's discourses with the following address:

> The Charter made the permanent collaboration of the political opinions of your government with the wishes of your people the indispensable condition for the regular functioning of public affairs. Sire, our loyalty and our devotion condemn us to tell you that this collaboration does not exist.

But what could the deputies, bourgeois and easily afraid, do against a monarchy that seemed so sure of itself that it sent a fleet, comprising two hundred three warships, to conquer Algiers (June 25)? They could only prepare new elections.

Alexandre wrote to Mélanie that he had finished *Antony* on June 9, and had read it either on the tenth or the eleventh to Mlle. Mars and Firmin for whom the parts of Adéle and Antony had been written. On June 16th, the reading took place before the committee. Alexandre went wild with joy:

> Dear love, it is three-thirty. I just returned from the Committee; I have been accepted unanimously. So here is *Antony* launched—they pretend that it will be played within a month's time—May God hear them and me, too, because I wish you health, which I cannot give you, and happiness and love, which I can give you.

He was irresistible. All surrendered before him—the powerful, the women and the reading committees.

He had met Belle Krelsamer and asked his friends to verify the beauty of the woman and her talent as an actress:

> My dear Alfred de Vigny
> I came to ask you whether you are free Tuesday at two o'clock. In which case we could go with Victor, Boulanger and Saint-Èvre to Versailles to see an actress act, with whom Firmin had played at Marseille. It is said that she has great talent. If

the three of us are satisfied we could introduce her into the Français where she could be very useful to us . . .

P. S. She is young and pretty.

With beautiful jet-black hair, eyes of deep azure, splendid teeth, a nose as straight as that of the Venus of Milo, Belle asked protection for her theatrical career. Who could resist her?

Certainly not Alexandre, all the more that Belle, if she were not as young as Dumas pretended—she was twenty-seven or thirty, according to her daughter's birth certificate, or to her death certificate—knew all the arts of seduction. Daughter of a small Jewish property owner of Mulhouse, Cerf Krelsamer, she had followed in the wake of her older sister to the life of demi-mondaine. Noticed by the Baron Taylor, she gave him a daughter, Mélanie-Adéle, who came after Jean-Paul (born November 3, 1825) of an unknown father. Taylor was not an ingrate; he had permitted his mistress to make her debuts at the Comédie-Française between July 15 and August 10, 1828, under the theater name of Mélanie Serre. Her speech had been found too slow and too painfully worked out and she had to go back to touring the provinces. Her meeting with Alexandre was her last chance in Paris. She made a play of resisting him for the sake of propriety. Dumas had expected a resistance of six weeks; all it took was three. No matter, he was loved.

On June 10, the King and the Queen of Naples, accompanied by the Duchesse de Berry, went to a perfomance of *Christine*. Alexandre kneeled before the Duchess to offer her a splendidly bound copy of the play. On the 15th, he danced at Madame Lafond's. She was a dark beauty, admirably well-preserved. In this same salon, during the preceding carnival, a young woman dressed as a Roman priestess crowned with verbena and cypress had come to him as he paraded in costume as Arnaute: coat and gaiters of red velvet embroidered with gold, a Greek white "fustanella" and arms of chased silver. The priestess was Marie Malibran. Desdemona, Rosina, La Somnambula and Norma on the opera stage, she demanded the secret of the remarkable turban Alexandre wore. She wanted to use it the next day in her *Othello*.

On June 18, Alexandre demanded that *Antony* be given preference for presentation on September 15. The Committee agreed. Yet, he vaguely told Mélanie that the Comédie-Française had not decided or that perhaps it would present the play immediately. This might have been an excuse to avoid going to La Jarrie and to stay in Paris near Belle. Successes seemed to come in pairs: Harel asked him to adapt *Édith* for the Odéon.

Audacious, Dumas dared to ask on July 1 that Belle be engaged as "pensionnaire" at the Comédie-Française. He attempted in vain to win one of the old "societaires" to his cause. Yet the engagement of Belle was postponed . . . next year, perhaps. Since even success had its limits, Belle could not reproach Alexandre for lack of trying.

Paris had lost its calm, the elections on June 23 and 24 were a triumph for the liberal oppositon. The Te Deum, the ringing of bells that celebrated the taking of Algiers, did not drown out the voices of the newly elected. Alexandre was thinking of following the invading army. But there was La Jarrie and Mélanie who complained, and cried, and asked for her Alex:

Paris, July 7 (from Alexandre to Mélanie)
I do not understand, my love, the four-day delay you mention. I have written to you with the most exact regularity, even when I could not write, when a drop of sweat fell on each letter and when I had to write every word twice to make it legible once. I do not understand the reproaches at the end of your letter, only that they are reproaches again. I cannot remember what I wrote you—It is happiness that you must read instead of recreation—and the sentence must be reconstructed: if love becomes a torment instead of happiness—yes, my friend, I repeat, I understand that in the beginning of a love of which one still doubts, one needs to be sure of it, even at the expense of one's tranquility. But after a bond of three years, which rests on sacred honor and love, that one could be still at the point of small inquiries, the small harassments of the beginning of love, that is what I do not understand.

Paris bored him. Mélanie bored him. The petty gossip exchanged in the salons exasperated him. Yes, he spent money, but had he not eight or ten persons to support? Yes, he considered withdrawing *Antony* from the Français which did not play it, which refused to engage Belle. Yes, he began to negotiate with Harel who promised him twenty-five thousand francs. Alexandre had already found his censors who, with the whip of criticism in their hands, would pursue him throughout his career, ignoring his work, attacking the extravagant, dissolute, spendthrift man. He rode around in a tilbury *all day long.* When did he write his dramas that he offered to the theaters? He was suspected of using collaborators before he even had thought of getting one. Ah, to leave Paris!

> If I were free from all, I would travel continuously alone; I would come to Paris only to have my plays acted, then I would go away immediately. (to Mélanie Waldor, around July 20, 1830)

It was then, when he was attempting to organize this new design for his life by leaving for Algiers, that Paris itself became once more a fascinating scene.

At Saint-Cloud, Charles X had signed the Ordinances of July 25. First Ordinance: the liberty of the periodical press was abolished. Second Ordinance: the Chambre des Députés of Departements was dissolved. Third Ordinance: A new electoral law was adopted. Fourth Ordinance: the next elections would take place on the 6th and the 28th of the following September. The response of Charles X and his minister, Polignac, to the votes of the electors was a simple and final refusal.

On Monday, July 26, at eight in the morning, Achille Comte, professor of natural sciences at the Lycée Charlemagne, friend of Mélanie and Alexandre, hurried to see Dumas:

> "The Ordinances are published in *Le Moniteur* . . . Are you still leaving for Algiers?"
> —"I'm not so foolish! What we are going to see here will be even more interesting than what I could see there."
>
> Alexandre called his servant, who rushed in. "Joseph, go to my gunsmith; bring back my two-hundred-shot rifle and two hundred twenty-calibre bullets!"

III

Decorated in July

Alexandre, why did you dispatch Joseph, your servant, a moron
and a cheat, to your gunsmith? What revolutionary bug had bitten
you? A few weeks ago you presented the Duchesse de Berry with
a copy of *Christine*, do you remember? It was the woman you
respected even more than the title. Good! But in whose service, for
what cause did you intend to use your gun? In the service of the
Duc d'Orléans, whose employee you were? The young Duc de
Chartres was your friend, the Duc d'Orléans flattered himself that
he was a liberal and loved the arts. In the service of the Bonapartes,
whose pale scion survived in Vienna? You often frequented the
Bonapartist salons but you withdrew from those Napoleonic liberals
who were too dedicated to classical literature. Would you serve the
Republic? There was no indication that you felt sympathy for the
Italian carbonieri, that you honored the memory of 1789, even less
that of 1793. Yet there are inherited obligations. The son of a
Republican general could do no less than his father. It was your
father's rifle that you wanted, that you locked up before going to
feel out the atmosphere of the streets.

It was ten in the morning when Alexandre came out from 25
Rue de l'Université into the bright summer sun. It was a short
distance to Belle's apartment. The young woman was sad because
of the postponement of the trip to Algiers. Why stay in Paris where

nothing was happening? Where nothing would happen, added Achille Comte. "Out of pure curiosity." Belle unpacked the trunks.

Alexandre walked along the quays, where no sign of unrest could be seen; he went briefly to the Palais-Royal. Nobody was there— the Duke was at Neuilly, his son at Joigny, Broval at Villers, Oudard no one knew where. Alexandre continued to the Café du Roi, whose habitués were Royalists who applauded the monarch's authority. Étienne Arago, son of a Conventionnel and a Republican himself, stopped by. His brother, a famous astronomer, was due to give a talk at the Institut. It was suggested that Alexandre also go to the lecture. On the Pont des Arts they heard that the liberal newspapers had begun a referendum against the Ordinance, which restricted the right to publish without previous authorization. At the Institut, the Immortals were in turmoil. They had great apprehension. Would François Arago speak or not? He did, begged by his colleagues who feared that his silence could be considered as factious. He delivered a vigorously applauded panegyric on the engineer Fresnel, with allusions to the present events which were as factious as silence could have been.

After a short visit to the charming Emma Guyet-Desfontaines, Alexandre went to the Grand Véfour for dinner. In the gardens of the Palais-Royal some young men unsuccessfully attempted to imitate Camille Desmoulins by reading *Le Moniteur* aloud. After dinner, Alexandre continued his erratic walk. He went to the Leuvens' where Madame de Leuven was worried; neither her husband nor her son had returned home. Alexandre rushed to the *Courrier Français* where M. de Leuven had a meeting. There they were drafting a protestation in the name of their Charter. They triumphantly announced that the President de Belleyme had judged in favor of the journalists' referendum: printers could print the previously suspended newspapers. Now they would either have to sign the protestation, printed before the president's decision, or simply stop it. The discussion was dragging. At last, at midnight, forty-five journalists risked their signatures and perhaps their heads as well. After Alexandre had reassured Madame de Leuven of her husband's health he rejoined Belle. It was a day wasted, the rifle remained in the closet.

Into splendid sunshine, on Tuesday the 27th, Alexandre emerged from the first floor of 7 Rue Madame where he had kissed his mother who felt a bit lonely since Mélanie, Madame de Villenave and the small Élisa had left for the country. Otherwise, she lived in perfect tranquility. Alexandre met Paul Foucher, whose terrible nearsightedness extended to politics; he claimed that the next day he would read the most beautiful drama in the world. Alexandre should hear it at once, but he escaped by calling for a cab: "To Carrel's!" Carrel, director of the *National,* was a figurehead of the Liberal, even Republican opposition. Carrel was eating lunch very peacefully. The revolution would not take place, he said. He intended to stay home, to read and to work. Alexandre succeeded, however, in dragging him out to the boulevards. At the Bourse the crowd seemed drawn toward the Rue Richelieu. There were rumors that the office of *Le Temps* had been pillaged by a squad of police. In fact, there were about twenty policemen in battle formation before the printing works, on whose closed door a superintendent with a white scarf was striking heavy blows. A giant of a man opened, his black mane of hair reached to his shoulders. Behind him followed editors, employees and the printers. Alexandre recognized Baude and squeezed the arm of Carrel, who shook his head. With a thundering voice, Baude reminded the slightly embarrassed superintendent of the Civil Code and its article on "effraction." The superintendent demanded, however, that a locksmith be called. A whisper, light as a breeze, ran through the crowd. People vaguely understood that what they saw was not the confrontation of Baude with a superintendent, but rather the battle of rights against arbitrary rule, of conscience against tyranny. The locksmith, brought in haste, slowly took out his tools while Baude read him the article of the Code. The man hesitated, fiddled with his peaked cap: "Hard labor! The galleys!" At each of his hesitant gestures the crowd applauded—offered to be witness at the Court if needed. The man put his cap back on his head and excused himself. A second locksmith came with a bunch of keys and hooks at his belt, but even before reaching the door he had hidden them. He said, "My hooks were stolen." "You lie!" replied the superintendent, ready to arrest him, but the crowd enfolded the threatened locksmith into its multiple swirls. A third locksmith, the man who riveted irons on convicts, a reliable man if such there were, was called. The crowd was evacuated; the people cried "Long live the Charter," but observed the police barricades.

Carrel and Alexandre let themselves drift into the office of the *National* on the Place des Italiens. There everybody was depressed: the people had not reacted as expected. Yet, they could feel a shiver in the air which announced the impending storm. One hundred thousand copies of the protest were distributed in the streets. The tide was swelling. Everywhere groups were assembling, according to their political affinities—Bonapartists, Liberals, Republicans. Carrel refused to join any of those, for he believed only in legal resistance. "Do we have a regiment we can trust?" he asked. He disdained the strength of public opinion.

As Carrel and Alexandre went up the boulevards, they heard a sound like shooting near the Palais-Royal. Was it a platoon? Carrel went back home while Alexandre ran toward the Bourse. There the lancers were charging into the crowd. Already three people lay dead on the Rue Saint-Honoré. Young men ran by—they had seen a tricolor flag on the Quai de l'École. When eight o'clock rang on the clock of the Bourse, the day was ending, but on the Rue Vivienne, bayonets were appearing, pushing away men, women and children. Women waving handkerchiefs from open windows cried: "Do not fire on the people!" As Alexandre could see from the Café des Nouveautés where he had taken refuge, the troops had deployed on the Place de la Bourse. A corps of guards was left in a ruin of a shelter made of planks, while the rest of the troops headed toward the Bastille. Street children invaded the square. First they threw insults, and then stones in the direction of the guards. They hurt a soldier who fired. A woman fell to the ground and there were cries of "Murder!" The square was evacuated, the shops closed, the lights extinguished. The only theater, still lit, seemed like an insult to this sudden mourning. A group of men carried a corpse to the peristyle steps and screamed, "No show tonight! Close the theaters! People are being slaughtered on the streets of Paris." The theater audience left slowly as they tried to avoid stepping on the slain woman, who appeared to be about thirty years old.

Alexandre ran into Étienne Arago, who was at the head of a small group. They decided to meet the next day at Arago's. Alexandre, who was famished, asked to have a supper served at the Café des Nouveautés. From table to table information was exchanged: some people had seen a barricade being built on the Rue Saint-Honoré. Would this riot only prove to be a prologue to revolution? A shot, followed by a tragic cry, "To arms!" interrupted the discussion. They all went up to the mezzanine. It was nine-forty. From the windows they could make out a chaotic fight. The soldiers had been surprised, surrounded, attacked and beaten. The assailants took their rifles, sacks and swords; they hoisted the woman's corpse onto a stretcher. The dismal procession, lighted by torches, moved ahead to the cries of "Revenge!" In the café, diners were finishing supper by the sinister light of the burning barracks, which shone like a puddle of blood on the dark square.

At midnight Alexandre headed back to the Rue de l'Université. Shadows moved in the darkness, a voice asked, "Who goes there?" Alexandre replied, "Friend!" and exchanged a few handshakes with the builders of the barricades. There was a vast encampment behind the fences of the Tuileries. A sentinel hollered, "Get away!" Once he had returned to the Rue de l'Université, Alexandre listened from his window to the beautiful summer night; all seemed silent.

Wednesday, July 28. Alexandre rubbed his eyes as a friend suddenly awakened him. The student quarter was in insurrection and the students stormed against Lafitte, Casimir Périer and La Fayette, who had slammed the doors in their faces. Once dressed, Alexandre ran to kiss his mother who enjoyed the calm of ignorance. When he did not find Cavaignac at home he went to the Place Dauphine, to the Joubert book shop where he expected to find him; he was not there. Belle expected Alexandre and he stopped by. He promised her whatever she wanted, that he would not get mixed up in the events, that he would continue to be only the witness he had always been. She kissed him tenderly before letting him go.

He joined a large crowd in the Rue de Beaune. They wanted to march on, but they did not have any arms. "No arms?" trumpeted Étienne Arago. "If you have no arms, there are plenty at the gunsmiths." Alexandre pointed out a gunsmith in the Rue de l'Université and then climbed to his fourth floor apartment. Joseph brought his master's hunting outfit and helped him put it on. A rumor had spread in the Rue du Bac: Étienne Arago and Gauja, who had located the gunsmith, sounded the call to arms. Two gendarmes on horseback ran them down. They had time to fire, and a gendarme fell, pierced with two bullets; the other turned back as fast as he could. Alexandre had donned his coat, taken his rifle, his game-bag, his pouch of gunpowder and had filled his pockets with bullets. In the street, he was surrounded and told to help build barricades. Taking a pair of pliers, he began to pry loose the blocks paving the Rue de l'Université. When some soldiers appeared, they were taken prisoners without any real opposition, but since nobody knew what to do with them, they were released; only their rifles were kept. The barricade builders went back to their project, but Alexandre was soon tired of this heroic work and loaned his pliers with pleasure to a tall young man, blonde and dressed in an apple-green morning coat. His name was Alexandre Bixio. With a handshake a friendship was born.

Once the barricade was finished, Alexandre the hunter retraced his familiar route along the Place de la Révolution and the Rue Saint-Honoré. All streets and passages were strategically guarded by the troops. Alexandre went up to his former office and found a cautious Jacques-Parfait Oudard at his post. When Alexandre insinuated that the title of "your Majesty" would fit the Duc d'Orléans very well, Oudard moaned with distress. When Alexandre made a play of aiming through the crack of a shade at a general passing in the street, Oudard, in agony, took hold of the rifle—whose trigger was not even cocked. When Alexandre opened a window, Oudard protested highly. Alexandre looked at the passing troops. The excitement he expressed was not shared by his ex-chief who, in allegiance to Louis-Philippe, did not like such open political maneuvering.

With his rifle on his shoulder, Alexandre went farther along the Rue de Richelieu as if he were going to open the hunting season in the Saint-Denis plain. Everywhere people erased the "fleurs de lys," everywhere they scratched off the King's monogram and scrawled graffiti on the sign-boards: "Down with the Bourbons" followed "Long live the Charter." Handkerchiefs were waved from the windows to passing civilians. A fever was communicated to the city. Alexandre shivered with pleasure.

On the threshold of the *National*, Alexandre and Carrel were joined by Jean-Baptiste Charras, a handsome young man about twenty years old who, at the beginning of the school year, had been expelled from the Polytechnique for having sung *La Marseillaise* during a dinner. He wanted to fight and, in the company of four school friends, had vainly tried to meet Lafitte and La Fayette. But where was the fight?—At City Hall. Alexandre went in the direction of the Faubourg Saint-Germain. At the café of Hiraux, the son of Alexandre's former violin teacher, he heard that Marmont, Duc de Raguse, had offered to the king his services as commander of Paris' armed forces. Had he not been a traitor before? On the Pont de la Révolution, people pointed toward Notre Dame: a tricolor flag waved from one of the towers. Alexandre leaned on the parapet, his arms taut as though petrified, and tears filled his eyes. The Republic, the Empire, lived again in this hanging rag—the great epic was reborn. He clasped his rifle tightly. A sharp fusillade burst from the Place de Grève. Because he carried a gun some men assembled around Alexandre, and asked him to lead their group. They went along the Rue de Lille growing in number as they advanced. By the time they reached the Rue du Bac, Alexandre commanded fifty men, plus two drummers with one flag. He wanted to go up to his apartment to take some money, but on the landlord's orders the porter refused to open the door to these dangerous revolutionaries. The group had no ammunition; a gunsmith mentioned that they could get cartridges at the back door of the Institut. They rushed there and, in fact, a gentleman distributed powder that could be obtained by standing in line: twelve rounds for each rifle, six per pistol. Then, on to the Place de Grève! On the Quai aux Fleurs, they found themselves face to face with the 15th Light Regiment, fifteen hundred men at least. They stopped. The Captain recognized Dumas ("Truly, Monsieur Dumas, I did not believe you were as crazy as that.") who asked that his men might simply pass through. The Captain stood fast and the group had to adopt another strategy.

When the insurgents reached the suspension bridge at City Hall, they totalled about one hundred men. They were just starting to cross the span when a cannon fired suddenly and mowed down a dozen of them. Sheltered behind the parapets, Alexandre's troop fired at the Place de Grève. The cannon fired for a second time, sweeping everything. "To the bridge!" cried a voice, and the little army sprang forward, but they had barely crossed a third of the bridge when the cannon fired yet again and the bayonets charged. The group dispersed, disappearing like smoke. On the bridge, dead and wounded men were now piled up. The soldiers advanced toward Notre-Dame to pull down the tricolor flag and silence the bourdon bell whose ringing dominated the sound of battle.

Alexandre had left the battlefield, rather pleased with his behavior in the face of gunfire; he was his father's worthy son. He went to knock at the door of the painter Léthière. The old man and Mlle. d'Herville welcomed him as a hero and offered him brimming glasses of "tafia," the raw rum from Guadeloupe. The drawing room clock showed three in the afternoon. Alexandre related the details of his insurrection and was asked for dinner. About five o'clock

Léthière's son brought a fresh batch of news: the boulevards were afire, half of the trees were cut down to build barricades, the soldiers were squashed under bedsteads, armoires, chests of drawers, pieces of marble, water basins thrown from the windows. The people, the petite bourgeoisie, the young had thrown themselves into the uprising. But what about the financiers? The army? The aristocrats? The Chambre des Députés palavered and sent delegations. Perhaps the victors of today would have to flee tomorrow, and Léthière asked Dumas: "Do you have money? A passport?" All those things were presently at the Rue de l'Université apartment from which Alexandre was now banned. Léthière's son was sent as a courier and he came back half an hour later with a wallet containing three thousand francs, a passport and about forty bullets. He told Alexandre that, considering the turn of events, his landlord was no longer opposed to his return.

Alexandre left his gun, powder and bullets with Léthière. "We must compromise the leaders of the opposition, who shiver undercover," thought the machiavellian Alexandre. He dressed for the occasion and crossed the bridge again. All the shops were closed but dim lights flickered at most windows; in the open air, the bourdon bell of Notre Dame, ceaseless and lugubrious, sounded like the flight of bronze birds. La Fayette was not home. Dumas turned back and in the dark he encountered shadows. He recognized the General, who confessed, "We can do nothing with the deputies ... If they let me act, I am ready." Alexandre ran to Arago's where there was a meeting of people who formed the nucleus of the revolution. He told the group, "La Fayette will accept the leadership. Good! Let's go to the *National*." There they put together a sublime forgery, a fake proclamation coming from a phony provisional government intended to be posted all over Paris and published in all newspapers. Then, exhausted but with a quieter mind, Alexandre went to bed. Some intermittent shooting could still be heard and accompanied the bourdon bell of Notre Dame.

Thursday, July 29. Joseph trembled and after some indecision woke up "Monsieur." There was fighting around the Rue de l'Université, mostly at the Musée de l'Artillerie where there was a corps of guards. "Dammit! They will pillage everything!" thought Alexandre while running to Saint-Thomas d'Aquin. Soldiers were driving off the intrepid bunch of attackers, and Alexandre advised them to attack through the garret above the post, showing them the way. Bullets rained on the guards, who were climbing the walls of the courtyards and gardens and running away. The insurgents were already in the museum. "Respect the arms!" roared Alexandre. But they were there *to take* the arms, and Alexandre knew that the most precious ones should be saved. He put François I's helmet on his own head; he fastened the king's shield to his arm, his sword at his side; he hoisted Charles IX's arquebus on his shoulders. Then, bent under this weight, he went back to his apartment where he astonished Joseph with all the metal with which he had saddled himself. With difficulty he removed the helmet which suffocated him and returned to the museum. He brought back the armor plate, the ax and the mace of François I. All the rest had disappeared.

Alexandre had smelled the odor of gun powder, heard the roar of the guns, seen the flow of blood in this great and tragic game of war and insurrection. He was slightly intoxicated. When he was told that there were gatherings at the Place de l'Odéon, he hurried there; five or six hundred men were milling about in the square. They surrounded two or three students of the Polytechnique School. Barrels of powder were smashed, and each man asked for a share which he put into his pocket, his handkerchief, his cap or his tobacco pouch. They melted lead from the rain gutters to make cartridges. They asked for paper and received it in sheets, in reams and in bulk. Soon three or four thousand cartridges were ready for distribution. Spirits soared on the Place de l'Odéon. The crowd became hoarse screaming "Long live the Charter!" "Long live the Republic!" When a horseman passed dressed in a morning coat, they cried in one voice, "Long live the Emperor!" One old woman fell on her knees, crossed herself and, exalted, cried "Oh! Jesus! I will not have to die without seeing him again!" Drums resounded, the crowd sang *La Marseillaise*. They got under way but soon the revolutionary army divided itself into three parts. Alexandre was with the corps which went straight to the Louvre via the Pont des Arts. It was now 10:30 by the institute clock. Across from it stood the formidable Louvre. Swiss mercenaries were on its balconies, in a double row behind the fences of the gardens, and along the parapet was a regiment of cuirassiers.

On the quay, under a sky white with heat, they scattered. Alexandre settled down behind one of the bronze lions on the central steps of the institute. He could see a cannon on the Pont des Arts and a regiment of cuirassiers offered a good target. The day before he had learned how to master his fear; he kept a cool head. Around him he could recognize simple people: store clerks, students, all with rifles, and some young boys . . . heroic street children who handled pistols, sabres and swords as best they could.

The heat was insufferable. Not a breath of air stirred while the shooting continued without interruption. A belt of gun smoke hid the royal troops on the other bank. As soon as it cleared, the shooting resumed. An insurgent fell, hit on the forehead; another, wounded in the abdomen, crawled toward Alexandre, who helped him to reach the basin of the fountain where he could drink. As the shooting continued with no great result, someone cried, "To the Louvre!" Alexandre kept his position as observer. Bullets whizzed past him. When a hidden cannon thundered on the Pont des Arts, wounded men whirled and fell or tried to get up, some trying to escape by jumping into the Seine. The young boys retreated like a flight of sparrows. Soon the quay was empty. The wounded man near Alexandre gave a last sigh—a second bullet had ended his life.

When Alexandre reached the small door of the Institut, he knocked with the butt of his rifle. The concierge opened and Alexandre slipped through the door. Saved! Madame Guyet-Desfontaines could hardly recognize him under the sweat, the whitish powder and the blood. He brandished his rifle and explained the situation. His hostess was wildly amused. Alexandre swallowed a large bowl of chocolate in one gulp and then the hero, stretched in a large armchair, narrated at length his iliad! When he returned to 25 Rue de l'Université, he was received as a conqueror. He had wanted to change his shirt and fill his pockets with gun powder and bullets, but when he peered through the window he saw thousands of sheets of paper flying in the blue sky. The Tuileries were taken and, brave Alexandre, you were not there! He put his coat back on without changing his shirt.

It was an image never forgotten: the Tuileries occupied, the tricolor flag on the top of the central pavilion; hundreds of women coming from everywhere; a polytechnician wounded in the chest had been seated on a throne decorated with fleurs de lys; embraces, sudden recognitions amongst the crowd; the revelry of people in the King's bed. Alexandre followed in the crowd's wake. In the Duchesse de Berry's bookcase he took the copy of *Christine* bound in violet Moroccan leather he had offered to the princess. In the courtyard, four men wearing dresses and feathered hats taken from the wardrobes of the King's daughters danced a quadrille.

It seemed that the revolution had succeeded, but what could be expected from the politicians? At the Lafittes' town house, the courtyards, gardens, antechambers and drawing rooms were overflowing with onlookers. Some of them had even found standing space on the roofs of surrounding buildings.

The crowd grumbled as the timorous liberal deputies gathered inside the house. Alexandre stole in, following some officers of the National Guard when they entered the council room. Lafitte, who had sprained his ankle the day before, was lying in an armchair. La Fayette and some forty deputies chatted in small groups. Suddenly, the frightening sound of shooting broke out. "The Royal Guard is marching on City Hall," it was rumored. As if sucked out, the deputies disappeared through exit doors and windows. Alexandre approached La Fayette. The shooting, he suggested, came from the confused Royal Guard. A better informed officer claimed that it was actually the shots of joyous celebrations. The deputies were mustered again; some had found refuge in the horse stables. A deputation came in—La Fayette had accepted the Paris command that had been offered. Alexandre was already flying from the antechamber, to the courtyard, to the streets, crying at the top of his lungs, "Make way for Général La Fayette who is going to City Hall!" The crowd cheered; 1830 was linked to 1789. La Fayette advanced slowly, with an escort of children, women and old people. He arrived at City Hall at three-thirty after a march of one and a half hours during which he experienced all the intoxication of popularity. When the General settled down, a swarm of peasants, students and newly appointed generals surrounded him. Messengers arrived in succession and La Fayette embraced them. Meat and bread were distributed; people camped on the square.

Alexandre was famished. He went to a wine merchant and talked him out of a bottle of wine, a piece of bread and a salami. From the windows of the cheap café, he could see all the events happening at City Hall. Once again an eyewitness after the battle, Alexandre did not want to miss anything. While the men from the suburbs, the young people from the schools and the students palavered, embraced and rested, the bourgeoisie schemed. They had named a municipal commission to counterbalance La Fayette's power. At Saint-Cloud, the King repealed the Ordinances, but it was too late.

When Alexandre had eaten his salami, he crossed through the multitudes camping on the square. In the large room of City Hall, Odilon Barrot, a gentleman with a hat adorned with feathers, had just been named Prefect of the Seine. He was writing across from a young man who had, as his only weapons, a powder pouch around his neck and a small dagger on his belt. Could one suppose that he loaded his dagger with gun powder? The municipal commission and the Commandant of the revolutionary armies glowered at each other. Alexandre had an office opened for his use and stole a pencil and paper to write notes on that memorable day. But his eyes closed in spite of the uproar around him. He arranged two armchairs like a camp bed and fell asleep.

Friday, July 30. It was the beginning of a great day. When he looked at himself in a mirror, Alexandre could recognize the traces of two days of fighting: a thick beard, a face burned by the sun, missing buttons on his twill coat and blood on his gaiters and shoes.

Gunpowder was becoming scarce. "If Charles X came back to Paris, we would not even have four thousand shots," La Fayette reported. Alexandre offered to find more gunpowder wherever he could. He asked for an order from La Fayette who, not wanting to have Alexandre's death on his conscience, at first refused. "At least give me a pass to reach Général Gérard," insisted Alexandre. This La Fayette accepted, and Alexandre wrote, "Let M. Alexandre Dumas pass to Général Gérard." La Fayette, the revolutionary of two worlds, signed and while he turned his back, Alexandre added "to whom we recommend the offer he just made to us." Général Gérard objected—it was very compromising to sign such an order. "And what about fulfilling it," retorted Alexandre, who gave the draft which the General then copied: "The authorities of the City of Soissons are asked to give at once to Alexandre Dumas all the gunpowder that can be found either in the powder magazine or elsewhere in the city."

Alexandre carried on with his falsifications by adding himself, above Gérard's signature, "Minister of War." That was sufficient for the military authorities, but there remained the civilian authorities. He had to convince La Fayette, who by now was rather tired, to give him the proclamation he asked for:

To the citizens of the city of Soissons:
Citizens,
You know what happened in Paris during the three last immortal days. The Bourbons were driven away; the Louvre was taken over; the people are now masters of the capital. But the victors of these three days may, through the lack of ammunition, lose the victory they have so dearly acquired. They turn to you, through the voice of M. Alexandre Dumas, with a fraternal call to your patriotism and your devotion.

All the gun powder you can send to your brothers in Paris will be considered as an offering to our fatherland.

At City Hall, Alexandre ran down four steps at a time. It was two in the afternoon and the gates of Soissons closed at eleven o'clock at night. There were about 60 miles between Paris and Soissons. On a square, Alexandre met one of his friends, Bard, an eighteen-year-old painter, and offered him an invitation: "Come with me to be shot." A meeting place was decided—the first post relay on the road to Soissons. There, the relay master immediately offered to hitch up a carriage which they could keep in case they needed it. Bard, who was expected to come with Alexandre's horse and pistols, was late. While waiting, a flag made with merino wool— half a yard white, half a yard blue and half a yard red—was sewn together, nailed to a broom handle and fixed to the hood of the cabriolet.

When Bard arrived full speed, they rushed into the cabriolet. The postilion mounted his saddle and the carriage sped away at a furious gallop. They traveled about 12 miles an hour, stopping only to get relays of horses. At each stop people gathered, attracted by the tricolor flag. At Nanteuil they changed the postilion. The replacement was Père Levasseur, a stubborn old man who claimed he knew his job because he had driven Général La Fayette, but preferred trotting to galloping. Alexandre, insisting on speed, threatened the man with his pistol, then pulled off the man's boots, mounted the horse himself and took off at a gallop! At Villers-Cotterêts the native son received an ovation. He was congratulated, interrogated: "He wants to enter Soissons? Soissons! A royalist city! No chance for him to get to Soissons before eleven o'clock!" "No matter," interjected a friend, Hutin, born in Soissons, "I know the guard there." In that case they might as well take time for supper. The two heroes sat at a table with a circle of people around them. Alexandre recognized the faces of old friends left behind seven years ago. Inexhaustible, he recounted the epic of the past three days of which very few details had yet reached Villers. They all embraced a last time, then Hutin, Bard and Alexandre climbed into the carriage. Two hours later, Hutin, as he had promised, had the gates of Soissons opened for them. It was eleven-thirty.

Saturday, July 31. They slept very little. At the first light of dawn they took down the red drapes in Hutins' dining room, and the blue drapes from their drawing room. From Madame Hutin's trousseau they took a heavy linen sheet: they had to make a new tricolor flag to replace the flag they had left at Villers for security reasons. Everyone sewed: Madame Hutin, her cook, Hutin, Bard, even Alexandre himself. At seven in the morning the plotters were in the streets. They reconnoitered by the ruins of the Cathedral Saint-Jean where the gunpowder was kept. By chinning up over the wall, they could see two soldiers in shirt sleeves working in the garden. They split up: Hutin would alert the liberal citizens of Soissons while Alexandre would rush to Dr. Missa's, one of the city's most enthusiastic patriots. The doctor was very cautious. In spite of all the proclamations Alexandre flourished, it was likely that the authorities would not give any help. As for the commander of the place, the Chevalier de Liniers, it was a good guess that he would oppose and resist. Hutin had alerted two friends; the small band jumped over the wall of the powder house to the extreme surprise of the soldier-gardeners. Threatening them with one hand, Alexandre waved with the other hand the order from Général Gérard. They recognized the signature and were ready to deliver the powder if they received an order from their commander. Alexandre inquired as to where he could find the commander's house, while under the pretense of admiring the view, Bard and Hutin climbed up the cathedral's tower to unfurl the makeshift tricolor flag.

The commander asked one of his officers about this tricolor rag that was waving in the sky of Soissons. His stupefaction redoubled when a strange figure burst into his office—a tie as twisted as a well-cord, a shirt stiff from four days' wear, a coat stripped of all its buttons: Alexandre Dumas, dramatist, author on a mission for the Provisional Government with an order signed by the General who was Minister of War. It was a suspicious signature, of course, not authenticated and with no seal. "I am ready, however, to believe you," Commandant Linier said with an ironic smile, "but there are no more than two hundred cartridges in the magazine." Vexed, Alexandre declared that he would verify that fact at once. The verification showed that there were two hundred pounds of powder in the magazine belonging to the artillery. While the commander was getting ready to show his authority, Alexandre burst into Linier's office and closed the door behind him. By now, the group included a lieutenant of police and a lieutenant colonel of engineering. The commander, ironic and stubborn, refused to deliver whatever was wanted, unless he was forced to do so. Alexandre was not ready to be mocked; he backed toward the door, cocked his pistols, pulled them out of his pockets and aimed them at the officers. "If in five minutes this order is not signed, I will blow out your brains, beginning with you, Monsieur le Lieutenant du Roi."

Alexandre began his count, "One, two, three . . ." The door crashed open; a woman, crazy with terror, hurled herself in, looked in stupefaction at Alexandre and screamed at the officer, "Oh my friend, give up! Give up! It is the second revolution of the negroes!"

Madame de Liniers, née Saint-Janvier, had seen her father's and mother's throats slit before her very eyes during the revolt of the Cap. The commander would have preferred to give up with honor. But how could he surrender a whole fortress and its garrison to a single man? Alexandre offered to sign an affidavit that the king's lieutenant had surrendered under duress with a pistol at his throat. Liniers preferred that they send for some more insurgents so it would appear he had been overpowered in numbers. Alexandre locked the door and called in his friends while the commander signed the order.

Despite the mayor's protestations and those of the storehouse manager, Alexandre rushed to the powder storeroom. He sent a friend to stop and requisition carts to be used for the transportation of the powder. With an ax and stones, he then attacked the door of the powder magazine. Dangerous sparks flew. The door was splintered and Alexandre sat on a barrel to wait for the arrival of some twenty young men and all the firemen of Soissons who loaded the powder in the carts.

It was four o'clock and they had not yet had any food. They ate at Madame Hutin's where the cabriolet was parked, and at six in the morning the convoy took to the road; the powder vehicle first, Hutin, Bard and Moreau behind in the cabriolet and finally Alexandre riding a horse. He had one of his hands on his holster, ready to blow up the convoy if there were any opposition to its leaving Soissons. Once past the city gates they drank some twenty bottles of wine to the health of La Fayette with the young men and the firemen who had decided to escort the heroes until Villers-Cotterêts. On the ramparts, the townspeople applauded the sight. At Verte-Feuille, Alexandre, dead with fatigue, sat in the cabriolet and fell asleep at once. He slept until Le Bourget where he awoke in the relay station courtyard.

Sunday, August 1. At nine o'clock the convoy entered the Paris City Hall. La Fayette was still at his post. His uniform gaped a bit, his vest was untidy and his tie was loose. He had lost his voice. When Alexandre appeared, he opened his arms to embrace him but could not get out one word. His secretary said in his place, "What trouble you damn Republicans gave us yesterday! Fortunately all is finished now." All finished? Louis-Philippe had stealthily come back to Paris during the night of July 30th. To the great relief of the bourgeoisie, he had accepted the general government of the Kingdom. Alexandre took a bath at the Deligny Swimming School to rub out all traces of three days of heroic adventures. Then, clean and freshly dressed, he succeeded in getting into the Lafitte town house. Four hundred people were packed into the dining room, the antechambers and the corridors. It was announced that henceforth the French king would be called Philippe VII. Alexandre jumped upon Béranger, the song writer, and ironically congratulated him on creating a king. "I have done what all the young people of Savoy do when there is a storm; I put a board over the brook," replied Béranger as an excuse.

On his way to the Palais-Royal Alexandre was dreamy; around him he heard more curses than acclamations. Louis-Philippe received those who had made him king: Casimir Périer, Broglie, Guizot, Dupin, Sébastiani, Molé, Gérard, Lafitte. The municipal commission had come to worship good fortune.

Monday, August 2. Charles X had retreated to Rambouillet and had abdicated in favor of his grandson. Alexandre had found Belle's arms and Belle's body again. He wrote to Mélanie:

Dear angel, dear love, all is ended. As I predicted twenty times to you, our revolution lasted only three days. I was fortunate enough to take an active part in it and was noticed by La Fayette and the Duc d'Orléans. Then, a mission to Soissons where I, alone, seized the gun powder, made my military reputation. Happily, it will end there. The Duc d'Orléans will probably be king . . . You can imagine how difficult it is for me to leave Paris at this moment. However, I need so much to see you that I will take the stagecoach as soon as possible, if only to clasp you in my arms—because, my love, after all this time I have a great need to see the only woman I love, and that I ever loved. Many things must change my position. I cannot tell you in a letter, however, I believe that you can hope a lot for your Alex.

The heroic action was ending; the sharing of the spoils had begun. Alexandre could not help hoping. That very morning he had visited Louis-Philippe, who, as soon as he had seen him, came to welcome him. Alexandre again told the epic of Soissons, and the Duke concluded, "Monsieur Dumas, you have just made your most beautiful drama!" Alexandre bowed, then left. The Duke went to the Palais-Royal courtyard to shake hands and embrace the holders of commissions and rag pickers alike. The Duc de Chartres had just arrived at the Palais, at the head of his regiment. From one of his gestures, Alexandre understood that the young prince shared with him the same disgust for this pleading for popularity. Hoping to advance himself, he was already betraying all those men of the people, those students who had fought as Alexandre did for an ideal. A very vague ideal, perhaps, but one that did not have the flaccid face of the Duc d'Orléans.

Tuesday, August 3. Fights were still raging in the streets. Cordelier-Delanoue burst into Alexandre's room, a repeating rifle in his hand. Alexandre was surprised to hear that Charles X was marching on Paris with twenty thousand men and cannons. Paris had risen to meet him. Alexandre jumped from his bed and put on his hunting clothes once again. He would be a part of this. Harel came in with an idea that he wanted to share with Dumas. He smiled for he knew very well that his royal resistance would be doubly advantageous to a still shaky power: it would frighten the fallen king and disperse the armed populace for a day or two. On the Place de l'Odéon Alexandre was surrounded, feasted, invited to take the head of a troop made up of stagehands. He treated them to drinks, to dinner; then they all piled up in Harel's cab, on the driver's seat, on the shafts, on the top deck. The horses neighed. For arms the heroes had only some prop spears but more arms were being distributed at the Palais-Royal. The streets were gridlocked with cabs requisitioned by the government. The heat was crushing and they quenched their thirst as often as possible. They roared, "Long live the Charter!"

"Bunch of assholes! That will fatten you as much as a crumb from a holy wafer!" cried Colonel Jacqueminot, who had been ordered to provoke this spontaneous expedition.

All they did was improvised; they had no map, no bread, no means of transportation, no spies, no rations of hay. They spread throughout Versailles where the royal regiments surrendered without resisting. At Saint-Cyr, they took over the eight cannons of the military school, although they had neither bags of powder nor bullets. The roads were now strewn with swords, haversacks and bearskin-hats that the demoralized soldiers had abandoned in their retreat. Alexandre and his men settled around a straw pile topped with the flag from the cab. Alexandre searched for food; the village priest gave him a three-pound piece of bread and some wine in a milk jar. The men of the band dispersed to the surrounding farms and came back, one bringing a hen, another two eggs. Once the meal was eaten they crawled into the hay to sleep.

Wednesday, August 4. At five o'clock, in their cabs rolling on the road to Paris, they heard a heavy fusillade. Although it was a false alarm, it left a few dead men on the field. They heard that Charles X had finally left Rambouillet and was traveling in the company of four commissioners in the direction of Cherbourg and to his exile. Alexandre and his friends sang *La Marseillaise* and continued on their own way. Alexandre's and Cordelier-Delanoue's cab had run away, and the two men had to walk across the fields to Versailles where they hired a carriage. Finally at home, an exhausted Alexandre gave Joseph orders not to wake him under any circumstances. Then he fell asleep. The revolution was over.

The July sun had set. For two days it had shone on the most exciting scenes. Alexandre would never forget those days during which, mere atoms themselves, they had participated in the movement of universal history. Of course, he had taken part in the action because of his antipathy for the Bourbons, who wanted to gag men's thinking. But it was mostly because of his taste for action itself. He had lived intensely, so intensely that the great, serious game had changed him forever. He would never betray this revolution which would betray its friends, the Republicans. Now the man of letters was giving way to the man of action. Where had his literary friends been? They had gone underground. Friendship now changed its course. The fire of action had forged a strong solidarity; the betrayal of the revolution by the middle-of-the-road bourgeoisie only reinforced it.

I V

Antony,
Passion in Modern Costume

What I have just seen is so beautifully poetic and dramatic, Madame, that there are moments when I believe I have now given up writing, even one word; what is there to be done after what has already been done? What theatrical drama can match that of the street? What medieval hero can equal the least citizen of our suburbs? (to Marceline Desbordes-Valmore, August 5, 1830)

The aftermaths of revolutions are sad. Once the excitement has abated, the petty human motives that greater events had hidden are exposed. Alexandre spurned Harel's request for a play entitled *Napoléon* to take advantage of the climate that followed the Bourbon flight. He spurned the musician Zimmermann's request for a cantata:

Ask this of a man who has not fought, of a man who has not seen anything. . . . But I, who have seen, who took part in the action, could write nothing good; it would always prove less than what I have seen.

He spurned Oudard's offer to send him to St. Petersburg with Louis-Philippe's envoy to Czar Nicolas I. What was the reason for these repeated refusals like those of a sulky child who despises all that is offered to him? Was he really ashamed of the shady dealings around the power? Or was he mostly disappointed with his share of the loot? There were disillusions, or worse, deceit. On August 11, he sent Mélanie Waldor *Le Moniteur* of August 9 which published his account of the expedition to Soissons. He was quite cocky because the evening before he had been a guest at a splendid dinner Louis-Philippe had given to celebrate having been proclaimed the new king of France. In a covering letter he told her: 'I have spent all the evening at the Court; all the family is as simple and as kind as before.' Mélanie wanted to return to Paris? Alexandre discouraged her: 'You would make a mistake . . . ; I would have gone to spend the end of this month and the following month with you.'

The trip to rejoin Mélanie was at least considered, but the hero of the Trois Glorieuses could not travel as a private citizen; he must have a mission. He explained his plans to La Fayette: to organize a National Guard in Vendée, for that province might get restless again. During their lunch together the next day, the poet pretended to be a politician. It was necessary, in Vendée, to encourage the support of small property owners to avoid a return to civil war. When coffee was served, La Fayette gave Alexandre the official passport for which he had asked.

Could he wear a uniform? "Have a uniform made for yourself that resembles that of an Aide-de-Camp," advised La Fayette. On the Place du Carrousel, the son of the director of the *Journal de Paris* paraded on a horse in the uniform of the National Guard, clothes he had probably just invented: shako with a flow of tricolor feathers, epaulets of silver, belt of silver, royal-blue coat and pants of the same color. Alexandre wanted the same. His departure depended solely on the thread of a tailor:

My love, I cannot tell you quite precisely the day of my arrival but could I not stop at Clisson and from there send you someone who will call for you? We could stay there two days, as we had planned. . . . Adieu, my angel, I am traveling for my work; understand that well. As far as new positions and openings go, I begin to believe that they are more rare than they were under the previous dynasty. (to Mélanie Waldor, August 16)

Alexandre resigned himself. He would not be a prefect or an ambassador; his new uniform was so beautiful and his official mission was an excuse to leave Belle without worrying her. Military men left their women at home.

I am leaving the day after tomorrow, my love. I'll make a small detour; then I'll meet you. I am rather pleased to leave Paris at this time. (to Mélanie Waldor, about August 20)

He left Paris, "with its streets so dynamic that one could believe them alive, with its population camping in the streets and its cannons on the Place de Grève." In the stagecoach his mind turned back to those exceptional days and each passing moment set them further away and soiled them. Ah! It was then that one should have died.

There was something intoxicating in those frequent embraces, given and received, that one could have believed that everyone passing by was a traveler coming back from a foreign soil who saw his fatherland once again. It is because we were emerging from despotism and, for some few moments, we entered freedom! Everyone was so pleased; we all loved one another. The tricolor flags were waving everywhere, and at each moment, at each corner where one was displayed, we started as if surprised to see it. Then, from time to time, a rifle shot in the streets made one remember that the people were the masters and that they were watching. (*La Vendée aprés le 29 Juillet*)

Alexandre became nostalgic for those few moments of liberty when the ephemeral sovereignty of the people created an atmosphere of universal love. At Blois, he visited the château which was now only a barracks on whose walls drunken cuirassiers had scratched with the tip of their swords, "I love Sophie" or "Long live Louis-Philippe." At Tours, when he came out of the stagecoach, he heard that three ministers of Charles X who had signed the Ordinances had just been arrested. Alexandre boarded the boat on the Loire for Angers where he lodged at the Hôtel du Faisan. He asked Victor Pavie, son of a printer of the town, to come to see him. Six months before, Victor had participated in the battle for *Christine*. They embraced each other as General and soldier of the battle; in the alcove, on hooks, hung the most stupendous uniform and a civilian coat. The two friends, arm in arm, climbed up the steep streets. Alexandre spoke inexhaustibly about the days in July. He suddenly wanted to hunt some waterfowl. He invaded the provincial shop of a seller of hunting apparatus and came back dressed with gaiters, belt and a game bag. But the snipes of the Baumette marsh had either hidden or run away. Alexandre had to be content with shooting a five-franc coin with Charles X's effigy that Pavie had thrown into the air. The coin fell, marked with four lead pellets on its face. The weather was hot. Alexandre took off his clothes and swam nude in the Maine river. Pavie, the prude, preferred to sit on the edge from where he feasted on the aquatic exploits of Dumas:

I admired his supple and robust physique which Providence seldom matched so well with the gifts of superiority of intelligence and thought.

I realized, with these discoveries, that he would have received no less applause as a stunt horseman in a circus act or as a virtuoso tight-rope walker at Madame Saqui's theater than as an author for leading stages. (Victor Pavie, *Souvenirs de Jeunesse et Revenants*)

When it came time for leaving, the traveler was escorted to the coach office; goodbyes were repeated on the steps of the coach for Nantes. They went through a village where a new mayor had just been inaugurated, where the cannon thundered and the houses displayed flags; the mayor was on his balcony surrounded by his family. From the coach Alexandre appreciated the pretty legs of the mayor's young wife.

Nantes also had had its revolution. The houses still showed the scars, a young man hit by a buckshot was dying, the eleventh of the patriots who had sacrificed their lives. The next day, with his rifle on his shoulder, Alexandre took the road for Clisson. The game was wiped out, by the awful winter of 1830, but snakes abounded. Between Torfou and Tiffauge, a guide—previously a *chouan*, a guerrilla of Vendée—showed Alexandre the stone commemorating the battle of Torfou, during which Kléber and his thirty-five thousand citizens of the Mayenne were defeated. The guide imitated the chouans' rallying cry of an owl. Not feeling quite safe, Alexandre avoided following the hedgerows too closely.

At La Jarrie, Alexandre's arrival was the occasion for a feast. The property was surrounded with oaks and cedars, a place where one could easily become a bit bored. Elisa, now five-and-a-half, hung on Alexandre's coattails and climbed on his lap. A dinner was arranged to meet the important people of the place. Alexandre wore his uniform; Mélanie's physician threatened to leave if Alexandre did not take off his costume that the doctor, who belonged to a legitimist committee, considered an insult. During the few days of his stay at La Jarrie, Alexandre went hunting. Mélanie was constantly in tears for Alexandre had admitted, under heavy questioning, that he had had an adventure with an actress. Adventure? He promised Mélanie he would leave the other woman. Was there not the small Antony now growing in Mélanie's womb? Alexandre was soon bored: he had left heroic drama for domestic drama. He tried to work again at *Édith*, but without enthusiasm. To Eugène Jamet he wrote:

> La Jarrie, Saturday evening, September 4, 1830
> My dear Eugène:
> I am writing to you from the country of the infidel and I give orders to pass my letter through vinegar so that you will not catch royalism as one catches a pestilence. What a country this Vendée is! First there is not a partridge, not a hare, only 6-foot hedges with thorns two inches long. Add to this, not the smallest tricolor flag anywhere to cheer one's eyes; the gendarmerie trains in police caps to avoid displaying the cockade. Pull me out of here, my friend, pull me out quickly. Here's how: Go to Firmin, my dear Eugène, and tell him to have Masson, secretary of the Comédie-Française, write to me that my presence in Paris is necessary for *Antony*. Do not tell anybody about it. You guess why I need to seem compelled to leave.

How long had Alexandre stayed at La Jarrie? Six days, a week, and already he wanted to run away. He did not love any more, yet he had to pretend to be in love. As his only diversion in the melo-drama *in camera*, he received a letter from an employee of Pavie's printing plant. Pavie had defended a poor peasant who had washed some coins with mercury to make them look like silver and had been condemned to the galleys for it; Pavie now called upon Alexandre to intervene. Alexandre wrote to Oudard, executive secretary of the kind Queen Marie-Amélie, and to Appert, under whom he had worked at the Office of Assistance. A royal pardon was granted. Grateful, the peasant came to throw himself at his protector's feet. Philanthropy made Alexandre forget, for a short time, a more intimate malaise.

On September 18, Mélanie had a miscarriage. On the morning of the 22nd, a carriage was harnessed for Alexandre's departure. Restrained by her mother's and daughter's presence, Mélanie could not, as she wanted to, throw herself in Alexandre's arms. At the first curb, the high hedges hid that house of which, today, there remains only a leveled tower, a room with a granite fireplace, some sections of walls and a gazebo near a pond. At Cholet, before a cup of coffee, Alexandre scrawled to the woman he had just left the same lies:

> You must have seen that it took nothing less than necessity to make me leave. Good God, dear angel, do not hurt yourself so much. Above all, believe in something more intimate than the love between us which will survive all our thousands of griefs. I will not see her again when arriving in Paris, my angel. It will, however, take a few days until I have a friendly visit to explain to her the cause of my separation—but it will take place, my angel, even if she must cry very hard and very long; her work in the theater will console her.

When he arrived in Paris, it was pouring rain. M. Guizot was now minister and he had had the facade of the Institut cleaned. The revolution was long over and so was Alexandre's love for Mélanie.

Alexandre sniffed out the atmosphere of Paris. The talk was mostly about the approaching trial of the Ministers. They were now locked up in the donjon de Vincennes. The crowd demanded death; the new government thought of suppressing the death penalty in political matters. At the Comédie-Française, Mazeras had been named provisional commissioner. Alexandre received the promise that rehearsals of *Antony* would soon begin. Belle was on a tour in Rouen. Alexandre devoted his time to a report on the Vendée. His conclusions were clear and he made three points:

1. Build roads . . .
2. Transfer ten or twelve priests to villages beyond the Loire river and send in their places . . . priests that the government can trust.
3. Cease paying pensions to nobles hostile to the government.

He gave this contribution to La Fayette. King Louis-Philippe must have it immediately. Mélanie tortured herself with the loss of the child who, she believed, was the only tie that could have held her lover. On September 28, 1830 Alexandre tried to console her:

Why does your broken geranium torment you? He was from another era; he had to be broken to live again as our love. Take care of your stalk, my angel, and you will see new leaves grow on it which, in future years, you will give to me topped with a kiss.

The popular commission had voted unanimously to give Alexandre the National Cross, called the Cross of July. He had again immersed himself in the Parisian brouhaha. He had been admitted with acclamation into the Mounted National Guard, the honorable corps whose uniform he wore already. He kept records of the chaotic spasms of parliamentary life; he went to all the meetings that his republican friends arranged. They palavered to try to forget the failure of their victory. The Sun of July was nothing but a remembrance to be kept between friends. Belle was back from Rouen. Alexandre made her read one of the letters he wrote to Mélanie:

There was . . . a quantity of tears, more from fear of her future than from true love. In brief, perhaps she will write to you for she cannot believe that you know everything; she thinks that you don't know about our relations and the letter I wrote her. But you know everything, so don't worry about anything. It has been decided that we are nothing to each other, only friends. She left me, however, in tears and in anger. (October 4.)

Alexandre had taken the *Édith* manuscript out of Mélanie's armoire. He said he intended to work at it further and would offer as a farewell gift to Belle the part of the princess in the play. Though Mélanie could hardly believe, even for an instant, these retractions of her fickle lover, he could not tell her the truth; Belle was pregnant and this news would be devastating to Mélanie, who still lamented her lost Antony.

Alexandre once again became very involved with the theater. *Antony* had been cast. Rehearsals would begin Saturday, October 9, and the first performance would take place "within three weeks or a month," he hoped. Harel, on his part, was not discouraged and had not given up his idea of a *Napoléon*. On October 11, after the first performance of *La Mére et la Fille*, Harel had invited Alexandre for supper with friends. Around three o'clock in the morning, Mlle. George, under a gracious pretense, took Alexandre to her room. When he returned to the dining room he found Harel there alone. Alexandre wanted to leave. Certainly not, Harel insisted, everyone was in bed and he took Alexandre to a room he had never seen before. Two candles burning on a table loaded with books of all sizes and with pens of all kinds illuminated a bed with a huge scarlet eiderdown, a bearskin rug, slippers, a small settee and a large armchair covered with tapestry—a beautiful room, indeed. Harel was satisfied that it pleased Alexandre, who would not get out of it until he had written *Napoléon*. Condemned to "hard labor," thanks to Napoléon! Was this reality or fable? The next day Alexandre wrote to Mélanie:

> I am frightfully busy—*Antony* in rehearsal and you also know this business of *Napoléon* which I did not dare to write under my name. All is settled. Delanoue will sign it, do the research, and this will give me some money without letting anyone know I am the author. Do not mention it, even to your brother. I am working like a poor horse.

Indeed, he had a play in rehearsal, a play in rewrites (*Édith*), a play in the making, a play for glory; a play for a mistress, a play for money—of which he was ashamed even before writing it. Alexandre spread himself thin, torn apart by all his self-created needs.

The king had read the Dumas Report on the Vendée and had annotated it but left Alexandre dawdling and asking again and again for an audience. Alexandre wanted to take advantage of this report to obtain authorization to write *Napoléon* as a political play. Was Alexandre finally received by Louis-Philippe? The interview, as related in *Mes mémoires*, could be true, or largely fiction.

Louis-Philippe had kept the easy-going manners he exhibited as the Duc d'Orléans. He was surprised that Alexandre, encouraged by La Fayette to study the possibility of establishing a National Guard in Vendée, had not mentioned this project in his report. The measure would be temporary and too expensive, Alexandre asserted. The King did not believe in a New Vendée. Alexandre not only believed the contrary but also that Louis-Philippe needed the situation in Vendée as a pretense for not intervening in Poland or on the Rhine. Leave the business of politics to the King and to his ministers, Louis-Philippe retorted. "You are a poet; so, make poetry." And the audience was ended.

On the bridge to the Tuileries, Alexandre met a friend from his first barricade, Bixio, dressed in a blue coat, trousers with a red band, shako with a flame of red horse hair. He belonged to the National Guard Artillery, Fourth Battery, nicknamed the "Murderer" because of the great number of physicians it contained. Alexandre could not resist a costume, especially when it was worn by a Republican. He wanted to belong but he was the king's assistant-librarian. At once he composed his notice of resignation:

> Sire,
> My political opinions not being in harmony with those Your Majesty has a right to demand from the persons who compose his staff, I beg Your Majesty to accept my resignation from the post of librarian.

All was confusion during that autumn, confusion in his private life, confusion in his creative work, confusion in his political life. Mélanie Waldor had come back to Paris about the middle of October. She had immediately understood that Alexandre's new affair was more than an adventure and could not accept that Belle lived only a few doors away from Alexandre. She cried, she ranted, she begged, she saw soon that the only solution was death. She wrote a will:

Nov. 1830
Monday 22, eleven o'clock in the morning.
Before *he* dies I want to have:
My letters to read them again—and my portrait.
Our chain and our ring.
La Prière, le Lac, la Jalousie.
His seal *Mi labia*
And if I die, I want all this, except the portrait, to be buried with me in the Ivry cemetery. I want only a white marble tombstone, with the day of my death written on it, my age, and then below: *Saro di te o di morte*, and at the four corners of the marble—these four dates—12 Sept. year 1827, 23 Sept. year 1827, 18 Sept. year 1830 and 22 Nov. year 1830. These four dates are the only ones that decided my fate and my life. I want, too, as long as my mother is alive, geraniums around me and I ask my child when she is grown up to replace my mother in this duty.
Instead of a shroud, I want to be dressed in my blue dress and my yellow scarf, I want our black chain around my neck, I want his watch and our ring to be on my heart with our broken geranium.
His poems and our letters at my feet.

She tried to bury herself in an oblivion of opium but recovered to suffer again; she accepted sharing her lover, but the thought of it tore her apart, and on December 9 she wrote:

Two o'clock, Thursday
Let me write to you, my Alex. I have no other thought far from you and I feel that life escapes me day by day. I do not reproach anything since you love me, you love only me but your weakness kills me and I am afraid to die . . . Take pity on me as I took pity on you, or you never loved me. Accept her reproaches, her anger, you are guilty, oh, know how to atone for this fault. Choose between a painful moment and the misery of all my life if I live. Can she love you as I love you? Is she for you what I am myself, a part of you?

Alexandre was fickle but he was not cruel. Certainly, he knew the proportions of blackmail and literature that made up this verbose despair. He was worried, though, for who knew where all this excessive emotion would take Mélanie? To what extremes?

As for leaving Belle, whose waist rounded a bit more each day, Alexandre was too proud of his generous virility to even dream of it. One more mouth to feed and he worked with all his strength.

Cordelier-Delanoue had cut a play from the imperial hagiography based on a pattern made by Alexandre—the dramatic device was a spy saved by Bonaparte in Toulon, who followed his career to Sainte-Hélène. Alexandre had begun the outlines on October 25; on November 2, the twenty-three scenes of *Napoléon Bonaparte ou Trente Ans de l'Histoire de France* were finished. They had to adapt it to the theater. There were more than one hundred acting parts and they had to disentangle this chaos. The director did not know where to start; he begged Dumas to condense several characters into one. They got down to sixty-six speaking parts interpreted by thirty-six actors and five actresses. Harel, who was dreaming about the money brought in by *Napoléon á Schoenbrünn* produced by a competitor and performed at the Théâtre Porte-Saint-Martin, emptied three snuff-boxes at each rehearsal. Frédérick Lemaître created the part of Napoléon. Whimsical, violent and a buffoon, Lemaître's terrifying rages frequently interrupted the work of the director. Alexandre sometimes left the hubbub of the theater for that of the street.

Dumas had been welcomed with open arms by his republican friends among the "Murderers." Three times a week he drilled from six to ten o'clock in the morning in the square court of the Louvre and twice a month he went to the shooting range at Vincennes. The artillerymen were always prepared for action. On December 8, the republican politician Benjamin Constant died. The artillerymen had been notified to be ready on December 10 for convoy duty. On the day of the funeral the boulevard was packed with a hundred thousand men who had joined the cortege. The flags were veiled with crepe, accompanied by the sinister sound of muffled drums. The crowd was like a surging sea with a storm brewing above. There were cries, "To the Panthéon!" But the Prefect of the Seine opposed a change in the order of the ceremony. On the edge of the grave, La Fayette had to be helped; overcome with fatigue and emotion he seemed ready to drop and follow the casket into the grave. It would have spared him a political death!

This funeral of Constant was only a rehearsal. On December 15, the trial of Charles X's ministers began. Alexandre never took off his beautiful uniform with the red trimmings. The troops of the National Guard had to open the way to the Court which was besieged by the crowd. On December 20, Alexandre sat in a reserved gallery and listened to the pleadings. Suddenly a drum rolled furiously outside. Alexandre rushed out and forced his way through a throng of people who had pushed into the yard of the Luxembourg Palace behind a carriage from the royal printing press. They screamed, "Death for the ministers!" The peers, shaking with fear, adjourned the trial. Alexandre went to the Louvre; the artillerymen were ready to march with the people but they had been notified of a Bonapartist plot to take over the twenty-four cannons of the park. To fight for the Republic, all right! But to fight for Napoléon II? Cartridges had been distributed; informers had been discovered. Jacques-Parfait Oudard summoned Alexandre, who went to the Palais-Royal. He was reassured that the artillerymen would defend themselves with their last cartridges against the Bonapartists, that they were ready to march with the people against the Luxembourg or against *any other palace.*

The next day, the twenty-fifth, Alexandre was at his post. The Latin Quarter was filled with troops and stolid bourgeois who were there as members of the National Guard, but feared for their shops. They savored the expected condemnation of the ministers. About two o'clock, the end of the pleading was announced. It was followed by a heavy silence, soon broken by cries of "To death! . . . Condemned to death!" The throng seemed to disperse but then surged back again. The ministers were condemned, but only to life imprisonment. The earlier false proclamation had been a stratagem to allow the condemned men to get safely back to Vincennes. The crowd rushed ahead. Cutting his way into the torrent of people, La Fayette attempted to speak to calm the anger that was swelling. Alexandre stayed near La Fayette until he heard the shot of a cannon. It could be the artillerymen asking for help. Alexandre let the old revolutionist face the rising tide of the people and, dagger in hand, he ran off—he was at the Pont-Neuf; he was at the Louvre. Seeing the dagger, people cried, "To arms!" At the Louvre the gates were closed and nearly six hundred artillerymen walked back and forth. Because there had been an attempt to steal the linchpins of the cannons, Alexandre was designated for duty that night. He was with another artilleryman he did not yet know and with whom he talked of literature and architecture, Prosper Mérimée. At the entrance, the revolutionists and the reactionaries were face to face, ready to fight. The purpose of all that excitement changed when it was heard that the National Guard and an army regiment surrounded the court of the Louvre. With a unanimous cry of "To arms!" Dumas' artillery contingent ran to get ammunition, but the reserves were empty. The Governor of the Louvre had taken all away during the day. Men settled, however, near their cannons; they slept with their muskets between their legs. At dawn, the artillerymen behind the gates were like wild, famished animals. Bakers, wine merchants, butchers fed them through the fences. The drums still beat, but the National Guard and the students called to the people for moderation. In the evening, the troops and Guards left the Louvre; the gates were opened; the artillerymen were free. Alexandre went back to the Rue de l'Université; the pale December sun had set long ago.

The political career of La Fayette had not survived the ministers' trial. He resigned December twenty-fifth, the very day when the artillerymen met to elect new officers for the Fourth Battery. Alexandre won the majority of the votes and was named Assistant Captain. He immediately exchanged his wool braids, stripes, and epaulets for new braids, stripes, and epaulets made of gold. When he went to the Palais-Royal for the traditional exchange of New Year's wishes, he was greeted with mocking laughter; the artillery had been dissolved by royal order the day before. He quickly cast off his military attire and wore the more fashionable clothes of the dramatic author.

After a long month of rehearsal, *Napoléon* began to take shape. From December tenth, Harel had peppered the press with communications announcing the "next day" opening of *Napoléon*. On January tenth, the Odéon had the appearance of a riot or preparation for a battle; the National Guard packed the theater. The raising of the curtain brought exclamations: the sets were splendid. Harel had not been stingy—they cost over eighty thousand francs! The Kremlin on fire! Ah! The crossing of the Beresina! Oh! During the intermissions, drums and trumpets blared martial tunes. The National Guard had left their shops for the epic. Frederick Lemaître did not look at all like the Emperor. He wore the small gray coat, he agonized at Sainte-Hélène. The crowd wept; then, its emotions stirred, they applauded loud enough to bring the house down. Dumas' worried ear picked up a few boos. Probably some people in the audience were truly fond of literature. Alexandre was not far from agreeing with them.

When the crowd came out to the Place de l'Odéon, some patriots stayed on the stairs to hoot Delaistre, not as the actor but as the character he played, Hudson Lowe, Napoléon's guardian. Alexandre felt a bit ashamed. One does not brag about a success due to circumstances in which there is not a trace of genius. He may have blushed, but his pockets were full. The play was long-lived—sixty-nine perfomances while its art . . .

Meanwhile, rehearsals for *Antony* had begun at the Comédie-Française but were dragging. All the actors were dissatisfied with their parts and the author was dissatisfied with the actors. How could the coquette Mlle. Mars express Mélanie's excess of passion and remorse projected into her double, Adèle d'Hervey? How could Firmin express the fatal character of Antony, "a big fool, who resembles me very much," as Alexandre said to Mélanie? The play was too long, he was told; he must cut out the second and the fourth acts. Why not kill the whole play? Mlle. Mars wanted to wait for the installation of a new chandelier because she had dresses made at the cost of fiftes n hundred francs and wanted them to show in the best light. All the shifting and delays discouraged Alexandre. Soon Mlle. Mars decided to retire from the play. Thinking the Comédie-Française was sinking, she abandoned ship. It is possible that, at this juncture, Dumas withdrew his play and took it to the Porte-Saint-Martin, although this is somewhat improbable since Dumas and Hugo intended to turn to their advantage the difficulties faced by the Comédie-Française and to put themselves at its helm. As he wrote to Hugo about March 3, 1831, Alexandre had found a backer:

My dear Victor,
Still the same enthusiasm—and the same affability on the part of our lender. He expects us tomorrow, Friday, at noon. . . .
To you, friend, Alex Dumas.

The two friends became busy; they contacted the people who had influence with decisionmakers. Jacques Laffite had left his position in favor of Casimir Périer, thus the outlook seemed more favorable. Also around March 15, 1831, Alexandre wrote to Victor Hugo:

> My dear Victor,
> Yesterday, the ministry had printed in the *Messager des Chambres* that we might become directors of the Théâtre-Français; this looks like a commitment. The change in the ministry offers us new opportunities. Therefore I have not written to Crosnier, thinking that it was better to wait than to engage ourselves.
> Your good friend.

In fact, Hugo had dealt with Crosnier, director of the Porte-Saint-Martin, for *Marion Delorme*. Censorship had momentarily fallen with the Old Regime. Hugo urged Dumas to follow him but Dumas had no play ready. Of course, there was *Antony*, if the Comédie-Française released it. The part of Adèle would fit Marie Dorval so well. The unfortunate attempt by Marie to seduce Alexandre in a cab had been forgotten. Alfred de Vigny, who was given to redeeming women of easy virtue, adored Marie. Alexandre became involved in a new liaison. He had established with Marie a companionship which did not exclude a shiver of sensuality. He read her *Antony*; leaning on Alexandre's shoulder, Marie read at the same time; at the end of the first act, she kissed him; at the end of the second act, as they pushed forward in the reading, he felt the actress trembling; her tears rolled onto the manuscript; by the fourth act, Marie had clasped Alexandre's neck and almost strangled him. "Where did you learn about women?" she murmured. The fifth act left her indifferent; it had to be redone. Would Alexandre stay overnight? M. le Comte de Vigny wouldn't have to know about it. The next morning, Alexandre was settled on Marie's bed. She clapped her hands joyously. Now the fifth act enchanted her—she already played some of the lines: "But I am lost" and "My daughter, I must kiss my daughter!" Marie wanted Bocage for Antony. They had lunch with this handsome, thirty-five-year-old man with black, hooded eyes which knew how to express, in turn, rudeness, will, and melancholy. The real Antony. Bocage found the work neither a play, nor a drama, nor a tragedy, nor a novel, but something that encompassed all of these forms. It was certainly gripping. They agreed to a reading for Crosnier—who fought against sleep for the third act, openly slept during the fourth, and snored during the fifth. The pressure of Marie Dorval and Bocage, however, triumphed over Crosnier's reservations. *Antony* could be played at the Porte-Saint-Martin. The future of the drama depended now upon the future of the Comédie-Française.

But Alexandre could not give himself entirely to the theater. The street was still there—reminding him ceaselessly of the revolution which had not yet run its agonizing course in so many hearts. Certainly he had forever broken with the king. After a last request for an audience had been refused, he had taken the opportunity offered by the Preface to his *Napoléon Bonaparte* publicly to send his resignation as Assistant Librarian on February 11, 1831.

Sire,
For a long time I have written that, as for myself, the man of letters was but a preface to the political man.

The age at which I could be a member of a regenerated Chambre is approaching. I am almost certain that the day I am thirty I will be named a Deputy. I am now twenty-eight, Sire. Unfortunately, the mass of people who see from below and from afar do not separate the intentions of the King from the acts of the ministers.

The acts of the ministers are arbitrary and kill freedom. Among the men who depend upon Your Majesty and who tell you everyday that they admire and love you, there is perhaps not one who loves you more than I do. They may say it but do not think it, while, as for me, I do not say it but I think it.

But, Sire, devotion to principles comes before devotion to men.

Alexandre had burned his bridges, he had taken sides. He could not live by literature alone. Fidelity to one's principles, when these principles are opposed everywhere, is social suicide. There was no more political future for the republicans than there was for the artillerymen who had been arrested for plotting against the state. But the government, in striking against the republicans, at the same time stirred up legitimist manifestations, perhaps for symmetry and seeming fair-handedness in dealing with repressions. A big blow for the left; a small blow for the right; this so-called middle-of-the-road was a political tightrope act. On February 14, 1831, a mass on the anniversary of the Duc de Berry's death was to be celebrated at the church Saint-Germain-l'Auxerrois. Alexandre attended a rehearsal of the *Vieux Sergeant* by Henri Monnier at the theater of the Vaudeville. The head claque of the theater warned Arago and Alexandre that something was brewing. A great number of carriages with coats of arms were stationed in front of the church; many Voltairian bourgeois stood on the church porch and grumbled against this legitimist provocation. Étienne Arago rushed into the church and, followed by the crowd, invaded the nave and the choir, broke the catafalque, tore the mortuary drapes, and knocked down the altar. The crowd all screamed and danced about grotesquely dressed in priestly vestments. Alexandre had remained at the door from which he had watched the blasphemous scene; he left, head down, worried, with a heavy heart. He had to push a wedge into the convulsing throng. The rioters believed they saw Jesuits everywhere, whom they wanted to throw into the river. On the Pont des Arts, Alexandre witnessed the pillage of the church and its vicarage. The cross with the fleur de lys which crowned the spire was toppled.

The next day, in spite of orders, Joseph came into his master's office: "They are pillaging the Archbishop's palace," he said. Once dressed, Alexandre ran to the Cité. From the Pont-Neuf space, Alexandre saw floating in the river furniture, books, chasubles, cassocks, and priests' robes, which, swelled by the water, looked like drowned men twitching for the last time. All the Archbishopric's treasures flowed toward the ocean. The notables of the regime witnessed the riot, very pleased with it or so they seemed:

It was not a riot of men in overalls, full of enthusiasm, risking their lives in the midst of the fire of fusillades and the thunder of artillery. It was a riot in yellow gloves, in morning coats, mocking and impious, demolishing, insulting, . . . it was a riot of the bourgeoisie, the most merciless as well as the most wretched of all riots. (*Mes mémoires*, ch. CXCVI)

Alexandre's heart protested, for this parody of the generous days of July stunned him. When, on his way back, he crossed the Palais-Royal, he saw that the fleurs de lys were erased, the coats of arms on the carriages were scratched, the wrought iron balconies were mutilated.

But love cannot be scraped off. Like those fleurs de lys branded on the shoulders of outcasts, it is indelible. Mélanie, from the arid shore on which Alexandre had abandoned her, went on complaining, even when he sometimes visited her out of pity.

She still fought to regain her Alex, trying to strike the thief of her love, Belle, with the pinpricks of calumny. Alexandre was irritated and wrote to Mélanie:

An explanation is necessary between you and Mme. Serre so that I find out who said the infamies that have been spread about. I am expecting you, as soon as you receive this letter, to come to Mme. Serre's. It is necessary. I have waited for you to feel better. You have improved. Come.

Alexandre was harsh with the forsaken woman, too harsh, she complained. On March 2, 1831 she withdrew, she wept her good-bye song:

Why see each other, my friend? It is useless, all is ended for you and me. I still love you but not with that love that once made my joy and my life. I love you; I miss you; but in the past. . . .

You tell me that you would like to break with her. I accept that this is not another of your ruses to keep me tied to you. Well, that break is impossible for you; you fear this woman. I have guessed that from all you told me about her. Do not fight anymore; it hurts when the strength or the means for breaking are missed. As for me, Alex, I will not make a scene; I will have only tears! And those tears you will not see since I beseech you not to come back to me. Alex, should I tell you? I am without strength against you when you are here. I know you lie and I believe you! It is a pity that so credulous a soul should be united with a soul so clever and deceiving; the only solution is to run away from you and not see you anymore. . . .

Burn and break everything that made our joy, this is the price of my pardon, and I will try to live, if not happily, at least at peace.

A love not quite extinct still burned under the ashes. Alexandre could not accept that the woman who had lived four years beside him could leave him forever. He did not want to burn her letters. "No, I will give them back to you but I will not burn them. If I ever burned them it would be to light the coal stove with which I would asphyxiate myself." Life brought a series of partings that he endured gracelessly. He had chosen the Republic against the Duc de Chartres's friendship and the gratitude he owed to the king; now he must choose Belle, who carried his child, or his previous mistress who had in part made him the man he was now. Ingratitude is a weapon of freedom. Alexandre slipped his bonds but remorse followed him.

On March fifth, Belle gave birth to a daughter who was named Marie-Alexandrine—"Marie" after Alexandre's mother. Alexandre recognized the child two days later. Marie-Alexandrine was at once sent to a nurse. Alexandre was accumulating bastards. And what about his son, Alexandre, whom he loved so much? It seemed that a cabal of women, probably headed by Mélanie Waldor, wanted to remove the child, not from Dumas, but from the immoral woman with whom he lived. Alexandre had not recognized his son at his birth; they could now take him away. He pressed his attorney to hurry the legal legitimization "without the mother knowing it." This was done on May seventeenth.

During all this the fate of the Comédie-Française had been decided. They had given up the idea of naming a director. Taylor returned to his position as a supervisor on March twenty-ninth. The plan of Victor Hugo and Dumas was rejected. Therefore the rehearsals for *Antony* could begin at the Porte-Saint-Martin with Alexandre directing Marie Dorval and Bocage. Bocage knew how to use everything, even his own faults, to bring originality to his character; Marie Dorval immediately had found the perfect interpretation for her part.

Dumas began once more to enjoy the play he had almost grown to dislike. *Antony*, five acts of love, jealousy, and anger, was an echo of the real, savage jealousy Alexandre had felt for Commandant Waldor at the beginning of his affair with Mélanie—an echo of a reality that had once been alive. Though transformed to fiction, it poured out from a heart still bleeding: "I was Antony, though not an assassin; she was Adèle, though she did not flee."

Mélanie had not run away, she had fallen. During the rehearsals, Alexandre was touched with the tenderness of the past which the play now carried to the stage. He wrote to Melanie. She was moved, too:

Oh, my Antony, on my knees I thank you. I do not want love anymore, but your neglect, that I attributed to scorn and hatred, was killing me. I am devoured by fever, but your letter brings balm for my suffering. Oh, yes, you are still the good, the noble A-Antony that I loved so much; you are only cruelly unhappy. I will be your friend. I will live to repair with a sweeter, less intoxicating, but less tempestuous life the harm I have done to your life.

Until this evening, if you can.

While Alexandre prepared to receive the public's verdict of his play, his friends, the artillerymen, were waiting for the judges' verdict. Their trial had begun on April sixth. The verdict reproached them more for their republican opinions than for their alleged plot.

"You accuse me of being a republican; I accept the accusation as a title of glory," claimed one of them named Cavaignac.

Alexandre had attended the trial's last four days. He had heard Pescheux d'Herbinville, a twenty-three-year-old man who used to wrap cartridges in silk paper and decorate them with pink ribbons, boast of having distributed arms. Alexandre felt his enthusiasm rise as each case was pled. On the fifteenth, when the accused men were declared not guilty, hands applauded, hats flew off; the crowd threw themselves over the benches to shake hands with them. The prisoners were freed.

During the last rehearsals, Marie Dorval could not find the right tone for her cue, "But I am lost, me!" How would Mlle. Mars say it? She would play it sitting and then she would get up. Marie Dorval, therefore, would begin standing and then sit down. As for the modern costumes? Antony, a child of the century, wore cravat, vest, and trousers, as did the common herd of men. For the theatrical effect he needed a costume that would at first sight show the eccentricity of the character. The key would be the cut of the vest and the knot of the tie. Alfred de Vigny, friend of Alexandre and lover of Marie Dorval, was asked to the rehearsals.

My dear Alfred,
Do me a favor. *Antony* is getting along, consider it as if it were yours, come to the rehearsals and give me and the actors all the advice you believe necessary for the good of your adopted son.

Vigny believed the play would be a great success. Alexandre doubted it. On the first of May, the last rehearsal on a closed set made a great impression. Stage hands, firemen on duty, walk-on actors were unanimous in their approval. Alexandre had sent seven tickets to Mélanie. He had not been able to bring them himself because he had to be at a meeting to debate the design of the Cross of July decoration. The revolution, be it only with its symbols, still interfered during days that Alexandre should have devoted exclusively to literary affairs. An ordinance proclaimed on May second stipulated that the July Cross would bear on its head side: "27, 28, and 29 July 1830" and the inscription "Given by the King of the French." Men receiving this Cross had to swear fidelity to the king. Another revolt was brewing. They met at Higonner's and adorned themselves with a red and black ribbon. Would Louis-Philippe, not satisfied with having stolen their revolution, ask again that they thank him?

On May third at the Porte-Saint-Martin all minds were filled with politics. When the curtain rose, the stage seemed quite dusty: no new rug, no new decoration. The drawing room furniture had already served for ten other plays. Crosnier had no faith in the play's success. In the first scenes, Marie Dorval in the gauze dress of a society woman clashed with the set as did her harsh voice and her slightly stooping shoulders. Bocage was carried on stage. He had fainted, but soon he tore off the bandages from his wounds and, before fainting again, had time to murmur, "And now, I will stay, won't I?" The audience, won over, applauded.

Dumas had shortened the intermissions, he hurried artists, stage managers, and stagehands and the curtain rose again. Bocage took hold of the scene, expressed admirably the bitter misanthropy of his character. Dumas congratulated him. The actor was beaming, the audience applauded again, they shivered and shuddered even more at the cruelty and violence of the third act: Antony chased Adèle, forced her to stop at an inn, entered her room, threw a handkerchief on her mouth, dragged her into a closet. The curtain fell. Rape, almost, on the stage! Silence in the theater, the audience was stunned; then came an immense clamor, frantic applause, gushing like a cataract. In their dressing rooms, the artists changed their costumes. Marie Dorval, half undressed, welcomed Alexandre and kissed him. The tension was too strong. Alexandre took Bixio, whom he had met in the corridors, for a walk toward the Bastille. The two friends chatted, laughed, almost forgot that in the overheated theater, half a mile away, Alexandre's fate was at stake. When he went back to his loge, Adèle was the prey onstage of the perfidious vicomtess's attacks and Marie Dorval was achieving the highest pathos. In the loges, society women tore their lace handkerchiefs, already wet with tears. Alexandre ran backstage—the curtain had to be raised for the fifth act before the applause stopped. He cried to a stage hand, "One hundred francs for you!"

Now the lovers Antony and Adèle struggled, crushed by grief. They had not even the tragic option of dying together, since double suicide would mean dishonor for Adèle. The husband came in and Adèle, dumbfounded, cried, "But I am lost!" and collapsed in an armchair that her partner should have conveniently placed. Bocage had forgotten this detail. Driven by passion, Marie Dorval stumbled over the arm of the chair with a flourish of underskirts. Her terror seemed all the more real. The audience stood, stamped its feet. The husband broke down the door and Adèle, stabbed by Antony, lay on the sofa. "Dead?" roared Colonel d'Hervey. "Yes, dead; she resisted me and I have killed her," Antony answered coldly as he threw his dagger at the feet of the husband. The gallows awaited him but Adèle's honor had been saved. The audience was caught between terror, fear, and grief; it could hardly restrain itself. They called passionately for the author. Bocage and Marie Dorval, both beaming, bowed to the crowd as it continued its applause. Alexandre ran toward the actors. He was recognized; the crowd pulled the buttons from his beautiful green coat; they tore his coattail into rags that they would keep as relics. Bocage was as gleeful as a child while Marie laughed, cried, seemed out of her mind in a triumphal rapture. Alexandre did not hear anything, did not see anything. He was swimming in a sea of light.

Antony was a triumph amid the rubble of the revolution. Alexandre might have second thoughts about abandoning literature for politics. The public, who had worn out its gloves with applause, sent the author back to his mission: not to change the world but to express it in fiction. *Antony* represented a revolution of sensibilities. Though author and play were accused of immorality and brutality, in truth it was the modern world that erupted on the stage. *Antony*, created from the wretched lot of Alexandre's life, was a synthesis, an archetype like Werther or Childe Harold. Under his coat beat the heart of modern man.

V

Retreats

On May 6, 1831, Alexandre, a red and black ribbon in the buttonhole of his coat—red for blood, black for mourning—looked about the room of the Grande Chaumière. All the men who had been decorated in July were there to elect a board of fourteen members, one for each district of Paris. Alexandre was designated to represent the suburbs. A very brief discussion resolved that there would be no pledge, no "Given by the King":

> It was impossible, without falling into the absurd, to suppose that the decoration was given by a King who did not exist at this time and for whom, we loudly avowed, we were not then fighting.

Did the government require a red and blue ribbon? Alexandre spoke and swore that the colors did not mean anything. He pulled out of his pocket three or four yards of blue ribbon with red piping. He cut them and decorated first all the members of the committee, then the nearest men present. Some of them went to a notion shop to buy fifty more yards of ribbon. An order of republican knighthood was thus formed whose knights could, if necessary, take to arms again as they did in July. On May ninth they met again at the Vendanges de Bourgogne, in Faubourg du Temple, to celebrate

the acquittal of the artillerymen. There were two hundred participants in the long, main floor room opening on a garden. Alexandre
sat next to Raspail. When they brought champagne, the men grew
more exuberant. All called, "Dumas! Dumas! A toast!" Alexandre
got up and, in spite of his reluctance to speak in public, gave a
speech the words of which seemed rather lukewarm to the high-
spirited audience:

> To art! If only the pen and the paint-brush could cooperate
> as effectively as the rifle and the sword in this social regen-
> eration to which we have devoted our life and for which we
> are ready to die!

Toast upon toast! Suddenly the name of Louis-Philippe was
heard, followed by boos from a young man who held in the same
hand a raised glass and an open dagger. Alexandre was concerned
by the turn the meeting had taken, and from the sill of the open
window jumped into the garden. The excited young man was Evar-
iste Galois who was arrested the next day.

For the moment their cause could not be defended by rifle and
sword. Alexandre would again have to arm himself with his pen.
Antony's triumphal run continued: 28,553 francs had bounced into
the cash registers for the first ten evenings. A slump in publishing
forced him to produce the book at his own expense but the sale
would compensate him. As a preface, he opened the book with
verses he had composed for Mélanie two years before.

Their frantic passion belonged now to the past; the previous
month's hysteria had subsided as if their love, expressed in *Antony*,
had delivered the lovers from the excess of their passion. Mélanie
invited Alexandre to an informal evening of talk with some friends.
Her love now had the majesty and serenity of things eternal. She
was at peace, if not happy. She could not, however, restrain a surge
of hope when Alexandre announced he intended to break with Belle.
Mélanie dared not believe that this break could be more than a
momentary falling out. She did not hope for passion any more, but
for the familiarity that four years of common life had formed. She
wanted to kiss the young Alexandre whom, at his father's instigation, a judgment had taken away from Laure Labay. He was put
in the Vauthier School, Rue de la Montagne-Sainte-Geneviève.

But Alexandre had not broken off his relationship; Belle

triumphed. Mélanie could no longer nurture her betrayed hopes; she accused Alexandre of gambling with her reputation. Her dearly acquired serenity was shattered.

Those first months of 1831 began a period of break-ups: the public break with the King; the private break with Mélanie, and again the break from Mlle. George, his statuesque interpreter of *Christine*.

He must leave Paris, where each evening a riot nearly exploded. Young boys threw garbage at guardsmen; there were uprisings and fights. A spark would be enough to ignite the city. He must leave Paris, where too many meetings infringed on the time he reserved for literature. He must write, for everything now depended on literature alone. Alexandre packed on July 5, 1831.

In the stagecoach that took them away from the backstages of theaters and their temptations, Belle had put her head on *her* Alexandre's shoulder, now hers alone. Now he was hers, but would she know how to keep him for long? She imagined a serene life that would end years of wandering; they would live with Alexandre's mother, his son, and the little girl who still gurgled in her swaddling clothes. During the fourteen hours it took for the coach to reach Rouen, Belle had time to imagine the future at least ten times.

Alexandre and Belle embarked on the ship for Le Hâvre; it passed the sail boats floating near Harfleur. On the left bank they could see the spire of the church of Honfleur. Trouville was hidden by the Villerville dunes and at Le Hâvre they transferred to another boat.

Alexandre had chosen to travel by water; a small, pretty boat with four strong oarsmen was waiting for low tide. Alexandre took time to shoot a few saltwater birds. A sailor pointed out to him some fishermen's houses crowded together on the right bank of a small river: Trouville. On the other bank, immense, swampy grazing fields: Deauville. The smooth beach shone like a mirror. Astride sailors' shoulders, they were carried to the dry sand. Children were filling up baskets of mussels. Women dug in the sand to find sand eels that they killed with a spade. Up to the waist in the sea, fisherwomen caught shrimp with long-handled nets. Alexandre breathed the sea air deeply.

At the inn, the hostess, Marie-Anne-Rose Ozerais, plump, pink, clean, and pleasant, did not look her fifty-three years. Alexandre introduced himself as a friend of the fisherman, Paul Huet. With a sly smile and an inquisitive look, Mère Ozerais stated her rules: forty sous a day for the rooms. Belle would take care of the cooking and, by being thrifty, they could bring the food budget down to four or five francs per day. At this time the couple had one hundred ninety-five francs to spend; the holiday at Trouville would balance the exorbitant expenses of life in Paris. Alexandre's room was a square space with whitewashed walls and a pine floor. For furniture, there was a walnut table and a bed of red-painted wood; on the mantel, a shaving mirror took the place of a formal mirror near two glass vases shaped like cornucopias. Under a glass bell, wax orange blossoms from the inn keeper's wedding bouquet still flowered afresh after twenty-eight years. The calico curtains were immaculately white as were the linen bed sheets.

For dinner they had a Norman potage, lamb chops, sole in "matelote," lobster with mayonnaise, a salad of shrimps and some roasted snipe. When they took a walk on the beach after dinner, the big clouds turned red from the setting sun. Small fishermen's boats were returning and were met by the fishermen's wives with large baskets hanging from each arm to carry the fish. They absorbed the sweetness of the evening on the shore until night closed upon them.

That same evening, Alexandre laid out on the walnut table his papers, ink, and pens. In bed, by the light of a candle, he wrote the first verses of a tragedy, *Charles VII chez ses grands vassaux*, that he had promised to Harel. He had to renew himself ceaselessly. Before beginning to write again, he had read a lot: *Les Marrons du feu* by Musset, selected scenes from *Andromaque* and *Le Cid*, others from *Götz von Berlichingen* by Goethe, and several novels by Sir Walter Scott. In the *Chronique du roi Charles VII* he had found an idea on which to hang several scenes. But he swore that the dramatic structures were entirely his own. Alexandre worked very quickly— by morning the one hundred beginning verses were written.

Alexandre had found what he was looking for in the uniformity and monotony of a spa, the evenness that he had lost in the storms of his political life and the restlessness of his social life. The sun, already high, woke him up. He took his pencil and continued the scene he had left the night before. After breakfast at ten, he took his rifle and went to shoot three or four snipe in the Deauville marshes; from two to four, he sat again at his work table; then he swam for an hour; at five-thirty they dined; then they walked on the beach. From nine to midnight he was at work on *Charles VII.* Soon he became acquainted with a few people also on holiday. He became friends with Bonnechose, a timid gentleman who shared Alexandre's love for hunting, the same Bonnechose who, six months later, was killed during the insurrection in the Vendée. Alexandre even slaughtered a porpoise which wanted to swim along beside them.

One day, M. Beudin, a banker who flattered himself as being a man of letters, arrived at Trouville. With his collaborator, Prosper Goubaux, he was also one-half of "Dinaux," a pseudonym: BeuDIN + GoubAUX. The two collaborators were writing *Trente ans ou la vie d'un joueur* but could not make the play work. "Dinaux," alias Beudin, asked the collaboration of Dumas, who accepted under the absolute condition that he would not be named.

A tacit understanding was established on July 24, 1831, the twenty-ninth birthday of Alexandre who, in spite of his optimistic expectations, was still and always in need of money. He wrote to Bixio:

My dear Bixio,
Are you dead? If this is true, beside the annoyance of losing you we will have that of dying from hunger.
Quickly, my friend, send us what you promised us.

During that time, Mélanie Waldor was on a holiday at the Château de Fontainebleu as guest of her daughter's godmother. Mélanie rowed on the lake and recited her poems to applause. The success was flattering. Each evening, she wrote endlessly to her ex-lover sentiments that she repeated again and again. What did she tell him, if not her confusion? Madame Villenave was dying of cancer. Mélanie implored pity; she asked for a "word from a friend, which will make my heart beat less painfully." Page followed page that she did not dare to send. The pathetic Mélanie could not help loving Alexandre still!

At Trouville, as the days passed with a rhythm of one hundred verses each day, *Charles VII chez ses grands vassaux* was nearly finished. On August tenth, Alexandre wrote its last verses.

When he read it back, the tragedy seemed a pastiche, but Alexandre did not yet admit it to himself. His task accomplished, he packed his bags. The same small boat took them to Honfleur where the poor Bonnechose accompanied him and told him goodbye forever. In the coach to Rouen, Alexandre learned from a journalist that Victor Hugo's *Marion Delorme* had been played on August eleventh. "You have not lost much. Cold audience, badly acted, weak poetry." Alexandre grew angry: "Weak, verses like those . . . ?" and he recited them in a tirade—he knew *Marion Delorme* by heart. Once he arrived in Paris, he hurried to see the play. When he did on August twentieth, the audience of the Théâtre Porte-Saint-Martin was amused to see the great Dumas, "as always crazy, as always excellent," talk and scream loudly to all the audience. Marie Dorval and Bocage had promised to play for him alone that evening, but the other actors were mediocre. Alexandre thought Hugo's marvelous poetry seemed lifeless; it was like breath upon a mirror that dulls its brilliance.

When Dumas read *Charles VII chez ses grands vassaux* to some of his friends, the lack of approval was so obvious that he later offered to refund Harel the thousand francs already advanced on the play; Harel protested. He believed that Dumas had been attracted to a larger advance of five thousand francs and wanted to sell his play to the Théâtre-Français. He offered the same amount. Dumas would read the next day for the actors. The result was fantastic, the actors fought for parts. Alexandre was confident again. To pose for his portrait by Boulanger he changed from the costume of Antony to the coat of Yaqoub. He again found the circle of his literary friends who had been dispersed by the July revolution. On August twenty-eighth at Marie Dorval's they sang, chatted, and recited melodramatic tirades; at midnight they drank tea, laughing at the follies of Charles Nodier, who was chasing girls backstage with the proposition, "I love you; do you want my blood?" Around Marie Dorval were Alfred de Vigny—number-two man in the house—Frédéric Soulié, Sainte-Beuve, Alexandre Dumas and Victor Hugo, who complained of the bad reception of *Marion Delorme*. He was accused of having imitated *Antony*. Alexandre publicly denied this accusation in *La Revue des deux mondes*: "M. Dumas asked us to record that *Marion Delorme* was written a year before he even thought of *Antony* and that consequently, if there was a plagiarism, it was on his part and not on Victor Hugo's"—laudable loyalty which would be remembered later on. The friends were fused together as before. Had Victor Hugo forgiven Alexandre for his great, too great triumph with *Antony*? All for one, one for all? For some time, yes.

Rehearsals had begun at the Odéon for *Charles VII chez ses grands vassaux*. Would this play cause another riot?

Mélanie had at last finished her long letter to Alexandre, the letter she had not dared to finish, as if the final period would mark the finale to her love. She entrusted its delivery to Casal, a friend and physician who would later leave medicine to manufacture umbrellas:

> September 1st
>
> Casal has had a letter for you for a long time; go to him, Alexandre. I cannot repeat to you the contents but I believe that you will be grateful for this last sign of trust. I count enough on your honor to believe that what I confess to you will die between you and me. It has cost me very much but I was suffering even more for being unable to open my soul and to admit at last that I have been unfair to you in various situations. . . .
>
> Be my friend, Alexandre, the feeling I have for you is sweet and deep; it will be as durable as it is sincere. Your happiness in exchange for mine; that is what I ceaselessly ask of God, yes, that at least one of us be happy! . . .
>
> Adieu Alexandre. Adieu; believe that whatever happens I will always be your friend, your best friend, and I hope soon to prove it to you.

Mélanie feared Belle: the secret letter was deposited with Casal; with it was a letter for Madame Dumas:

> Here is a note for monsieur your son; it is important that he receive it. Please believe that it will give him more pleasure than pain and give it to him when you are alone with him.

When Alexandre held in his slightly shaking hand the sheets of Mélanie's letter, he recognized her feverish handwriting. He did not love her anymore, or so he believed, but does one ever end loving? A sweet emotion invaded him slowly:

May I hope that the length of this letter does not frighten you? Alexandre, my friend, you are worth more, in spite of your faults, more than most men. I compare you to them and I do not blush anymore for having loved you; for you, you have for excuse your age and your African blood and when you loved me you still had a young and pure soul; you have not coldly premeditated my destruction; you have not accumulated ruse upon ruse to bring me to it . . . your love was without artifice, without scheme. Alexandre, your love was not the kind that degrades a soul. Ah! I would give millions to hide my forehead on your chest and cry to you that I do not despise you anymore, that far from hate, I will always be, whatever happens, your friend, your best friend! Oh! Can you conceive that because I have loved you, *you*, people believe they have a right to debase me by trying to drag me into a cowardly intrigue! You have said it, something better than love survives true love . . . Is it not what you feel sometimes? Is it not true that I am not a stranger to you, that you remember sometimes our days of happiness which will still last if your passion and an unbridled love of pleasure does not come between you and me? Because it is quite true that you have deceived me constantly and this from the first day you swore to be mine only and forever. Ah! Go, I forgive you. You have deceived me but all those women who have ruined you while amusing you, you will forget them. But I, don't you see, myself alone, if I should die, would become again your sole thought and would bring regrets in your heart and tears in your eyes!

Your friend.

Alexandre quickly refolded the sheets of paper and gave them to his mother to keep. He shook off all those remembrances which tried to clutch him, and that unhappiness which would cling to him. He was not yet thirty and had a frantic taste for happiness. The cult of the past grows only in later years.

The rehearsals for *Charles VII* continued; Harel did not believe in its success. So generous when it came to *Napoléon*, he now showed a rare stinginess. He did not want to spend anything for the sets, the costumes, the accessories.

Alexandre had found a dream of an apartment on the Square d'Orléans, entirely new with an entrance at No. 42, Rue Saint-

Lazare. The rooms, vast and with high ceilings, looked over a large square court with a garden. In the heart of Paris, Edward Cresy, an English architect, had adapted the comfort of his own country. The apartment was large enough for Madame Dumas to live with little Alexandre and Belle. It was the true family nest of which Belle had dreamed.

Painters, paperhangers, carpenters began work; money was needed. Alexandre threw himself into a collaboration with Beudin and Goubeaux, his first such serious collaboration. The three authors dined together, and Alexandre read his prologue for the new play. It was all that Beudin and Goubeaux had hoped for. The outline of the play was quickly put together. They split the work: to Dinaux went the scene of the election; to Alexandre the means necessary to depict the motivations of an ambitious man. How could he get rid of his wife, the sweet Jenny, who could prevent him from rising in politics? "He chucks her through the window!" retorted Alexandre.

Charles VII chez ses grands vassaux was ready for the audience, yet the avarice of Harel persisted tenaciously—Raymond killed a deer during the first act, but there was no deer. Alexandre became the hunter of props: he killed a deer in the forest and had it stuffed at his expense. He also negotiated with the Musée d'Artillerie— which owed him after his services rendered on July 29, 1830—for the loan of a complete breastplate. On October twentieth, the evening of the premiere, the theater was filled with the usual troop of men with beards and moustaches, invariably present at first-night performances; in a loge, Mélanie Waldor, ghastly in a red dress; in a corner of the balcony, Baron Taylor looking ferocious. The eight-year-old Alexandre sat beside his father.

The five acts unfolded in dullish silence. The play was too classical for the romanticists, too violent for the classicists. Nobody could sympathize with this "originality of patchwork"; it was a literary compromise. The audience's polite attention was rewarded, however, in the middle of Act III, when the visor of Charles VII's helmet dropped abruptly and muffled his tirade into a lugubrious croak. Everyone laughed, but Charles VII's squire bounced up, dagger in his fist, and succeeded in working the springs of the visor. Charles VII, red as a peony, half suffocated, resumed his discourse. All applauded; they believed they had seen a theatrical trick.

Alexandre took his son by the hand when they returned home

across nocturnal Paris. The child felt his father's hand shake. He did not say anything, but the little Alexandre felt that Papa was unhappy. *Charles VII* was not, however, a failure; it was only a half-success. People did not come in a rush, but they came: twenty-six performances in 1831 was an honorable run—even though it did not net Alexandre a sou.

Like Antaeus, Alexandre had touched the earth again, he had regained his strength. He had finally discovered the dramatic mechanism that would permit him to throw Jenny through the window. He thus finished *Richard Darlington* and took it to the Théâtre Porte-Saint-Martin where it was accepted, but under a new title, *Le Divorce*. Marie Dorval was to play Jenny, Bocage would be Richard. The drama finally was mounted at the Odéon where Frédérick Lemaître and Mlle. Noblet played the main parts in the drama, now renamed *Orgueil et passion* by "M. Dinaux." Dumas was not even mentioned in the press.

Footlights, the excitement of the audiences, the intoxication brought by applause were now Alexandre's world. He did not belong any more to Belle than he belonged to himself; he had become a "name" that brought money. He was losing himself and could recognize himself only through remembered loyalties. He visited Raspail at Sainte-Pélagie, a gloomy and dark jail where the republicans who had not accepted Louis-Philippe's coup were imprisoned.

The former fighters had nothing left except fraternity; Poland had been betrayed. The pompous sot, Sébastiani, now Minister of Foreign Affairs, had proclaimed in the Chambre des Députés that order reigned in Warsaw as it would soon reign at Lyons, where the famished silk workers were ready to revolt. Maréchal Soult's army would gloriously put down a few thousand needy people. With Raspail's shoulder against his own, Alexandre felt the warmth between them, in spite of the icy autumn, and extinguished hopes.

Alexandre never neglected his duty as a man in fashion and he showed himself where he should be seen. On November 21, 1831, he was at the Opéra for the premiere of Meyerbeer's *Robert le Diable*. There he cheered up the unlucky tenor, Adolphe Nourrit, who had crashed down into the first basement of the theater when a badly set trapdoor had opened under him. Sullen, Meyerbeer was less worried about the fall of his tenor than for the fall of his opera, which was coolly received. The musician loved success more than he loved music. That winter was not good for dramatic works. A sort of black plague seemed to hit dramatic productions. Would *Richard Darlington* also be affected? This drama had followed Harel to the Porte-Saint-Martin, where he was now assistant to Crosnier while he kept the direction of the Odéon. The general rehearsal on December ninth had attracted its usual lot of "Jeunes-France" in leather hats, morning coats with wide lapels, and overcoats made of green oilcloth. Dumas observed the emotions aroused by his polished melodrama. Belle paraded at his side. The play caused a great commotion in Paris, which, deprived of a revolution, was now ready to create a storm at any opportunity. *Richard* was a political play that flogged the corruption of public mores. A crowd pushed at the box office to get tickets. The Théâtre Porte-Saint-Martin resembled a boat lashed by a tempest. Frédérick Lemaître's genius soared well above the undercurrents. He was the ferociously ambitious Richard Darlington, who had chosen cynical success because the corrupted society offered him no alternative other than shady dealings, bribes, promises, and betrayals. Though set in England, the French audience understood and responded to this direct, bold picture of corrupt parliamentarianiam. Alexandre would not become a Deputy at thirty; he would not be the people's hero, fair and unselfish, who "comes out poor and naked from the Chambre des Députés, as a fighter from the arena." Richard was his negative image—a man who accepted the pervasive decay. Alexandre would not share in the spoils of corruption. A man of the people, he had "written in the blood of revolutions his own letters of nobility," which permitted him to deal, like a member of the old aristocracy, as an equal with royalty. In the large loge where he was sitting, the roar of the crowd came to him as if muted by the voices of the heroes of July. Harel was presiding over success and he knew that it would be greater still if Alexandre allowed himself to be identified as the author. Harel begged Alexandre; Goubaux and Beudin begged him, too. Harel tempted him with the crisp sound of three one-thousand-franc bills. Alexandre stubbornly refused. He had not yet shed his cloak of self-respect; he still held on to some shreds of integrity.

When the curtain fell in a frenzy of applause, Alexandre ran to the actors to kiss them. He was stopped in the corridor by a pale, haggard Alfred de Musset, who said he was suffocating. It was the most beautiful homage anyone could render.

It was a triumph; there were seventy-one performances in 1831 and 1832. But it left Alexandre with a bitter aftertaste, for the play did not entirely belong to him. He was not the complete creator. Because he needed money, he had agreed to stoop to collaboration and he had even repeated it:

The misfortune of a first collaboration is that it brings a second one; the man who has collaborated is like the man who lets the tip of one finger be caught in a rolling-mill; after the finger, the hand; after the hand, the arm; after the arm, the whole body! All must go through the mill; on going in, one was a man; when coming out, one had become a mass of wire. (*Mes Mémoires*, chap. CCXXII)

If *Richard Darlington* had been the finger, *Térésa* was the hand. Bocage wanted a part, the part of an old man. It was a strange idea for a thirty-year-old actor. Anicet Bourgeois had written an outline. Alexandre put the outline aside. He preferred another story, that of a generous old man, Delaunay, his wife, Térésa, and her lover, Arthur, who seduces Delaunay's pure young daughter, Amélie. It was a rather poor melodrama that Dumas agreed to revise only to please Bocage. From Anicet's first draft, he manufactured the drama in a few short weeks spent probably at Villers-Cotterêts, where he had gone again to see old friends. During the day, Alexandre rediscovered the traces of his adolescence; he recognized the paths, the thickets, and the strong scent of dead leaves. Evenings, he visited the homes of friends, where they drank copiously, sang, and he was surrounded—the hero of their rustic celebration—while they measured the distance each had covered. Far from Paris and its tumult, Alexandre sometimes had the impression that real life was under those trees in Villers-Cotterêts, frozen in time. But he soon threw himself once again into fiction. Bocage had found a theater for *Térésa*, the Variétés. From a suburban theater he enticed a young, slightly overweight woman, Mlle. Ida. At the end of November, the rehearsals had begun, but the theater sank into bankruptcy. Bocage started his search for a theater all over again.

The few subscribers of *La Revue des deux mondes* were the first to read the new *Scènes historiques* in the December 15, 1831 issue.

Lively and brisk, they informed and entertained. They were signed by Alex. Dumas, the scandalous dramatic author. Was he tired of the theater? Was he afraid of becoming over-exposed in the foot-lights? Some said that his imagination was drying up and so he used collaborators. But the historical chronicles were inexhaustible.

VI

Hell and Damnation

A lexandre was now thirty. He was famous—recognized in the streets, restaurants, and cafés; theater directors increased business merely by using his name. He still had friends, but *Richard Darlington* and *Térésa*, melodramas in collaboration, made the mouths of his dear friends Vigny and Hugo pucker with distaste. He had money and would have it again tomorrow. He had two children, one mistress—tomorrow he would most probably have two, since the young Ida had already made most promising eyes at him. He was envied, an object of jealousy, but it is not good to appear too happy when one's political ambition was definitively compromised. Louis-Philippe had muzzled the Republic. Alexandre wore the mourning of a great unsatisfied ambition. He had been sent back to literature, a special but not really serious calling.

Bocage had convinced the director of the Théâtre Royal de l'Opéra-Comique, which was in collapse, to loan him the Salle Ventadour. They even booked one of the singers from the theater to replace Guyon, who was too weak. During the day, Guyon was young Alexandre's junior master at the boarding school of Saint-Victor. Laure Labay, in order to stay with her son, had taken work as a seamstress at that institution. During rehearsals, Alexandre brooded over Ida, a fine talent—plump and simple, of course, but mostly a blonde with a delicious avoirdupois. Blonde and plump like Aglaé, and like Laure.

Alexandre did not believe that the play *Térésa* had any literary worth. He accepted the wishes of the actors. He surrendered himself, figuratively with hands and fists tied, as if he had no other desire than to please the directors and the artists who should have been his servants. Too tired to fight and to defend a literary doctrine which he did not believe anymore, he squandered his talent as a thing of little value.

But the drama was by Dumas. The crowd fought at the door of the Opéra-Comique; the beautiful scenes of the fourth act were greatly effective and they applauded the eruption of Vesuvius. Even the ending, the fiddling about between the adulterous wife and the amorous valet, turned out well. Ida had thrown herself at Alexandre's neck, and after such success she could not refuse him anything. Alexandre clearly heard the applause that rose from the audience but did not enjoy it any longer, he despised those who applauded. He was in the fatal decline into which everyone had pushed him: directors and actors who demanded shocking melodramatic situations; actresses who coaxed him for parts; an audience that wanted strong emotions even if they were slightly vulgar. To produce. To show off. On February sixteenth, at Delphine Gay's, Alexandre talked seriously with Balzac about the Republic and the revolution. Then he had to be seen, on February eighteenth, marvelously costumed at the ball given by Duponchel, who was the theater designer.

Mlle. Dupont, who had the perennial part of the maid at the Comédie-Française, had obtained Baron Taylor's consent to give a benefit performance; for that occasion she wanted a comedy in one act to pique the audience. Of course she asked Dumas, who would bring a substantial cash receipt. As Dumas relates it, the genesis of this small comedy seems quite confusing. It was probably Eugène Durieu who had originated the basic story line: the unexpected return of Vertpré, whose wife, Adèle, had pretended to be his widow, upsets the dalliances of the triangle—Léon d'Auvray, Adèle de Vertpré, and her niece, Pauline. Dumas agreed to collaborate, but on the condition that Anicet Bourgeois, co-author of *Térésa*, would also be a partner. Bourgeois wanted to get his start at the Théâtre-Français. Durieu and Anicet put together a scenario and then, with Dumas, revised, and rearranged the scenes. They left the first preparatory writing to Dumas who, in twenty-four hours, had ready *La Jeune tante*, which, rebaptized with the more enigmatic and compelling title *Le Mari de la veuve*, was accepted by the Comédie-Française on March 8, 1832.

Although Alexandre was entering the Comédie-Française through the back door, Mlle. Mars agreed to play Adèle, a conciliatory gesture after the unfortunate mishap of *Antony*. Mlle. Mars was artistic integrity personified: she was prompt for each rehearsal and quick to quibble, demand cuts and corrections. Alexandre had given in to the demands of much less prestigious artists. Each evening he took the manuscript under his arm. He corrected and cut.

Meanwhile, a cholera epidemic from India had made its way through Persia, reached St. Petersburg, and was now in London. The French shrugged and reassured themselves, "There is the Channel," and people went about their business as usual. Dumas was reelected a member of the Society of Dramatic Authors. He intervened so that the luscious Ida was engaged at the Porte-Saint-Martin. Would it be a slander to infer that she gave much of herself to balance the scales in her favor?

For good measure, Alexandre stressed that he "would find for this theater, where he expected to give at least two of his works during the year, a talented actress who pleased him and who had already been very useful to him." In fact, on the previous October fourteenth, he had made a deal with François-Louis Crosnier: he promised to give to the Théâtre-Porte-Saint-Martin two plays each year for two years. In exchange, he would receive 18 percent of the receipts and some bonuses in proportion to the play's success.

Paris basked in the light of an early spring; women in their new clothes dappled the grass of the Tuileries. The few last riots were just ending when, suddenly, the newly reborn happiness was shattered by a cry of alarm: "The cholera is now in Paris." In the Rue Chauchat, a man had died. It seemed only a false alarm, but a few days later the number of tragic casualties grew. On March twenty-sixth, there were four deaths reported. The plague started with a slight shivering, then a feeling of cold, cramps, and endless diarrhea. The blood thickened, the capillaries were affected, the victims turned black and died. No effective medicine was known. Absurd rumors were going around: the government had poisoned the fountains of Paris to get rid of the city's excess population, or to get rid of the republicans.

It was no time to put a new comedy on the stage, yet, on April 4, 1832, *Le Mari de la veuve* opened at the Comédie-Française. Some five hundred persons were courageous enough to endure the smell of camphor and chlorine that floated over the audience. In spite of the crowd's lugubrious appearance, the play was greatly applauded. Monrose stepped to the front of the stage and announced that the author desired to remain anonymous. From his loge, Alexandre had heard the boo that resounded when the husband had declared, "What weather! Here I am, as watered down as college wine!" A boarding-school master, no doubt.

The Odéon had to close its doors on April second. Black hearses rolled across Paris. The casket makers were soon short of coffins. Alexandre fled Paris for Nogent-le-Rotrou, where his brother-in-law Victor Letellier had been named Controller of Indirect Taxes. Alexandre lodged at the Cour du Croissant, where almost immediately the cholera was carried by a nurse arriving from Paris. He saw that it was futile to run away from the cholera since the disease followed him. He went back to Paris. From his window on the Rue Saint-Lazare he could see fifty or sixty funeral processions pass each day on their way to the Montmartre cemetery.

Harel visited and pressed him to collaborate in reworking a drama by Gaillardet, a young man who had written *La Tour de Nesle*. Harel had asked Jules Janin to work on the play, but Janin had given up after composing one long and beautiful speech. Harel still believed that the play could revolutionize Paris. He had asked Gaillardet to cut the drama into scenes and add new subject matter. He handed it to Alexandre, "I have this scenario in my pocket. Do you want to read it?" Alexandre did not accept, but asked that this young man come to see him. Impossible—he had left to bury his father at Tonnerre. Maybe later. . . .

On April 15, 1832, Franz Liszt and Louis Boulanger came to spend the evening at Rue Saint-Lazare. Belle served very black tea—excellent, it was said, against the epidemic. When Alexandre accompanied his friends to the stairs, he felt dizzy; he shook and held on to a table to avoid falling. The cholera! Catherine, the maid, rushed in, "A lump of sugar and some ether!" Alexandre, very pale, went to bed; he could not speak, he simply shivered. He swallowed the contents of the glass that Catherine gave to him and then fainted. He had absorbed one-half glass of pure ether. When he woke up he was rolled into a large fur rug, a boiling water-bottle at his feet.

Belle and Catherine rubbed every inch of his body with a bed-warmer full of embers. Alexandre burned inside while he was roasted outside, and finally the shivering subsided. He was saved.

There had been seven thousand deaths, and from twelve to thirteen thousand sick persons reported by April fourteenth. While Alexandre began his convalescence, the Théâtre-Porte-Saint-Martin was near death itself. Harel harassed Alexandre: "Too weak! Come off it! Your condition is most favorable for inspiration."

Dumas gave in on April eighteenth and promised the play would be ready in two weeks. Shaking with fever he made the effort to read Gaillardet's manuscript. He interrupted his reading at the second scene. He had found the play's essence, the battle between a queen and an adventurer, between power and genius. No matter now what was in the original manuscript. The drama took over his imagination. He called Harel and settled the conditions of collaboration.

There was one sine qua non: in spite of Harel's insistence, Dumas refused to be named as an author. With a bad conscience, he had weakened and agreed to write melodramas. He needed money, that was understood. But he could not go so far as to prostitute his name!

Propped up by two pillows, Alexandre lay in bed with his writing kit before him. Each morning a messenger picked up the fruits of the preceding day. When he was too tired or feverish, he dictated a scene a day.

Hearses no longer passed under his windows; instead there passed moving vans into which ten, fifteen, twenty corpses had been piled. Collective masses were recited before the van load was dumped into a common grave. Instead of a shroud, they were covered with a coat of lime. There was a ceaseless, sinister croaking of wheels on the pavement! An implacable sun bleached the blue sky. An odor of putrefaction spread over the city. *La Tour de Nesle* was, also, a chronicle of cholera, for was not cholera itself the image of the decay of a power that only an unclean hero could confront?

Alexandre was still very sick. Afraid of the cholera, Frédérick Lemaître had retreated to the country and ignored the notices for rehearsals with which he was bombarded. The play could not wait for the epidemic's end. Harel engaged Bocage, who was free. When he heard about it, Frédérick, braving the plague, rushed back to town. He foamed at the mouth, threatened and pleaded but to no avail. Bocage kept the part. Still very weak, Alexandre dragged himself to the theater; he was touched by the despair of the temperamental actor.

When on May fifteenth, at Tonnerre, Gaillardet heard that Harel had taken the liberty of giving his *La Tour de Nesle* to Dumas without notifying him, he too raved and ranted, threatening to summon Harel and Dumas to court to have the play forbidden. Innocent young man! Harel did not even take the trouble to reply. Alexandre, not as cynical as the director, wrote to Gaillardet, reassuring him: "I have done everything necessary to smooth the difficulties and the play, as it is now, seems to me a possible success."

Yet, on May nineteenth, Gaillardet burst into Harel's office in his traveling clothes and threatened to have the play stopped. "You won't succeed," declared Harel. "I will change the title and play it anyway. If you sue me, you might obtain twelve hundred francs as damages. If you let it play, you will earn twelve thousand francs." They called in Dumas. The meeting was tempestuous—they flaunted threats of duels; then they calmed down and reached a compromise. Gaillardet and Dumas agreed to be recognized as joint authors of *La Tour de Nesle*. The play would be performed and printed under the name of Gaillardet alone but Harel would reserve the right to have posters with the author's name followed by stars, leading the viewer to believe that a second name could be added.

The cholera seemed to diminish, but the grave diggers were still busy. The pestilence of civil war dawned on the horizon. The Duchesse de Berry was trying to stir up the Vendée. At the Théâtre de la Porte-Saint-Martin, Mlle. George and Bocage had taken hold of their parts magnificently. Alexandre had sent a loge ticket to the previous Prefect of the Seine, Odilon Barrot, who asked him to dinner before the performance. The dinner seemed endless to Dumas, who was on tenterhooks. When they arrived at the theater, he could smell success. The room was like a boiling caldron, and Bocage was blowing fire. The actor was fantastic. The dramatic terror reached a peak. When the curtain was lowered, the audience breathed deeply to better cry its bravos; all seemed exultant, freed— freed from the cholera, freed from riots, freed from the limp tyranny of the "happy middle." The stage was an immense distorting mirror in which could be recognized the specters of oppression and the unhappiness of the time. A frantic melodrama, perhaps, but one that was thrown like a curse at the face of power. Bocage had announced to the public that the author was the unknown M. Gaillardet. In his loge, the young man from Tonnerre blushed and bowed, a bit stiff. He was not so sure that the play was quite his own. He remained certain that his own version would have been much more striking. Madame Odilon Barrot, however, was enchanted; she had been entertained as if she were a boarding-school girl. Alexandre smiled at her exuberance. Once more he had shown how he could dominate his public, how he could arouse emotion. Who could believe that a beginning author could, with his first attempt, unleash such passion? That evening, Alexandre sinned through pride; he was the deus ex-machina and that was enough. He had no regret in not being named.

But Harel did not agree. The name of Dumas was an asset that he did not intend to neglect. He had printed a new poster for the second performance: *Le Tour de Nesle* by MM.*** and Gaillardet. Alexandre was not named but under the transparency, the three stars, the primordial part of his collaboration was recognized. Gaillardet protested. A scandal? It would transform a tremendous success into a triumph. Gaillardet, in fact, got into action; with legal papers he summoned Harel before the Tribunal of Commerce. He swamped the newspapers with letters of protest:

> Announce, if you please, that in my contract, as on the stage, and, as I hope, on tomorrow's poster, that I am and will be the sole author of *La Tour de Nesle*. (to M. Charles Maurice, Director of the Courrier des Théâtres, May 30, 1832)

The war of the notices had broken out. Harel retorted to Gaillardet:

> The play, for the whole of its style and for nineteen-twentieths, at least, of its composition, belongs to the famous collaborator who, for his own reasons, has not wanted to be named following an immense success. Of M. Gaillardet's primitive work, nothing or almost nothing remains; this is what I swear and what will prove to be the case if one compares the performed manuscript with M. Gaillardet's manuscript.

Gaillardet was strangling with rage; he wanted to fight. Alexandre, who wanted to stay neutral in the near exchange of blows between the director and the crazed young author, had to come out from his shell. Gaillardet had his letter published: *Le Corsaire* attacked him and he had to threaten the manager to a duel; he did not eat anymore, and each evening, he had seizures of fever. Since Gaillardet had not been wise enough to stop fighting with Harel, Alexandre turned his own bad mood against the novice. In a communiqué to *Le Courrier des Théâtres*, dated June 4, 1833, he wrote:

I have not read the work of M. Gaillardet; the manuscript was in the hands of M. Harel and has not left him for an instant. When accepting an assignment with a given title and plot, I fear being influenced by a work previous to mine and, therefore, of losing the verve which is so necessary for me to achieve my own work.

Now, if M. Gaillardet finds that the public is not yet informed enough of this puny affair, let him ask arbitration of three men of letters of his choice; let him go to them with his manuscript and I with mine; they will judge on which side lies tact and on which side lies ingratitude.

To remain faithful to the end to the conditions I have voluntarily imposed on myself in my letter to M. Gaillardet, permit me, Monsieur l'Editeur, not to name myself here either, no more than I have done on the poster.

[signed] The Author of the manuscript performed as *La Tour de Nesle.*

Alexandre extended the tact even further. He claimed that Gaillardet's demand was right, that the controversial stars should return to their earlier, inferior position on the poster. He backed up Gaillardet, who did not want to give an inch in his quarrel with Harel. Gaillardet thanked his "dear master."

Exhausted by these piqued vanities, these shameful transactions, this publicity fluff, Dumas dreamed of Switzerland, of Italy! Of leaving pestilential Paris, that hell of mediocrity! But on June first, Général Lamarque, the last epic hero of the Republic, died. A relief for the government of Louis-Philippe. The organization of his funeral was left to the family and friends, and Alexandre was named representative of the artillery commission.

On June 5, 1832, with a branch of laurel, he sprinkled some holy water on the body of the general, who was dressed in his parade uniform, lying with gloved hand on his bared épée. Then Alexandre left the crowd and sat in a café to drink a cup of chocolate. All of his limbs were weak but he had to get up at the sound of the drum. The casket was under a doorway draped in black. The flow of National Guardsmen, artillerymen, students, workmen, veterans of wars, Polish, Italian, Portuguese refugees had finally sorted themselves out and each group had assembled around its own banner. The heat was suffocating; huge black clouds rolled over Paris; thunder resounded like a cannon; the rain poured over the hearse which began to move, dragged by some thirty young men harnessed to long cords. La Fayette, staggering, held to a corner of the funeral drapery. Deputies, generals, outlaws, six hundred artillerymen with loaded rifles, ten thousand National Guardsmen armed with swords, workmen, members of secret societies, a river of forty, perhaps fifty thousand men passed silently, interrupted now and then by a space for a banner, "Honor to Général Lamarque." Alexandre marched on the flank of the artillerymen who impatiently shook the red flame of their shakos. Suddenly the procession turned toward the Place Vendôme in a unintelligible brouhaha. "The soldiers of Napoléon around the column! To the column!" The squad of guards, willingly or perforce, had to render final honors in a salute. The Commander of the post, either out of fear or sympathy, granted the wishes of the crowd.

On the terrace of the Cercle des Arts, the Duc de Fitz-James had kept his hat on as if screwed to his head. A hail of stones broke the glass panes of the building. The crowd growled dully amidst the drums' veiled rolling. The rain had stopped. The crowd was incited to anger by the provocative look of policemen posted at regular intervals. One of them hit a flag bearer who had stepped on a symbolic gallic rooster and was immediately surrounded with twenty raised daggers. To save him, Alexandre pushed through the rows of artillerymen. The wounded flag bearer had taken off his tie. Blood ran from his throat onto his coat and reddened his Cross of July.

Everything seemed to cry, "To arms": the wailing of the drums, the swinging of the flags beaten by the storm, the shouts of menacing voices which roared again and again, "Honor to Général Lamarque!" The crowd pulled out the stakes that held the newly planted trees on the boulevards to use as clubs.

On the Place de la Bastille they sang *"La Marseillaise,"* banned for a year now. Fifty thousand voices in chorus sang, "Aux armes, citoyens," while the procession went up to the dais erected at the entrance of the Austerlitz bridge, where the memorial speeches were to be given. Lamarque's body was to be sent to the department of the Landes, where it would be buried.

At three o'clock in the afternoon, Alexandre, dying with hunger and fatigue, took two artillerymen to dinner. He leaned on them, he was so weak; he fainted briefly. A glass of ice water, then a gigantic "matelote," an eel stew, revived him. Did they hear a fusillade? Alexandre raised his glass to the memory of Lamarque and rushed to the quay, climbing atop a stone marker. It was nothing serious yet, only a great commotion on the Austerlitz bridge. The friends threw ten francs to the tavern keeper and ran toward the barricade as the fusillade increased. People in overalls welcomed them. Some artillerymen returned fire and cried, "Long live the Republic." Paris was soon on fire. Alexandre went up the deserted boulevards to the Rue de Menilmontant, which now was obstructed by a barricade. Farther on, at the Faubourg Saint-Martin, Alexandre recognized one of his ex-battalion comrades, dressed in a rounded coat and trousers with buttons, a police cap on his head. Alexandre came to him with a gesture of friendship but the ex-comrade took aim at him. Believing it was in jest, Alexandre continued to advance. A bullet whistled past his ear while a cloud of smoke hid the man who fired.

Alexandre broke open the door of the Théâtre de la Porte-Saint-Martin which displayed the poster for the seventh performance of *La Tour de Nesle* by MM.*** and Gaillardet. Alexandre wanted his rifle or at least the pistols he had loaned for *Richard Darlington*. Harel made his body a barrier in front of the prop room door. Did Alexandre want to have the theater burned down? Then, from a small window on the second floor, Alexandre saw a child hidden behind a tree throw a stone which rebounded off a dragoon's helmet. The child's mother caught him and shook him violently. If women were not going to take part in the revolt, all was lost!

In a lamenting voice, Harel called Alexandre; some twenty men, demanding arms, had invaded the theater. Alexandre harangued them and then arranged for a distribution of twenty rifles that they swore they would bring back, if they survived. With a piece of chalk they wrote on the theater's doors: "Arms given." Harel could breathe again; the theater was saved. Mlle. George was afraid and balked when she saw Alexandre in an artilleryman uniform. He sent a messenger to his home to fetch civilian clothes so that he could go to Laffitte's townhouse, center of the opposition, without difficulty. Alexandre and Lafayette arrived at Laffitte's at the same time. La Fayette said, "Find me a place for a chair and I'll wait to be killed in it." The other deputies were far from showing such quiet heroism. Alexandre had nothing to do there and he returned to the boulevards. He could hardly stand up. He burned with fever; he took a carriage and having arrived at home he fainted between the first and second floors. Belle and their servant hoisted him to his apartment, undressed him, and put him to bed.

June 6, 1832. During the night the insurrection had been stopped and was now concentrated in two neighborhoods—on the Place de la Bastille and around the Church Saint-Merri. The government reassembled its troops. In spite of his fever, Alexandre went out to see what was happening. He dragged himself to Laffitte's again and, in the courtyard, shared his indignation with Savary, the astronomer and fellow sympathizer. When it was heard that the revolutionaries had capitulated and decided to send two representatives to the King to plead for clemency, Alexandre and Savary protested vehemently. They found the deputies guilty of treason to their country, too quick to disavow the revolt of the people. Was it all finished? No, they heard the bell at Saint-Merri and, as long as a sick man rattled, he was not dead! Alexandre was exhausted with fever, disgust, indignation, and despair. He sat on a chair at the Café de Paris. Even his body betrayed him and did not allow him to use a rifle effectively or to join the last fighters in the cloister of Saint-Merri where they were trapped.

Was it in an ironic dream that he heard shouts of "Long live the King!" No. It was really Louis-Philippe on a horse, surrounded with his Ministers of the Interior, of War, and of Commerce. Calm, smiling, unconcerned, he was shaking hands with National Guardsmen, armed and screaming ferociously to better flatter him. It did not matter that they had blood on their hands!

The men in the Saint-Merri cloisters had fallen as heroes. The Republic, as it had been dreamed of in 1830, was very dead. With rage in his heart, Alexandre had to accept that a part of his inner self no longer existed:

On the ninth of June, I read in a legitimist newspaper that I had been caught, weapons in hand, in the Saint-Merri cloister, court-martialed during the night, and shot at three o'clock in the morning.

The news had such an official tone, the narrative of my execution—which, it was reported, I accepted with great courage—was so detailed; the information came from such a good source, that I had a moment of doubt; besides, the editor was so strongly convinced that for the first time he said something good about me in his newspaper; it was therefore evident that he believed me dead.

I threw off my blanket, I jumped out of my bed, and I ran to my mirror to prove to myself my own existence. (*Impressions de voyage,* I, p.3)

He saw a frightfully emaciated body and burning eyes which seemed to have wept too often. The image was Alexandre, but mirrors do not reflect the state of the soul.

PART
IV

An Artist's Pilgrimages

I

Switzerland, a Republican in a Republic

Alexandre was convalescing. His physician advised him to get some of his strength back, then to pull himself out of pestilential Paris where riots killed those whom cholera spared. Thanks to *La Tour de Nesle*, the summer looked financially superb. Prudently, however, Alexandre took advantage of the necessary rest to finish a drama that Mlle. George had commissioned. Tired of her stage roles as queens, the artist wanted to play a woman of the people. Before the insurrection Dumas had already written the first three acts. But he felt crushed by fatigue, his mind was blank. In spite of Harel's promises of money and advances, Alexandre sulked. Once more Anicet Bourgeois was called in with an idea for a plot: an émigré who hates the common people seduces and impregnates the wife of the gunsmith of Brientz. Later she bears a legitimate child by her husband. Yet some twenty years later, the son of the émigré and the son of the gunsmith confront one another. The ex-émigré, who has become an informer, is condemned as a forger while his son is sentenced to the gallows as a thief and a murderer. Betrayal, debauchery, lewdness, crime in generous doses! On June seventh and eighth Alexandre and Anicet set to work on the last two acts, conscious that their work was abominable. But it would bring them an advance of three thousand francs. Still it was hardly enough for the planned trip. Alexandre sold *La Tour de Nesle* to a bookseller:

seven hundred francs for him, as much for Gaillardet. He offered
to the publisher Gosselin two volumes to be written about his
upcoming trip to Switzerland. The publisher shrugged, Switzerland was overdone as a subject.

While Alexandre scraped the bottom of his purse, Belle had
packed the trunks, relieved to get away from the resurging cholera.
Alexandre rushed about saying his goodbyes—long embraces and
promises for Ida; kisses for the young Alexandre who cried and
was desolate in his boarding school; a visit to the little Marie at
her nurse's, where she had hardly begun to walk. The government
looked favorably on the departure of a writer who had been seen
on the boulevards in the uniform of an artilleryman and who had
distributed arms at the Porte-Saint-Martin. Even an arrest had been
suggested, as an aide-de-camp of the King had warned Alexandre.
When he returned, and with time, all would be forgotten.

On the evening of July twenty-first, Alexandre and Belle climbed
into the coach for Montereau. The writer had an album in which
he would write his observations. Gosselin's rejection had not discouraged him.

Dumas traveled as he lived, at a gallop. Rather than follow him
step by step across Switzerland, it is better to look over the ninety-
nine vignettes he left as his *Impressions de voyage*, as if, 150 years
later, one were receiving a series of postcards from him.

July 29: "The estate of Voltaire at Ferney. Inscription on the small
chapel, *Deo erexit Voltaire*. God reconciled with Voltaire? Each time
he named M. Arouet de Voltaire, the guide touched his hat. He
offered a chip from a tree planted by the very hand of M. Arouet
de Voltaire and, as a bonus for a *louis*, *his* cane that the guard had
kept religiously since the death of the great man."

August 20: "At Lax I read in the *Nouvelliste Vaudois* the sentencing
to death of two republicans involved in the Saint-Merri cloister.
Heads roll, either on the flagstones of the Tuileries or on the pavement of the Place de Grève, a double entry bookkeeping kept for
the benefit of death, between the people and royalty and written in
red ink by the executioner. When will this book be closed, when
will it be sealed with the world "liberty" and cast into the grave of
the last martyr?"

August 25: "Chateaubriand is at Lucerne, in voluntary exile, at the Hôtel de l'Aigle. Had my card given to him."

August 26: "Chateaubriand has invited me for lunch. Admiration for him was my childhood religion. He has cleared the way for young writers. On his landing, I must stop; my heart beats violently. He, himself, opened the door. I stammer like a provincial. Let us talk of France. He considers his party as lost and believes all the future is in social republicanism. Stays attached to his cause because it is unfortunate. 'I have marched, without willing it, like a rock rolled by a torrent, and now I find myself nearer to you than you are to me,' he said."

Les Poules de M. de Chateaubriand. On the bridge of the Cour: "We stopped about two-thirds of the way onto the span at some distance from a place covered with reeds. M. de Chateaubriand pulled from his pocket a piece of bread that he had put there after lunch and began to make crumbs of it into the lake; soon a dozen waterhens came from a sort of island formed by the reeds and rushed to fight for the meal prepared for them, at that moment, by the hand that had written *Le Génie du christianisme*, *Les Martyrs* and *Le Dernier des Abencérages*. I looked for a long time, without saying anything, at the strange sight of this man, leaning over the bridge, with smiling lips, but with sad, grave eyes. Little by little his occupation became completely mechanical; his face took on an expression of deep melancholy; his thoughts passed over his forehead as clouds in the sky . . . I respected this meditation as long as it lasted. At the end, he moved and sighed. I came near him; he remembered I was there and held out his hand to me.

" 'But if you miss Paris so much,' I asked him, 'why not go back? Nothing exiles you and everything calls you back.'

" 'What do you want me to do there?' he asked. 'I was at Cauteretz when the July revolution began. I went back to Paris. I saw there a throne of blood, another one of mud, lawyers making a charter, a King shaking the hands of rag pickers. It was deadly sad, especially for one filled, as I am, with the great traditions of monarchy. I left.' . . .

" 'I thought that you recognized the sovereignty of the people.'

" 'Yes, perhaps it is good that from time to time royalty dips down into its source through an election; but this time they skipped a branch of their tree, a link of their chain; it was Henri V that should have been elected, not Louis-Philippe.' . . .

" 'Won't you come back to France?'

" 'If the Duchesse de Berry, after having committed the folly of coming to the Vendée, commits the stupidity of letting herself be caught, I will go back to Paris to defend her before her judges, since my advice would not have prevented her from appearing before the Court.'

" 'If not?'

" 'If not,' M. de Chateaubriand continued, while breaking a second piece of bread, 'I will continue to feed my waterhens.' "

August 28: "Sarnen, the shooting range. My first try passed three hundred feet above the target because of the extreme precision of the trigger on the training rifles. Laughter from the crowd injured my honor as marksman. A man from Linthal, half in German, half in Italian, but mostly with gestures, taught me how to handle the delicate rifle. I hit the mark at my second try. Bizarre self-conceit; I have no use for the Sarnen peasants' admiration, but how my heart was beating."

September 1: "The curiosity of the Zurichois focused above all on income. The good Fritz Haguemann, who asked me how I earn my money, was shocked when I answered, 'In the morning, I take a pen and an exercise book; then as long as I have ideas in my head, I write, and when that makes a book or a drama, I take the bundle to a publisher or a theater.' And I earn twenty-five to thirty thousand francs! The Athens of the North, or so its inhabitants call it, hardly deserves its reputation."

September 12: "Constance evokes a dream town of palaces with frail rows of columns, cathedrals with daring spires. 'Where is it?' I wanted to scream when confronted with this modern, poor and sad city. Imagination always goes beyond reality."

September 13: "Sent my card to Queen Hortense who lives in exile at the Chateau d'Arenenberg. Upon my return from the island of Reichenau, I find a dinner invitation.

"The daughter of Josephine possesses the greatness of the dream I had of her. Gracious, kind with emotions made of all the generous feelings: love, respect, piety. I would have fallen on my knees before her if she had not been accompanied by her reader. She showed me the souvenirs of her imperial past. After dinner, Mme. Récamier, black dress, head and neck wrapped in a black veil. How old is she? From the youth in her voice, the beauty of her eyes, the shape of her hand, twenty-five. The Queen sat at the piano; she sang for me, 'You Leave Me to March to Glory,' which, when I was five, my sister sang to me; it was my favorite sentimental song."

September 14: "Before lunch the Queen took me for a walk in the park and asked me:

" 'I believe you are republican,' she said.

" 'You are right, Madame la Duchesse. However, because the meanings and the shades of opinions that the newspapers representing the party to which I belong and whose sympathies I share— though not all their methods—have given to this word, before accepting the republican qualifications you give me, I will ask your permission to explain the principles. . . . I will not hesitate to tell you on which points I agree with the social republicans and on which I disagree with revolutionary republicans.'

" 'Are not all of you in agreement?'

" 'Our hope is the same, Madame, but the means each wants to use are different. Some speak of decapitation and dividing properties; those are the ignorant and the insane. It may seem surprising to you that I do not use stronger words to qualify them; it is not necessary. They are neither feared nor to be feared; they believe that they are way ahead and yet they are quite backward; they date from 1793 and we are in 1832. The government makes a pretense of dreading them but it would be very sorry if they did not exist because their theories form the quiver from which the government takes its arms. These are not republicans: they are *"republiqueurs."* Some others forget that France is the eldest sister of all nations; they do not remember that her past is rich in tradition and they look upon the Swiss, English, and American constitutions for the one that would best apply to our country; these are the dreamers and the utopians. Completely absorbed in their armchair theories, they do not perceive, in their imaginary applications, that the constitution of a people can be durable only if it is born from its geographical location, that it comes with its national traits, that it harmonizes with its customs. The result is that, as there are not two peoples under heaven with identical geographical location, with identical nationality and customs, the more perfect a constitution is, the more it is individual and less applicable to a locality other than where it was born. These people are not republicans, they are *"republiquinistes."*

" 'Many others believe that an opinion is clothed with a severe mullet-blue coat, a vest with large lapels, a flying cravat, and a pointed hat; those are the parodists and the barkers; they cause riots but are very careful not to join them. They build barricades and let others be killed behind them; they compromise their friends and go into hiding, as if they were compromised themselves. Those are not yet republicans; those are the *"republiquets."*

" 'But there are others, Madame, for whom the honor of France is holy and untouchable, others for whom the word given is a sacred unbreakable commitment from the King to his people. This vast and noble fraternity stretches to all countries that suffer and all the nations that awaken; they went to pour their blood in Belgium, in Italy, and in Poland and they came back to be killed or made prisoners in the Saint-Merri cloister; those, Madame, are the puritans and the martyrs. A day will come when not only the prison doors will open for those who are captives but when the bodies of those who are now dead will be sought and graves will be built for them; all that can be reproached to them is that they were ahead of their times, were born thirty years too early; those, Madame, are true republicans.'

" 'I have no need to ask you,' the Queen told me, 'if you belong to the last group.'

" 'Alas! Madame,' I answered, 'I cannot honestly boast of that honor; yes, certainly all my sympathy goes out to the latter, but instead of letting my feelings carry me off, I call on my reason; I wanted to do for politics what Faust did for science, go deep and touch the bottom. I have remained a year immersed in the abyss of the past; I went with an instinctive opinion; I came out with a reasoned conviction. I saw that the revolution of 1830 had made us take a definite step forward, but this step had taken us simply from the aristocratic monarchy to the bourgeois monarchy and the bourgeois monarchy was an era we had to live through before arriving at a more popular structure of government. Since, Madame, without doing anything to get closer to a government from which I have distanced myself, I ceased to be its enemy; I quietly watch it proceed into its era, the end of which I probably will not see. I applaud the good it does; I protest what is bad; but all this with no enthusiasm and no hatred; I neither accept it nor reject it; I endure it. I do not look at it as a form of happiness but I believe it a necessity.' "

September 19: "Neufchatel. Visited the island of Saint-Pierre, Rousseau's room, a small, square room lighted on the south by a window opening on the lake of Bienne. Thirteen straw chairs, two tables, a chest of drawers, a bed, a desk painted in white, a stove made of green faïence, walls covered with the names of Jean-Jacques' admirers."

September 23: "Left the Hôtel de la Poste at Marigny at six in the morning. Three days before my sojourn here an ambushed hunter was killed by a wounded bear. Did the *'biftek'* I was served come from this bear?"

September 29: "Chamonix in the black of night. Excursion to the Cross of Flegère and to the sea of ice. At dinner, Jacques Balmat, an intrepid guide, told how he conquered Mont-Blanc.

"Left Chamonix on the morning of the thirtieth, return by the Tete-Noire . . . half way on the road one meets a stone shaped like an enormous mushroom whose stem rests on the earth and whose umbrella top presses on one side of the mountain and on the other side it hangs over the road and forms an arch; an inscription informs the passerby that this stone belongs, full title, to a young lady and an English Lord who bought it in equal shares. Their arms, surmounted with the coronet of a count, used to ornament the property but, as it seems that bronze is valuable in Savoy, their armorial plaque was removed. Our guide told us that the same English couple had bought two pine trees near Sierre, and as we showed our surprise at this peculiarity, he told us that they were lovers who had thus consecrated the resting places where they had stopped— but not always because of fatigue.

"Twelve shelters are dispersed along the road to provide help to travelers during the winter. It is there that in winter, in the middle of a stable or rather an apartment ninety feet long by thirty-five feet wide, that seventy horses can find shelter and food, while in front of the gothic fireplace thirty people can sit and warm up. The fireplace throws the needed heat into this immense building whose roof is held up by two larch beams, eighteen inches wide and fifty feet long. . . ."

From Isola Bella, on Lac Majeur, on October third, Alexandre sent a note to his mother:

> This trip will have been very useful for my health which you saw was so frail and which is now excellent, then useful also for the literary work which all during the winter will permit me to avoid working on the dramas which tire me so much. We are in a very beautiful country and under a very beautiful sky; if you were here with us, we would stay all winter. Adieu, dear Maman, keep yourself well so that I find you again fat and gay.

He spent happy days on Lake Maggiore, then resumed his trip. Very rapidly he visited the north of Italy: Milan, Pavie and its Cartesian monastery, and Turin.

Once the trip ended, the album was closed. It is possible that Alexandre, as he had planned, also stopped at Marseille before reaching Paris.

The cholera was considered extinct. The macabre balance sheet totaled 18,402 deaths. After his three months' vacation, Alexandre hastened to get the news: Harel was making a long face. In spite of changes and cuts, *Le Fils de l'émigré* had held the stage for only nine days. It was a flop, the most bitter yet for the previously unbowed Alexandre, but the Porte-Saint-Martin had great expectations from the adaptation of the historic scene Dumas had published in the January issue of *La Revue des deux mondes*. Anicet Bourgeois and Lockroy had worked well. The cast was brilliant. Moreover, the catastrophe of *Le Fils de l'émigré* was only a half-disaster; the everlasting *Tour de Nesle* had gone back into service. A steady income producer, that play!

Paris was bustling as usual. With Ida managing to be fired from the Palais-Royal, the political undercurrents, the trapped Duchesse de Berry, Antwerp besieged, attempts against Louis-Philippe's life . . . Alexandre, the tireless walker charging along the mountain peaks, had forgotten everything. There was also Laure, who, worried about the income paid to her by her ex-lover, wanted to get a certificate as a librarian, "to provide," she said, "her young son with a profitable occupation." Alexandre intervened with the Director of Libraries. There was, too, Victor Hugo who was preparing for the performances of *Le Roi s'amuse*, but Alexandre's absence had opened the way to Parisian slanders and Hugo gave Alexandre a cold shoulder. Harel had proposed that Dumas write a new drama. Alexandre refused. Drama tired him too much; he wanted to expand his talent in other directions. His historic scenes were very successful with the readers of *La Revue des deux mondes*. He wrote three new ones which appeared in the December fifteenth issue. But mostly he went back to the great work he had drafted before leaving for Switzerland—*Gaule et France*. He had researched chronicles. An idea, or rather a desire, was germinating, limitless, as all his desires were at first: to compose a series of novels that would spread over the reign of Charles VI to the contemporary scene. In this panorama, *Gaule et France* would be the gateway of this work: how Gaul became France. At the end of 1832, Dumas wrote little, but he read the *Lettres sur l'histoire de France* by Augustin Thierry and the *Études Historiques* by Chateaubriand. He took notes, he imagined a majestic series of novels which would teach history to the people, which would show the inevitable trend of this history toward liberty and fraternity. His career as a man of letters would not be a mere preface to a career in politics, for politics was forbidden him. Rather the man of letters would be the political man. Insurrection did not lead to anything, except to mass killing of the insurgents. The time had come to educate the people.

Dumas' triumphant plays filled up his cash-box. He could support his four households: his mother, Laure Labay and his son, Belle and her little girl, and Ida, without prostituting his talent. He wanted to abandon the theater before the theater abandoned him. The failure of *Le fils de l'emigré* was a warning, as was the fate of Hugo's *Le Roi s'amuse*, stopped after the second performance by a reestablished censorship.

Antaeus had touched Earth. In Switzerland Alexandre had again found the strength necessary to attempt new projects. This was the price of survival.

II

Balls, Duels, and Litigations

W hen the public violence died out, it made way for private furor. With no more barricades or insurrections, deeply hostile to the new regime which had stolen their revolution from them, the republicans confronted another disillusioned party, the legitimists who were mourning their King like widowers. To Louis-Philippe's great enjoyment, the vanquished tore one another apart. Betrayed by Deutz, the Duchesse de Berry was arrested on November 6, 1832, at Nantes by Général Dermoncourt, who was once the companion of Général Dumas in Egypt. The royalist newspapers screeched loudly against the inhumane treatment inflicted on the Princess. Was she not imprisoned in the gloomy fortress of Blaye? Already Eugène Briffault, writer for *Le Corsaire*, had been challenged to a duel and had paid with a wound for his reply to the royalist editor of *Le Revenant*. Preliminary skirmishes increased when it was heard that physicians had been sent to Blaye. Did it mean that the Duchess's health had worsened? Could it not rather be a pregnancy? insinuated *Le Corsaire*. The legitimists sent at once a collective challenge to the editors. The republican newspapers supported their colleague, *Le National*'s Armand Carrel, who had been included in the collective challenge.

A collective duel? Alexandre would join, too. There was a crowd at Carrel's door, but Alexandre's name gained him access to Carrel, to whom he confessed that he would fight only because of his republican allegiance although he found their cause ridiculous. Carrel took him to a drawing room where they put on their fencing masks, took their foils, practiced a few thrusts. The evident anger in Carrel's attack was dangerous! Even if he had no intention of accepting the collective challenge, Carrel had singled out his own adversary in a list of names: it was Roux-Laborie.

On February second, Alexandre was a very busy man. In the morning, Carrel's duel took place near the island Saint-Ouen. It was a short, quick action. At the third pass the adversaries lunged at the same time. Carrel's foil went through Roux-Laborie's arm, but Carrel himself received a grave wound in the groin. Alexandre ran to *Le National* where M. de Beauterne, nervous and excited, wanted to be included in the list of republican duelists who would avenge Carrel at all costs. But the list was filled up. All right, so he would challenge Alfred Nettement of *La Quotidienne*. He wrote his challenge at Alexandre's apartment. To make a full measure, Alexandre believed he himself had to challenge a legitimist—his friend Alcide-Hyacinthe du Bois de Beauchesne, ex-head of the office of Sosthene de La Rochefoucauld—who at that time was in the country, which made the encounter more uncertain. In the evening, Alexandre was at the Porte-Saint-Martin, where Victor Hugo attempted to compete with *La Tour de Nesle* by showing one of those "fables of the people" which "are the reality of the poet," *Lucrèce Borgia*. The play was short; Harel had the idea of preceding it with a farce. The "Jeunes-France" stamped their feet, protested, clamored for the drama. The curtain was quickly lowered, then immediately went up again on the poisonings, the adulteries, the sinister monks that Victor Hugo had put on the stage.

The students and young painters were delirious. They waited for the author to come out of the theatre, unharnessed the horses of his cab, singing raucously while they escorted him home. In truth, it was not only as the author of *Lucrèce Borgia* that he was thus acclaimed, but also as that of *Le Roi s'amuse* which had been censored by the government. Literature was really a political arm, the only weapon that Hugo could use at that time.

The duelists had lost all restraint: cries of hatred filled the newspapers, grave and lugubrious witnesses went back and forth to arrange encounters. The government paternally put an end to this restlessness by arresting the belligerents. Only Beauterne was still able to stick his épée into Nettement's arm—in a duel on February 4, 1833. Carrel was recuperating—"Tout-Paris" was at his door and left calling cards. Alexandre visited Carrel, that republican martyr, who, when his convalescence had ended, paid his first social visit to Roux-Laborie, his adversary. Once Carrel had cooled his head, his duel seemed to him slightly laughable. In his newspaper he printed an open letter which ended the frenzy. Alexandre did not have to fight Beauchesne and was relieved. These sudden misdirected hatreds became ludicrous when *Le Moniteur* printed a declaration from the Duchesse de Berry announcing that she had been secretly married in Italy and that she was very much pregnant. Being a princess did not make her less of a woman.

Alexandre had abandoned the theater. He wanted to prove that he was a writer of prose who could seduce with his verve and talent without having recourse to the extremes of dramaturgy. Buloz had offered to publish his trip to Switzerland in *La Revue des deux mondes*. Would it be an historic subject? Geographic? Artistic? Anecdotic? Dumas was not a man who could limit himself; it would be all of this together. However, to rejuvenate a worn-out genre it would be also an epic of the self in a new setting: *Impressions de voyage*, an affirmation of subjectivity. Dumas had opened his album and, without worrying about the chronological order, chose to give to *La Revue* some articles which were already semi-polished: first, *Une Pêche de nuit* (February 15, 1833); then *Un Bifteck d'ours*, the *Col de Balme*, *Jacques Balmat* (March 15), *Le Mont Saint-Bernard* (May 1). It was like beginning a trip with its ending. Buloz was enchanted—the *Impressions de voyage* had brought him new subscribers.

Paris had forgotten insurrections and cholera. On February eighteenth there was a ball at the Tuileries. The republicans were, of course, not invited, nor were the young romantics. The guests were only those doctrinaires who were as arrogant as morticians. It was necessary to show the universe that France, republican, romantic, and alive, could still triumph over the sumptuous yet dull festivities of Louis-Philippe. "Why don't you give a ball?" Bocage had asked Alexandre. A ball, or rather a counter-ball, a nose thumbed at the bourgeois monarchy. The idea bounced around and all the illustrious people of the arts promised to come, but the Rue Saint-Lazare accommodations were too small. It happened that there was on the same landing an empty, undecorated apartment. The owner agreed to give it to Alexandre, who trusted his artist-painter friends with the decoration. Ciceri, decorator for the Théâtre-Français and the Opéra, would stretch his canvas on the walls and bring brushes, rules, and paints. The invitations were sent: "M. Alex. Dumas asks M. . . . to do him the honor of coming to spend the evening at his home, Saturday, March thirtieth. Costume strictly required. We will meet at ten o'clock, Rue Saint-Lazare, No. 40." Two hundred? Three hundred? Supper should be served to this large gathering of people. Alexandre obtained a permit to hunt in the forest of Ferté-Vidame. The supper would feature venison. His hunting bag came back full and splendid. Alexandre called Chevet the caterer and proposed a barter: three deer against a thirty-pound salmon, a deer against a giant galantine. The three last deer would be roasted whole by the caterer.

The rooms were heated to dry the canvas. The painters climbed on chairs, stools, and double ladders. They laughed, they chatted. They were still young and had talent.

And Delacroix? "Don't worry," he said, "I will come at lunchtime." He didn't take off his little black morning coat. He did not roll up his sleeves or cuffs. He took a charcoal crayon and sketched in four strokes a horse, then a horseman, a landscape, and dead, dying, and fleeing soldiers: *Le Roi Rodrigue après la bataille.*

While the canvas dried, Chevet's employees began to set the tables. Three hundred bottles of Bordeaux were warming up, three hundred bottles of Bourgogne were cooling off, five hundred bottles of champagne were on ice.

Alexandre and Belle were in their bedroom putting on their costumes. A 1525 costume for Alexandre: pale green jerkin brocaded with gold; the shirt front laced with gold, tied to the shoulders and with matching golden lace at the elbows; silk short pants, half red, half white; velvet shoes embroidered with gold. For a long time he contemplated himself in the mirror: his hair, shaped and hanging to his shoulder, was held by a circlet of gold. Belle had fitted a starched collar on her black velvet dress; she was fitting a large black felt hat with black feathers on her beautiful brown hair. She was so beautiful! Why was it that Alexandre loved her less?

The two orchestras were settling down little by little, one in each of the two apartments. Alexandre welcomed the guests, who were all in costume. There were the sculptors, represented by Barye as a Bengal tiger; the musicians, with Rossini as Figaro; the painters, with Alfred Johannot as young Louis XI, Louis Boulanger as a courtier of King Jean, Delacroix as Dante. Among the writers, Paul de Musset came as a Russian. The publishers offered Ladvocat as Henry II. To mingle with this company of artists, society women had been permitted to wear masks.

In a shimmer of colors, quadrilles were organized. The music could hardly be heard over the brouhaha of conversation and laughter. Cigar smoke danced lazily in the light of the oil lamps. Some very grave men came in domino—multicolored for Eugène Sue, black for Odilon Barot, exprefect of the Seine. Little by little, as their theater performances ended, the singers and actors of Paris arrived: Mlles. Mars and Firmin in their costumes of *Henri III et sa cour*; Mlle. George as a shepherdess; Bocage as Didier from *Marion Delorme*; Cornelie Falcon as Rebecca; Nourrit as an abbé of the Court.

The apartments looked like a Champs-Elysées where a collection of historical and literary heroes of all times and all countries had gathered at once. Gracious actresses made a garland of women around La Fayette, who had donned a domino. Simple, gentle, smart, gallant, the revolutionary of two worlds was the king of the feast. He was the embodiment of the republicans. He sat at a table to play "écarté" against Bois de Beauchesne, disguised as a Vendéen. "By what privilege are you the only one here not in disguise?" asked the old republican of the young legitimist.

Wine poured in steady streams, and the dancers were caught in a sarabande. Youth, beauty, pleasure, this ball in the middle of carnival appeared as a silky and bright lining for the gloomy, dull, and lugubrious mantle that enveloped the France of Louis-Philippe. Who was disguised as a sick man? It was M. Tissot, of the Académie Française, chased by a mortician who followed each step and insisted every five minutes, "I am waiting." They had supper at three o'clock in the morning in the two bedrooms of the empty apartment made into a dining room. The flowers began to wilt and fade. In spite of her duties as a hostess, Belle had noticed that Alexandre took in his arms for a waltz a luscious blonde young woman who was masked. Too luscious to be a woman of society, she was the specter at the end of Belle's love affair. Ida, of course! The ball had started again, the dances languished—it was nine o'clock the next morning. Led by the orchestras, the dancers came out on the Rue des Trois-

Frères in a last gallop whose head reached the boulevard while the tail still wriggled on the Square Saint-Lazare.

Two important figures were missing from the list of guests: Victor Hugo and Alfred de Vigny. Vigny, whose image had been painted by Nanteuil on the panel of the doors, was at the bedside of his mother who had suffered a paralytic stroke.

But why didn't Alexandre list Victor Hugo among his guests? Most probably Hugo had brought his masked Juliette to this supreme feast of romanticism triumphant, but Alexandre, tactfully thinking of Adele Hugo, refrained from identifying his friend.

And with this ball *Mes Mémoires* ends, as if very suddenly the memory refused to persist further. Was it by chance? Or rather a refusal to relate to 1833 and those days of calumny, slander, and raillery—those days when friendship, which had once been sworn for eternity, faded because of minor differences.

Artistic and literary Paris was one big village of which *La Revue des deux mondes* was figuratively the steeple. Alfred de Vigny loved Marie Dorval, who was a devoted friend of George Sand, who had just broken off with Jules Sandeau.

Marie Dorval was attracted to Alexandre and wrote to Sainte-Beuve:

By the way, thinking of it, I do not want you to bring me Alfred de Musset. He is very much a dandy; we would not suit each other and I was more curious than really interested in seeing him. I think it is imprudent to satisfy all of one's curiosities and better to obey only one's first inclination. Instead of him, pray, bring me Dumas in whose art I have found both a soul and talent. He has shown the same desire to meet me as you have. So you have only to mention a word from me; but come with him the first time because first times are always fatal for me.

With dull colors Sainte-Beuve painted for her the picture of a liaison with this Dumas who was already wearing out two or three mistresses. The soul of Dumas that Marie Dorval had discovered inhabited too passionate a body. George Sand threw herself at Prosper Mérimée one April evening; it was a disappointment and a fiasco. Alexandre, not personally used to these accidents, had a witty comment: "Prosper Mérimée is five feet, five thumbs. . . ." He was still laughing at a dinner offered on June nineteenth to the collaborators of *La Revue des deux mondes*. Buloz, Gustave Planche, George Sand and Dumas were around the table. What joke did Alexandre dare? George Sand nearly choked with rage, "He insulted my honor," she stormed. Gustave Planche, her knight-in-waiting, took her home and fanned her anger. We must, they decided, get this insolent Dumas to retract his offensive words. On the twenty-first Dumas was peacefully standing in the garden of *La Revue des deux mondes*, when suddenly and theatrically, George Sand pounced down upon him. She demanded reparations. A man does not fight with the weaker sex and moreover, "Madame, when a woman comes, accompanied by a man, to demand explanations, it makes the man responsible for the consequences. I am ready to make responsible the man who accompanied you but he does not want to face me, he even turns his back to me. Otherwise, I would willingly fight a duel with him." Gustave Planche was on the first floor. Bitterly, George repeated to him this new insult. "I will come down," he boasted chivalrously, but soon he allowed himself to be calmed by Buloz and, once George Sand had left, his ardor fell little by little.

George Sand was not pleased. She scolded Marie Dorval and pardoned her indiscretion. She spread bitter tales about Alexandre. Planche, on his side, had not digested the insulting words of Dumas. But as he suffered from an eye infection, he had to ask a friend to write a public demand of reparation.

Alexandre replied graciously, even made a show of gentlemanly manners (he was, remember, the grandson of the Marquis de la Pailleterie), and chose his seconds. Planche had asked six questions for Dumas to answer "clearly, in writing, and with his signature." "Ridiculous," commented the seconds. In his first excitement, he had gone too far, he would like to withdraw. Alexandre, the good sport, opened a way for him to retreat.

There is only one condition under which I will admit that I was wrong to say what I said; that since you are not Mme. G. Sand's lover, you cannot be responsible either for her past remarks or her future remarks.

The coward, Gustave Planche, could now take care of his eyes in peace. The case was closed, but the gossip was just beginning. "Sainte-Beuve told me all about the looseness of Mme. Dudevant [George Sand] who had given herself to Mérimée. During a meal she was insulted by Dumas who was supposed to fight a duel over it with Planche. To scotch the rumor, Dumas asked that Planche declare officially that he was not Mme. Dudevant's lover." (from the journal of Charles Didier, June 28)

"You know that the Planche/Dumas affair has been settled, as it was easy to foresee. Planche has denied, in writing, that he was Madame Sand's lover (which I consider to be a cowardly lie since they live together) and Dumas then replied that if such were the case, he had been wrong." (Letter from Bixio to Bocage, August 5, 1833.) "Planche had almost fought a duel with Dumas about Mme. D[udevant], which is all slightly ridiculous and slightly scandalous and to Planche's obvious disadvantage, although Dumas was certainly wrong." (Sainte-Beuve to Victor Pavie, July 13)

Though life seemed a patchwork of insane follies, Dumas obstinately pursued work in the midst of quarrels. Besides *Gaule et France*, which promised to bring him recognition as a serious author, he was taking advantage of current circumstances. He had started a publishing business with Buloz. Général Dermoncourt had arrested the Duchesse de Berry at Nantes and the General was an ex-comrade-in-arms of Général Dumas. Why shouldn't Alexandre collect Général Dermoncourt's remembrances in a book? It promised to be a great success. The salons of the noble quarters and the chateaux, cold to the new régime, would provide the most natural buyers. The General and Dumas spent long evenings together. Narrated by a republican general, written by a republican author, this tale of the misfortunes of a legitimate princess became an act of opposition. The new regime was shown as capable, certainly, but with none of the chivalrous virtues which honored the French tradition. Was it not a traitor, a Jewish renegade, who helped to trap the princess? This Judas did not appear by name, but kept the lion's share of the spoil.

In the meantime, spurred by his collaborator Anicet Bourgeois and probably even more by Ida, who wanted a prominent part, Dumas put together a new drama: *L'Échelle des femmes*. Bocage asked him why he had not offered it to the Théâtre-Français. On July 28, 1832 he responded:

The first reason is that the rehearsals I have just finished there exasperated me more than ever before and made me swear that it would not see either my prose or my verses for a very long time. The second reason is that Mlle. Mars leaves in the month of June; I do not know anyone who would take her part. The third is that Anicet was so fearful of losing *Térésa* that he tormented me every day to finish with Harel who would only take on *Térésa* on the condition that he might have *L'Échelle*. He came twice with the contract for me to sign.

The summer of 1833 arrived, and with it the usual exodus of townspeople from the city. Alexandre took care of his pressing affairs, then took the road to Dauphine, probably leaving Belle in Paris. It was their first separation, and a portent of the final abandonment. He was invited to stay at Vizille by Edmond Badon, author of *Un Duel sous Richelieu*. Badon's father and mother were enchanted with this big eccentric Parisian who left behind him a trail of gaiety. Badon's sisters and other society ladies were not insensitive either, especially the gracious and melancholic Henriette de Bremont. Alexandre rediscovered the delights of long walks on the slopes of the Alps. It is probable that there he finished *L'Échelle des femmes*, which he had already rebaptized *Angèle*, and he ended the seventh part of his *Impressions de voyage (La Mer de Glace)*. He even thought of broadening his *Impressions* to include the relation of Dom Julien's ascension of Mount Aiguille and the story of the Emperor's entrance into Grenoble, taken from Colonel Edouard Ney's eyewitness account. Alexandre almost succeeded in forgetting the clouds that were gathering. He had read a pamphlet in *L'Europe litteraire* by Granier de Cassagnac who, under the pretense of reviewing *Gaule et France*, violently accused Dumas of being a shameless plagiarist. Dumas would have to take care of his enemies when he returned to Paris. Granier de Cassagnac was a protégé of Victor Hugo who had helped him join the *Journal des débats*. Alexandre was not worried by the venom of the scribbler, but by what he sensed as the betrayal of a friend.

At this time Hugo was resting at the Roches, guest of the owner of the *Débats*, known as Bertin l'Aîné. In the sweetness of the Chevreuse Valley, Hugo was troubled only by his host, who had brought to his famous writer the galley proofs of a literary column he wanted to print. The author was Granier de Cassagnac. For

Hugo, who smiled with pleasure, there was exalted praise; for Dumas, only ferocious hostility.

Granier had expanded his article of *L'Europe Litteraire*. According to him, Dumas was a vile plagiarist who only had a talent for borrowing from Walter Scott, Schiller, and Lope de Vega. Victor Hugo did not admit, even to himself, that he was not sorry for this trashing of a friend. Had not Dumas sometimes claimed that he was Hugo's equal? Hugo preferred vassals to friends. Yet, perhaps in a gesture of friendship, he advised against the publication of the article. Moreover, it would be also against his interest. It would be dangerous to outrage Dumas when Hugo's *Marie Tudor*, just finished, would be on stage before long. Dumas' help and his trusty friends were not to be neglected. The article was put in reserve. Bertin himself would give the authorization to publish.

Alexandre was back in Paris at the beginning of October. *La Vendée et Madame* was published—eighteen hundred copies were sold in eight days; a second edition was on the press. After Victor Hugo's *Marie Tudor* at the Porte-Saint-Martin would come *Angèle*. "It will be a good winter, I believe, for literature; there is at present a real reaction to art," Alexandre confided to Edmond Badon. He had not returned to the Rue Saint-Lazare; he had left that apartment to Belle until the time she would leave on a tour. He went back to his bachelor routine, living in furnished rooms. Ida lived in the Rue Lancry. She was happy for Harel had engaged her for the title role of *Angèle*.

But Dumas' world was hardly an idyllic scene—not with Harel's flair for publicity. The scandal of *La Tour de Nesle* had served him well. He knew how to manipulate the strings of puppet authors. On November first, he wrote: "Very soon *Marie Tudor*; coming attraction, *Angèle*." That clearly suggested the failure of Hugo's play. Victor foamed at the mouth. Since it had come to that, since Dumas had without a doubt his part in this infamy, let Cassagnac's article be printed! It appeared! Deeply saddened, Alexandre wrote to Hugo:

Today [November 1] the article was brought to me to read and I must admit that I do not understand that, since you are so close to M. Bertin, an article about me was accepted without it being first shown to you; therefore I am convinced that you knew about this article.

What could I say to you, my friend, if not that I would never have allowed, especially on the eve of the performance of one of my plays, an article to appear in a newspaper on which I had the influence you have with *Les Débats*, against—I would not say my rival—but my friend.

Consolation did not come from Victor Hugo, who took pleasure in creating ambiguities:

[November 2] There are many more facts against me, my dear Dumas, than you guessed or than you supposed. The author of the article is one of my friends; it is I who urged his employment at the *Débats*. The article had been shown to me by M. Bertin Aîné at the Roches, about six weeks ago. Those are the facts against me. As for the facts in my favor, I will not write them to you in detail; I want . . . to let you suppose or guess them.

Victor Hugo

Alexandre hated this quarrel which, however, brought him the sympathy of most people. Dumas stabbed in the back by his dearest friend! Everybody was eager to rub salt in the wound. Harel understood where his own interest lay; the public was behind Dumas and also behind Harel. He did not hide his disapproval to Hugo and did not bring to the production of *Marie Tudor* all the care it needed. Mlle. George, who had reacted badly to Ida's engagement, took Hugo's side. The cabal mushroomed. On the evening of the premiere of *Marie Tudor*, the audience violently demonstrated their hostility to Hugo: the final scene was booed from beginning to end, and when the traditional announcement was made, the author's name was booed again. Juliette Drouet (Hugo's mistress, who had a role in the play) who had been blamed, in part, for the failure of the play, was very upset and called in sick the next day. The theater had to post "no performance tonight." As a substitute for Mlle. Drouet, there was only the new member of the Porte-Saint-Martin company: Ida. All during that day, November seventh, Alexandre made his mistress rehearse the part of Jane. He was not detached enough to be amused by this reversal of situations.

He had been present at the premiere. The equivocation of Victor Hugo, even if it had satisfied one of his baser emotions, had deeply affected him. He knew that any blow that struck one romantic wounded all the group. During those tempestuous days he tried to find a means of reconciliation. To Hugo, who wanted to defend himself by publishing the letter he had sent to Dumas (and which the latter denied receiving), Alexandre wrote:

> Victor, a last word of advice, advice not from a previous friend but from a true friend; Victor, do not publish your letter. It will destroy you. How do you expect to disown the article when it will be known that the author is one of your friends; that you had sponsored him for the *Débats* and that you had knowledge of the article two months before? It will be thought that you had delayed it, so that it arrived on the eve of the day your play opened. It will be wondered how you did not have enough influence over a man you sponsored at the *Débats* to stop his pen; or, supposing that this influence did not exist, how was it that you did not warn me?

Alexandre was quite ready to forgive but he had to deal with Hugo's immense pride. Hugo, who preferred to trample on a friendship rather than admit that he was wrong, who refused to confess that, in his anger, he had allowed this article to appear, and worse, had consented to its publishing. He had his letter and that of Dumas printed in *L'Europe littéraire*, the November fourteenth issue. He pushed Garnier de Cassagnac to write in *Les Débats* a denial of all Victor Hugo's participation in this controversy. It was a complete falling out, but there was no hatred on Alexandre's side, only an incurably sad nostalgia.

When friendship fails, love alone can fill the emptiness. Ida was now his and he had offered her a theater engagement that would very soon be a leading part. He judged they were even for the time being. Love for him, in that month of December 1833, had the expressive face and eyes of Marie Dorval. "Not beautiful. Worse," said Victor Hugo. But had not Marie a husband, Merle, nicknamed the "white merle" because of his legitimist allegiances? And had she not a lover, more official than her husband, Alfred de Vigny, who had started her on the way of regeneration and virtue? Yes, Marie had all that and above all a whimsical sensuality. She had always been attracted to Alexandre, and their familiarity as neighbors had made them closer. Alexandre had left the Rue Saint-

Lazare, but not with the hope of possessing Marie, who was so much like him that their love was almost incestuous. They were so good together and so free, too. Marie came back from Le Havre where she had acted in *Antony*. During her absence Merle had signed, in her name, a contract on November 1 with the Comédie-Française. Was it possible to imagine Marie not being cast in *Antony*?

Dumas also signed a contract. *Antony* would become a part of the repertoire at the Comédie. Alexandre would write a comedy and a tragedy for the theater and, by an addendum to Marie's contract, her debut at the Comédie would be in *Antony*. In the middle of these many transactions, Alexandre and Marie became attracted to one another. A wrist was touched, a kiss given, but they had to be careful, Alfred and Ida were jealous. To live this kind of love was also to know the taste of betrayal. For the first time Marie knew the feeling of being an adulteress. "It is not right," she said, "to deceive a love so strong and so whole; and Alfred is your brother in art." Alexandre and Marie knew that their good intentions would not hold against their inclinations. Even the scruples were delicious.

Louise, Marie's chambermaid, a true soubrette of comedy, was tolerant of the wayward ways of her mistress. She knew how to maneuver the encounters so that the husband (Merle) and M. le Vicomte (de Vigny) did not suspect anything. When Merle was away, Alexandre came to spend the night at 44 Rue Saint-Lazare. It was probably with his head on Marie's bosom that he gave his last touches to *Angèle*. *Marie Tudor* was badly received and held the stage for so short a time that Harel was prompted to put Dumas' play in rehearsal. Alexandre began to love life again and to fight. What better way to reply to Garnier de Cassagnac than to publish in the December 1833 issue of *La Revue des deux mondes*, simply and humbly, the story of his life and of his plays, under the title, "How I Became a Dramatic Author." But Marie was not there to help him. She had to fulfill her contracts with the theater of Rouen. "As soon as *Angèle* closes, I will go to meet you," Alexandre had promised. In the meantime he swamped her with letters. She answered, adopting the style of her theatrical parts:

[Rouen, December 27 and 28, 1833. Friday]
Oh! it is not by defiance that I do not write to you. No, my God! But it is that in an instant I was put into a terrible

position that I have not the audacity to hold. No, Alexandre, no, I could not; if I were not loved as I am, as you know it, this deception would not be as revolting as it is to me; but to receive so many marks of attachment, of trust, and to have a secret such as we have created is awful.

I dared to give myself to you; I dare not write to you because I do not dare to think. One is very much alone when one writes and to betray, I need the two of us. Even then I don't know; when we are together, we are so good that all takes a kind of childishness; it does not seem that we are very guilty. You, no; but I have no excuse. And if you were told this about another woman, you would despise her! Fortunately, and that is what saves me, our friendship is stronger than our love. It is friendship, believe it well, that you have for me; the constraint under which we have to live has given our relationship some of the characteristics of love: you have become my lover because we had to hide to see one another.

[Saturday]

You really will come? You really want to come? To begin the year thus will bring us bad luck. The love I have for you cannot ease my heart because fear takes all the space. Will you chase it away? Tell me. I do not believe so! Do come, since you want it, come and let it be an adieu since I cannot be your mistress any longer. As for you, remember that you did not want it. You said that you would be too jealous. That you would not deceive him, and it was for one time only . . . one time! You asked me what would assure our friendship for always. What do you want now? You speak to me only of love and what future is there in this love? Do not write me anymore, I pray you! Your morning letter never comes alone. It is awful, I assure you. Come to speak to me, to understand me as a friend, to reassure me, me who never in my life has had a remorse and who believed that it existed only in a poet's imagination! It is very true, however, and I would love you well but with all my soul if you could cure this illness. When arriving at the hotel, send me a short note and I will come to meet you. But do not come to my door. My chambermaid is here, very near to me and in the evening she takes my key. It must be me who goes to meet you.

. . . Burn this letter, if you love me, burn it, take away from

me this worry that you might lose it . . . or that it could be
found upon you.

Marie

On this same December 28, at the Porte-Saint-Martin, *Angèle*
was played. Gabrielle-Anne Cisterne du Poilloue de Saint Mars
had a loge seat. She remembered:

The great talent of Dumas is mostly to move souls; one does
not worry about the means; one cries and one is happy. This
young girl, betrayed, abandoned [Angèle] has sublime accents
of pain.
. . . It was audacious to put on the stage this pregnant girl
whose time of delivery was approaching; when Mlle. Ida came
on stage, covered with her ample coat, there was a kind of
shivering amongst the audience. Some censors tried to murmur; the enthusiasts made them remain silent.
Mlle. Ida began to get fat; she was so pretty she was forgiven.
Angèle is her best part; she was very good in it. She cannot
be ranked as a talented actress although she is very intelligent.
Her voice was not pleasant; her pronunciation was faulty.

Nobles and commoners alike cried and applauded the actors as
well as Dumas. The young men—students, painter-apprentices—
"Jeune-France," applauded, too, but against Hugo. Lost and anonymous in that throng, was Belle, sad-eyed, rejected, unhappy. Before going on with her vagabond life she had to settle the sinister
account of the breaking off. She wrote Dumas on January 2, 1834:

I have only a few days to remain in Paris and I was very
anxious to speak with you before my departure which is fixed
between the 6th and the 8th of this month. I am moving out;
this keeps me occupied and I could not go to your home,
where, anyway, I will not find you.
. . . I ask you to send me the month's allowance for the little
girl; you know that it's due on the first and this man [the
nurse's husband] comes Friday morning. If you can manage
it, you might do me the pleasure of giving me, too, 350 francs.
You know, I have to borrow for the rent and I would not want
to leave while owing that amount; you have time for that until

the 6th. Believe me, Alex, that it embarrasses me to ask you for this money. If you want to come to see me I will be home today from 5 to 8 o'clock, or tomorrow at the same time. I do not need to tell you all the happiness I have had to see your great success, although, perched in a loge in the gallery.

Your friend, Mélanie Serre.

But the "true leader of the new dramatic school" was at that time swooping down upon Rouen in a mail-coach. The sound of his triumph had already reached Marie, who waited for him, split between desire and apprehension:

[Monday evening]

Since you had such great success that you were given flowers, I will send you my crown from *Antony* which heard last Thursday as much applause at your name, as at your play, and as much as the four actors received. Keep it as a double remembrance. How is it that every one here tells me of your arrival? You are insane! . . . Is it possible, do you want me to leave at once . . . and another thing: it is very unfortunate because I do not play Wednesday; yesterday evening I would have written to you to come but this morning I must tell you, come one day later. I am telling you things that I had not decided to let you read. Could you come one or two days later? It is very simple; come to the same hotel but do not come to my room. I am not locked up in it, but Josephine has the key to come in during the morning. You will send me a very short word to tell me where your room will be. I play *Henri III* Thursday for the first time. Who could play it as badly! I could not undertake *Angèle*; I have too little time. The Bordeaux business cannot be fixed; I must leave on the 15th. I am sorry to go so far; it seems to me that one can never return from there.

I send you, too, with my crown, an ugly little purse that I sewed yesterday near my fireplace. It is all I have to send you. For your ring I need your hand. . . .

Marie received Alexandre's little word. He was there, a few rooms away; a few moments later she was in his arms. Marie and Alexandre had already pressed many bodies against their own, yet they rediscovered the pleasures of love as if they were still adolescents. Alexandre was radiant. Marie, the sublime actress he had admired from his very arrival in Paris, was here beside him. He could touch her shoulder, her breasts. After three days, he left and did not write. Was he angry because Marie had told him that she was unhappy, or remorseful for deceiving Alfred or did he wait for her to return the same love he had given her at Rouen? She wrote:

> I spent my time in re-reading your adorable short letters instead of answering them. O, I love your letters! Almost as much as you . . . yes, I had thought of giving you this day and this night that you asked me. I believed it and now it cannot be. I ought to have ended my rehearsal Tuesday and I would have left Wednesday evening and I would have stayed with you Friday all day and also the entire night. I have announced my return for Saturday morning and it is impossible for me to change or to postpone.

Marie had lied. She had not returned on Saturday but on Thursday. She had put herself in the position of having to lie each day. She had slept alone. She was in despair. She had been told that Alexandre had again taken up his relationship with Ida, moreover that he was Eugénie Sauvage's lover. She quarreled with Alfred. Marie was sad and humiliated. Alexandre forgave the lie, and what is more, he accompanied her to her theatrical engagement in Bordeaux. The postcoach left at six o'clock in the evening of January 24, 1834. Alexandre was unable to board at the terminal, but did at the first stop. They had three days of intimate conversations, sweet talk and hand holding. A week of stolen happiness at Bordeaux, slightly spoiled by a swelling on poor Marie's cheek. She could not act; she belonged entirely to her Alexandre. He loved her, but he had to leave her again.

Since December, Alexandre lived at No. 30, Rue Bleu. A comfortable and elegant apartment—a bedroom with walls covered in fawn-colored silk trimmed with embroidery, a ceiling made of a single mirror, blue velvet drapes, furniture made of lemon wood, animal skins instead of rugs. He distractedly flipped through the January fifteenth issue of *La Revue des deux mondes* which featured his portrait, the one Marie had seen reproduced in *La Gazette des comédiens*:

M. Dumas . . . is one of the strangest phenomena of the present time. Passionate by disposition, shrewd by instinct, courageous by vanity, kind of heart, weak in reason, improvident in character, superstitious when he thinks, religious when he writes, skeptic when he speaks; Negro by origin and French by birth, he is light even in his most fiery ardors; his blood is made of lava; his thinking is a spark. He's the least of logicians extant, the most anti-musical man I know. A liar in his quality of poet, avid in his quality of artist, generous because he is artist and poet; too liberal in friendship, too despotic in love; vain as a woman, hard as a man, selfish as God, honest with indiscretion, obliging without discernment, forgetful to the point of carelessness, vagabond in body and soul, cosmopolitan by taste, patriotic in opinion, rich in delusions and in whims, poor in wisdom and experience, gay in spirit, slanderer in talk, witty in repartee, Don Juan at night, Alcibiades during the day, a true Proteus escaping from all and from himself, as lovable for his faults as for his qualities, more seductive for his vices than for his virtues: Such is M. Dumas, as he is loved, as he is, or at least as he appears to me at this time.

A seductive bad lot—was that the way he was seen? Marie found the portrait faithful. Alexandre felt like a prisoner of the thousands of looks focused upon him.

He and Marie had admitted that it would be better to separate to escape Alfred and Ida's inquisition and also the remorse of deceiving them, but friendship survived, stronger than this secret that bound them. The welcome Marie received at the Comédie lacked warmth; Mlle. Mars reluctantly accepted the intrusion of this queen of the boulevards, the only rival she had to fear. Marie had to return to the ranks, for she was considered an apprentice in *Antony*. All right, she would follow all the common rules, she would play the parts given to her, the Eugénie of Beaumarchais, for example. Since he attracted the public Alexandre was a power to be reckoned with; he protested in a letter to Marie Dorval:

Madame and friend:
. . . You would begin at the Théâtre-Français as a woman who has been given conditions and not as a woman who imposes her own. You would begin without triumph, for the work will

cool off your most enthusiastic friends. The next day the newspapers will say that Mme. Dorval came to the Théâtre-Français to kill herself. *Antony* raises all the questions left asleep by *Eugénie*. Combined with the admirable creation you made of the part of *Adèle*, *Antony* places you today at the celebrity level at the Théâtre-Français. In *Antony* you can be compared only to yourself and as every day you will find some new way to act, the Adèle of today will always be superior to the *Adèle* of yesterday. Do not desert. Hold on to your real part. Go back under the flag where you won all your crowns, or else—you know my contract with the Comédie-Française—I will save you in spite of yourself as those soldiers who are forced, with a sword to their backs, to walk ahead and win the cross because they have been frightened into doing it.

The affair was larger then Marie Dorval or Alexandre Dumas, himself: it was a literary question. After the great success of *Henri III et sa cour* and of *Hernani*, the romantics had abandoned the Comédie-Française where they had been considered intruders. Because of this ostracism, the Comédie-Française was barely able to survive, while the Porte-Saint-Martin triumphed. It was, therefore, necessary to go back to this temple on the Rue de Richelieu with one's head high. Alexandre threatened, both sides compromised. Marie Dorval would debut in *Une Liaison* by Empis and Mazares, but *Antony* would be put into rehearsal at once. The best French actors had agreed to play the parts. Alexandre had his revenge; the play was announced for April eighteenth.

On that same day, a Monday, young Alexandre arrived at his father's apartment with a copy of *Le Constitutionnel* in his hand. His school master had sent him as a messenger. Why *Le Constitutionnel*? Alexandre understood immediately: on the front page there was a vitriolic article by the academician Antoine Jay expressing his indignation that the subsidy of the Théâtre-Français had been increased to two hundred thousand francs—"a spirit of dizziness seems to hover above this unfortunate theater. The performance of *Antony* is officially announced for tomorrow, Monday; *Antony*, the most blatantly obscene work which has appeared in our obscene times," thundered M. Jay, who was not an ordinary journalist. He was also a deputy and Recorder of the Theatrical Budget. The classicists were gathering for their offensive. On that same day, at the Chambre des Députés, deputies threatened to abstain from voting the budget of the Théâtre-Français if *Antony* was played there. Prime Minister Thiers was not unfavorable to artistic innovation, but he could not gamble his political career on *Antony*. He reversed his decision and gave orders to stop the performance.

Roaring, Alexandre bounded over to the Ministry. If those were the facts, he would not give new plays; he would sue the Comédie before the Tribunal of Commerce. Poor Marie Dorval, "the money-pump of her family," could only protest symbolically. She sent a virgin's crown to M. Jay. It was in a box with a short letter, wrapped and tied with a white ribbon:

Sir,
Here is a crown that was thrown at my feet in *Antony*; permit me to lay it upon your head:

'I did owe you this homage.
No one knows better
How much you have deserved it.'

Irony is the last weapon of the vanquished.

During this spring of 1834, Alexandre was a constant feature of the judiciary chronicle. He had opened a suit against the Comédie-Française for breach of contract, but he was in turn attacked by Barba, the publisher, who had bought the rights for the publication of *Christine ou Stockholm, Fontainebleau et Rome* and *Henri III* without reservation. Despite that agreement Alexandre had contracted with the publisher Charpentier for an edition of his complete works. The first volume, which included *Henri III et sa cour*, and the second, *Christine*, were announced in bookstores. Barba summoned Alexandre and his new publisher before the Tribunal of Commerce.

Alexandre learned the arcane ways of justice, for he acquired a taste and became a frantic litigant. Very soon he became the principal hero of the *Gazette des tribunaux* and the Tribunal of Commerce, which initially condemned him together with Charpentier to a five-franc fine and twelve hundred francs for damages and interest and to the seizure of all copies of *Christine* and of *Henri III*. Immediately Dumas and Charpentier launched an appeal. The pending suit was sent back to the Royal Court on the twenty-eighth of June. Small newspapers dote on the judicial dealings of men in the public eye. For instance, L'Ours, a publicaton that boasted to be "a journal edited by an association of beasts," exercised its special wit:

First it is good you know one thing: M. Alexandre Dumas is a nobleman, count, viscount, or baron at least. Let's say viscount! Aside from being a nobleman, M. le Vicomte Alexandre Dumas is the worst creature you can imagine, having no worry, no care, a man of pleasure, of feasting, of throwing through the window gold, wine and women.

Alexandre did not read L'Ours but a friend showed him the article. Alexandre at once took a pen:

Your article entitled 'Alex Dumas and the Publisher Barba' fell into my hands. I accept the title of nobleman that you gave me. The weapon of a nobleman is an épée. I await you with two épées to know whether you are a knave or not.

Alexandre, the republican, could not allow his qualities as a nobleman and as an honest man to be doubted. He sent his seconds, but they were refused on the grounds that nobody knew them. Alexandre raged; he himself went to the office of the journal, thundering and threatening. He demanded satisfaction. The manager of the journal and his editors declared themselves ready to meet Dumas on the field of honor, but they asked the favor of a day's delay, time for the author of the article to make himself known and take over the responsibility for his prose.

At once ridiculous and solemn—since his life was at stake—Alexandre turned to Victor Hugo:

Victor, whatever our present relationships are, I hope you won't refuse the favor I will ask of you. I do not know the knave who personally insulted me in a miserable four-legged journal called L'Ours.

This morning he refused to come out because, he said, he did not know the name of my seconds. I am writing to de Vigny also, lest, in case he were tempted to use the same ploy, it should become a joke. I will expect you tomorrow at seven. A word to the messenger so I know that I can count on you. Moreover, this is perhaps a means for us to shake hands once more, for I do miss you.

So much repressed love under false off-handedness! Victor, whose initial anger was now spent, was not without some remorse himself and was not going to lose this opportunity. At seven o'clock in the morning he was at Alexandre's. Still, he coldly kissed his ex-friend and shook hands with the two other seconds chosen by Alexandre, Alexandre Bixio and Général Dermoncourt. In the office of the newspaper they confronted the seconds of Maurice Alhoy, who would fight the duel instead of the writer of the article, who was absent. The manager and the editors of *L'Ours*, through the mediation of the seconds, swore that "the attack was not at all directed against the character and the person of M. Alexandre Dumas." On both sides, the seconds concluded that this matter should not continue.

But Alexandre did not see it that way. He wanted to show off his strength and his courage before Victor. There would be a duel— he wanted one. On Monday, July sixth, in the early morning, with their épées ready, Alexandre and Alhoy had taken off their coats. If the venomous Jacquot de Mirecourt can be believed, this duel was fixed in advance. But Maurice Alhoy, carried away by the heat of the fight, reportedly kept so close to Alexandre that the latter cried, "But, dear friend, this is not the way it was understood." This being the only testimony that remains of this duel, it should be accepted with reservations.

Duel on the field, litigation before the court. On June thirtieth, before the Tribunal of Commerce, Dumas pleaded his case against the Comédie-Française, or rather against Thiers, "who had put *Antony* on the index without knowing anything about it, as he had admitted himself at the Chambre des Députés." Alexandre had been offered a performance of another one of his plays, but he wanted *Antony*, his favorite work and the favorite, too, of many young people who looked to Alexandre as their representative. The case was set for deliberation. On July second, the judgment on appeal of the plagiarism case by Barba against Charpentier and Dumas was rendered. The publisher and the author were condemned together, three thousand francs in damages and interest to the plaintiff! Alone, Dumas was fined one thousand francs, but the judges considered that there was no reason to confiscate the Charpentier edition of the complete works. What a relief!

During this tumult, the copies of that edition were almost all sold but Dumas' dramatic production that spring was of a very mediocre vintage: *La Vénitienne*. In spite of Mlle. George's impressive presence, it had not been much of a success on March eighteenth and was followed with twenty-two performances in March and five in April. Dumas had denied having anything to do with this drama by Anicet Bourgeois; Dumas' usual collaborator had blown open the secret when he had dedicated the book of the play to Alexandre. *Catherine Howard*, played for the first time on June second, at the Porte-Saint-Martin, was only a patchwork put together from *Édith*, a play written and refused in 1829, changed from verse to prose, transposed from the Middle Ages of Harold the Saxon to the Renaissance of Henry VIII of England. But, said Dumas, history did not matter: "*Catherine Howard* is an extra-historic drama, a work of imagination, born from my fancy; *Henri VIII* was but a nail for me on which I hung my picture." The critics remained sullen, and in his publicity, Alexandre complained that they asked of him the kind of work that he could not produce at his age, an age during which imagination takes over reason, the green years, between twenty-five and thirty-five during which one invents *Hamlet, Le Cid, Les Brigands*. Wait a while, gentlemen critics. The time will arrive, between thirty-five and forty-five, for *King Lear, Cinna, Wallenstein*! And finally, during the third age when one descends from forty-five down to fifty-five, the age of reflection is when one composes *Richard III, Polyeucte, William Tell*. Alexandre was just thirty-two, for heaven's sake! But the theatergoers, who had given an honorable welcome to Ida in spite of her flawed elocution and her voice that sounded as though she had a continual head cold, became fewer and fewer. There were but fifteen performances in June, only two in July.

Such a life would wear anyone out. The countless chicaneries which made the dearest friends disappear, the incoherent loves which, once the first sparks of pleasure doused, left a very empty heart. Of course there was Ida, who had been forgiven when she had been unfaithful with Roger de Beauvoir. But Alexandre had so much to be forgiven, himself! This fickle man, however, was sometimes as jealous as a tiger. Ida's opulent plumpness attracted some clients of a high-tone procuress who was ready to act as a go-between. Alexandre was furious: "The first time that this person sends a further proposition, she will encounter someone who will thank her with a riding whip."

The procuress took this with great arrogance:

> The virtue of this woman at No. 12, Rue de Lancy does not date back far enough for her past to be forgotten. Her private conduct is known; she does not ask your permission to make you a CUCKOLD when it pleases her; moreover, she would do well to do it more often so she would be able to pay her thirty thousand frances of debt. A jealous man is an imbecile; a CUCKOLD is a man of wit when he knows when to shut up.

His love of pleasure and his improvidence enveloped him in an insuperable disgust. Once again he was moved to leave quickly, very quickly, to break off with Paris, which corrupted those who attempt to conquer it. He would make money, then leave. Fortunately, on July fourteenth, the Comédie-Française had been condemned to pay Dumas ten thousand francs as damages and interest for not performing *Antony*. The theater manager appealed, but all was settled amiably; Dumas received six thousand francs and agreed to withdraw *Antony*. He could then leave for the Mediterranean coast as he had planned. He had asked and received a grant from the Ministry of Public Instruction, "five thousand francs ascribable to the funds to encourage education, to subsidize the expenses of the scientific trip he will undertake on the Mediterranean coast." The rest of the sum would be paid in three installments at the end of the months of October, November, and December. "I am leaving," he wrote on September eleventh to the director of the *Courrier des théâtres*.

One last matter of business was still pending. Gaillardet had published in the twenty-first issue of the *Musée des familles* a very anodyne article, *Lectures du soir*, on *La Tour de Nesle* and its history. Very anodyne, certainly, but the signature was followed with "It is useless to bring back to mind that M. Gaillardet is the author of *La Tour de Nesle*, the modern drama performed with so much success and brilliance at the Porte-Saint-Martin." There was a crime! At first, Alexandre did not appear to have been upset. He was then very involved in the last rehearsals for *Catherine Howard* and in litigation. The arrow Alexandre let fly at Gaillardet was all the more sharp and pointed for being postponed. In the thirty-sixth issue of *Le Musée des familles* (September 4, 1834) appeared a letter from Dumas in which he recounted, with an often mordant irony, the origins of *La Tour de Nesle* and Gaillardet's contribution: a shapeless and quite ridiculous manuscript that Alexandre had rapidly closed before beginning the composition of his play. After this letter was published, Alexandre heard that Gaillardet went to practice on the shooting range each morning, which gave an inkling of how he was preparing his reply.

In *Le Musée des familles*, No 111, October sixteenth, Gaillardet detailed the melee between Harel, Janin, Dumas, and himself which gave birth to the very popular *La Tour de Nesle*. He vituperated against the thieves of glory and money in an article prickly with notes and pieces which discouraged its readers. On a good subject, which could have attracted everyone's sympathy, the young author had innocently built a very bad melodrama.

Alexandre was, as he expected, the injured party. On October fourteenth, he wrote to Gaillardet: "Your first letter was an insolence; the second is a joke. Wednesday morning my seconds will be at your house."

Alexandre wanted to fight with épées. Gaillardet, an apprentice in arms as he was in literature, demanded pistols. Gaillardet's seconds finally decided that Dumas was the first offender, therefore Gaillardet would have choice of the weapons. Pistols it would be. The encounter was set for noon at Saint-Mandé on October seventeenth. During the night Alexandre prepared for the eventuality of a tragic end, with instructions to his son and his daughter. For his mother, he composed some twenty letters supposedly from Italy, to postpone the pain that disastrous news would cause her.

At Saint-Mandé, Gaillardet stepped down from a cab, dressed in a black morning coat, black pants and a black vest, not a dot of white that could make a target. "He has cotton in his ears," whispered Alexandre to Bixio who, in his capacity as physician, accompanied Dumas to all his duels. They all left their carriages and went deep into the forest to a convenient path, straight and sunless. The seconds discussed the conditions of the duel: the combatants were to be placed at fifty steps from each other and would advance up to a distance of fifteen steps.

The pistols were loaded. The distances marked with canes. One of the seconds tapped three times with his hands. Gaillardet rushed foolishly to his limit and waited while Alexandre marched toward him prudently. Gaillardet fired. Alexandre saluted with his head, no hit. Alexandre wanted to take eight or nine steps but his conscience held him back. He must shoot from the place where he was when Gaillardet shot. Alexandre shot without aiming and was furious to have missed his adversary, more so because of his vanity as a good shot than because of true hatred. He did not want to stop there. He wanted to fight to the death. Let the pistols be reloaded! The seconds refused and left. Épées, then? Alexandre proposed them to Gaillardet who had remained on the field. No!

In the carriage returning them to Paris, Bixio speculated. Does the impact of a bullet hitting a man cause him to turn around or not? Alexandre's awkward miss had not allowed Bixio to get an answer to the question. In 1848, on the June barricades, he would make the experiment himself. One turns, he could confirm.

III

Discovery of the Mediterranean Sea

To attract eventual participants in his new project, Dumas composed a prospectus dated October 10, 1834:

An idea came to mind; it appears to us great and national in scope; here it is:

France and Europe have always lacked a voyage around the Mediterranean sea, recounting all of its poetry, history, and science. Many people have skimmed over a few pages of the great book of world history but no one has read it in sequence from Homer to Byron, Achilles to Bonaparte, from Herodotus to Cuvier.

In our time, when it is said that art and science are smothered by politics, we will attempt an art and science expedition. To all those who accuse our time of being materialistic and anti-poetry, we will answer that it is only now that we have found a government to accredit us; three of our best artists will leave their studios to help us with their brushes; a sculptor will leave his personal studies unfinished to reproduce, by molding, foreign masterpieces; an architect will abandon his professional trade for a work of art; a physician and a geologist will leave behind classes and clients they perhaps will not find again when they return; and finally a banker will open his wallet for us, without thinking that death could come to erase our signatures from his foreign drafts.

Very well! Thanks to help from the government, to artistic assistance, to financial trust, we will now make this trip that no one has dared before.

It was a grandiose project but a meager caravan which left Paris on November 6 or 7, 1834, via stagecoach. Where were the sculptor, the architect, the physician, and the geologist? There was one painter, however, the landscapist Godefroy Jadin (and his dog, Mylord, redoubtable strangler of cats). At Fontainebleau, Alexandre met Jules Lecomte, a young man who claimed to be prosecuted for political activities and whom Dumas had hidden for a month at Rue Bleu. Alexandre had a passport made for Lecomte, using the false name of Leuven. At Fontainebleau, Lecomte had pretended to be Alfred de Musset and offered a banquet to young men of that town. When night fell, Alexandre took this masquarader in his coach, but not before having to pay the bill for the banquet (four hundred francs). Alexandre forgave him. As for the artistic pilgrimage, they stopped everywhere for a picturesque sight, an historical remembrance, or wherever folk tradition demanded some imagination. Then Alexandre pulled out his album, and Jadin his crayons, for a joint version of poet and painter.

In Lyons, he would encounter two women: the first, Marceline Desbordes-Valmore, sweet and unhappy, kept in that city by the rocky career of her husband, the actor Prosper Valmore. She wrote to her friend, Mélanie Waldor, who liked to follow the moves of her ex-lover: "Monsieur Dumas spent three days in Lyons." Of Marceline, Dumas wrote:

In the middle of this population entirely preoccupied with material interests, I knew however that, chained in Lyons by her duties as mother and wife, I would find one of the most poetic circles of our time. The poor exiled prophetess who in Paris would be the pride of our salons, here in Lyons was as ignored as if she had inhabited a small village in the Landes or Brittany. . . . She received me in Lyons as a fellow-worshipper of an unknown god to whom she dared address her sublime prayers only in solitude and loneliness. By begging her, I succeeded in having her open a secret drawer in a small secretaire in which, hidden to all eyes, she kept these flowers born in the shade.

On Friday, November fourteenth, Alexandre attended, by chance, a performance of *Antony* at the Gymnase Théatrè of Lyons. He had eyes only for Mme. Meinier who was so touching and so real in the part of Adèle. He said, when speaking of her, "This woman acts well because she feels her part well." A young artist, married, a mother, she provided, by her acting, support for her family's needs. She was radiant when she received the poet's compliments. Perhaps she was ready for love, too. Alexandre had not been used to resistance from actresses. The very next day he invited her to come to his hotel room. Offended, Hyacinthe Meinier returned his letter. The dramatic author came to the aid of the lover; he contrived a false departure in haste, refused the invitation he had received from Hyacinthe's husband, and wrote her:

My friends leave without me. Everybody in Lyons believes I have left with them. I stay, however; I stay for you alone. I must see you. I will not leave my Room No. 3. I will wait for you there.

Hyacinthe came. She did not give herself; she rested her head against Alexandre's chest and their lips touched for a goodbye kiss. Alexandre had nothing. He still hoped for everything.

Hyacinthe, dearest, I could not believe that a man could be made so unhappy by being refused everything. Listen, this time I do not believe I am wrong. You love me a little bit more and you admire me a little bit less. Your eyes would lie, your hands would lie if it were not so.

Who told you that I was forgetful? Oh! You will see. I want you to love me as only your heart can love; your heart is full of love; I am certain. Why is it that I have to leave? My God! Oh! But in six weeks, on my return, you will come and nobody will be there anymore to prevent me from pressing you to my heart and kissing your beloved lips.

Alexandre traveled along the River Rhône, feverish with this new love. Each stop now would be for him an opportunity for a letter to Hyacinthe, as if his desire increased with distance.

Another letter that same evening, from a hotel in Vienne. Jadin and Lecomte smiled at this amorous rapture. They knew that Alexandre loved mostly because he had been resisted. He wanted Hyacinthe. The hunter hunted his prey. When he met a traveler going back to Lyon, he trusted him with a third letter:

> We will see who will be tired, you from laughing, I from loving you. For it is an *idée fixe* my beautiful angel, and never have I felt my heart so stubborn.
>
> Do you know, dear child, that you are admirably organized for defense and this worries me very much. You have spirit and no love. How do you want me to approach you? I must find among your friends someone who can tell me what is your weak side. If one of your letters could betray this, you would make me very joyful, my love.

At Orange, a letter from Hyacinthe waited for him in care of General Delivery, the first one in reply to his which were so passionate:

> Can you be serious when you say that you want me to love you and could you believe that I could become insane enough to do it? What? I should give you the present, so clean, so pure, in exchange for a future of despair? For it is so, Monsieur. What a misfortune if I should love you! Because I could not stand your forgetting me and you would forget me. All that my heart can contain of love, all that my soul can conceive of exaltation, all must be compressed into one feeling: maternal love. It is sufficient for me; it makes me happy and my life must stop there. One needs remembrances, you said—but, Monsieur, you have already made me rich for eternity. All that you could do for my happiness, you have already done; it is outside your power to add to it. You cannot do any more for me, and I, I can bless you and pray for you.
>
> Cease, therefore, to believe that a day will come when I will respond to the tenderness you imagine you are feeling. A word, a look from you will make my life?—No, this will not happen

and if your letters would bring trouble in my soul, I would not read them anymore and I would run away from you.

You reproach me for playing with your passion; you are wrong again; It frightens me and that is all.

H.M.

Cities dotted the trip now. Alexandre concentrated on the trip to forget this unachieved adventure in love; Châteauneuf, Avignon, Fontaine de Vaucluse, Villeneuve lez-Avignon, the bridge of the Gard, Nîmes, Aigues-Mortes, Beaucaire, Tarascon, Arles, Port-de-Bouc. At Marseille Alexandre stayed at the Hôtel des Ambassadeurs. He met his old friend Méry and found a second letter from Hyacinthe at the General Delivery. She loved, but did not want to love. To give a greater price to her fall, Alexandre thought cynically. Marseille was a feast, with Méry its host. The great man of letters was acclaimed, the theater put on his plays, his presence in the audience piqued people's curiosity. The cash registers filled. But why did not Alexandre embark, as arranged, for Genoa? Did the caravan lack money to leave France? Perhaps. The Minister of Public Instruction had postponed a second payment of 1,666 francs "until he had received information related to M. Dumas' trip." They retraced their steps at a gallop. They were to stay three hours in Lyons: "I am arriving—I have only three hours to spend here. Hyacinthe, come to see me, I beg of you."

Hyacinthe did not ask for anything, but Alexandre promised her everything: his recommendation and the glory which would certainly come from it, and even his love. He left the young woman awestruck on the banks of the River Saône. She waited for him now. She wrote to him often; he replied parsimoniously.

On December twenty-seventh, she complained, "It is ten days that I have been crying. Also I suffer and I am lost and wondering—what have I done that makes you forget?"

"I have not forgotten you," he answered.

I am much under the spell and benumbed by love: I do hear this sweet voice that speaks to me of those tender years of my life. It comes to me as an echo from another time, pure and sweet, in the midst of the capital's noise. How I listen for it to arrive. . . . You have made my heart pound as if it were only fifteen years old when it is actually thirty.

Must she exile herself to St. Petersburg or Bruxelles to get an engagement? Or should she remain in Lyons? He replied:

If in one of these three cities I were there to watch over you, to fend off the unhappiness that could come, by offering my chest against it, I would not hesitate and would decide for you at this instant. (January 2, 1835)

In turn, Alexandre complained, not of his distant lover but of Paris:

What shall I tell you about the cause [of my deep sadness]? My God, it is the eternal fight of spirit against shadow. If you could know what intrigues and what coteries, in Paris, surround all those who bear a well-known name, to crush this name, all those who have a heart, to de-poetize this heart, you would know the secret of these hours of mortal sadness, which, at times, make me fear falling into a complete despondency decid- ing . . . , to leave everything behind, to run away. It is the end of spring. What do you want . . . a kiss and all will melt in your breath, sorrow, sadness, worries, and I will be again an eigh- teen-year-old, beautiful eighteen which I spent in a world which seemed to me a garden whose flowers I wished to shower upon the heads of all men. (January 10, 1835)

Nostalgia is a refuge when the world around resists—recourse to the past to endure the present. The angel "who is still my love and not yet my mistress," chaffed him a bit: "You, you have present sorrows but your future is vast and magnificent! Your name is a halo of glory and this heart, so kind, so generous, will beat with love for a woman really worth sharing your life! Friendship, love, admiration, glory, fortune, all these are yours!" (January 15, 1835). Alexandre recommended his lover to the director of the theater of Rouen. Was it only gratitude? Hyacinthe now joined Alexandre in erotic rapture:

If you knew with what ecstasy I place my lips on each line your hand has traced—then your letter sleeps on my heart *with your chain and your hair*; it is only during the night that I sometimes take it off—for it seems that it burns my chest—it

gave me bad thoughts—in spite of myself I murmured your
name as a prayer—my mouth was thirsty for your forehead—
I was pressing you in my arms—then, in the morning, I cried—
I asked mercy from God—for it must be wrong to love in such
a way—and perhaps even more wrong to dare to tell it to you!
. . . When could I tell you—I love you, give you caresses,
kisses. But that will be all, won't it? (January 20)

Improbable candor? False ingenuity?

In Paris Alexandre fought to obtain financing for his trip. On
January 29, 1835, he formed an association with André Drouot de
Charlieu, the publisher:

> M. Dumas has formed a project to take a trip around the
> Mediterranean and to write from this material a work of po-
> etry, history and science which, because of its low price, should
> be well within everyone's reach. The government, having
> given its support for this enterprise with grants and letters of
> credit, the persons appearing before us conceived the idea of
> forming a corporation and offering shares as a means of allow-
> ing the participation of persons whose fortunes have always
> been used to encourage worthwhile projects. After calculation,
> an amount of 100,000 francs would be more than sufficient
> to face foreseen expenses.

One hundred shares at one thousand francs a share to be sold!
Alexandre did not doubt for an instant that he could do it. He was
getting his itinerary ready and asked three illustrious travelers for
information. One of them, Alphonese de Lamartine, would trace a
road leading to remnants of the past in Corsica, Italy, Sicily, Greece,
Turkey, Asia Minor, Syria, Palestine and Egypt. More prosaically,
he asked Hyacinthe to get information regarding the best roads to
Italy: "By ship, when embarking in Marseille, you must stay in
quarantine in the first port where you stop; by surface from there
to Rome, it takes fifteen days—the roads are suitable for traveling.
Here are the details that you asked me for—do I need to tell you
that I looked for them with chagrin! My God, I who complained
about waiting eight days; how many will I count now. . . ." Alexandre scarcely had enough time to keep up with corresponding;
he had taken a trip for the "cursed business." "All is so horribly

long to conclude in this cursed Paris. Shall I begin to believe that misfortune might befall me? All that turned out well until now begins to turn out badly . . . I had believed I could see you from the fifteenth to the eighteenth, but now I don't know when I can leave; I will send you, to amuse you or to bore you, two volumes that I have been forced to write since my return" (February 9).

These two books are *Chroniques de France* and *Isabel de Bourgogne* (*Règne de Charles VI*) which covered again the historical scenes published in *La Revue des deux mondes* in 1831–1832, lengthened with fifteen beginning chapters, an intermediate chapter (XIV) and a concluding chapter, "Infernal amount of work, of which I will soon send you the evidence," he wrote to Hyacinthe on January tenth. Alexandre neglected his lover. Eleven days without a letter! But the forgetful, great man protected her anyway. She received an engagement at the theater of Rouen:

Eighty miles from Paris! My God—how near to you I will be—your name will resound in my ear—I am crazy! If only I could press my lips to your big, kind eyes! make you feel my heart—No matter if you have mistresses—no matter if you have no more love for me—I cannot remain unknown, indifferent to you—Oh, no—it is so difficult to understand the phantom of a poet.

The phantom of the touching actress, conjured up for an instant, also faded away after this last letter. Some erratic tracks, however, show that Alexandre continued to protect her career.

Again he had to begin the financing of the trip. The Ministry canceled the two last payments because Dumas "had not undertaken the trip for which this sum was granted." But Alexandre still had hope with the new Ministry.

Charlieu had left his position with the Publishing Society to Amédée Pichot, Director of *La Revue britannique*. Dumas sold some shares to Victor Hugo—their falling out was a thing of the past, but there was not yet quite a complete reconciliation. Hugo had subscribed for 250 francs against a note. Gérard de Nerval who, thanks to an inheritance would found the review *Le Monde dramatique*, signed an agreement with Dumas; he took one thousand franc shares in M. Alex. Dumas's trip, which "will deal especially with the theater." Jadin will again accompany Dumas and "will give him 15 to 25 drawings, finished enough for engraving, for a total amount of 2,500 francs." Alexandre made money with everything he could put his hands on. He had put together short stories which the publisher Dumont offered for sale under the attractive title: *Souvenirs d'Antony*. He had collaborated in *Cromwell et Charles Premier*, a five-act drama that Cordelier Delanoue endorsed and Harel put on the stage of Porte-Saint-Martin. He promised the same theatre another drama and had probably received an advance.

The road was open. After many entreaties, Ida was allowed to join the travelers. The caravan crossed France from north to south at a furious pace: having left Paris Tuesday, May twelfth at four o'clock, it reached Châlons to take the steamboat down the Rhône for arrival in Lyons on Wednesday. Then they departed Thursday at four in the morning for Avignon, from which they reached Aix on Friday at ten in the morning. They arrived the same evening in Marseille, the day after in Toulon, all very rapidly as Dumas noted in his album. In Toulon they settled in a provincial cottage above the harbor, Villa Lamalgue. There Ida frittered away her time, Jadin sketched, and Alexandre worked on his drama, *Don Juan de Marana*, or *La Chute d'un ange*, a religious play in five acts, the theme of which owed a bit to Mérimée's *Âmes du purgatoire*. Dumas described this "mystery" in Nerval's *Monde dramatique* as "a naïve representation of religious scenes from the Old Testament or from the Gospel (or linked to it) and also from pagan history; still keeping the connection with the revelation and development of Catholicism." He said that he applied to it mostly "the faculties given by God to man: poetry, imagination, style." But this grafting upon older traditions or myths took hold very badly. "Finished my drama June 12. Sent it to Paris on the 14 evening—displeased. Jadin consoles me. However, I do not expect a great success, especially without Frédérick (Lamaître)." Between writing two acts, Alexandre amused himself. He visited the famous penitentiary, dined with a vice-admiral, but once his drama was mailed, he, too, sailed away.

Leave Toulon July 15 at 7 in the morning; sleep at Draguignan, arrive at Grasse on the 16, visit Golfe Juan where Napoléon had debarked. In the coach from Toulon to Luc we find ourselves with Capitaine Langlet, a freethinker, strongly Provençal, greedy of mouth. . . . Arrive at Antibes. Visit the port the next day. We are awakened by the funeral procession of a child, its head uncovered, carried in its coffin by his friends. Sad impression. Distraction brought by the captain's voice and his mouth that we perceive under his cowl; when he gets ready to sing the "Liberere," he lifts up his hood and puts his eyeglasses on and we recognize him. He tells us he belongs to the fraternity of the Saint-Esprit and of Sainte Claire. . . . The parents did not accompany the body. . . .

Arrive at Nice on the 17, Fête-Dieu—Ignorant clergy: necessity for the bishop to ask for vicars from Turin. Departure on the 15, morning.

Furtive impressions from this trip, sketched in the album which revised, amplified, magnified during the sojourn in Florence would be included in the six volumes of *Impressions de voyage*. The caravan ascended La Turbie, touched Oneille, then Savone:

Genoa. Arrived on the evening of the 21; from about 20 to 25 miles away we could see it—magnificent palaces, but falling into ruins; marble and plaster, greatness and misery. Palace for 30,000 francs with its furnishings, the gardens and a duchess included in the bargain. The stairs were made to be descended by brocade dresses and velvet coats. . . .

The palaces, the processions ("all the windows draped with damask. They brought us bouquets and ices."). The Theatre Diurne (open air) is playing, this evening, *La Mort de Marie Stuart*:

Dresses of the Emperor's sisters and the princes' and peers' coats. On each side of the theater, the landscape of green trees and of charming villas. The sound of carriages. The houses around hurt the theater by renting their windows at half the price of the loges. At the time for signing the death sentence, the wind blew the paper away. The queen ran after it. Leicester wears pants of cherry color satin to which he added ties above the ankles to give a foreign look. Leicester decorated with two garters.

Near the free port, Alexandre noticed hostility. An emissary of the Sardinian *buon governo* firmly advised him to take a boat for

Livorno. Livorno contains "about 80,000 souls, most of them Jews. No society; the only society is the English society, tradesmen who receive foreigners. Fortunes of two or three million are quite frequent. I met one of these heiresses who walked on foot in a frightful mud."

Pisa. Night at the Campanile: "Marvel—the lightning bleaches all this square into a Sodom with its colossal monuments." The next day when Alexandre conscientiously visited the Dome, the cicerone pulled lottery tickets from all his pockets and made large signs of the cross when passing before the altar.

In Florence, they contacted all the writers and scholars of the city. Evening parties at the Contessa Nencini's, visits to the wonders of Santa Maria del Fiore, the Palázzo Vecchio, Palázzo Medici-Riccardi. In the evening, walk to the Cascine gardens to get the fresh air; opera and ballet at La Pergola. Florence prefers feasting to pleasure, rest to the feast. Under the scorching sun, the city is a sleeping beauty.

At Perugia, he admired Perugino's splendid frescoes. A penniless student came to see Alexandre. Did he possess French books? *Le Contrat social* of Jean Jacques Rouseau. "Keep my secret because if I had the misfortune to be convicted of possessing such a book, I probably would get ten or fifteen years of galleys." In Rome, Alexandre saw the Pope, a banisher of revolutionary books, but Rome was the only way to Naples and Sicily.

Naples' ambassador to Rome, M. de Ludorff, refused a visa for Naples and Sicily. With the reticent complicity of M. Ingres, the painter, director of the French School in Rome, Alexandre borrowed the passport of a student of the School, Joseph-Benoit Guichard. The next day, August first, Jadin and his pseudo-colleague took the Augrisani coach and were in Naples the next night. A magnificent moon glowed above the crater of Vesuvius. They had rooms at the Hotel de la Vittoria, but they hardly set foot there; they ran along the streets of Naples, the beach and the bay. With Maurice Schlesinger, director of *La Revue et gazette musicale de Paris*, Alexandre had made an "engagement to narrate . . . everything that has some relation to music during this long trip." He could not ignore the Teatro San Carlo, the most prestigious lyric theater of Europe. He became rapidly familiar with the company of perfomers which enchanted Naples, where people go to the opera to enjoy it, whereas in France they go to show themselves. Such singers! Gilbert-Louis Duprez who, the next year after a long exile, would reign at the Paris Opera; Georgio Ronconi, promising young baritone; La Malibran, sublime Maria; Fanny Tacchinardi, latest glory of bel canto under the name of Mme. Persiani. And also a great and beautiful diva, about thirty years old who triumphed in *Norma*: Caroline Ungher, whom Alexandre had too briefly met during the 1834 carnival in Paris where she was making her debut at the Théâtre-Italien. What had she told him then? "In forty-eight hours I will have time to show you that you please me, but not enough time to prove to you that I love you." They had now more than forty-eight hours in Naples, but there was Ida, the official mistress. There was also Henri-Catherine-Camile, Vicomte de Ruolz-Monchal, Alexandre's friend, a musician who was getting ready to present his opera, *Lara*, at the San Carlo.

Henri was in love with Caroline, and through much begging, had obtained from her a promise of marriage. Caroline had an engagement with the Opera of Palermo. The marriage would be done in that "happy city." What a strange coincidence! Alexandre, too, was embarking for Sicily. He had made reservation for a *speronare*, a charming boat, *La Madonna del pie de la grotta*, manned by six sailors. Alexandre invited Caroline and Ruolz on board.

In spite of bad omens warning the travelers, the boat hoisted its anchor and glided on an azure sea past Capri. The boat seemed to float on air. Caroline enchanted the sailors with her voice. But the wind changed; the pilot, who was called "The Prophet," announced a squall. At the time of the "Ave Maria," a big, black cloud came up from the southwest. The sea waves lapped against the boat. Alexandre and Ferdinand were invited under Caroline's awning. Soon it rained and thundered, the *speronare* heaved and yawed. Ferdinand was seasick and had to stay on deck. Alexandre and Caroline were alone under the awning, lying on the mattress, face to face, separated by the space of a yard. The lamp, for lack of oil, was soon out. The tempest became stronger. From time to time, Caroline, panting, cried: *"Non c'é pericolo, capitano?"* Suddenly an enormous wave raised the craft. Caroline slipped from her mattress into Alexandre's arms. *"Questa volta, c'é pericolo,"* he murmured into her ear. The tempest lasted all night, from August twenty-fourth to the twenty-fifth. When the sea was calm once more, Ferdinand was able to leave his sick station. Was it only one instant of rapture? No, Caroline would confess everything—she would break with Ruolz, she would wait for Alexandre in Palermo after he finished his circumnavigation of Sicily. Marvelous nights passed, starry, transparent nights; Alexandre and Caroline exchanged furtive kisses and, at Messina, the lovers separated.

Even from Dumas' impressions, it would be impossible to depict the following days, "if not the happiest, at least the most sensual," that he spent with Jadin and his Sicilian sailors in exploring the coasts of Sicily. A short odyssey, with ports of call such as Taormina, Acireale, the grotto of Polyphemus, Catania, Syracuse, Ortygia, Porri, the island of Pantelleria, Agrigento. Alexandre and Jadin climbed Mount Etna, they visited the ancient remains of Syracuse and Agrigento, they swam in the sea of the gods and lazily rested on the deck of the *speronare*. Sometimes Alexandre imagined that the breeze brought Caroline's perfume to him. When he closed his eyes he could almost feel her body against his own body. Caroline! The only delight missing at this time, but missing so strongly that at Agrigento he decided to leave the *Pie de la grotta* and to take a shortcut to Palermo. On foot or on mules led by a guide that they suspected of complicity with innumerable bandits, Alexandre and Jadin did not stop and in three days were in Palermo. Alexandre went to the Hotel Quatre-Nations where Caroline was also stopping. She was in rehearsal. Alexandre booked a suite near hers, hurried to the bath, then leaned on the bannister at the top of the stairs to wait for her. When she was told that a gentleman asked for her, she flew over the steps crying, "It's him!" When Alexandre's arms closed around her, she cried out, "I am free, I am free!"

When much later, Alexandre reminisced in writing about it under the title, *Adventure d'amour*, he had only a few words to evoke the twenty following days:

> Caroline had promised a month of happiness in the most beautiful country in the world; she gave me fifteen days more than she had promised. After twenty years, I say, thank you. No debtor had ever paid capital and interest as you did! As for Palermo, what can I say? It is a paradise of the world. Let the poets' blessing be on Palermo!

His memory, unconcerned with the chronological truth, kept only a flashing image: happiness in Palermo during this ending of August 1835. Caroline triumphed at the opera in *Norma* and in

Parisina. The lovers loved and spread joy around them. In Santa Rosalia, a chapel above Palermo, they exchanged promises of marriage. Separation was wrenching—the awakening from a delicious dream.

The *speronare*, when Alexandre was back on board, floated on quiet water. The night was filled with wonders—deep sky, starry sea, the perfumes of the beach, the shivering of the invisible. This same evening, Caroline was sublime on the stage in the fourth act of *Norma*, when Pollione leaves. Alexandre was asleep when, in the morning, she came in a small boat to ask for a day's reprieve, a last night. The sailors celebrated, danced, and sang while Alexandre and Caroline lay in their tent. When they had to separate again, Caroline, in her boat, kept her arms stretched toward her lover, as on the stage. Alexandre cried to her at the top of his voice, "I love you, you are beautiful! You are beautiful, I love you!" This beauty stood above any despair. Alexandre was more enthusiastic than sad. Life, sometimes, brings more drama than the theater. He could almost have applauded.

On October sixth, the *speronare* floated toward Lipari and the archipelago of volcanos. Jadin was back at his sketching board, Alexandre at his traveling album. For him all the landscape was but a metaphor of Caroline's body and soul—from Lipari to Vulcano, from the island of Basiluzzo to Stromboli. A storm kept the travelers at San Giovanni on the coast of the Straits of Messina. The crew has improvised an encampment. The idle sailors wondered what had come over this big Moor. Why was he always writing? In fact, Dumas had recovered his taste for writing. Perhaps it was a remnant of his dizziness, but he was back working on a new drama, *Le Capitaine Paul*, for Harel and the actors of the Porte-Saint-Martin. It was a dramatic sequel to *The Pilot* of James Fenimore Cooper, whose traces he had once searched for from Brest to Lorient.

On October eighteenth, a very strong storm was accompanied by an earthquake. There was no question of continuing by sea, and Alexandre and Jadin decided to go by the roads. With guides they went along the inhospitable roads of Calabria on mules, took a succession of incredibly narrow shorcuts and stopped at huts masquerading as inns. At Pizzo, Alexandre relived the last days of Murat, the landless king of Naples, who, when he returned to his kingdom, had been met by a firing squad. Alexandre passed through the Provençal Maida and the Albanaisian Vena amid storms, torrents swelling, fatigue, and exhaustion. Once, having reached an inn, Alexandre collapsed, semiconscious, on an armchair. Jadin lay on a mattress made of corn husks. From another traveler Alexandre heard, "Bellini is dead!" The friend who had given him a letter of recommendation for the Marquis de Noia! Perhaps it was only a nightmare, but in the morning Jadin confirmed the fact; all the newpapers of France and Italy had announced the sad news:

> I remembered his beautiful blond hair, his melancholic face; I heard him speak to me the French he spoke so badly with such a soft accent; I could see him put his hand on the paper (of the letter). This paper kept his handwriting, his name. This paper was alive, and he, he was dead.

"*Oh! Di qual sei tu vittima*," the trio in the first act of *Norma* haunted his mind. He was still in Palermo; it was Caroline who sang—Caroline, now alone, who multiplied the pilgrimages to Santa Rosalia:

> What name to give to the feeling that penetrates you when you again see a place where, a few days before, you had spoken with a dear friend? I don't know whether it is more pain than tenderness! The sea was before me and I searched it for you. Oh, absence is insufferable! . . . I prayed with all my heart wet with tears. My God, make him love me; see that he comes back to me and that I am worthy of him.

She feared that Alexandre, in Naples again, would be caught once more in Ida's nets:

> My nights are awful, always sad dreams. When will I have a letter from you from Naples? That letter will be for me a new proof of your love and a most assuring one; then I will be less oppressed by my visions, my fears. Oh! I have never loved before because I never felt what I feel today, both love and jealousy. I count the hours and there will be months to spend, and yet, when I think again of all that has happened to me, I believe that it is providence which brought you to me; in this chaos of my emotions and ideas, what is certain is my love for

you and my continuing prayer to God: 'My God, see that he comes back to me loving me as he told me and that I am worthy of him.'

She sent him her portrait, "me, in person, looking for you with my eyes." She sang *Norma*, and in the cavatina in which she called Pollione back to her arms, she thought of Alexandre and was inspired by love. She was wild with joy, she had received letters from her love:

You made me laugh when you told me that you bore me with your letters. My God, if you wrote me one hundred letters a day, I still would find them too few—dear love, believe me, never, no never have I loved before—one says this often but from me they are not idle words—I feel in love with all that is deep and holy; and if you forget me, if your heart should change, I could not live.

Alexandre had received this bundle of letters, sent to General Delivery under an assumed name, only upon his return to Naples about November fifth. He had first waited for the arrival of the *speronare* at Cosenza, a town that the earthquake of October eighteenth had partially destroyed. The town was an immense encampment which seemed to be preparing for an apocalypse. The *speronare* embarked again: they passed Paestum and Salerno; then, at Amalfi, they returned to terra firma; a curricle took the travelers from Cava to Naples.

Naples again after two and a half months of beauty, adventures, love, and there was Ida welcoming him with open arms. Alexandre could hardly confess that a siren had held him back at Palermo. He did not say anything; he did not write to Caroline. He again mixed in with the San Carlo company which spoke only of the forthcoming perfomance of an opera, composed by a young French musician, the Marquis de Ruolz, the unfortunate fiancé of Caroline. There would be a *gran gala*. "And this means?" asked Alexandre. The royal family will be present at the performance.

On such a day, in the theater there are twelve hundred candles which blind you and whose smoke catches the singers' throats. . . . The overture must be played with the curtain up because

His Majesty cannot wait. . . . All the Court attends this performance and the audience can applaud only after His Majesty applauds and His Majesty never applauds.

This was the reply to his question;, and Alexandre decided to help his ex-rival. He went to all the rehearsals and did not spare his encouragement or the expression of his admiration. Did he want to be forgiven? The modest, kind, timid Ruolz was overwhelmed with gratitude. On the nineteenth, *Lara* was finally delivered to the Neapolitan public for whom "life was made of happiness, pleasure and feelings" and who feared that boredom might tarnish some of these moments if they had to face unfamiliar music. Alexandre fixed his eyes on the royal loge: at first the King turned his back to the actors; then he opened a book; then he lifted his pince-nez to his eyes and pointed out a dilettante to one of his aides-de-camp. An officer in civilian clothes had come to the theater and His Majesty wanted him confined to quarters. Then he had a discussion with his brother. The first act ended; the King did not applaud. Desperate, Ruolz ran away. The music and the voice of Duprez took hold of the audience of three thousand during the second act. They threw glances at the King, pleading him to applaud. The King put his two hands together and a torrent of applause, bravos, and cries broke the dam. They clamored for the author, they looked for him and could not find him.

He was in the arms of Donizetti, who attempted to console him for his unsuccessful drama. He came back at the end of the third act to savor his glory.

Finally, Alexandre wrote Caroline a letter in which he affected to be jealous to better conceal that he had not broken off with Ida. Caroline replied on November nineteenth:

Do you believe that I have so many *relationships* to break off? My God, none certainly resembles the kind *you have*, and I am scrupulous in friendship; I do not want anyone else in the world but you. . . . You scare me when you say that perhaps for a long time you won't be able to break off with her—but once you have settled her in Paris, if you loved me, shouldn't you tell her goodbye and come to your wife? If you don't, you do not love me and then it would be better for me to die.

Caroline was soon to leave Palermo to go to Venice, where she had been engaged by the Teatro Fenice. Then, the follwing year, there would be Florence where she dreamed of a house in which she would live with Alexandre:

> You see that I begin to dare to shape some plans. But if you knew how much I fear that my happiness, present and future, is a dream and how much I convince myself all the day long and at the end I tell myself: 'You are insane; it is true, *he loves you*, he is your husband' and then I cry, My God, this is too much happiness!
> (Caroline to Alexandre circa November twentieth)

But Alexandre had already left Naples. He had to leave this city which resembled him so much in its voluptuous moods, its sensual abundance, its frivolous excesses. He had been arrested there by the police when his forged identity had been discovered—which, indeed, was a secret only to the police. Jadin contacted the French Chargé d'Affaires, and Alexandre was freed on the condition he would leave Naples within the next twenty-four hours.

Burnt by the sun, drunk with exicitement, Alexandre left quickly during the night. In the coach, Jadin and Ida remained almost silent; it was not easy to awaken from such beautiful dreams. Life now seemed to them like the sinister malaria-ridden Pontine marshes that they were now crossing at a gallop. Next, Rome, where thanks to the First Secretary to the Holy See, Alexandre had an audience with Pope Gregory XVI. His Holiness received him, dressed in his long, buttoned white dress, coiffed with his white skullcap, while on his feet he wore red velvet slippers embroidered with the Grecian cross. Impressed, Alexandre had fallen on his knees when passing the threshold, ready to kiss the Pope's slippers, but Gregory XVI held only his hand to him. They sat down, they talked. The Pope recognized that if this libertine had not the stuff to make a good Christian, at least he had a generous heart. When the audience was ending, the Pope dug into a kind of barrel to pull out a handful of rosaries (made with the pits of olives supposedly picked up on the Mount of Olives), filled Alexandre's hand with them and blessed the whole. It was said of His Holiness, "Wine and women were his gospel." As for Alexandre, he drank wine with great moderation.

In Rome, he met Caroline furtively as she passed on her way to Venice. They decided that they would meet again in the City of the Doges, which was at this time under the Austrian boot. He would embark at Ancona. He was already at Civita Castellana, trying to decipher a half-erased inscription at the foot of a statue, when he was approached and arrested by two of the Pope's carabinieri and taken to an office. There, threatened with five years of galley punishment, he was ordered to leave the Pontifical States at once and never to set foot there again. Alexandre protested, argued, mentioned the audience granted by His Holiness just the day before. Nothing worked, and Alexandre was put into a carriage with two carabinieri as escorts. At Perugia, the *"prigionere politico"* was received with the greatest regard: a less than unpalatable dinner, fine wine, the theater. Alexandre promised not to try to escape from his loge. His entrance into the theater was greeted with a burst of enthusiastic applause. It was not for the author of *Henri III* and *Antony*, but for the political prisoner of the Pope. Alexandre rose and saluted. When he woke up the next morning, a crowd gave him an ovation when he appeared at his window, and accompanied him to the gates of the city. At the border, the prisoner gave an ecu to his guardian angels, who kissed his hand with gratitude.

The Papal police had crossed up love. Alexandre was at Florence, Caroline expected him in Venice:

> I am waiting for you in one of the thousands of gothic houses, with a view of the Grand Canal, vis-á-vis the Toscarini Palace, the Rialto on the right—How many centuries will I have to wait for this poetic city to become alive with your presence?— See, I am sure that in Venice you will love me much more; the tranquility here, interrupted only by the song of a gondolier would suit you.
>
> (Caroline to Alexandre, December ninth)

Her mother died on December tenth in Florence. "You must love me also for my poor Mother whom I have lost," she begged him, but Alexandre was already on his way. He wrote to her from Genoa and sent her back to her solitude. She was rehearsing a new opera that she detested; from the Venetian government she obtained an assurance that Alexandre could come to Venice without being disturbed. After a letter from Genoa, there was no more words from

Alexandre. Through the frigid canals, Caroline rode alone in her gondola. Winter in Venice brought death to her soul and a jealousy that corroded like a cancer.

She did, however, finally receive a note from Alexandre, who was in Paris. Her hopes revived—he promised to come to Venice, he still loved her. Caroline exulted, but her joy was short-lived. January sixth she wrote Alexandre:

> You would have me believe that you could come to Venice if your plays [*Don Juan de Marana*, written in Toulon, and *Kean*] will only be staged by April, with Mlle. Ida; it won't be until March that I could expect your return. Then she stays in Paris without engagement. You will provide for all her expenses. It is not the money that concerns me but the fear that you would make her pay the interest personally. Three more months—Paris—the distractions—and Ida—could the remembrance of a saint—of a woman who has the misfortune to long for a legitimate love, hold against so many seductions.

Caroline could predict her future. Her triumph in Donizetti's *Belisario* (February 4) uplifted her but did not make her forget the abandonment that threatened. She was "as Hero in the legend looking at the wave that would bring her lover Leander." Fifteen days without one letter, then a note, written in haste, to let her know that Alexandre had sojourned in Rouen. What! Without telling her: "Do you see, I am unfortunately too old not to see that absence has for you a fatal influence on my love. I do not mention how I suffer from this idea which, vainly, I would like to push away, but the efforts it takes you to tell me 'I love you' do not resemble the pouring out of this blissful work from you in Messina, and Lipari, and in Rome."

Betrayed by Pollione, her one-time lover, Norma [Caroline] took her pen up March 4, 1836 for a last time. She knew what she owed to her own glory:

> It is almost a month since you took your pen for the last time, to write two lines after you returned from Rouen. . . . I cannot doubt anymore that I was very far-sighted when I left you the freedom to dispose of my future; at least you won't have any remorse since you will not see my pain and you can say, 'I

was sincere.' I would, however, have preferred two words from you and not this silence which enlightens me perfectly but which prolongs my agony from mail to mail. I have made a rule for myself not to disturb you, to write to you only in response to your letters, but this morning it is impossible to keep this resolution; my poor heart overflows. I do not want you to be unaware that I understand you and that I have reached the point of telling myself, 'He does not love me anymore!' And you could not persuade me of the contrary for there is no reason that justifies such a prolonged silence. . . .

Therefore, take back your freedom; I am going to wear my bracelet as a nun wears a hairshirt and, I assure you, it hurts! I will be for you the best of friends. I will not forget that you have opened the doors of paradise for me; I have seen it—I cannot inhabit it; your happiness is my only desire, that your will be done!

Laure, Mélanie, Belle, Marie, Hyacinthe, Caroline: the number hardly hid the same amorous pattern. The obstinate will be loved, then the rapid fall into indifference when the woman had given herself. The lover was a hunter who loved only the pursuit; a Don Juan devastated, doubtlessly, by a necessary cruelty. The demand of his senses distressed his heart.

After six months' absence, wandering, loving, Alexandre was back in Paris. Had he discovered the Mediterranean Sea, as the prospectus claimed? At most, a little of Italy and Sicily. Yet he had lived, sometimes he had felt the touch of happiness. He had divined the harmony of the world.

IV

A New Press

Dumas did not come back emptyhanded: He brought back two plays, a novel, and the album of souvenirs of his voyage. The gambler could hope to recoup his fortune. In Lyon, he spent a long day in the attic of Marceline Desbordes-Valmore. The tender Marceline convinced him to devote himself to one of his victims: He promised to write a biography of Mélanie Waldor. Dead love affairs can be transmuted into literature. Back to the Rue Bleu, where Ida had probably preceded him, to the pavement of the boulevards, to the brightly lighted theaters, to Buloz and to *La Revue des deux mondes*. He found Paris unchanged; Paris was petrified. Louis-Philippe had repressed the republican riots. Romanticism had survived the suppression of republican supporters; romanticism was diffused; it was everywhere; it was nowhere. Paris forgot so rapidly those it had flattered that Alexandre had to pick up the threads where he left off, to prove himself again, almost to debut once more. Had not the newspapers announced his death a few times without excessive chagrin! Women's hearts were more faithful. Why had he made the trip to Rouen, inviting reproaches from Caroline, if not to rejoin Hyacinthe?

Almost timidly, Dumas' name reappeared in *La Revue des deux mondes* (*Guelfes et Gibelins*, and *Dante et la Divine Comédie*, March 1, 1836; *Voyages de Gabriel Payot*, April 1). But he had to win back his place in the theater world. Harel had received *Don Juan de Marana*, the Christian mystery play that Dumas had sent him from Toulon and had accepted Ida for the leading role. At the same time, Frédérick Lemaître, who was acting at the Théâtre des Variétés, was also looking for a major role. He brought Dumas the manuscript of a play that had been proposed to him: *Kean*, a drama with no substance. The bitterness of the frustrating return to Paris, the financial worries and his scorned genius all spurred Dumas on. Kean was himself the friend of princes, the seducer of grand women. In a scene in the second act, Dumas could see himself spewing out the hack journalists who clutched his coat tails. And had not the young heroine, Anna, the dangerous purity of Hyacinthe?

Alexandre had two irons in the fire. *Don Juan de Marana* opened first. Ida played the angel, but her waistline had become rather rounded. "A leaden flight," was the sarcastic comment of the tabloids. No matter how unusual and beautiful, a play cannot survive ridicule. Alexandre sighed: Paris had been easier to conquer than it was now to re-conquer. If the theater could suddenly lift an author into glory, it very seldom guaranteed him the permanence that was assured to an ambassador, a minister, or a deputy. But the power of the press remained. Émile de Girardin had recently launched a newspaper which would be a compromise between the dull, established press and the small tabloids. He had his eyes on Dumas for the literary section. The two men signed a contract:

1. M. Dumas engages himself to review for *La Presse* all the important plays shown at the Théâtre-Français and the Porte-Saint-Martin. M. Dumas will select the most important himself but retains the right to notify M. de Girardin as to who would substitute for him so that these two theaters will be critiqued from a uniform point of view—to discuss in *La Presse* all the important questions of dramatic literature raised by theatrical grants—and to report the openings of new theaters and show-places.

2. M. Émile de Girardin reserves for M. Alexandre Dumas the Sunday morning columns in which will appear his historic scenes which will review the most important reigns in French history, beginning with Philippe de Valois—for his part, M. Alexandre Dumas accepts the obligation never to leave the space of these columns empty.

3. As for the political articles, their subjects will be settled in advance by M. Alexandre Dumas and Émile de Girardin— once settled by verbal convention, M. Dumas will be free to give his articles the tone that pleases him, understanding that the articles, always signed by him, are his sole responsibility. (June 26, 1836)

As for the conditions: one franc per line for the articles, one franc twenty-five centimes for the columns, a loge at the Français or at the Porte-Saint-Martin paid for by the newspaper, and eight warrants of 250 francs that Dumas would receive after one year of collaboration with the newspaper.

Dumas can be considered, therefore, one of the fathers of the modern journalism that Girardin invented. His belated claims can be justified:

About 1835 [actually 1836], I believe, *La Presse* was founded and for it I invented the *roman-feuilleton* [serial]. It is true that it had not been a happy project. Girardin had accepted from me only one weekly article and I had begun with *La Comtesse de Salisbury*, which was not one of my best works. In a daily serial, the novel would have had a chance. In a weekly serial, it had no success. Nevertheless, other newspapers adopted this new mode of publishing.

(*Le Capitaine Paul*, Preface)

In fact, after discussing his conceptions of his historical serial in *La Presse* on July fifteenth, Dumas published, from July 17, 1836 to August twenty-eighth, *Règnes de Philippe VI de France et d'Édouard III d'Angleterre* (seven columns), and on September eleventh, *Règnes d'Édouard III, de David Bruce d'Écosse et de Philippe de Valois*, which later were published in book form under the title, *La Comtesse de Salisbury*.

Dumas' collaboration with *La Presse* had hardly begun when it hit an obstacle. The established newspapers fired cannonballs against *La Presse* which, they claimed, planned to change a sacred vocation into a vulgar trafficking that would confuse readers with deceptive advice, and banal and cynical recommendations, instead of enlightening them. One of the newspapers, *Le bon sens*, left to Capo de Feuillide the task of dealing with Émile de Girardin, who sued him for defamation. In spite of his scornful arrogance, Armand Carrel was recognized as the head of republican opinion, and retorted in *Le National* of July twentieth that Capo de Feuillide had every right to judge M. de Girardin's enterprise as a bad one and accused the latter of having taking advantage of the September regulations that choked the free press. The polemic worsened: de Girardin seemed to call into doubt the republican's loyalty. A duel of words can only end on the field of honor and on July twenty-second, in the Vincennes' woods, shots fired simultaneously hurt both adversaries who fell wounded, one in the leg and the other in the groin. A bullet had hit Carrel's intestine and he was in agony. The republicans turned wildly against de Girardin who, they accused, had used this encounter solely for publicity and speculation. Carrel died, murmuring some confused words among which some believed they recognized: "France, friend, republic." Legend made a martyr of him. Châteaubriand and Béranger shed tears at his tomb, which Carrel's murderer himself, Émile de Girardin, approached with a halting limp.

Alexandre was a republican and he admired Carrel and felt close to him. Could he continue his collaboration now with *La Presse*? There was a conflict between his sympathies and his interests. But on July twenty-eighth, *La Presse* announced with relief:

> M. Alexandre Dumas has just sent us the following historical serials he had contracted to write for appearance four times per month in *La Presse*. This is the best answer that we can give to the rumors, which several newspapers welcomed too hastily, about his breaking his ties with our publication.

A taste of betrayal cannot ever be forgotten. Yet Dumas, in the columns entitled *Scènes Historiques* or *Variétés*, continued to offer in *La Presse* his best works, mostly parts of the notes he took during his trip in Italy: *Murat* (October 3, 9, 16, 1836); *Pascal Bruno* (January 23 to February 3, 1837); or again, experiences he lived and immediately grasped: *Mes infortunes de Garde National* (September 28 and October 6, 1836). However, the activity of Dumas at *La Presse* soon took a more traditional turn. For this new newspaper he was what Jules Janin was for *Les Débats*: the prestigious critic for the more important theaters, the Comédie-Française and the Porte-Saint-Martin, while Frédéric Soulié had the less glamorous work of covering the second-class theaters. Thus, from September 1836 to March 1838, Dumas took the pulse of the contemporary theatrical productions, attentive as a doctor at the bedside of a sick man. For once the romantic fever had passed, the theater was agonizing. On evenings of premieres, in his loge—not provided by the theater but paid for by the newspaper, as he had wanted it—Dumas was bored with looking at dramas or comedies that were almost all predestined to fall into deep oblivion.

Ephemeral criticism of no-less ephemeral works! Judging other writers' mediocre creations was more suited to a laborer than to a creative man. Dumas' dramatic column would not deserve much attention if it were not a platform as well, from which he could expose his ideas on contemporary art and defend them violently. In fact, the new plays at the Théâtre-Français and at the Porte-Saint-Martin could not even fill up a weekly column. So the Sunday space, when nothing new deserved review, offered an opportunity for dissertations on the state of the theater. Sometimes Dumas treated subjects such as "From Aristocratic Tragedy to Bourgeois Comedy and the Popular Drama" (July 3, 1836), or he resolved the question, "How Did Our Theater Cease to Be Original and Become an Imitator?" (July 25, 1836), or he claimed "The Necessity for a Second Théâtre-Français" (September 25 and November 30, 1836). Or he questioned himself at length about dramatic studies, "Did Tragedy Die with Talma?" (from December 4, 1836 to January 1st, 1837).

Less ephemeral than the simple columns—since Dumas subsequently put them together in a book he called *Souvenirs Dramatiques*—these studies, disinterested in appearance, had a practical and immediate purpose, Dumas was not alone in his fight; he was working hand in hand with Hugo. Their goal was the opening of a theater for drama in Paris. Adèle Hugo had arranged a meeting and a reconciliation between Victor and Alexandre in June of 1836 and now their collaboration in *La Presse* kept Alexandre in Paris. Yet it was at this time (January 22, 1837), he reviewed Scribe's *Camaraderie* in *La Presse* with this tirade against the curse of having a collaborator:

Collaborators do not push one ahead; they hold one back; collaborators generously grant you the failures and modestly keep for themselves the beauties; although they share the success and the money, they assume the attitude of the victim and of the oppressed; finally, between two collaborators there is almost always a dupe and this dupe is the man of talent; because the collaborator is an intrepid passenger, embarking on the same craft as you, who lets you perceive, little by little that he does not swim, while he must be supported above the water at the time of the shipwreck with the risk to you of drowning with him and who, reaching the shore, goes everywhere saying that without him, you were a lost man. . . .

Why didn't Alexandre avoid the very same dangers that he denounced! Did the triumphs of *La Tour de Nesle* and of *Angèle* make him forget the fall of *Le Fils de l'émigré?*

Dumas the journalist had to support the position of Dumas the dramatic author, always at the mercy of a reversal. Often he felt discouraged. Against the success of *Kean*, there was the failure of *Don Juan de Marana* and the rejection of *Le Capitaine Paul* at the Porte-Saint-Martin by Harel and Mlle. George, although they were struggling to survive in mediocrity by showing a company of performing Bedouins in their theater. The journalist was the new, modern hero who made and destroyed reputations and opinions and therefore gave birth to the society of the future.

At Rue Bleu, Ida assumed the management of the household. She was bringing up Belle's daughter, the little Marie, who had her father's beautiful sapphire eyes and thick black hair. Although Ida tried to win over the young Alexandre, who was twelve at that time and impervious to all her approaches of friendship, she was jealous of the slightly excessive love of the father for the son. She received admirably well her lover's friends: Theophile Gautier and the tender Gérard de Nerval, who had a passionate admiration for her blond fairness and her triumphant plumpness. Without much success, she attempted to exclude the parasites who stuck to her great man. But mostly she watched vigilantly for women who might take him away from her, newcomers or ghosts from the past such as that Virginie Bourbier whom Alexandre had loved at the time of *Henri III*. She had been touring in Russia but came back to France in September 1836 with the intention of staying a while. From St. Petersburg she had brought her ex-lover a beautiful dressing gown and some Turkish tobacco. Ida confiscated the dressing gown and replaced the Turkish tobacco with French *caporal* which caused coughing, spitting and cursing among the unfortunate friends to whom Alexandre offered it. Ida was jealous of Caroline, jealous of Marie Dorval whom she called "the old monster." Alexandre could hardly stand this perpetual emotional storm; he grew irritable. Ida made him almost entirely lose his natural gaiety.

In this same month of September 1836, Alexandre was put in jail. He had refused to join Louis-Philippe's National Guard and was condemned to one week in the Saint-Bernard House of Detention. Hugo tried, in vain, to visit him there. But the jailer had pity on female visitors. Ida took over the cell as a legal wife and introduced Alexander to a young woman whose head had been turned by literature, the future Comtesse Dash. Virginie Bourbier, too, crept into her poet's den but she believed that "she had been spied upon by two persons who, positively, had seen her come out." Ida was watching. Locked up, Alexandre dreamed of escape, not only from these four temporary walls but from Paris. Perhaps he would accompany Virginie, who planned to leave? Virginie was rushing around Paris; she needed hats, embroidered handkerchiefs and, above all, autographs. She pestered Alexandre to help her acquire them from his friends. She even, pleasantly, insulted him: "Miserable manufacturer of comic opera!" Indeed, the musician Hippolyte Monpou plagued Alexandre to write a libretto, and he used his days in jail to create *Piquillo*. Nerval would give it the needed polish.

Alexandre served his week-long sentence. Virginie left for St. Petersburg, where she soon felt disgusted by that city for its lack of vitality and action.

Had Paris, too, become insufferable? Alexandre's every move was watched. Everywhere there was talk of his follies and his absurdities. Had he not the incredible idea of writing a drama for Adolphe, the trained horse of the Franconi Circus, a *Caligula*, of course? But the horse died.

The core of the tragedy remained, and Alexandre worked on it, with his visions of Italy, Pompeii, Girgenti, Paestum, Rome, and also with a more serious project intended to humor "Son Étrange Sainteté Grégoire XVI" by putting the theater to the service of the development of the principles of Christianity. His work was not for the circus, but for the Comédie-Française. *La Presse* had fifteen thousand subscribers and as its theater critic, Dumas had to be treated with consideration. The provisory director of the Comédie deemed it diplomatic to engage Alexandre to write this tragedy. He was, therefore, granted all he desired, and he desired a lot: five thousand francs advance and Ida's engagement. Take it or leave it. The Comédie took Ida, who was engaged on February twenty-fourth for the season lasting from October 1, 1837, to March 31, 1838, with a yearly salary of four thousand francs. Through his journalist friends, Alexandre trumpeted this news all over Paris.

"And why not a tragedy?" he claimed in his publicity for *Catherine Howard*. He was thirty-five, the age of mature creativity. He, however, exploited his advantages first. The new manager of the Comédie, Védel, was weak. Dumas imposed on his a revivial of *Charles VII chez ses grands vassaux*, created at the Odéon in 1831. As the author, he reigned as master on the stage; he made the actors rehearse mercilessly.

He had four more days in jail to serve for sanctions from the National Guard. He begged General Jacqueminot to give him a few days' delay. He must attend rehearsals, he claimed: "In eight days I will have finished a task much more unpleasant than going to prison; then, General, I will be ready for orders from headquarters."

On April eighteenth, the performance of *Charles VII* raised neither emotion, nor interest, nor dread in the audience, as a critic was prompt to report, rather pleased to return the hail of blows Alexandre had distributed upon him and colleagues in *Kean*. At long last, the critics could get their vengeance on the author. This man, Dumas, was irritating with his candid vanity: critic and columnist in an important newspaper (*La Presse*), subsidized by the government for vague missions, principal tenant on the stage of the Comédie-Française, it was too much!

After *Charles VII*, Alexandre withdrew *Angèle* from Harel and offered the play to the Comédie-Française. Why such haste? The smith wanted to leave the anvil—Paris. He had already dreamed of his goal: after antiquity, the Middle Ages; after Italy, Germany. Ida would accompany him, taking advantage of her three free months from the Théâtre-Français to "play two or three German roles at the same time as her French repertory " (May 2, 1837). But would it be a trip as a couple or a "voyage à trois"? The discreet shadow of Gerard de Nerval, Alexandre's whimsical friend and collaborator, had appeared adoring and tender with Ida.

Dumas had at last harnessed himself to a tragedy based on Anicet Bourgeois' scenario. The subject was the Rome of the debauched Caesars, of Caligula, Messalina, Claudius, and Cherea, lover of Messalina, in contrast to the Christian purity of Stella, daughter of Julia who had been nurse to Caligula. It is possible that Alexandre had begun his tragedy while he was in the National Guard's House of Detention, between May eighth and tenth. On June twenty-ninth, he coolly rejected a proposition of collaboration with Armand Durantin, because:

> I am so preoccupied with my tragedy, *Caligula* (which I expect to read for the Théâtre-Français), that I cannot be as useful to you as I would like to be. In any case . . . it would never be for a collaboration. I have entirely given up this kind of work which debases art into a trade.

Dumas was not so preoccupied with his tragedy that he gave up the comedy of vanities! The Dear Duc d'Orléans had married the romantic Hélène de Mecklenbourg-Schwerin. A formal dinner, followed by a ball, would be offered to all the glorious names of France. On the program, promotions to the order of the Légion d'Honneur: *Victor Hugo, Officier*; *Dumas, Chevalier*, were on the list. But Louis-Philippe was tenacious in his resentment. He erased the name of his ex-employee who had so loudly declared himself for the Republic. Alexandre returned his invitation card for the reception in Versailles. Hugo sided with his friend. But a celebration for the greats of France without Dumas, without Hugo, the two top personalities of the new form of art was a farce. In consternation the Duc d'Orléans dared to contradict his father. Louis-Philippe gave up.

For a fete at Versailles, uniforms were compulsory; Alexandre and Victor donned their National Guard uniforms. They toured the Salon des Batailles, they met Delacroix and Balzac, who was dressed as a marquis in clothes rented from a secondhand clothing store. The King was charming, the dear Duke was most gracious. Like a young girl, Alexandre had an attack of vapors simply seeing and talking to him. The feast ended in a gridlock of carriages. It was dawn when Alexandre and Victor went home. With the Prince's friendship, and Hugo's friendship, Alexandre recovered his equilibrium. With such supporters, nothing could resist him. "Why not a theater for both of us?" he proposed to Victor Hugo, the same project they promoted in 1831.

Dumas went back to work on his *Caligula*. The Duc d'Orléans had invited him to the camp at Compiègne which he commanded for the summer army maneuvers. Dumas had accepted but had settled in a guard house at Saint-Corneille. He was completely involved in his work, as he wrote to his son on August nineteenth: "I am reaching my fourth act." He asked the young boy to come and spend a holiday with Aimée Letellier (Dumas' sister) at Bethisy–Saint-Pierre, at the house of his dying cousin Marianne.

Dumas sometimes left Caligula and the court of the Caesars for a picnic on the grass with the Duc d'Orléans. Once Dr. Pasquier carved the chicken. The Duke shivered, "One day it will be me." They all laughed awkwardly. And there was the charming Duchess. She turned the heads of the poets, who all dreamed of being the Alain Chartier who would receive a kiss from this new Mary of Scotland.

On September twenty-sixth the actor Ligier, who was expected to play Caligula, invited Baron Taylor in his and in Dumas' name to attend the reading of the play for the committee of the Comédie-Française which would take place two days hence. The play was unanimously accepted. *Le Moniteur des Théâtres* commented, that its premiere was imposing and added that the show was as new as it was majestic. "Money for my winter," Alexandre mentioned, more prosaically, to Meurice. Advance on advance: six-hundred francs on September twenty-eighth, five thousand francs in October, three hundred francs on October twentieth (advanced for the sketches of the costumes), one thousand two hundred fifty francs on October twenty-seventh. For the Comédie it was ruinous. The rehearsals began on November fifteenth after the censors, in spite of some objections, had authorized the performance. Philoclès Regnier gave his opinion:

> For three months Dumas made us lose our heads with his demands, his follies, his incoherences, to the point that we were thinking that the work he had put into his *Caligula* had made him catch the malady of his hero.

Dumas required Caligula's chariot to be pulled on stage by four white horses. It was refused, and he threatened litigation. The theater offered to replace the horses with women. Dumas did not resist anymore, but invented symbolic characters, the Hour of Day and the Hour of Night, The set designers were on edge: five sets of "rich architecture, decorated with figures," inspired by the frescoes of Pompeii and Herculaneum would be required. The costume makers tore their hair; more than one hundred sixty costumes had been sketched. Paris was enthralled by such extravagances. The loges were booked two months in advance. On December twenty-sixth there was nearly a riot. The regular police force had been increased. The dear Duc and the dear Duchesse d'Orléans were in the royal loge surrounded by the young princes; all the actors of Paris were in the audience. Scandalous gossips, cabals which, Ida insinuated, had been encouraged behind the scenes by Hugo or incited by some of Mlle. George's friends. The head of the claque did not know which way to turn. He had received contradictory orders; he compromised by having his claque applaud with two hands and boo with their lips. The audience had come to be scandalized and they were when a drunken Roman stumbled on stage and when Caligula threw himself upon Stella. They had come to boo and they booed the poor Mme. Paradol, who looked more like a wet nurse than her role required; they came to mock and they mocked Ida, a "callipigian martyr," who, once or twice, caught her feet in her long dresses and almost fell. They were scandalized and railed at Alexandre's arrogance, for available in the lobby during the intermission was a commemorative lead medal with his own left profile on the face and the inscription: *Caligula tragédie en V actes et en vers Ligier cr.*; and on the back side: *Théâtre-Français lre repr. de Caligula d'Alexandre Dumas. MDCCCXXXVII, XXVI dec.* "Nothing of the sort has ever been seen before," the audience growled.

But who had listened to the text? There was a battle over *Caligula*, but only an echo, in parody, of the great romantic battles. The fighters, on whatever side they were, believed no longer in the excellence of their cause. Alexandre was dismayed and said a definitive goodbye to tragedy. Ida was enraged when she read the reviews of the press, which reproached her monstrous plumpness. Delphine de Girardin's stabbed her in the heart.

How can one accept the profession of an ingenue with such a waistline? One should at least be movable when one intends to be lifted up every evening.

Alexandre had offered the Duchesse d'Orléans an illustrated manuscript for which he was thanked, as early as the next day, with a bronze by Boulanger de Barye, with the monogram of the Duke and Duchess—*his* bronze, that he would keep lovingly through all the adventures of his life. The edition of the tragedy was dedicated to an unknown spectator, present at the premiere: "The public instinctively has understood that under this visible envelope, there was something mysterious and holy; it listened for four hours with veneration and religion," wrote Dumas who still tried to mask the failure from himself. After twenty performances, however, by February sixteenth, the sales had amounted to less than one thousand francs. Much to Dumas' frustration, Vedel was forced to cancel the overly onerous performances. He attacked Védel's administration violently in *La Presse* of February twenty-third. "I have a drum roll to beat out on M. Védel's skin," he said to Émile de Girardin.

The revival of *Angèle* took place at the Odéon on January fourteenth and was marked by an almost tragic incident—the curtain fell, first on a candle and then on Mlle. Verneuil's head. She was in pain with the bruise for several days. The fault was Ida's, who, to be nearer her audience, wanted the furniture and accessories placed too close to the footlights. At any rate, assailed by the critics, vetoed by the censors who had not been consulted, the play could not survive. With failure after failure, bitterness upon bitterness, Alexandre had developed the temper of a watchdog. Nothing was right; he even had a horrid toothache. Ida avenged herself for the attacks with an excessive jealousy. Alexandre now kept only parasites as friends. Time to leave Paris? Yes, but he needed money.

The friendship of princes had gone to his head. He had left the modest apartment on Rue Bleu for 22 Rue de Rivoli, almost facing the Tuileries. The fourth floor apartment with a balcony had a magnificent view. Large and practical, it was furnished with great taste by Ida. But where to find the money? First, he would sell the columns from *La Presse* to bookstores. Then he would help Dauzats to write *Quinze jours au Sinai* from notes the latter took during a trip he made in 1830 with Baron Taylor. Then sell this work to *La Revue de Paris*, then to the bookseller Dumont. What else? Use

Le Capitaine Paul, a drama written in Calabria, refused by Harel and offered to Porcher in exchange for paying a debt. Then Le Siècle wanted a serial and Le Capitaine Paul became a novel.

Alexandre gathered in all he could. He wrote as much as possible. If he chose the romantic style, it was because it sold well. The noble genre remained for the theater. He followed the tendency of his time and, if sometimes he seemed even to anticipate it, it was because he was more sensitive than anyone to the modifications of contemporary taste. Dumas, the novelist, was born from his need for money and from the historical chronicle.

More money came with the treatise on La Vie de Napoléon that he signed with Édouard Mennechet, director of the Plutarque Français—five hundred francs cash on June 2, 1838, plus five francs upon the delivery of each part. He sold L'Histoire d'un ténor to La Revue et gazette musicale de Paris; he utilized the research on the Roman Empire that he did for Caligula to produce income by telling the story of Nero and his freed slave, Acté—who finally would give his name to the novel. This novel would appear in the Dumas bibliography as his first historic novel. Romantic fiction took precedence over the simple dramatized chronicle.

The master of the literary section of La Presse and, through this platform a master of public opinion, Dumas had broken off with Girardin and became the property of another newspaper, Le Siècle, for which he had to produce. A master, or almost, at the Comédie-Française, which was looking for a king, Alexandre had by his exigencies and his extravagances alienated the good Védel and the members of the theater. He was now reduced to lean toward foreign works, such as this Bourgeois de Gand by Hippolyte Romand, which triumphantly opened at the Odéon on May 21, 1838. This multiplication of odd works at the beginning of 1838 might have had financial advantages but it was also a manifestation of confusion. Dumas would find his way, though, even when he believed he was going astray.

V

A Dark Page

Madame Dumas was dying. Since her stroke in 1829, she had been bedridden in her distant apartment at No. 118, Faubourg Saint-Denis. Her very brief time of happiness had been followed by twenty years of widowhood, spent in apprehension for her son—her so tender, so good, but so foolish son—who dragged behind him so many dissolute women. Some of them had been kind to her, Mélanie Waldor, for example; but the others who exhibited themselves in theaters: that Belle and now this Ida! Her joys were few: Alexandre's hurried visits, dinners with her grandson on Sundays when the boarding school let him free. He was a well-behaved child, too well-behaved, in fact. It was a time when almost every day brought a new reason to mourn. Their cousin, Marianne Fortier died on March 25, 1838, in the small house at Bethisy–Saint-Pierre.

Alexandre did not want to cease being a child; he did not want his mother to die. To protect her as she became weaker, he brought her nearer to him. He asked his cousin Deviolaine to take the very sick woman into her apartment in the Faubourg du Roule. Death was a family affair and all Villers-Cotterêts grouped around the dying woman.

Paris was basking in the sun. Alexandre had celebrated his thirty-sixth birthday. He cried for long periods. Ida was irritated by this sentimentality; she detested the Dumas family, so Alexandre found consolation elsewhere. In his sorrow he wrote to his dear Duke, "At the bedside of my dying mother, I pray God to keep for you your father and your mother."

Somewhat later a footman came to the apartment. Alexandre followed him to a carriage, the door of which was open. Alexandre threw himself on the lap of the Prince and cried. The Prince himself would cause Alexandre's next tears.

Alexandre also called the painter Amaury Duval, so that at least his mother's memory did not disappear: "My mother is dying, my dear Amaury. I have no portrait of her; I count on your friendship to do me this last favor."

Madame Dumas heaved her last breath on August 1, 1838. She would rest beside her husband in the small cemetery of Villers-Cotterêts, where she used to make her daily pilgrimage. Alexandre was so prostrated that his sister Aimée had to organize the funeral. The sad procession left Paris on the third. On the next day, all of Villers-Cotterêts was assembled for the last rites and to carry Marie-Louise to her grave. Alexandre sobbed heavily. "You expressed regrets which could sweeten my pain, if the pain of a son who loses his mother could be sweetened," he wrote the next day, on his return to Paris, to the Haitians who intended to raise a statue of his father, Général Dumas, in Haiti.

"A great sorrow made me leave Paris and look for solitude on the banks of the Rhine." This was the official and definitive version. The truth was that the trip had been prepared long before. Alexandre was almost ashamed to pull himself away from his grief and leave Paris on the eighth or the ninth of August, 1838, as he did. As proof, there was the erasure on the manuscript of his *Excursions sur les bords du Rhin*. He had previously written: "I arrived at Brussels on August 10." Over the "1" he wrote a "2" and it remained as "August 20," to suggest a longer sorrow. Ida and Alexandre stayed at the Hôtel de la Reine de Suède. Brussels was the central point for their excursions in Belgium. It was a very well-filled week in which they strolled about the city, which was only a provincial town with a King with whom it was very easy to visit at Laeken. This taste for princes may seem out of character for a republican, but was he still a republican, this 1830 firebrand, this artilleryman of popular conspiracies? Probably he was, but his opinions were now more nuanced. The friendships with princes colored it:

Belonging myself to an old family whose name that, through strange circumstances, I do not bear anymore and in spite of my nearly republican opinions, I always made it my duty to glorify our old nobility instead of diminishing it. . . . Unbecoming attacks against the nobility came in part through the fault of those who reigned; they degraded France; they have torn off her arms piece by piece to throw them to barking rioters; they have scratched her coat of arms, the oldest, the most beautiful of all, to put on it a notary's book or a banker's register and I do not even know what kind of billboard.

(to the Duc d'Auffray, June 1838)

Yet the republican in him meant he would not miss the compulsory pilgrimage to Waterloo! The national epic transcended the political chasms. In Anvers, the superb Rubens in the cathedral and the museum; at Gand, the Quai aux herbes in the moonlight; at Bruges, the sleeping town of Arabian tales, the tomb of Charles le Téméraire; at Malines, the parades and feast for the Jubilee of Notre-Dame d'Hanswyck. The railroad now permitted rapid travel between towns. However, as Alexandre deplored, "It is possible that the railroad is a marvelous invention for traveling salesmen and luggage, but it is also the surest way to ruin the picturesque and the poetic." He filled his travel album with what he saw, with stories, legends, new impressions. Again, in four hours, the train took them about fifty-five miles away, to Liège, an execrable dinner and a hard bed. They visited the city, then took a carriage to Aix-la-Chapelle. Prussian discipline required that the border be crossed only at the designated hour and that travelers not exchange seats with the next person. At Aix-la-Chapelle, in the cathedral, before Charlemagne's mausoleum, Alexandre bent his head and recited to himself the beautiful monologue of Charles the Fifth from Act IV of *Hernani*. At Cologne, the next day, they stayed in a hovel bearing the pompous name of Hôtel de Hollande and they saw the still unfinished, yet imposing cathedral. And, most important for them, the Rhine:

It is difficult for us French to understand the Germans' deep veneration for the Rhine. For them it is a sort of protective divinity which . . . contains in its waters a quantity of naiads, ondines, good or evil genii that the people's poetic imagination sees during the day through the veil of its blue waters and at night, sometimes sitting, sometimes wandering on its banks. For them, the Rhine is a universal symbol; the Rhine is strength; the Rhine is independence; the Rhine is liberty.

Alexandre embarked for the land of legends on a steamer which spat fire and smoke with, of course, a *Taschenbuch* in his pocket and his album always at hand. It may seem surprising that Alexandre knew enough German to pick up the legends of the country. But there was Ida who, with her considerable heftiness and her jealousy, would earn the role of a detestable heavyweight in future biographies.

Ida had been brought up in a boarding school in Strasbourg by German canonesses. She had an excellent education, spoke and wrote German admirably. Between Cologne and Bonn, the landscape seemed to pass on each side of the boat, as if the view had no time to stop. Capricious, full of curves, the Rhine "abruptly hides from you behind some of its angles, the village or the castle you were following with your eyes. . . . Then other villages, other towns, other castles pass by." At Bonn the travelers went to the Hôtel de l'Étoile, managed by the poet Simrock's brother who took the role of cicerone for the French poet. Unfortunately, there was nothing remarkable about Bonn, so they made an excursion into the surrounding countryside. And, wonder of wonders, Simrock had reserved for the night "a real bed, with a real box spring, real mattresses, real sheets, a real blanket, a real pillow." A bed for the French taste, in fact.

They again took the amphibious "dragon-boat" for Coblenz where Alexandre wanted to salute the grave of Général Marceau, his father's companion in arms. On Saturday, August twenty-fifth, they stopped at Holzenfels to visit the ancient castle recently restored by the Prince of Prussia. The curator, hearing the name of Dumas, opened the doors wide and offered grand hospitality, the most exquisite food, the finest wine, and a bed which probably had belonged to Frederick Barbarossa. "If you come to Paris," promised Alexandre, "I will somehow or other try to match your hospitality."—"And for you the same, if you come to Berlin." And whom to ask for? Quite simple, ask for the Royal Prince. The curator was none other than the future Frederick-William IV of Prussia.

The banks of the Rhine rose, clothed with vineyards and topped by castles in ruin, vestiges of the ancient frontier outposts. The travelers leaned over the river to see the Lorelei with her blonde hair. Frankfurt was the goal for the first part of the trip. They settled down at the Hôtel de l'Empereur Romain. The *Journal de Frankfurt* immediately called attention to the arrival of such a distinguished guest. Its director, Charles Durand, was a strange character who had been prosecutor for the King at Bastia and alternately novelist, author of operettas in the provinces, then itinerant professor of literature, then director of the newspaper of La Haye. Charles Durand generously opened his house to Alexandre. His wife was twenty-three, and had the "chest of a sphinx." Could Alexandre resist? Of course, he won over the beautiful Octavia's heart and soon had the husband in the palm of his hand. He had not been twelve hours in the free city of Frankfurt and already he was master in the Durand household. But neither Octavia's charm nor the importance of the town could explain Dumas' long stay in Frankfurt. Alexandre was expecting Gérard de Nerval.

He spent time by writing ("I have 20 letters to write about Belgium and the Rhine provinces. Do you want them for 2,000 francs? Half of the letters are already done"—to Achille Bindeau of the *Messager*, August thirty-first); by walking and excursions in the Taunus and the Duchy of Nassau; by making love. Under the pretense that he was not at ease for writing at the Hôtel de l'Empereur Romain because of the noise and thanks to three thousand francs he had borrowed from Durand, he had rented a small apartment. A woman, face veiled, came sometimes to meet him: Mme. Durand.

But in spite of a pleasant and pressing letter Alexandre had sent to him about August twenty-seventh, de Nerval did not arrive:

> Dear friend, out of consideration for you, I have chosen Frankfurt-sur-le-Main, fatherland of Goethe, for sitting upon the egg you have laid. Although the town is not large and I am not hard to find here, remember carefully that I am staying at the Hôtel de l'Empereur Romain. It takes five days to come here, pleasantly amusing yourself along the way; try not to take fifteen days.

What was the egg laid by Gérard de Nerval on which Alexandre was sitting? It was the scenario for a drama, *Léo Burckart*, which has as its subject the German secret societies.

At last, Gérard arrived around September fifteenth; he was lodged in the small lovenest. Alexandre was not too displeased with the delay, which had permitted him to prolong the intoxicating first moments of his new affair. De Nerval was fascinated by his illustrious collaborator's social life—evenings spent at the Bethmanns' or at the Rothschilds'. Gérard was soon drawn into this whirl. For instance, an evening and supper at the house of the Russian envoy who had Durand on his payroll; a carriage trip to the principality of Hamburg where the French Protestants had regrouped, keeping their native language and their peculiarities; an evening at the theater; a hunting party offered by M. de Rothschild for the writer. Gérard was getting quite dizzy from this glory in which he shared.

The egg stirred. They had met Mme. de Rothschild's physician who claimed to have been a schoolmate of Karl-Ludwig Sand, the young German patriot who had murdered the dramatist Kotzebue, a traitor to the German nation. Alexandre had to go to Mannheim to reconstitute, little by little, the passionate life of Sand and his martyrdom. On the boat there were two women, Octavia Durand and Ida, and three men, Alexandre, Gérard, and the young Alexandre Weill. In appearance they seemed very conventional travelers, yet they were held together by the strangest sentimental ties: the two women belonged to the same man but kept their jealousy silent; Gérard was enamored of Ida; A. Weill desired the beautiful Octavia Durand; all sighed secretly, but the fame of the master kept a lid on all overt demonstrations. At Mannheim they visited Sand's house and the *Sandhimmelfahrt*, the place where his torture was memorialized. They met the director of the prison who had attended to Sand's last wishes.

At the hotel, Ida and Dumas were in the room next to the one occupied by de Nerval. Around midnight, Alexandre, in his nightgown, too quickly opened the creaking door. "Where are you going" cried Ida, abruptly awakened. "I have an atrocious colic," answered Alexandre, who dropped to the floor squealing loudly enough to break one's heart. Ida and Gérard helped him to get up and back to bed. One hour later, he again went through the door. "Leave this damned door open," he whispered to Gérard while he went stealthily to the room in which Mme. Durand feigned sleep.

Drama followed farce! The next day, Alexandre and Gérard piously listened to the testimony of the prison director who recounted Karl-Ludwig Sand's last hours. They copied the official documents, then they were taken to the small cemetery where the traitor, Kotzebue, and the martyr, Sand, rested. Alexandre broke a frond from a wild plum tree which was growing on Sand's grave, picked up a piece of ivy that clung on Kotzebue's monument and took both with him, twisted together.

Alexandre said goodbye to Octavia. He had promised the world to her husband: the direction of a newspaper in Paris, perhaps. They would meet to love one another again.

At Heidelberg, Alexandre and Gérard rushed to see the son of Sand's executioner. Gérard did not understand German well enough to keep up a conversation and had to ask Ida for help. But the young Wideman was only fourteen when the tragedy took place and he could not remember or say much about it. His father had arranged that the scaffold, sanctified by the martyr's blood, would be retired from use; the young man showed them the épée used for the beheading, rusted where Sand's blood had stained it.

Nothing now could keep the friends longer on the banks of the Rhine. They stopped in Strasbourg on their way back and took a coach which left at seven in the evening and brought them three days later to Paris. It seems that Gérard, perhaps tired from a long and dull trip had left them at Troyes. Alexandre and Ida reached Paris on the evening of October second.

Now that the trip had ended, it was time to exploit it. Dumas did not practice gratuitous tourism; he intended to extract all the profit he could from the literary culture of the countries he had visited. First he gave his letters, each dedicated to one of his painter friends, to the *Revue de Paris* under the title *La Belgique et la Conféderation Germanique* (September–November 1838). A little later he offered the readers of *Le Siècle* the legends extracted from medieval Germanic folklore (*Othon l'archer*, *Chronique du roi Pépin*, *Chronique de Charlemagne*). In spite of tentative romantic chronicles, he remained preoccupied with drama. Upon his return to Paris he was thrown into a violent rage when he heard that the inimitable Porcher had taken advantage of his absence to turn out *Paul Jones*. Alexandre, during one of his frequent periods of penury, had entrusted the work to Porcher against an advance of money. Porcher "entrusted" it to the director of the Panthéon theater who was Porcher's son-in-law. A Dumas play in a third-class theater!

Not only was it played, but to make it absolutely convincing that the play was from the famous Dumas, his manuscript was exhibited in the theater lobby. Still it was better to have a solid success in a third-class theater than a flop at the Comédie-Française! Besides, Dumas was in demand for much more important projects. The theatrical scene was changing that autumn: Buloz, director of *La Revue des deux mondes*, had been named royal superintendent to the Théâtre-Français on October seventeenth. Furthermore, the theater of La Renaissance would open its season on November eighth with *Ruy Blas*. The theater of La Renaissance? A temple in which the genius of Dumas and Hugo, as heads of the Romantic School would be honored. An old dream at last realized! In 1836, at Alexandre's request, the dear Duc d'Orléans had obtained the privilege of having a theater consecrated to the romantic repertory. Alexandre and Victor Hugo chose Anténor Joly as director, granting the privilege of founding what would become a second Théâtre-Français.

But a privilege is not sufficient to create a theater. A location is of first necessity. They could lease the Odéon, but it took time to gather the funds and the Comédie-Française had taken the building over. The Salle Ventadour, near the Porte-Saint-Martin, was the second choice. It was baptized with a solemn name: Théâtre de la Renaissance. Renaissance of the theater, of course. They had, therefore, to think of the production to follow *Ruy Blas*. Alexandre offered *Léo Burckart* which was greeted with long faces. He had to try again. To deal with the most urgent matters first, he took over a three-act drama, *Un Soir de carnaval*, whose author had been one of Gérard's friends in the past. This man used the name of Augustus Mac-Keat, but his real name was Auguste Maquet. His play had been refused everywhere. He had asked Gérard de Nerval's help, but he preferred to turn the project over to Dumas. Alexandre had at the moment two plays in progress, *L'Alchimiste* and *Mademoiselle de Belle-Isle*. He agreed to consider this *Soir de carnaval*, perhaps to give in to Gérard's wish or to please Ida. Maquet's drama had the kind of female part that she liked, a young girl, pure and unhappy. An ironic antithesis! Alexandre rewrote everything, even the title, which became *Bathilde*, and Ida made her debut at the

Renaissance in the title role. Maquet had now broken into Dumas' pattern of work but was only a short-lived collaborator, quickly forgotten because the great event during the last months of 1838 was the return to the Théâtre-Français. If tragedy had been a resounding failure, would comedy prove anything more than a gamble? A comedy from the pen of the author of *Henri III*, *Antony*, and *Angèle*? What pushed the master of drama to poach on these preserves when one of his dramas was recognized by the opening of the Théâtre de la Renaissance? It was a dire and urgent need. He owed a play to the Théâtre-Français which, though bad at tragedy, was excellent at comedy.

The plot of *Mademoiselle de Belle-Isle* was not new. It was based on a farce by Brunswick that had been refused once by the Porte-Saint-Martin: a young girl leaves home over night to visit her father who is in prison. Because the next day she cannot say where she went, she is compromised. Brunswick had taken his rejected comedy to the perennial play doctor, Dumas, who asked to think about it and thought for a long time. Discouraged, Brunswick sold his rights to a bookseller, but soon Dumas found the right introductory scene, the "scene of the sequin (gold coin)." From it, the comedy reeled off rapidly. Within fifteen days it was complete in Dumas' head and in an even shorter time it was in manuscript. The play pretended to be a drama, but if the title roles still belonged to this genre, the part of the Duke de Richelieu, that most mythical companion of Grandfather Davy de la Pailleterie, pulled the play toward a comedy of intrigue. The play was ready at the beginning of December and was read and unanimously accepted on January fifteenth. To embellish the raw facts, Dumas would later pretend that he had recited the text when not a line of it had yet been written. This is of course legend to amuse his audience. The reality was an advance of two thousand five hundred francs that fell into his money pouch on January nineteenth.

It was a play for Mlle. Mars, but in which role? The witty Mme. de Prie? Mlle. de Belle-Isle? Mlle. Mars' most respectable age favored the first, but the part of Gabrielle de Belle-Isle was younger and longer. Again an ironic contradiction. The small world of the actresses of the Comédie and their protectors was all in a flutter. Mlle. Mars, whom wishful thinkers had been pushing toward retirement, still had enough power to impose her will. At sixty, she would be Mlle. de Belle-Isle, the ingenue who had not yet reached twenty.

During the last rehearsal, the door of the loge where Dumas was enthroned had opened; a tall and rather handsome woman sat down to the author's left and looked at Mlle. Mars, who seemed to have drunk nectar. At the end of the act, the visitor turned to Alexandre:

"Oh!" she said with blazing eyes, "these swinish authors would not throw roles of that kind my way!"

Marie Dorval, the dear and whimsical Marie, had come from the provinces where she was more the "money pump" than ever, to take in the première of *Mademoiselle de Belle-Isle*.

Slightly licentious, very amusing and witty, the comedy attracted "the beautiful ladies" who applauded this reincarnation of Antony. "Great success!" recorded the stage manager on the evening of the premiere, April 2, 1839. The critics of the important and the smaller newspapers followed suit. The prince of them all, Jules Janin, who had so violently attacked *Caligula* that Alexandre had challenged him to a duel, gushed praises.

Alexandre dedicated his comedy to Mlle. Mars, so that "comedy could go back to its source." Did this sudden unanimity of opinion mean that the former angry young man had settled down?

VI
The Death of Byron

At age thirty-seven, Byron died at Missolonghi. It was a blessing to die young, in full glory. Alexandre had to endure. His *Alchimiste* was played at the Renaissance on April 10, 1839, a week after *Mademoiselle de Belle-Isle*, with a mixed success in spite of a remarkable character created by Frédérick Lemaître. Still, it was a success while at the Porte-Saint-Martin *Léo Burckart* was a total failure which distressed the poor Gérard de Nerval. He had rewritten the play completely, leaving hardly two hundred lines from his famous collaborator. The theater would not save him from insanity.

Alexandre filled *Le Siècle* with his prose. He also gave *Le Capitaine Pamphile* to the *Journal des enfants* and the *Mémoires d'un maître d'armes* to *La Revue de Paris*. He also offered in bookstores a translation of the *Dernières lettres de Jacques Ortis* by Ugo Foscolo, a *Napoléon* appeared in the *Panthéon littéraire* and he participated in the *Crimes célèbres*, written jointly by Alexandre Dumas, Arnould, Fournier, Fiorentino, and Mallefille.

His work poured forth in a flow of ink, poured, too, from the veins of secret collaborators among whom one could guess was Pier-Angelo Fiorentino, a young Neapolitan Alexandre had met in Naples, who had emigrated to Paris. But it was difficult to recognize in this chaos any thread of purpose—besides a need for money. Alexandre was sinking in an ocean of debts.

A savior had appeared in the person of Jacques Domange, son of a jeweler from Metz, who had come to Paris to make a fortune constructing drains and sewers. He was Ida's distant relative. The sprightly Domange had purchased a large part of Alexandre's debts and had loaned him great amounts of money. He was a businessman and intended to be repaid. Alexandre had to pledge his author's rights to Domange. Thus it was Domange who benefited from the fabulous success of *Mademoiselle de Belle-Isle* and he alone. As for Alexandre, he had shiny baubles of glory for consolation, for King Charles-Jean of Sweden decorated him with the order of Gustave Wasa.

Domange might also be credited with pulling the strings behind a rather grotesque marriage which legalized Alexandre's and Ida's eight years of living together. Certainly the demon in Alexandre had not yet retreated, for it still yielded to the slightest temptation, to any desirable woman passing by, even if she left only a scant trace of her passage, such as letters like the ones from the mysterious Ad (Adèle) in April of 1838:

You are so very worthy of all the love of a woman who would know how to appreciate you that I am afraid to abandon myself to such a sentiment. I feel all the danger of having a fleeting liaison with you. There are so many reasons to fear that you would not love me, or at least, that it would be only a fancy or a whim for you. For two days I have wanted to write you at least twenty times. I do not know what fear kept me back; I tremble to be without a reply from you; I tremble to destroy in you a feeling in which I did not believe but that, nonetheless, I was pleased to attribute to you and in the middle of my wavering your letter came. I read it, read it again with a happiness that nothing can describe to you and I do not hesitate anymore—I am writing to you; I follow the impulse of my heart, very certain that you will not take advantage of it.

Or again, later, at the time of the sweetest kisses:

It is impossible for me to go today to the Rue de Rivoli; I am a bit sick; I play tonight and I hardly have the strength to stand up. Tomorrow or later I will write to you and we will fix a day—until then, send me news from you, your letters are my only comfort; they make me accept your absence; they make me believe in your love; they make me as happy as I can be so far from you. Adieu, my dear friend, a thousand tender kisses.

Your Ad. Friday, April thirteenth.

An actress ("I play tonight"), a woman free after leaving yesterday's lover for Alexandre, was waiting at Rue de Rivoli for an unlikely love. Is it possible to imagine, even for an instant, that a man who so loved women could get married? Moreover, with an old mistress! However, it has to be accepted, and an explanation must be suggested for the unexplainable. It was said that the dear Duke, during a great reception, had told Dumas, who introduced Ida to him, "I am charmed to know Mme. Dumas. I hope that you will introduce your wife to us at a more intimate reunion." A legend, surely, even if the royal castle was then under a spell of matrimania. It was said, too, that Alexandre had answered a question about his reasons for this most surprising union, "My dear, it is to get rid of her." The boorishness cannot be understood as only a witticism, and the bilious critic, Viel-Castel, can be believed when he reported that Ida had bought all her lover's debts and had asked him to choose between marriage and debtors' prison. This malice contained a great deal of truth. In Ida, Jacques Domange had a guarantor for his loans. The marriage was accompanied by financial bargainings.

Domange saved Alexandre from bankruptcy and gave back to Ida the accessories of her splendor:

As I presume Ida will be very pleased to have sooner than later her beautiful diamond ring, add 1,500 francs to the sum you will bring me tomorrow. (to Jacques Domange, February 1840)

The banns were now officially published. Paris was amused by the unbelievable, while in other circles, there was indignation that the liaison with the "vampire" had become a legitimate union. Mélanie Waldor headed an offensive in the name of the young Alexandre, who was then at the Hénon boarding school and took courses at the Collège Bourbon. The adolescent hated Ida, and she returned the feeling tenfold. In a letter, he solemnly let it be known that he was opposed to the planned marriage. Mélanie Waldor had her husband's orderly deliver this ultimatum to the house of Domange where, it was believed, Dumas was hiding out. Again it was Mélanie who decided to intervene with the witnesses for the marriage: Chateaubriand, Villemain, the Vicomte de Narbonne-Lara and the Baron de la Bonnardière, to let them know that the illegitimate son was clearly opposed to his father's marriage. Mélanie's romantic imagination was in full flight. She could not accept that her Antony of 1830 could sink into such a sordid marriage. Alexandre was hurt that his marriage for economic reasons could raise so much passion. In January of 1840 he wrote to his son:

My dear child,
It is not my fault but yours if the relations between father and son have suddenly ceased between us. You came to our house; you were well received by everybody. Then, suddenly, it pleased you, excited by I don't know whose advice, to stop greeting the person I consider my wife because I lived with her. From this day, since it was not my intention to take advice, even indirectly, from you, the condition you complain about had begun and, to my great regret, has lasted six years. Now, this condition will stop the day you want it to stop: Write a letter to Madame Ida, ask her to be for you what she is to your sister and you will always and eternally be welcome. The happiest thing that could happen for you is that this liaison should last, because, as I have not had any children for six years now, I have *the certitude* of not having any and you will thus remain my only son, my eldest son.
                              I kiss you with all my heart,
                                            Alex Dumas
P.S. You should, instead of signing Alex Dumas as I do which could cause us both some great inconvenience some day, since our two handwritings are similar, sign Dumas Davy. My name is too well known, you understand, to risk any doubt and I cannot add 'père.' I am too young for that.

The adolescent's recriminations did not prevent the affair from following its course. The marriage contract was signed February first: Alexandre "brings in marriage and personally considers as his dowry the property of all his literary and dramatic work, appraised at two hundred thousand francs." Ida, who was identified as without a profession, on her side brought "clothes, linen, jewelry and silver for her use; the whole of a value of twenty thousand francs and a sum of one hundred thousand francs in cash" (of which she had not the first cent). To ennoble this fallacious contract were the signatures of the most illustrious of witnesses: M. François-Auguste, Vicomte de Chateaubriand, peer of France and M. Abel-François Villemain, peer of France, Minister of Public Instruction, friends of the future husband; M. Nicolas-Roger-Maurique, Vicomte de Narbonne-Lara and M. Gaspard Couret de la Bonnardière, officier de la Légion d'Honneur, Counselor of State, friends of the future wife. Paul Lacroix's commentary on the symbolic importance of the presence of Chateaubriand and Villemain was aimed at Alexandre: here are two names that can be translated "young men who have obtained and deserved the most beautiful dramatic success of our time; you, poet, you, novelist, you, traveler, you must pass under the Caudine Forks of classical Hymen in order to reach ministerial employment and to enter the Academy!"

On February fifth, the betrothed couple went to the city hall of their district for their civil marriage. To this ceremony of middling solemnity, they were accompanied by their witnesses and by the good Nodier who took advantage of the proximity of a bookstore to buy a few books. Chateaubriand and Villemain had passed along the chore of being witnesses at the religious ceremony to Louis Boulanger and to the architect Robelin. Nevertheless, the vicar of Saint Roch read his discourse as he had prepared it:

'Illustrious author of the *Génie du christianisme!*'—and he turned to Louis Boulanger who displayed a magnificent beard in the style "Jeune-France"—'and you, correct and polite writer who holds in your hands the destiny of our language and of public instruction!'—and he addressed Charles Robelin whose hands were adorned with yellow gloves worth two francs fifty centimes a pair—'yours is a noble and honorable patronage, gentlemen, for this young neophyte who comes to the foot of the altar to implore a sacred baptism of marriage!

Young man, I will repeat to you the words of the great Bishop Rémy to King Clovis: "Bend your head, proud Sicambre; adore what you have burnt, burn what you adored!" Be it now that from your pen comes only Christian work, edifying, evangelical! Leave behind you now those dangerous emotions of the theater, those perfidious sirens of passion, those abominable pomps of Satan; M. le Vicomte de Chateaubriand and M. Villemain, I regret that M. Charles Nodier has not come but you will answer before God and before men for the literary conversion of this fiery romantic heresiarch. Do become the godparents of his books and of his children. This is what I wish for him, my dear brothers. And so be it!'

After this parody of a sermon, as reported by Paul Lacroix, the good vicar of Saint Roch asked the newlyweds and their witnesses to sign the church register; he then noticed his mistakes and cheered up only when he remembered Alexandre's general confession.

"Thanks to the sacrament of marriage licensed by Her Majesty the Queen of the French, one can achieve anything in this golden age of the civil list," was Lacroix's ironic comment. What was Alexandre's goal? The Academy? Without a doubt. The end of disorder in his life? Perhaps. A healthier financial position, which would take away the fear of meeting a process server or a creditor at each bend of the road? Certainly. He had obtained the glory and money he had so much desired during his adolescence but, if he had known how to renew the tools of his glory, he had never known how to hold on to the flow of money that ran through his fingers. He was now cornered. His only way out was voluntary exile. According to Ida in a letter to Jacques Domange, November 2, 1840,

When I met my husband six years ago, he had already enjoyed his greatest successes and had earned enormous amounts of money. He had just left Mme. Serre, however, and I found him without a sou: no furniture because he was having new furniture made to fill his apartment, no silver, no linen, nothing at all, nothing but debts! ! ! . . . these debts had increased at once by his agreeing to a support arrangement of 20,000 francs, as you know, and by assuming the responsibility of the child's boarding school which made, *from that side alone,* a small regular allowance of one thousand ecus per year which did nothing but increase since the child was growing up. On the other side he had his invalid mother who depended on him alone and cost him at least another thousand ecus per year. Then again, there were Mme. Labbé [sic] and his son for whom, at the same time, he had set up a literary office which was very costly to him, to speak of all that they grabbed from him through the year and the boarding school of M. his son.—*For five consecutive years*, he has had to support a M. Fontaine [servant] who had to be clothed, fed and lodged while doing nothing and who, moreover, had swindled him out of enormous sums of money from funds my husband gave him to pay for bills *that he did not pay*, and up to sums of *five hundred francs* at one time that he gambled and lost. Here is, therefore, a regular amount of expenses of some *ten thousand francs per year* of which not a sou was for us. But that is nothing in comparison to the following: There were M. Rusconi, M. Lecomte, etc., etc., etc., whom he has had in his charge for years. I remember having paid myself *with my money* the account of M. Lecomte's tailor to an amount of 1,300 francs with the extras. Not to speak of notes he cosigned and the cash money they swindled from him every day. And of all that I am telling you, I have proof in my hands. Add to this his sister for whom he opened accounts in all the stores which supplied us, *the cousins, the nephews, the mistresses* and tell me, when one has already a considerable amount of debt and because of one's position one must keep up a rather elegant life and that, above all, one does not know what order means, tell me whether it is not possible to fall into a bottomless abyss.

One thing more that must be taken into account: this trip to Italy that we took five years ago which was intended to be a speculation and which, as with so many other projects, was a mistake. For this trip he created shares of stock for a rather high sum; he remained absent a year, without working, which already caused a deficit of some thirty thousand francs. He commissioned and paid for drawings which are, at present, I don't know where and which will never be used for anything. It was necessary to refund these shares little by little and you know that has not been done . . . finally . . . I could write you volumes about these causes for ruin for which, with my hand raised before God, I can swear I am not responsible. And just think that to pay all these expenses there is only the profit from work that varies constantly and the return from which is most irregular, especially when the business is kept in the greatest disorder, the signing right and left of notes and letters of credit that were hidden from me because his motives were concealed from me. How do you expect me to be able to do anything for or against such deplorable conditions?

Autopsy of a bankruptcy: parasitism, disorder.
In that year, 1840, order took the face of a city—Florence.

PART
V

The Capitol and the
Tarpeian Rock

I

One Year at Florence

"Midway in the journey of our life, I found myself in a dark wood, for the straight way was lost."

(Dante, *The Divine Comedy*)

Florence, if it was not Hell, was at least Purgatory. Alexandre had not actually run away. Glory imposed its obligations; he had majestically prepared his exile and the work he would have to write to redeem himself. He had to take advantage of his travel albums stuffed with notes. He also took with him scenarios of plays to mend or to rebuild, among them one of Latour's dramas that Maquet had submitted to him.

He offered a working method to Buloz (May 15, 1840):

Please, present on my behalf to the committee of the Théâtre-Français the following propositions:
A five-act drama for the month of December.
Plus: I would like to translate and imitate, in verses, Shakespeare's *Hamlet*, *Macbeth*, and *Julius Caesar*, so that these plays take the place of Ducis' and Voltaire's plays in the repertory, which are seldom or not at all shown—and it is not I who give the reason but I have heard it from the very mouths of some of your Gentlemen Members—that these plays have aged.

During his absence, Dumas' interests were to be in the hands of Jacques Domange, of course, "proprietor of my author's rights" and "moreover bearer of my general power."

Alexandre and Ida had said goodbye to everyone at the end of May. They had boarded ship at Marseille on June fifth and settled in Florence on June seventh.

We arrived in good health at Florence, not on the second, as we had hoped because we stayed five days in Marseille to rest, but on the evening of the seventh. Three days later we were settled. Now, please God grant me the eloquence of the serpent, for I would very much like to persuade you and convince you to come spend a month with us. . . . You would take the State-operated boat; the accommodations would cost 80F for you and 80F for your carriage, plus 60F for each one of your servants; it will take you straight to Livorno in twenty-six hours. Among the state boats which leave on the first, eleventh, and twenty-first of each month there is no choice; all are good.

When arriving in Livorno, try, if possible, to leave your carriage fully loaded so you will need to use the *facchini* as little as possible. They are, together with those of Avignon, the greatest scoundrels on earth; there is nothing to see in Livorno so call on two customs men; give them ten francs to seal your luggage and they will take you for some kind of queen traveling incognito, call you 'Your Majesty,' will not rumple one of your handkerchiefs and will wish you a good trip. You will make this good trip in six hours; in six hours, not one minute more, not a minute less, you will be with your good friends who will be very happy to see you and who will do all they can to avoid crying with joy when kissing you. . . . For 855F therefore, and I figure generously, you will have arrived; you will have yourself driven to Porta alla Croce, Pallazzo Lagestverde—we kiss you and we talk of your getting settled.

Either you will have a charming main-floor opening on a garden with a double drawing room, double boudoir, double bedroom, double bathroom, double dining room and five or six other rooms that I do not mention, all of them for 300F a month, furnished, of course; or you could accept in our own apartment a bedroom, boudoir, small drawing room, bathroom and dressing room which we can spare for you . . . and in this case you would pay per month half of our rent which is 200F. . . . We have an excellent cook; we spend 500F per month for our table. . . . Finally we have a carriage at our disposal from eight o'clock in the morning until midnight, for 264F per month. . . .

What do you think of my letter? I hope a manager would not have done better and certainly would have robbed you much more. (to Mlle. Mars, June 1840)

An Eden, this palace with a belvedere and a theater, plus twelve rooms and a garden as large as the Luxembourg gardens, with water works, fountains, naiads, tritons, laurel groves, lemon tree groves and a gardener named Demetrium. What could Adam and Eve lack to taste fully this paradise, dreamed of once before by Caroline Ungher? Their Parisian friends: Louis Boulanger, Jadin, Mlle. Mars. But Florence was the meeting place of princes in exile, prestigious society that Alexandre very soon was frequenting. He met Jérome Bonaparte, ex-King of Westphalia, who deplored not having his name on the Arc de Triomphe. Alexandre boasted he would intervene with Villemain to repair this oversight. Exiled himself, he dreamed of glorious comebacks, the French Academy, for instance.

In the meantime, he "works like a poor horse to face everything." And on what does he work? From a letter to Maguet, of August 13, 1840 increasingly promoted to his chief collaborator, it is known:

First, you must have received (money) regularly at Dumont's since I have sent already four volumes. Try to get for me the *Voyage* of Mr. de Bussieres in Sicily. (Alexandre, therefore, was preparing the draft of his *Speronare*. . . .)

Now, old boy, here is a small bit of news that must be played up: the City of Florence, having decided that it would have a booklet on its magnificent Galleria degli Uffizi, the most beautiful of all in Italy . . . and that there will be two texts, one Italian, the other French, has contacted your servant for the French text and offered ten thousand francs that he certainly didn't refuse; however, he has accepted only on the condition that he would be free to dedicate the work to M. le Duc d'Orléans. . . .

The work will be made of 350 portraits from Cimabue to M. Ingres by painters who have sent their work to the Galleria.

When he heard from Dumas himself on the terrific deal for *La Galerie de Florence*, Edouard Charton, Director of the *Magasin Pittoresque*, could not hide his indignation.

Alexandre had found a collaborator, Hector de Garriod; he also invited Amaury Duval to execute the drawings which would later be engraved. While the *Impressions de Voyage* refunded Domange in Paris, *La Galerie de Florence* would assure Alexandre the means to live like a prince. "The feasts at Florence do not prevent me from working," he wrote to Collin, whom he would soon entrust with a mission to approach the Comédie-Française, in spite of the "state of anarchy" in which the theater survived. He added, "When have you seen Alexandre (his son)? The stubbornness of this unhappy child is almost my only sorrow; it is he alone who practically forced me to leave Paris."

Hostile Paris, distant Paris, but he still wanted to hold onto it with imperious letters. His hand traced upon the handsome writing paper stamped with his initials on twin shields, personal letters to the unhappy child who seemed to repent of his mistakes:

Your letter brought me a great pleasure because it tells me that you are well and your health is what worries me the most in the world. In any case, I won't go to Paris before the end of January; my absence is very necessary for my finances; you must therefore be patient; and it costs me as much as it does you. . . . Learn German well—it is one of the things that will serve you best; do not neglect the Greek either. The ancient Greek will give you great ease with modern Greek. You know that I would be very pleased if you learned an Oriental language. . . . (to Alexandre fils, September 1840)

There were business letters, too, of which Jacques Domange was the principal addressee. The Mariani affair had to be settled, the privilege at the Opéra-Comique requested from the Duc d'Orléans, an unsuccessful trip to London settled with no scandal and no litigation that could upset the dear Duke, his protector. Dumas continued his hard work. He had finished his impressions of the trip to Belgium and the Rhine and could mail the last pages on

October nineteenth. He would also try, within the ten following days, to send at least three-quarters of the volume on his trip to Italy to Buloz (*La Revue de Paris*) and to the book seller Dumont. He offered his *Medicis* that he had written for *La Galerie de Florence* to *La Revue de Paris*.

In spite of this frantic work, the financial ease they had known before did not return, and Ida choked with indignation when a rumor reached her from Paris, spread by one of Mlle. Mars' confidantes, that the Dumas couple was living in ostentatious luxury. She wrote to Constance Domange, November fourth:

[Domange] knows our meager resources. . . . I impose on myself deprivations of all kinds to keep up the appearance of a decent life here. I do only what is *strictly and indispensably* necessary. It must be realized that some positions demand a display of exterior ease. My husband with his name, finds himself in contact with the highest society and willy-nilly we cannot be impolite with people who seek us out and overwhelm us with politeness. Even without offering *a glass of water* in our home to the people who invite us continually, we must have a fairly decent apartment. To do this as cheaply as possible I have left the good and convenient apartment we had when we arrived here to take another one of rather good appearance but as inconvenient and cold as possible which, because of this, is rented to us quite cheaply. I broke off little by little with all the acquaintances we made when arriving here in all the great households which receive and give parties. . . . We did not leave Florence during the greatest heat when everybody went to spas and to the surrounding countryside where we were invited everywhere. The fear of the smallest expense has nailed me here. I have not bought *one pair of gloves* since I am in Florence and I have ordered only a few pairs of shoes from Paris.

Goodbye to the palazzo's naiades and tritons. Alexandre now has a much more modest house in the via Rondinelli where he settled in a small room. As he will later remember it "with its water-painted walls, its framing garlands, its sober arabesques, its immense bed surrounded by a mosquito net. . . . There I wrote the first volumes of the *Chevalier d'Harmental*, all *Le Corricolo*, all *Le Speronare*. It was a charming white cubicle . . . with white curtains, whose window was opened at eight in the morning onto a courtyard full of the spring sun and wandering breezes and opened let in the branches of an immense jasmine whose flowers, attracted to me, came to paper and perfume my wall, while the two twittering sparrows which give their name to the street built their nest in the corner of the window" (*L'Indépendance Belge*, March 20, 1852).

Farewell the excursions across sweet Italy—although Alexandre had indulged in a short jaunt to the island of Elba in October and prepared to travel again in March from the south to the north of Corsica. But travels and business were then tightly connected. He thought of including Elba and Corsica in his *Impressions de Voyage en Méditerranée*. Goodbye, too, to feasts and magnificence.

Dumas lost himself in his work. He begged Domange for money so he could devote himself again to the theater. He needed to live two months without having to earn money, "Two months, two and one-half months are not too much, I hope; I hope to write two plays," he added bitterly. He thought as much as he could about his plays while doing other work but he had great difficulty putting his ideas in order while he had to plough through other furrows. He was thinking of the casting of plays that were not yet written and on October 20, 1840, he wrote to Domange, "I believe that I can work two more years as I work now and still hold on. It is more than I need to pull myself out of trouble."

Let only Buloz take his *Impressions de Voyage* for *La Revue de Paris*; let Mlle. Mars and the Comédie play his repertory and, as he wrote to Buloz, November 4, 1840,

> I will put myself immediately . . . to a three-act comedy with Louis XV costumes, which everybody already has, and which will take place in one drawing room only.

But while Dumas was sixteen hundred miles away, the vexations in Paris accumulated. Dumont did not keep his promise about the drafts, Buloz seemed to lack honesty, Domange sniveled. Alexandre became angry, gave his statement of account and in a letter to Domange dated November 4, 1850, concluded:

> Send me two thousand francs . . . and I could send first a three-act comedy. . . . As for a second one in five acts, you

must let me have a bit of peace as I really cannot ruin my health and my reputation at the same time. . . . In six months I will have sent you 14,405F worth in manuscripts. . . . What more do you want; what can I do? I cannot work longer than ten hours a day and it is impossible to have eyes and entrails that hurt more than mine do. . . . I expect to cash in my chips soon and then I will be perfectly at peace.

Tortured by stomach pains, half-blinded by a kind of ophthalmia, Alexandre thought back upon his recent past, the already distant happiness of the trips from 1834 to 1835, Hyacinthe, Caroline; his writing, denying the sad present, was the key to those lost paradises.

The five volumes of *Excursions sur les bords du Rhin*, were published serially in *Le Siècle* from August 13 to December 25, 1840; three volumes of *Souvenirs de voyage (Le Midi de la France)* enchanted the subscribers to *La Revue de Paris*, starting November twenty-second. The poor Alexandre was "as an ox to the plough except that I drag my plough both day and night" (to Domange, November 23, 1840). His son's reborn tenderness was a single glimmer in this obscurity:

Rest assured, it is not for six months; it is not for a year; it is not for two years; it is for always that I will take care of you until you can be on your own. (to Alexandre fils, November 30, 1840)

At last, some money came from Paris, and Alexandre could devote himself entirely to his comedy. Almost immediately he sent a bulletin of victory to Domange, December 2, 1840:

My play is finished in my head; which means that on the eighteenth of December it will be sent and will arrive for you on the twenty-ninth—it is Mlle. Mars' New Year's gift; I hope she will be pleased. Instead of writing three acts, to give it all the importance of a farewell performance, I have made it in five acts, . . . the play should be read during the first days of January. . . . I suffer so much from my eyes that I am afraid it is becoming serious.

And to Domange, ten days later, December 9, 1840:

I applied myself to my comedy and already three acts are done. Do not worry about all the vexations they will give you at the Théâtre-Français; hold on firmly. . . . It will be a great success, all the more if Mademoiselle Mars plays it . . . Anseline will make a copy of it and he will keep my manuscript for the Duchesse—the manuscript will arrive the twenty-second or the twenty-fourth.

As for the "embryo of three acts," of which he sketched the plot for Maquet:

A young girl, very young, very naive, had married a young man almost as young as she who is preoccupied with that very modern idea that a man's life is nothing without passion. It's a kind of 'ape' of *Antony*.

The embryo had become a five-act comedy in a single night, the first to the second of December, at Pisa, where Alexandre had gone to search for inspiration. By the twelfth, the fifth act was finished. It was read on a December evening to a choice audience, the Duchesse de Choiseul, M. de Laborde, the Prince Galitzine, the Duc de Lucques, with the best society of Florence and some talented artists. On December 16, 1840, Ida wrote to Domange:

The play . . . created a sensation of which you cannot have any idea. I have never seen such enthusiasm. Truly and without any partiality, it is the best comedy of our time. He has surpassed himself and I believe that it is superior to *Mlle. de Belle-Isle*, that's my opinion and that of all the people who have heard it. Therefore, I ask you, my dear Domange, do not let yourself be fooled by all the clamoring at the Théâtre-Français or by that imbecile Buloz, or by the newspapers.

The next day, the Duc de Lucques sent Alexander the Great Cross, a decoration of his small duchy. It was the fourth Cross for Dumas who some days later wrote to Domange: "Be kind enough to buy for me about a yard of the green ribbon of Vasa, another yard of the ribbon of Isabelle la Catholique, matching the samples that I am sending you, and also some of the ribbon of July, about this length. . . . There is a ball at the Court—and there is no ribbon to be had here." Feasts, trips, and mostly some rest:

> He has worked with such great effort that his health has been attacked rather gravely and, besides, he has caught an eye disease that worries me. He has consulted with three physicians and all unanimously have prescribed, before everything else, a complete rest, at least for the moment.

A comeback, at last! Still the theater may often bring a success which, under the influence of various coteries, may turn later into a fiasco. Alexandre, the old fighter, rallied his troops. He wrote to Collin, December 16, 1840:

> Now they will turn against me a thousand filthy tricks . . . I will send you a list of our friends who must be at the première . . . I recommend Alexandre (fils): he is old enough to go with you to the orchestra; besides they will give him two first galleries. I will put my nephew in the musicians' orchestra; it would not be bad if some zealots went there. . . . Tell our Minister that he should take advantage of the triple vacancies to make me enter the Académie—What the devil! They must be calling for candidates in the streets of Paris by now—and the three serious candidates should be Hugo, myself, and de Vigny.

He had sent duplicate copies of his comedy on the fifteenth or the sixteenth, one to Asseline, the secretary of the Duc d'Orléans, the other to Jacques Domange. In spite of a "few difficulties in its acceptance, because Mlles. the mistresses of ministers or others did not play in it," he was certain of its success. He could already count on box-office receipts of four thousand francs for forty performances if Mlle. Mars was in the cast. He asked Domange to distribute letters to help with the performance. But mostly he demanded money: three thousand francs on account of the expected five thousand francs, the advance from the October first agreement with Buloz.

The time for complaining was past. Alexandre forgot his pains and made his plans for the future: the performances of his play, the continuation of his *Impression de voyages*, a novel that he owed to

Dumont, which would be titled *Le Chevalier d'Harmental* (first draft by Maquet), the elections to the Comédie-Française, and especially his son's education that he too much neglected. At the end of December 1840, he wrote to his son:

> The Latin verses that they make you do and whose usefulness you ask me about are not very important. However, learn their rhythm, so that you can scan the language and feel all the harmony there is in the verses of Virgil and the ease in those of Horace. Then this habit of scanning the language will be useful to you again if you have to give a speech—in Hungary, for example, where the least peasant speaks Latin. Learn Greek thoroughly so you can read Homer, Sophocles, Euripides in the original and you will be able to learn modern Greek in three months. Finally, practice well how to pronounce German; later you will learn English and Italian. Then, and when you know all this, we will together judge for ourselves which career fits you best. By the way, do not neglect drawing.
>
> Tell Charlieu to give you not only Shakespeare but also Dante and Schiller. Study the Bible, as a religious, historic and poetic book. Through the translation, look for the high and magnificent poetry it contains—in Saul and in Joseph. Read Corneille, learn passages by heart. Corneille is not always poetic but he always speaks a beautiful tongue, colored and concise. Tell Charpentier to give you, from me, an André Chenier. Read Hugo and Lamartine—but only *Méditations* and *Les Harmonies*. Then make for yourself a little portfolio of whatever you find good or what you find bad; you will show me this work when I return. Work, then rest with the very variety of your work: take care of your health and be good.

Alexandre, the wild young boy of Villers-Cotterêts, wanted to impose on Alexandre fils the education of an academician's son. The program almost rang as a disavowal, a return to the classics, still retaining some idols from his younger years. But why deprive the son of Chateaubriand, Goethe and Byron, who had formed the father? What remained of romanticism? Some of Lamartine, almost all of Hugo and himself, Alexandre Dumas.

Alexandre Dumas' *Un Mariage sous Louis XV* was read at the

Comédie-Française on December twenty-seventh and received with reservation for corrections, as if he were the village scribbler! It was a big letdown. Although he would not accept corrections as if he were a nobody, he did agree to accept advice.

More serious, perhaps, Mlle. Mars seemed to refuse the role of the countess. Piqued, Dumas consoled himself as best he could and claimed that he would rather work for a young, talented, and beautiful woman (Mlle. Plessy) than for anyone else. Yet, when he heard that Mlle. Mars' refusal was not yet certain, he rapidly changed his tone and wrote her on January 7, 1841:

The play has been made for you alone, for your sake alone. The role is young because it is especially in the dodgings, in the disappointments, in the contradictions and in the passions of youth that you are admirable. . . . The role is forever yours.

Dumas had rapidly rewritten the fourth act, "more dramatic and more gay now." To avoid any blunder from Domange and to renew his notes with the booksellers, he decided to throw himself again into the Parisian furnace: "I will be there on February fifth because I must wait for the state-operated boat (which leaves on January twenty-ninth)." But, for lack of money, he postponed again and again this necessary trip. In the meantime, he went back to his galley slave's work. "There is no money coming in," complained Domange, who had not obtained the expected two thousand five hundred francs advance from Buloz. "We have money coming as long as there is one pen and some paper in the world," replied Alexandre superbly. He was back to his *Impressions de voyage*; he finished the third volume of *Speronare*; he had finished the first volume of the novel, *Bathilde*, which was the same as *d'Harmental*; he wanted to forget that mess of a Comédie-Française.

His vanity now took the Académie Française as its objective. Domange was asked to consult Victor Hugo on the subject and to take this letter to him:

What do you think of my candidacy at this time? Would it not be beautiful to get in together? I know that you will be as pleased to see me follow you as I to see you precede me.

He must also ask Asseline to nudge Casimir Delavigne and again to see Nodier, his neighbor at the Arsenal.

> Do you believe that I now have a chance for the Académie? Hugo was accepted. All his friends, more or less, are mine. . . . If you see things taking shape, go up to the academic platform and tell your honorable colleagues in my name, how much I desire to sit among them: (To Nodier, January 1841)

With great financial sacrifices, at last Dumas could announce to Domange on March first:

> I shall arrive, my very dear friend, but to tell you when and how is not yet possible. I will bring with me the first two volumes of the novel, *Le Chevalier d'Harmental* still titled *Bathilde ou histoire de la régence*; arrange all this so I can find 500F., General Delivery at Marseille. Hurry the rehearsals, my dear Domange; I will take them in hand wherever they are and press them on. Then, when in Paris, I will do two other volumes, the five-act drama and I will leave again. I have nothing else to tell you except that around March twentieth my wife and I will be in Paris; she wants to stay in a hotel and I am afraid that, as it is a perfectly ridiculous idea, she will hold to it stubbornly.

The lease on the apartment at the Rue de Rivoli had most probably been canceled or was going to be.

The draconian savings did not spare this luxurious apartment in which Ida had been pleased to receive the best society and Alexandre's best friends no more than they spared a secret place, the apartment in the Faubourg du Roule where Mme. Dumas had died.

Alexandre wrote to Domange on November 23, 1840:

> Do what you want in the Rue du Roule apartment . . . but please do not forget that there are thousands of things there that are precious to me, among them one of my father's hats and there is a black box in which are about fifty autographed letters from Napoléon, Bernadotte, Murat, etc. The commode

drawers are full of books that my mother read and that I would like to keep. . . . Rich people alone have a right to these kinds of follies; it is true that they do not commit them.

Money's cruelty does not even respect memories.

II

Death of the Prince

A round March twentieth, Alexandre was again pounding the Parisian pavement. He had seen Victor Hugo and Charles Nodier: there was no hope for his nomination to the Académie Française. On the other hand, on March fourth, Domange and Buloz had settled their disagreement with the Comédie-Française. The cast for the new play had been named.

After a ten-month absence, Alexandre was met with indifference. His booksellers were almost hostile; he broke off from *La Revue de Paris* and it would ultimately be *Le Siècle* which would publish *Le Chevalier d'Harmental* as a serial of which Alexandre was finishing the last two installments, with Maquet's help. He got rid of Dumont and took on Max de Bethune, the publisher to whom he promised his next *Impressions de voyage (Le Capitaine Aréna)* and the future glory of publishing *Les Trois Mousquetaires*.

Only one person brought Alexandre the comfort he needed. His son, almost eighteen, was trying to write for the first time, and the father marveled at this double of himself.

As soon as his business was settled, he left, disappointed with the Comédie-Française. To show his irritation more strongly, he did not attend the premiere of *Un Mariage sous Louis XV*, on which he had built so many expectations. The "success" noted in the theater register June 1, 1841, was a bit premature. The critics were split in their opinion; the theater goers did not show much interest. Ah! if Mlle. Mars had only used *Un Mariage sous Louis XV* as the play marking her retirement!

Back in Florence, to which he had dedicated his next comedy, he worked on his drama, *Lorenzino*, an answer to Alfred de Musset's *Lorenzaccio.* Nothing much has been left to record this spring of 1841 except letters to the son he had found again. They were anxious letters:

Go to my sister's for your vacation; nowhere could you be better off than there. I wish that you would not hunt; but should you really want to hunt as a man who knows how to shoot a gun, go to Devisme. . . . (I would like it better if you would wait for me for this—because it might be possible that in the month of October, after my play . . . I could take you to Corsica.)

If you hunt, since you will be at my brother-in-law's some fifteen days before the hunting season, ask him to give you some lessons. Your two cousins are scatterbrains who would shoot lead into your buttocks. . . . You know that I positively forbid you to swim in a river.

Lorenzino was written for glory and next to it, *Jeannic-le-Breton* was written for money. Frédérick Lemaître had convinced Alexandre to revise this drama written by a young author, Eugène Bourgeois.

With his *Lorenzino* under his arm, Dumas, who had not much trust in Domange any more, went himself to deal with the Théâtre-Français. He read on the fifteenth of October of 1841—the play was accepted and, as it was made very clear to him, for the last time he received two thousand five hundred francs in advance. *Jeannic-le-Breton, ou le gérant responsable* was played at the Porte-Saint-Martin in November of 1841. It was Bocage and not the whimsical Frédérick Lemaître who interpreted Jeannic-le-Chouan, just as he had substituted for Lemaître in *La Tour de Nesle.* Dumas haunted the Théâtre-Français, the ministers, the academicians. He was driven by one idea: to come back to Paris only if he were surrounded by his previous glory and with his financial position firmly reestablished.

At the beginning of January, with his drama in full rehearsal, he left Paris, after asking Taylor to supervise his play. From Florence he invited Alexandre fils—in fact he delegated him—to attend the last rehearsals.

The five sets were repainted and regilded, the sumptuous costumes were ready. On Thursday, February twenty-fourth, *Lorenzino* unreeled its Florentine luxury and cruelty, but the audience remained as cold as marble. The register noted a "Disputed success." Worse, the play had only seven performances.

It was probably the day after this unfortunate premiere that Buloz received a surprising letter from Dumas, dated February eighteenth:

> Descend into your own conscience: see how many promises have been made and have not been kept; then judge me. I am withdrawing *Lorenzino*. It can be done only in two ways: I offer to substitute *Hamlet* for *Lorenzino* and then the advance will remain for *Hamlet*. Or I offer an entire break, complete, definitive, and I will refund the advance.

Buloz was stupefied. What could have happened to bring about this ultimatum? At most, it can be guessed by reading between the lines of a letter to Alexandre fils:

> I do not know whether you wrote me because for seven days I have been held back by a swelling of the right side of my face which prevents me from going out and I have nobody to send to get your letters.
>
> Most probably I will leave with the ship on the thirtieth. I will be at Marseille on the first—and in Paris on the morning of the fourth. You have seen that *Macbeth* was refused by the Français. I have finished *Hamlet*. Let Meurice know it—verbally, no letters and tell him that he has been admirably useful to me and that if the Théâtre keeps its word, he will be pleased with me. . . . Send the enclosed letter. [the letter to Buloz]

Alexandre had undertaken adaptations from Shakespeare, as projected long ago. *Macbeth* was given to the Comédie in December and was refused. Dumas was furious and apparently had little trust in the success of *Lorenzino*. He also feared the loss of the two thousand five hundred francs. Thus, this *Hamlet*, rewritten in haste from a first version of the young Paul Meurice, was finished, he said. Yet on March eighth he announced to Domange that "within four days I will have finished *Hamlet*." His agent had to inform Buloz of this and also inform him of Dumas' impending arrival.

The trips between Florence and Paris multiplied. No doubt the financial reasons suggested explained them in part, but there may have been other motives. Conjugal life under the jealous watch of Ida was monotonous. Alexandre missed the Parisian life that he cursed. A new liaison with a young Virginie had begun in December and would soon be revealed. To Domange, whose "eternal doubts about the security of the advance hurt him too much," he swore he would "work a month in Paris only to refund you."

Few traces of his third trip remain. What was he working on? Was it *Corricolo*, which *La Revue de Paris* began to print June twenty-fourth? What business had to be settled? Had he tried to strengthen his collaboration with Bethune, the bookseller Dumont was suing? A most unproductive trip, it seems, since Buloz had not accepted the projected arrangement.

Called back by the languishing Ida, Alexandre left Paris once more for Florence with the tender Virginie in his arms as far as Lyons.

The wonders of a new friendship were waiting for him with the prince of a new dynasty, the young Prince Napoléon, son of the ex-King Jérome Bonaparte of Naples, who had left the Court of his uncle, the King of Würtemberg, to spend a year with his father.

I did appreciate exceptional qualities in him, a young man who had not yet reached twenty. These qualities are a deep and precise intelligence, a poetic and lofty spirit, a liberal, extensive education, and finally a strangely exact knowledge of Europe.

With an affectation of democratic simplicity, the young man asked to be called simply Napoléon Bonaparte, no titles, no decorations. Dumas, the mentor, had discovered in him a very new Telemachus with whom he could meditate and chat in front of Florence's old republican monuments, a Telemachus whom it was pleasure to indulge. Alexandre wrote to the gunsmith Rouart, June 25, 1842:

Do me the favor of making a hunting equipment similar to mine and for the same price as mine, for the Prince Napoléon— nephew of the Emperor.

In Paris, new dimensions of his emotional life developed: extreme tenderness for Virginie whom Alexandre smothered with gifts—a missal, bound by Curmer, a burnoose and also the renewed love for his dear son, Alexandre, whom he guided in his first poems: "Your verses are very good . . . and you see from the progress you are making every day that there is little worth keeping from your first work."

At Florence, Alexandre and Prince Napoléon planned an excursion, or rather a pilgrimage, since the goal was the Isle of Elba. The two men, each with one thousand francs in his pocket, leased a small shell of a boat, *Le Duc de Reichstadt* at Livorno and embarked for Porto Ferrajo. On their way, they shot a few sea gulls and albatrosses. They went through a picturesque small storm that drenched them to the bones; they walked the length and the width of Elba, where there is nothing save great nostalgia and they decided to have a hunting party on nearby Pianosa Island. In the distance lay an island, Monte Cristo, shaped like a sugar loaf, on which they were told, herds of wild goats wandered. The next day, while their boat turned around the island, Alexandre promised to Napoléon that, in celebration of this trip, he would entitle one of his next novels, *L'Île de Monte-Cristo.*

When they arrived again in sight of Elba, on June twenty-eighth, two dynasties crossed paths. Napoléon and Alexandre could see the sails of the French fleet, commanded by the Prince de Joinville, third son of Louis-Philippe. The ships had dragged with them the nets of two poor fishermen from Pianosa. Alexandre later pleaded their cause with the "sainte" Marie-Amélie, Queen of France, on July 13, 1842.

On that same day, the Duc d'Orléans was killed when he fell from a carriage. Alexandre did not hear of it immediately; he worked, he rushed to parties and to dinners. On the eighteenth, he was invited to see King Jérome, and his heart was calm and joyous. Prince Napoléon, sad and worried, was waiting for him. The Duc d'Orléans, he said, was dead! Alexandre grew pale, staggered, leaned upon his young friend and cried.

Dead! What a terrible juxtaposition of letters, always; yet in some cases it becomes even more terrible! Dead at thirty-one, dead so young, so beautiful, so noble, so great, so full of expectations!—I said aloud, 'Oh, my prince, my poor prince!'

And I added more softly, with the voice of my heart . . . 'my dear prince!' Many loved him, without a doubt, . . . but few knew him as I had known him, few loved him as I had loved him!

In spite of the grief that overwhelmed him, Alexandre took upon himself the duty to go to the Duke's funeral and left Florence sick of heart. He wrote to his son, Alexandre, on July twenty-second:

You are right, I have greatly suffered since the day my mother died. I had never before had such pains. Please God to keep you from any accident because I believe I would blow my brains out!

He took the steamboat at Genoa on the twenty-seventh. The next day at Marseille, there was no space to be had in the mail coach, so he leased a carriage and traveled day and night, not wasting a second getting to Lyon, where he had reserved a seat. On the morning of August third, he was back in Paris. Then it was on to Notre-Dame Cathedral, covered with black drapes, thirty thousand candles, forty thousand persons inside and outside. Alexandre could not approach the catafalque, which he wanted to kiss and from which he wanted to cut a piece of velvet as a relic.

In the carriage going to Dreux, Alexandre met three of the Prince's college friends. The towns they passed had all displayed flags at half-mast, temporary altars, mortuary arches. At Dreux, Alexandre, who had not slept the last nine nights, threw himself upon a mattress. He was awakened by the drums of the National Guard. The urn, containing the heart of the prince, preceded the casket. In the chapel, a man was sobbing, biting a handkerchief between his teeth: it was King Louis-Philippe. Then the ceremony, the *De Profundis*, the absolution, the slow descent to the grave. It was August 4, 1842, exactly four years from the day when Alexandre had led the mourning cortège at his mother's funeral.

When he left the chapel of Dreux, Alexandre was a shattered man. Even more than a friendship broken by death, it was perhaps the collapse of his dearest hopes. The Duc d'Orleans represented the republic and the arts ascending the future throne, he was the desired conjunction of progress and harmony, the calm transition of monarchy to republic. Alexandre was surrounded by the ruins of his dreams. Would he be able to recover? The end of the year 1842 is veiled with shadows: Dumas must have gone back to Florence to Ida and to work to survive. In a letter to Domange, February 12, 1843, he summed up the work he did at the end of 1842:

> In the two and a half months since we made our new contract, here is what I have done and what I have given you:
>
> 2 volumes of *Georges Halifax*
> *La Vivandière*, which is in rehearsal
> Five volumes and two plays.

To which must be added *Souvenirs de Florence*, printed in *La Presse* (August 5 to November 27, 1842); *Le Seducteur et le Mari*, a three-act drama by Charles Lafont to which he had given some help; *Sylvandire*, a charming novel set in the time of Mme. de Maintenon on a subject Maquet had found in *Les Mémoires de Madame la Marquise de Fresne* by Gatien de Courtilz; *Georges*, the only novel in which Dumas touched the question of race. Local color was obviously provided by Felicien Mallefille, a native of Maurice Island, but it was a multiple collaboration based on a rough manuscript by Maquet or by Mallefille that Dumas rewrote entirely.

The novels began to supersede theatrical work, perhaps because the profit from the theater went to Domange, except for the advances. *Halifax*, a three-act comedy mixed with songs about a good man gone wrong, was presented on the stage of the Théâtre des Variétés on December 2, 1842. It was a resounding failure. Dumas shared this displeasure with his collaborator, Adolphe d'Ennery. During the final rehearsal Dumas had sensed that the play needed a prologue. As soon sensed, as soon done, and the actors had to learn the new lines in haste. *La Vivandière* does not figure in Dumas's bibliography, but in Leuven's or Brunswick's works under the title *Le Mariage au tambour*. It was played for the first time at the Théâtre des Variétés on March 9, 1843. It had been a play written for Virginie Dejazet's return to the stage, but she did not act in it. It was also a play that reaffirmed the friendship and the collaboration of Dumas and Leuven. They were twenty years older, that's all! From his adolescent days and the first farces, Adolphe had followed, in a minor key, the scintillating trajectory of his friend's career. He had become himself a secondary master in the theater of the boulevards.

The ink on the manuscript of *Le Mariage au tambour* was hardly dry when Leuven proposed another subject to Dumas: a young girl, a boarder at the school of Saint-Cyr, was abducted by a nobleman who, by the king's order, had to marry her; the husband at first felt only dislike for her, but by the end of the play he adored her. The collaborators (Dumas, Leuven, Brunswick) allocated the work—the last polishing was Dumas's share and Dumas, growling, got the advance (which Domange could not touch).

Alexandre read the play for the committee on April 20, 1843. According to Dumas fils, only the first four acts were then written. Dumas expected to finish the end in a few words, but the success of the reading was such that, pretending to decipher the words from paper actually blank, Dumas at once faked them fluently and loudly and improvised an entire fifth act on the spot. The casting of the major quartet of characters was done with no difficulty but not without jealousy. Anaïs (Pauline-Nathalie Aubert) the "serpent" had coiled herself so well around Alexandre that he could not refuse her the role she wanted. Her rival, Mlle. Doze, was indignant and wrote to Mlle. Mars on May 3, 1843:

> In his whirl of gallant pleasures he became so closely involved with the 'serpent,' that he gave her the best role in the play he had just read . . . ; you can guess all the chattering, gossip and meanness this shameful intimacy brought him.

To satisfy the actors to whom he had promised a comedy for August and a drama for January 1844, Alexandre packed his trunks again and followed Ida who had preceded him to Florence. This was revealed in his letter received April eighth by M. Belloc, his business agent in Florence:

> You know that Paris is a pit—once you reach the bottom you do not know when you will get back up to the rim. It is now seven months that I am climbing up with all my strength and I cannot get out.
>
> However, I expect to leave at the end of this month—but Mme. Dumas wants to leave, herself, with Mme. la Baronne

de Talleyrand. I will only pass through Florence and then meet her in Venice.

Thus, since September, Alexandre had been held in Paris with an *idée fixe*: to leave again as soon as possible. He had been from play to play, from collaborator to collaborator, from embrace to embrace. Had he even had time during that spring to grasp the importance of a great literary event? The romantic drama to which he had, in great part, given birth had died with the failure of Hugo's *Burgraves* in March, while neo-classicism was triumphant with the *Lucrèce* of Ponsard (April 22), and Dumas had hardly perceived it. He had sent his son as his delegate to the premiere of Victor Hugo's gigantic drama.

In Dumas' biography, *Les Burgraves* is mentioned only with a witticism which shows how much worn his first enthusiasms had become. Swept along by Mélanie Waldor into a tumultuous waltz, Alexandre had fallen on the floor. "Just like *Les Burgraves*," he heard someone say. "But I, I get up again," he replied. A humorous word, a punctuation at the end of a great ambition.

Alexandre had run away from the Parisian pit on May second. During his absence Leuven directed the rehearsals of the *Demoiselles de Saint-Cyr* from which the Comédie-Française, at this point starved for money, expected a great deal. He ran, not to Venice but to Florence, where one of the heroic-comic adventures he always attracted awaited him. Jules Lecomte, who was paying for the mistakes of his youth with exile, had stopped in town. Forgetting the pranks of Fontainebleau and his letters of Van Engelgom which were not kind to Dumas, he came to Alexandre to offer his services. Grandly, Alexandre refused and loudly made known his reasons for refusing. On May eleventh, he was asked to come to the embassy to confirm his accusations. Lecomte, later chased from Florence, was furious. About seven o'clock, in the Cascine gardens, Alexandre was talking at the door of the Comtesse de Wurtemberg's carriage. With a commotion, Jules Lecomte advanced, accompanied by Prince Doudoukoff-Korsakoff. Lecomte had a heavy cane in his hands. Alexandre took a position of defense, avoided the blow with his left arm and, with his own cane, hit Lecomte's face so hard the blood poured from it. Then Alexandre put his hand on Korsakoff's shoulder, "Prince, you accompanied Monsieur, therefore you are his second. I will not fight against Monsieur who is a crook, but I will fight against you." The Prince accepted the challenge, but after inquiries, asked to be excused.

A more redoubtable adversary awaited Alexandre at Marseille on his return—the young Rachel, whom he had seen triumph in *Lucrèce*. From this day, she had "remained hidden in a fold of his heart." For her, he had changed the plans of his trip so he could see her again in Marseille where she was on a tour. At the beginning of July, Alexandre and Rachel dined at the Prado with Méry and the actress's official lover, Waleski. They walked on the beach, Rachel leaned on Alexandre's arm. She picked up a small marble pebble and gave it to him. Alexandre left Marseille fired with a new love. He gushed in the letters he sent Rachel from Paris:

Ah you, antique enchantress, you have revived everything, made everything alive again in this heart, if not dead, at least very dulled; a squeeze of your hand made it bounce; your mouth, so close to mine when I was at your knees in the theater, caused even the smallest of my fibers to vibrate. I love you, Rachel, I love you so much and this is so true that while I write to you I repeat these words to myself aloud to hear myself say them.

But Rachel did not intend to pick up this handkerchief, which had been too frequently dropped before. On July 16, 1843, she let it be known dryly:

I had hoped that my silence would be enough proof to you that you judged me wrongly; it is not the case; I must therefore ask you to cease a correspondence from which I am and I must be hurt. You tell me, Monsieur, that you would not dare repeat close to me what you write; I have only one regret; it is that I do not inspire you from a distance with as much deference as when near.

The dream of love had passed, leaving a slight wound to Dumas' self-esteem:

Since you absolutely want it, let us remain where we were; it still is a part of the way taken for the future. Your admirer and above all, your friend.

Alexandre had learned not to believe in the virtue of actresses. Wound for wound: Rachel to Dumas:

I return to you the two lines you did not hesitate to send me; when a woman has decided not to ask anyone for help, she has no other means to reply to an offense; if I am mistaken about your intentions, if you have inadvertently, in the middle of other occupations, let fall these two lines from your pen, you will be charmed to have them back.

Alexandre was indeed very busy with the first performance of *Les Demoiselles de Saint-Cyr*. It was very hot in Paris on Tuesday, July twenty-fifth. Alexandre had celebrated his forty-first year the day before (in the company of the "serpent" Anaïs?). The audience enjoyed the comedy, light and sparkling with wit, and applauded loudly, but the critics sulked, especially their "prince," Jules Janin, who denounced it as "this insipid and aborted comedy." Dumas replied in *La Presse* on July thirtieth: "What! Monsieur Janin, you slaughtered my comedy as you have slaughtered my tragedy! You, who were chatting during the show with your colleagues in the corridor. You shouldn't be surprised that you understood nothing!"

Janin did not let the diatribe pass and commented in *Les Débats*, August 7, 1843, that it was "A play with thirty-six fathers, which is only a farce which was refused by the Variétés under the title *Les Deux Mousquetaires*."

Alexandre sent his witnesses and seconds for a challenge in a duel. Jules Janin had acquired some corpulence and lost his youthful ardor. He and Alexandre were reconciled. All considered, in spite of a bad season and bad critics, the success of the comedy was more honorable with thirty-six performances in 1843. Alexandre could again dream of the Académie.

Goodbye, Florence. The packing cases full of clothes, of arms, and of books—the portable library—were opened at 45, Rue du Mont-Blanc, where Alexandre had taken up his new domicile. Once more, it was Dumas versus Paris. Glory demands an eternal reconquering.

III

All for One

The control of Jacques Domange had at last loosened up, for the debts were almost entirely paid. Alexandre no longer had to give an account to anybody except his son, whose hatred for his stepmother had not diminished. Alexandre had to deal with the young man's harassment:

> My friend, I will answer by writing to you, as you asked, and at length. You know that Mme. Dumas is Mme. Dumas in name only while you, you are truly my son and not only my son, but about the only happiness and distraction I have. You ask to go to live in Italy or Spain. I do not mention the kind of ingratitude you show in leaving me in the midst of people that I do not love and to whom I am chained only by social relationships. . . .
> Your situation in Paris, you say, is stupid and humiliating. In what way, I ask you. You are the only friend I have. We are seen so much together that it has come to the point where our two names are never separated. If some decent future awaits you, it is in Paris. Work seriously, compose, and in two or three years you will earn some ten thousand francs per year. I see in this nothing that is stupid or humiliating.
> For the rest, you know well that I, who am so used to

imposing upon myself for the happiness of those who are around me and for their well-being for which I took responsibility before God and risked all possible moral deprivations—I will do whatever you want. One day you will be able to say, if you are unhappy, that I turned you away from a path you wanted to follow and sacrificed you to the selfishness of paternal love, the first and the last love that had remained in my heart and that will be frustrated by you, in turn, as it has been by others.

The writing paper was bordered with the black edge of mourning. Another death had been added to his griefs, probably Victor Letellier's, his brother-in-law, who had ended his career as Director of Indirect Taxes in Senlis. Alexandre took his nephew, Alfred, as his secretary, not a negligible position, toward the end of the year, 1843, when Dumas seemed to be writing with four hands. There was *Ascanio* (*Le Siècle*, between July 31 and October 4, 1843) and *Le Château d'Eppstein*; there was *Amaury* (*La Presse*, between December 29, 1843 and February 4, 1844) and *Gabriel Lambert* (*Revue Pittoresque*, *Musée Littéraire*, 1843); and there was a romantic quartet which seemed to be a sampling of all the possibilities of a novel since it mixed historical romance, inspired by the *Memoirs of Benvenuto Cellini* (*Ascanio*), a novel of the fantastic (*Le Château d'Eppstein*), a sentimental novel (*Amaury*), and a realistic novel (*Gabriel Lambert*). It was as if Dumas, in his search for new avenues after the various successes of his plays and the exhaustion of his vein of inspiration after his *Impressions de voyage*, was groping blindly. Or it was perhaps from chance meetings and collaborations. Dumas seemed to want to take possession of the novel as he did of the theater, annexing successively farce, drama, comedy, and tragedy.

Number 45, Rue du Mont-Blanc was a beehive to which young writers came to beg Dumas to loan them his pen and, above all, his name, as a warranty for the success of their own modest efforts. Alexandre promised and more often than not, kept his word. He promised Paul Meurice, his translator of *Macbeth* and of *Hamlet*, to work again on *Ascanio*; he promised Hippolyte Auger to try his hand at a society novel, *Fernande*; he promised Louis Lefèvre to restructure *L'École des princes*, a five-act comedy (Odéon, November 29, 1843); he promised Leuven and Lherie to finish *Louise*

Bernard, a five-act drama (Porte-Saint-Martin, November 18, 1843); he promised Auguste Maquet, who was still just a collaborator among many others, to write again an historical compilation, *Louis XIV et son siècle*, and to begin the adaptation of *Une Conspiration sous le régent*, a comedy accepted by the Comédie-Française but closed by the censors. All these young men came to Dumas and came out with tales about a character who became a fable that all Paris seemed soon to accept. It was Alexandre Dumas' black servant, a harassed slave, dying of hunger, who wrote the novels while his master strutted about the boulevards, hardly making the effort to sign his works. The myth was kneaded with a mixture of admiration, envy, malice, plus a touch of boulevard froth and very little reality. However, it was a fact that there was as much collaboration as there were collaborators. It all suggested that Dumas did not have an inventive but rather a combinative imagination; most of the subjects he developed came from others who often had nothing more to sell than a primordial idea. Dumas executed the work, repaired the plans and then his hand took off on the paper. Auguste Maquet alone was perhaps more than a supplier of ideas. He participated in the elaboration of the basic plan and delivered, after Dumas' return from Florence, first drafts that Dumas amplified or tightened according to the principles of theater aesthetics (cutting scenes, enlivening dialogues, giving rough indications of sets and movements). Maquet, a theatrical jobber with good historical knowledge, tried his hand in the writing of novels. Dumas, the very genius of theater, could galvanize a very dead text. Let the dramatic take over the literary text, and the true recipe for the serial was discovered to be served at a theater matinee to a spectator in an orchestra seat.

Dumas still did not realize that his alliance with the hard-up Maquet was opening the way for a renaissance. His last theatrical attempt, *Le Laird de Dumbicky*, in spite of all its amusing gaiety, had turned into a disaster at the Odéon on December 30, 1843. It ended the year rather badly. But Dumas could get a better chance with an idea for a novel, an idea that had come to him while reading the *Mémoires de M. d'Artagnan*, a book written by Gatien Courtilz de Sandras, whose first volume he had rented at the library of Marseille. Thanks to his own *Louis XIV et son siècle*, he had already carefully explored the historical background. There remained only to create the heroes, d'Artagnan, Athos, Porthos, Aramis—friends united in the same purpose. Dumas, Hugo, Balzac, Vigny . . . why not reconcile the ancient and the modern, and ally the past and the recent past—all for one, one for all, as it was at the time of the barricades of 1830.

Alexandre promised this novel to *Le Siècle* for which Louis Desnoyers was director of the literary section that enjoyed twenty to twenty-five thousand subscribers. Who knows when writing the first lines of a book whether it will live for posterity? When the first serial appeared on March 14, 1844, *Les Trois Mousquetaires* were heroes promised a normal destiny: publication in serial, then in book by Baudry and copies by Belgian bookstores. Literary myths are born modestly. The few notes exchanged between Dumas and Maquet, most of them laconic, were scant in details: "Send me as soon as possible the d'Artagnan volume," or "Do not forget to get a book on Louis XIII. . . . Bring me at the same time the work you prepared for Athos." or again:

> It is strange, I had written you this morning to introduce the executioner in this scene; then I threw the letter in the fire, thinking that I will introduce him myself.
>
> And the first work I read proves to me that our minds have met. Yours, and buckle down for it is now two hours that I am without work. Let me have enough to last to eleven in the evening.

Or again:

> In our next chapter we have to learn from Aramis who has promised to inquire for d'Artagnan in which convent is Madame Bonacieux and what protection of the queen surrounds her.

It was a novel like any other, begun while the preceding one was not yet finished. ("Send me material as soon as possible, even if it is only some ten pages [of *Une Fille du régent*], and especially the first volume of d'Artagnan.") A novel not yet finished even when its successors were already in the works with *Monte-Cristo* and *La Guerre des femmes*. And yet, a novel becoming quite special by the will of its readers. The sales of *Le Siècle* had progressed, first with the street vendors who offered it to passersby, then through the follow-up subscriptions. The subscriber, the real king of the bourgeois monarchy, had decided: a bored France had chosen the thrill of Dumas' small epics—"gripping drama, warm passion, true dialogue, sparkling style" (Victor Hugo). At Dumas' home, the directors of newspapers followed one another, for they adored Dumas, or rather the profit they expected from his signature. Even if he had wished to, Dumas could not, for commercial reasons, associate his research assistant, Maquet, with his own romantic creations. Alexandre let himself be adored and never refused anything—he never had known how to refuse, not dinners, duels, amorous dalliances, collaborations, nor friendships. He was the anti-Faust, a spirit who always said yes. There was *Le Comte de Monte-Cristo* for *Les Débats*, *Fernande* for *La Revue de Paris*, *La Reine Margot* for *La Presse*, *Vingt ans après* for *Le Siècle*, *La Guerre des femmes* for *La Patrie*, *Le Chevalier de Maison-Rouge* for *La Démocratie pacifique*, *La Dame de Monsoreau* for *Le Constitutionnel*. Two fabulous years.

But where was the happiness in this ocean of hard labor? His heart was silent, or almost. Alexandre fils had gone to eat out his resentment for being merely Dumas' son at Méry's in Marseille, halfway to Italy, where he had planned to expatriate himself. He was resting from his dissipated life. His father feared he might catch one of the nineteenth-century plagues, syphilis or pulmonary tuberculosis. There was, however, much gaiety in the letter he wrote to his son on April 17, 1844, while he finished dressing for dinner with Liszt "who gave yesterday, all alone, a concert which brought in 13,080 francs." He promised the earth to his son:

My trip is not a supposition . . . we can see in a month—either Corsica or Barcelona, Seville, Granada—or Rome and Venice.

If Méry chooses Rome and Venice, here is what you should do—leave directly for Naples where I cannot go; then return to Rome where I will be on a fixed day—from there, after eight days, we will leave for Ancona, from Ancona we will reach Venice by steamer in five or six days; then we would come back through Padua and Ferrara and Mantua; there still will be Algiers.

Trips were conditionally planned with varied itineraries all during that spring of 1844, as if Alexandre, held down by the chains of the serials, could escape only into what was imaginary.

The young Alexandre extended his stay in Marseille while the trip remained an idle dream. His father would have liked to put him immediately to work on *La Galerie de Florence*, a project long postponed, which was moving again—or on *Une Histoire du chateau de Versailles* "with all the anecdotal adventures which happened there."

Alexandre urged his son to dispense with letters in verse in which there were always "personalities or eroticism so heavy that they cannot be put into newspapers where they would cut a fine figure" (May 15, 1844). For Dumas, income came first. But the son was camping at Méry's and was very eager to take his first trip with his father. Their plans multiplied. Switzerland and Holland: "I will leave for Switzerland; I will rendezvous with you somewhere and we will go together to Holland." Corsica and Sardinia "to keep the incognito"; Switzerland and Holland again:

Leave Marseille when I tell you; go to Geneva . . .; go to Shinznach near Basel. There reserve an apartment with three or four rooms for Mme. Dumas and your sister—plus a room for me—with another staircase if it is possible—if not, on another floor. . . . We will leave three or four days later for Strasbourg and from Strasbourg we will go to Holland to see the tulips. (to Alexandre fils, June 1844)

A separate staircase, more than long explanations, depicts the destruction of the Dumases as a couple, Alexandre and Ida; they held together because of the conventions they had ratified with their marriage. Ida also was a second mother for the young Marie, now thirteen. But Alexandre stole away by the secret staircase to new loves. New names incarnated his erotic fantasies: Mlle. Doze, Mlle. Mars' talented pupil, confessed to her protectress that she was tempted by Alexandre who, however, said to his son, "You are strongly mistaken if you believe that Doze could ever be something for me—she is going to throw herself into uncontrolled circulation and already does marvelously well on that score" (May 14, 1844).

Exit Mlle. Doze, to give way to Eugénie Scrivaneck, who was

enchanted with the honor the great man paid to her. On July 1844 she wrote to Alexandre fils:

> I am at the height of happiness; I will not leave your father! He agrees to take me with him; I will travel with you, *as a boy!* The tailor just took my measurements. Ah! I am crazy with joy. Excuse me, my good, my excellent friend, for not having told you this before but from day to day I intended to talk for a few moments with you and always there were obstacles. Your father makes me work hard; I take his dictation; I am very proud, very happy to serve as secretary to *him*, the *universal* man. . . .

To better train her before crossing Corsica and Sardinia, Alexandre took Eugénie to Trouville. Trouville, more than ten years after; the young Antony had acquired some weight but had lost nothing of his vigor. Jules Janin met Alexandre in the return coach "with a horrible girl, half-Prussian, half-Dutch, who spoke a real gibberish." Alexandre was returning from Trouville where he bathed and brought back novels, he said to the astonished Janin, worth eight to ten thousand francs! Dumas had accumulated enough pages for *Monte-Cristo*, so that he could relax in the delights of a trip with Eugénie, disguised as a young man, and his son. Ida stayed in Paris and ruminated on plans for a separation while the father, mistress, and son traveled around Belgium and probably also along the Rhine.

At the beginning of autumn, Alexandre divided his time between the Chaussée d'Antin and Saint-Germain-en-Laye, where he rented the Villa Medicis, Rue du Boulingrin. He was far enough from Paris to accomplish his titanic task without disturbance or temptation, near enough for the necessary exchanges with newspapers and booksellers, near to Maquet who had settled his summer quarters at Bougival.

But the Villa Medicis was not quite a hermitage. There was a gardener, François-Augustin Michel, and his wife, Augustine, who cooked; Rusconi had been for some ten years the butler; Alfred Letellier was secretary to his uncle; the young Alexandre, of course, had definitely hoisted his anchor to float on the literary waves; there were real or pretended friends, mistresses for an hour or for some months. As with all of Alexandre's residences, this offered a mixture of pleasure and work with no definite organization. The newspapers had priority above all. When Maquet sent his copy, Alexandre left the dinner table or the party, locked himself in the small pavilion with stained-glass windows and a table fixed to the wall, and his hand took off along the paper.

In spite of stables, a coachhouse, a garden with a chicken coop, a monkey "palace," bird cages, a greenhouse, games, and flowers, the Villa Medicis did not equal the dimensions of the writer's success. Alexandre Dumas Davy de la Pailleterie's ambitions turned to real estate. At Port-Marly, patiently he bought at the place called Montferrands, lot after lot, expanding the property which was planted with fruit trees, poplars, and ash trees. But the proprietor did not see his property that way. He saw on the heights the château and, higher yet, a working pavilion above the Seine; he saw fountains and waterfalls and, across the road to Versailles, stables and out buildings. He had chosen an architect, Hippolyte Durand. Not to build a house, but a monument to his glory, that is to say, to the glory of literature.

For the time being, he had to activate the "finance pump." *Le Comte de Monte Cristo* created an interest unheard of before as much in the cubicles of concierges as in the salons of the noble Faubourg. *La Guerre des femmes* brought subscribers to *La Patrie*. Maquet and Dumas had hardly time to tie their outlines. In 1844, he wrote to Maquet:

A word, dear friend.

First, very good.

Then, here it is.

Cauvignac demands of Lenet and of Larochefoucault the 30,000 livres still due to him.

Larochefoucault replies that he first must pay the malcontents, etc.

Cauvignac gives him eight days.

The eighth day, he puts Cauvignac off until doomsday.

The ninth, Cauvignac goes to the Queen.

Here is what we want, I believe, that Cauvignac was thrown out by the queen for being insolent.

Cauvignac regards the attack as an outsider.

The royal troops are pushed back; come back then to Cauvignac.

I will try to finish the volume with what I have.

Tomorrow, before one o'clock, you will have your 500 francs. Buckle down and when I have finished I will have something like 1,500 francs to give you in one swoop.

Similarly, Dumas traced a plan for his collaborator, who would develop it into a draft novel using the *Mémoires* of *M.L.* (Pierre Lenet) *conseiller d'état* as the historical background. Each novel was treated in its own special manner. The work devoured the creator, who was now only what he was writing. His biography was almost completely blended with his bibliography. The universal glory, all of a sudden, commanded like a mistress, imposing upon him postures and relationships. Alexandre did not belong to himself anymore; he was the slave of his readers, of his critics, of his detractors. Popularity, like a demon, had taken possession of him. And yet, he had to live. He had to part from Ida—poor, neglected Ida who had become monumentally fat. With her disappeared a last principle of order, the imitation of a home life which had more or less kept Alexandre within the borders of reason. Ten years of married life, marked with flashes of jealousy, deadly fallings out and sentimental reconciliations. The friend of the good Théo and of the tender Gérard, the intelligent and cultured woman was eclipsed to make way for demimondaines, second-class actresses who asked the great man's patronage. The son gloated; the father signed a contract of separation:

M. Dumas, according to the conventions already determined and signed between his wife and himself—will give, beginning [blank] to Mme. Dumas an amount of 1,000 francs per month. Moreover, he will also pay for her carriage.

If Mme. Dumas leaves for Italy and leaves her room and her dressing room, etc.—that is to say, her personal furniture— M. Dumas will give her an indemnity of 3,000 francs at the time of departure.

Besides he will add a sum of 500 francs during the twelve first months so he will have paid 9,000 francs in exchange for furniture.

It is well understood that, in consideration of this amount of 12,000 francs per year to which M. Dumas, of his own will, adds 3,000 francs for the carriage, Mme. Dumas agrees to take care of the education and upkeep of Mlle. Marie Dumas. (Memorandum for M. Gandaz, October 15, 1844.)

Ida had chosen Italy because it was the country where she was loved. Her discreet lover was Eduardo Alliata, Prince de Villafranca, Duc de Salapurta, first-ranking Grandee of Spain, Prince de Montereale, Duc de Saponara, Marquis de Santa Lucia, Baron de Mastra, Seigneur de Mangiavacea, Viagrande, etc. He was a young man of twenty-six, noble, rich, very much in love. It was in April of 1845 that Ida left Alexandre forever, taking with her, far away from her father, the young Marie.

Alexandre's generosity was taken for granted. The Dumas-Maquet novel factory produced at maximum capacity. The rapid exchange of notes, written in haste between two chapters increased:

Don't be afraid, there is no padding.
Do, with all its details, the scene of the first attack, of the arrival of the legate, etc.
'Quick, quick, dear friend, send me that: we must do the things this month.'
'More bastard, more bastard, more bastard.
This week will not pass without financial arrangement.

It was *Le Bâtard de Mauléon* which appeared in *L'Espagnol*, a Madrid newspaper, before being taken over by *Le Commerce* which had already published *Une Fille du régent.*

Yes, yes, yes, my child, one hundred yeses; we must finish the volume with d'Artagnan's and Porthos' departure; they met in Boulogne and now leave together.
Could we arrange that Lord de Winter and Lord Montrose were both Montroses through the mother? A house without issue—Charles I's authorization to use the name. But then it must be de Winter who comes to France to ask for help. The absence of love will hamper us; I begin to see that.

Vingt ans après, published by *Le Siècle*, gave a triumphal continuation to *Les Trois Mousquetaires*:

We must, you know these two charming words, don't you? I must end *La Reine Margot* on the first of next month. Let us go back to work.

I am sending you your last pages so that you can take off from there.

Tomorrow, my friend, tomorrow more work and a vigorous pull on the harness.

La Reine Margot, which had begun its career in *La Presse* on December 25, 1844, replaced *Les Paysans* by Balzac which, to Girardin's great despair, was boring readers at the fateful time of subscription renewals.

"Novel factory," was the incendiary bomb that Jacquot de Mirecourt had, in February, flung against Dumas' majestic armada—who would never forget this impertinence and turned to the Comité des Gens de Lettres, defender of chagrined writers:

Is it an abuse for two persons to join together to produce according to personal conventions which have constantly pleased and still please the two associates?

Now, this question: Has the association harmed someone or something? . . . In two years, Maquet and I wrote *Les Mousquetaires*, 8 volumes; the continuation of *Les Mousquetaires*, 10 volumes; *La Fille du régent*, 4 volumes; *La Reine Margot*, 6 volumes. I will not mention *Sylvandire* and *d'Harmental* written before: in all 42 volumes. Has *Les Mousquetaires* harmed *Le Siècle* which printed it and M. Baudry who published it? Has *La Fille du régent* harmed *Le Commerce* which had printed it and M. Cadot who published it?

Have the other works harmed the newspapers and the publishers who had purchased them simply on their titles? No, for the public has judged them favorably in this strange suit in which a judgment was rendered when there was no accusation. M. Maquet wrote under his name alone *Le Beau d'Angennes*, 2 volumes; *Deux trahisons*, 2 volumes; *Leurs mots sont un mur—Bastille, Vincennes, Bicètre*; two months of serials at *La Revue de Paris*, in all 15 volumes. I have produced *Georges*, three volumes; *Fernande*, three volumes; *Gabriel Lambert*, seven volumes; *Les Frères Corses*, three volumes; *Cecile*, three volumes; *Le Siècle de Louis XIV*, ten volumes; *Albine*, three volumes; *La Galerie de Florence*, four volumes—thirty-three volumes; without counting the theater and the current work.

This is a sample of what two men can produce who, either alone or in collaboration, are in the habit of working twelve to fourteen hours a day.

(to Comité des Gens de Lettres, February seventeenth)

Dumas counter-attacked, too, on the legal level. He subpoenaed Jacquot de Mirecourt before the tribunals. He wrote to Maquet at the beginning of March 1845:

I have no news from you. What is happening? The complaint is lodged; the brochure will be seized this evening. Do not worry; we will have a sweet and good revenge—and if a year in prison and a 3,000 franc fine are not enough, ah, well, we will give him a thrust from our épée.

"Shopkeepers' manners," added Viennet, president of the Société des Gens de Lettres, whose words scored in the salons at the Chaussée d'Antin, the offices of the journalists and in the foyer of the Comédie-Française. "Artist's atelier," Dumas rejoined superbly, sending Jacquot to oblivion. Considering the satire of the time, perhaps Jacquot was only the parrot of Buloz, superintendent of the Théâtre-Français, who, armed with his two magazines, reigned through terror over the literary world. Displeased with the Comédie, which did not revive *Christine* as planned, and because he had been refused an advance of five thousand francs, Dumas was not afraid to confront this potentate with considerable violence via letters to M.D.L., editor of *La Démocratie pacifique* (November 4, 5, 6, and December 26, 1844). He wanted to be the spokesman for all literature which was either raised to a pinnacle or dragged in the mud, according to the interest of the moment. He portrayed French literature, primary in the world, as vilified by this brutal, ignorant, impudent man from Savoy. He appealed to Victor Hugo, to Balzac, to George Sand, to Eugène Sue, to Frédéric Soulié, to Alexandre Soumet, to Alfred de Vigny. Buloz, a puppet of the regime, murdered literature! Popularity against power. Alexandre did not hesitate, although he knew that Buloz would return blow for blow; the Comédie-Française threatened Dumas with a suit for nonexecution of contract; Buloz' courtiers dipped their pens in bile.

Dumas' popularity against Buloz' power? The one-eyed Buloz, as considerable as he was, was still mediocre game for Dumas, who was aiming beyond the royal superintendent for the King himself, "responsible in matters of art," who neither loved nor feared poets and, with his indifference to artistic matters, had let wither, little by little, their flowering of 1830. Dumas began his campaign of banquets early. Soon the people, guided by artists, would dethrone the King! Some protested his inconsistency. They claimed that Dumas had received an inheritance from the Duc d'Orléans, the friendship of the young Duc de Montpensier who had honored his brother's friend by attending the revival of *Christine* at the Odéon on December 9, 1844. According to Dumas, the Republic loved young princes who admired art; it enjoyed fine dinners, the evenings at the Opéra, the balls and feasts which Alexandre frequented in the company of his son. On March seventh, Anaïs Lievenne, actress at the Vaudeville and mistress of Alexandre fils, invited the gayest group in town for supper at the Frères provençaux. They gambled, and a suspicious winning caused Dujarier, editor of *La Presse*, to feel insulted and to challenge Beauvallon, editor of *Le Globe*, to a duel. It would have been a most banal episode of that time if, on March eleventh, Dujarier had not been killed and if, before the duel, Beauvallon had not previously tried his pistols. A duel? A treacherous assassination, public opinion decided. The motive? A war of the serials that was raging. Rumors had it that *Le Globe* had taken vengeance upon *La Presse*, which was stealing its subscribers. The duel was followed by endless and scandalous suits in which Dumas was involved as a witness.

With Dujarier hardly buried, Dumas offered Girardin "12 volumes: *La Dame de Monsoreau*, four volumes; *Les Quarante-cinq*, four volumes; *Jacques Ravaignac*, four volumes; which made 5,626 lines to be paid in twelve installments at eighty centimes a line, or 4,350 francs per volume." The volumes would be delivered in June and in January.

Fifty-two thousand francs was a large sum and Girardin hesitated. He also wanted to obtain exclusive rights but he could not afford it. Why wouldn't he enter into a partnership with Véron who was trying to put the old *Constitutionnel* back on its feet. "The arrangement with Véron will work," assured Dumas on March twenty-sixth, a few hours before signing the contract by which he sold to Véron and Girardin twice nine volumes at 3,500 francs each, payable in cash: eighteen volumes, or 63,500 francs, plus 45,000 francs for the rental library edition, plus 36,000 for export to foreign countries, a total of 144,000 francs. The order book was full; now to work. Of course, there remained the backlog, too: five volumes of *Le Comte de Monte-Cristo* for *Les Débats*; *Le Fils de Milady ou vingt ans après*, in process in *Le Siècle*, as well as *Le Vicomte de Bragelonne*, which would be delivered within three months to the same newspaper (six volumes expected); *Le Chevalier de Maison-Rouge*, already delivered to *La Démocratie Pacifique*. But what was that for two men who worked twelve hours a day! Therefore Dumas felt free to ask some advance on his future production (5,000 francs) and hoped to settle very soon and definitively his debt to Domange.

Needless to say, *Le Chevalier de Maison-Rouge* was only delivered in part to *La Démocratie*. Maquet and Dumas labored on two novels at once because Véron and *Le Constitutionnel* were both waiting for *La Dame de Monsoreau*, and there was also *Monte-Cristo* to complete. The large blue sheets of paper were pulled out of their reams, the pens rasped:

> It is now two days that you have left me without copy and consequently that makes two days that you are making of me the most unhappy man on earth. Had I *Monte-Cristo*, I would have worked.
>
> A roll of copy has been lost; it is a disgrace, on my word of honor! Impossible, you understand, for me to go tomorrow to Paris. Do it again, dear friend. My servant will sleep in Paris, if necessary, to bring me the two parcels together. Spend the night, dear friend, and see to it that *Les Débats* is informed by messenger that the serial is lost and that I have to redo it. Then spur on or have someone spur on to a rapid gallop those railroad people.

These bulletins insisted mostly on the mishaps. It could happen that the copy had not time to go round-trip between 40, Boulevard du Temple, domicile of Maquet, and the Villa Medicis and the office of the newspaper to which it was destined. In such a case, Maquet sent directly his own work on Dumas' large paper. Such occurrences, however, cannot be considered as the norm. The mechanics were perfectly well adjusted. The collaboration between Dumas and Maquet had been tested and Dumas had rejected all other collaborators, as well as the entire romantic genre other than the historical novel.

Dumas fell out with Buloz and the Comédie was no longer at his beck and call. Now and then he helped Leuven in some short-lived productions but the novelist was more and more choking the playwright. When he decided to return to the stage, it was to adapt the novel that had ended as a serial in *Le Siècle*, *Vingt ans après*. As a play, it was titled *Les Mousquetaires* and had found refuge at the Ambigu-Comique theater. On the evening of the premiere, October 27, 1845, the curtain rose at six-thirty and did not go down before one in the morning. The audience's enthusiasm was not shared by the Duc de Montpensier who, when Dumas came to his loge to be congratulated, showed his surprise that his dear Alexandre had allowed his play to be performed on a second-rate stage. "I do not have my own theater and I am compelled to play wherever I can," replied Alexandre. But why not ask for the privilege of having his own theater? If His Highness supported his overtures. . . .

If Dumas suffered from dizziness when reaching physical heights, he delighted in altitude when it came to social adventures. Master of the serial, he reigned over newspapers on which he could impose his own conditions. Only the small tabloids which could not afford a Dumas serial continued to attack him, mosquito bites on an elephant's skin! But did he not have enough? Could he not, on life's path, stop along the road's edge and enjoy the immense income he was producing? "Enrich yourself," said the statesman/historian François Guizot from the dais of the Chambre des Deputés. To economize, to reduce oneself? Alexandre burst forth in titanic laughter. He despised Guizot; he despised the Louis-Philippish shopkeeper's mentality; he despised his contemporaries' hoarding schemes. His ideal was elsewhere. He was of the race of conquerors and with his pen, he carried on a replica of the Imperial epic. Always more. Not more money, not more power, although he pursued both as a means. Always more life.

IV

The Coronation of Alexandre

H e kept every newspaper reader in France in suspense. When he indulged in a moment of rest on the terrace at Saint-Germain-en-Laye, he saw on the hill at Port-Marly the shape of a building which blended the gothic style with Renaissance architecture. Each day the walls became higher. The contractor's masons were busy under the orders of the architect, Durand. Slow, too slow, thought Alexandre. In his mind, he imagined a frieze of medallions running along the facades: Homer, Sophocles, Shakespeare, Goethe, Byron, Victor Hugo. Above the porch, his emblem: *J'aime qui m'aime* (I love who loves me). It was a château to the measurements of his dreams, and much more, the tangible sign of his empire. These medallions were portraits of ancestors, of brothers who gave foundation to his legitimacy.

On February 18, 1846, he had asked the privilege of having a theater directed by Hippolyte Hostein. He had signed his request Alex. Dumas, Marquis de la Pailleterie.

On March fourteenth, with his privilege in his pocket, Dumas met with Hostein. They put together a limited partnership that would build the future king of theaters on the Boulevards. Even before the creation of the financial society the theater had a name, Théâtre Montpensier. Gratitude had its obligations. In April, the partners bought the old Foulon townhouse for six hundred thousand francs and expected that eight hundred thousand francs more would be needed for construction and for *objets d'art*. The architects were chosen: Dreux and Sechan, admirable theater decorators. The Foulon townhouse had been torn down and also the famous small café *L'Epi-scié*, a well-known meeting place of convicts who broke their bans. There was building on the Boulevards, there was building at Port-Marly. Like Orpheus, Alexandre seemed to have the power of moving stones.

And also the power to shake up the dullest places. Saint-Germain was asleep, Saint-Germain was waking up. Each day the railroad carried friends, mistresses, parasites, process servers, and on Sunday the gapers, who hoped to see, even from a distance, even only in profile, the great man who had monopolized the theater, where he captured the artists of the Comédie-Française themselves. In April they played *Les Demoiselles de Saint-Cyr* in the garden of the Villa Medicis for the friends of the master. The actresses crossed the path of the celebrated Atala Beauchesne who had a soft heart for her host.

Feasts, day and night—Alexandre trailed behind him the scent of scandal. On March twenty-eighth, called before the Tribunal of Rouen as a witness in the Beauvallon suit, he had antagonized the Court by answering the President who asked him his profession: "I would say dramatic author if I were not in the native land of Corneille." Then, trenchant as a noblemen, he had given a long dissertation on a point of honor. The newspapers took pleasure in mentioning his eccentricities. They pointed out that Dumas père and fils had taken to Rouen their respective mistresses. More than the high society set which was already used to flirting with the demimonde, the middle class was shocked by such immorality flaunted in a public place in the very face of justice. Once this bomb had been thrown, Alexandre kissed the hand of the very illegitimate widow of Dujarier, the dark Lola Montes, and left for Paris. Not only was he not ostracized, as might be expected, but on April twenty-fifth he dined at the Duc Decazes' and sat next to Victor Hugo, peer of France. Among the other guests were Lord and Lady Palmerston, Lord Lansdown, and M. de Montalivet.

It was not the men in power who reproached Dumas for his unbecoming conduct, it was the public who violently booed *Une Fille du régent* when it was finally performed on Wednesday, April first at the Théâtre-Français. Each time the word *gentilhomme* was heard, the boos redoubled. Take that, Dumas! Pay for being too popular. And only sixteen miserable performances! But who cared for the Théâtre-Français, rheumatic and decrepit as it was. The first foundations of the Théâtre Montpensier were rising from the ground and already Dumas was building up his company. To Adolphe Laferrière, whom nasty tongues had nicknamed *"La Derrière,"* Dumas wrote,

Yes, no doubt, it would please me to have you, but how much? It is not one juvenile lead I want; it is, with my way of writing dramas, five or six young male leads.

Before his splendid theater opened, while Léon Guichard, who years ago had lent him his passport, was making the first sketches for the frescoes, Dumas continued to feed the Paris newspapers with his serials. *Le Comte de Monte-Cristo* was ending in *Les Débats* on January 15, 1846, a month before the last chapters of *La Dame de Monsoreau* appeared in *Le Constitutionnel*, but *La Presse* had already begun *Les Mémoires d'un Médecin, Joseph Balsamo.*

Alexandre was getting tired of incessantly writing new theatrical productions and dramatic situations mentioned only at the foot of newspaper columns. It was now three years since his return to Paris; he suffered from the daily wear, the small change life left him. Again, he wanted to leave. Giraud, the painter, and Desbarolles had dropped by the Villa Medicis before embarking for Spain. Looking at the soft landscape of the Île de France, Alexandre, his son, Maquet, and Louis Boulanger had for a long time dreamed of desolate sierras and dusty plains. Alexandre, with a heavy sigh, went to lock himself in his pavilion to finish the next day's serial. His desire to travel was burrowing its way when circumstances brought opportunities. The colonial politics of the government, which wanted to make Algeria better known in order to attract settlers, coincided with Alexandre's itching for a trip. M. de Salvandy had visited Algeria: "Magnificent country! It must be popularized!" he had reported and it was suggested to him, "Let Dumas write two or three volumes about it; out of three million readers perhaps fifty or sixty thousand of them will develop a yearning for Algeria."

M. de Salvandy applied the idea upon his return. He invited Alexandre and offered him a mission in Algeria which would permit him, while traveling through Madrid, to attend the double wedding of Queen Isabella II with the Infant Don Francois d'Assise and the marriage of the Infanta Louise-Fernande with the Duc de Montpensier. Alexandre did not refuse in spite of his projects for *Balsamo* and the theater under construction. As for the financing of the trip, Victor Hugo commented in *Choses Vues*:

The Minister of Public Instruction gave fifteen hundred francs, taken out of the funds for Encouragement and Help to Men of Letters, plus fifteen hundred francs of the funds for Literary Missions. The Minister of the Interior gave three thousand francs, out of the funds for special projects. M. de Montpensier gave twelve hundred francs. When he received these sums, Dumas said, "Good! It will at least pay for my guides!"

Alexandre did not travel as he used to in his youth, with sack on his back and a stick in his hand; he traveled with an escort. He had called on his son, on his collaborator, the stiff and loyal Maquet, on his friend, Louis Boulanger. All answered, "Present!" They had enough money for the guides; as for the rest, Dumas sold his author's rights for one hundred thousand francs, with a clause for repurchase (October 2, 1846).

The next day, about six in the evening, the coach of Laffite and Caillard was hauled upon a flat railroad wagon and the engine puffed and zoomed. There was no time to waste, for the Duc de Montpensier's marriage was set to depart October tenth. If delays made the travelers miss a coach, Alexandre rented a private carriage. They passed the terrible Spanish Customs as if it were a child's game; the Customs officers had read on the trunks the magic name, Alexandre Dumas, and profusely offered their services. With twelve trotting mules they reached Madrid, outlined in a violet haze. They lodged at Monnier's, a French bookseller who was amazed by the apparition of "our" Alexandre Dumas.

In the middle of a frenzy of feasts, illuminations, corridas, ballets, the writer experienced the intoxication of a European popularity. The Duc de Montpensier was charming; the Duc d'Ossuna, "thirteen or fourteen times" Spanish grandee, invited Dumas for lunch. In his *De Paris à Cadix*, however, Dumas was silent about the marriage ceremonies: benediction in the Ambassadors' Room of the Orient Palace; solemn rebenediction the next day in the Cathedral

Nuestra Senora de los Atocha; dinner in the Colonnes room on October seventeenth, during which Alexandre was wedged between the ugliest of the bishops and a chamberlain with his key hanging on his back. Neither knew a single word of French and, frustrated for the wit he could not exhibit, Dumas devoured food like a glutton. In spite of his desire to treat his readers with the narration of the nuptial festivities, he had to disappoint them because the French newspapers had maliciously announced that he was taking the trip as the historian of His Highness, the Duc de Montpensier! Nonsense! He certainly wanted to be the friend of princes, but their servant? Never! He sulked and absorbed a great quantity of corridas; he witnessed the deaths of forty-six bulls, he said, by the hands of the sublime Montes, Cuchares, and Lucas Blanco. Dumas saw nothing of Madrid beyond the blood of men and beasts in the arena, the intoxication of his own glory and the infinite sweetness of a group in which "one completes the other." Once the festivities ended, the princes took flight. After a picturesque visit to the Escorial, Dumas and his friends took the road to Toledo. The good Gautier had already passed on those abominable trails and had already depicted those magnificent cities whose past radiated on the miserable present. Alexandre discouraged anyone thinking of attempting the trip in his *De Paris à Cadix, XXXVII*.

> You know, Madame, what is meant by a curiosity: it is a certain number of stones, one posed on the top of the others in a more or less capricious manner, more or less fanciful, that all travelers see, one after the other, led by the same cicerone who tells to all the same story that they will in turn relate, in their fashion, uniform or different, depending if they have more or less imagination.

Alexandre and his friends escaped, the best they could, the cicerone, and Spain became for them only a stage for a delightful friendship, in a splendid decor: Granada and the Alhambra, Cordoba and the Sierra Morena, Seville and its Giralda, white Cadiz. But the play was mostly worth what the actors put into it, and their roles were admirably distributed: Alexandre, the *amo* (the master) leading his troop among the population's reverence of all of Spain; Dumas fils, the juvenile lead, lazy, whimsical, loving, who was always late or disappearing to sleep longer or to make love;

Desbarolles, the juvenile lead's grotesque confidant, the "man with the rifle," constantly branded on the cheek by the recoil of his gun; Boulanger, friend of the *amo*, a ridiculous rider who had to be strapped to his mule like a sack, who was harassed by the fervent love of a courtesan; Maquet, whose stiffness bent only when seasick, the fastidious treasurer of the caravan; Giraud, the historian-painter who sketched the ephemeral moments; Pierre-Théodore-Marie Rihan, better known as Paul or Benzoin-Water, the exotic valet born in far-away Somalia, who lost everything, especially his balance, from his unconquerable lust for rum and Spanish wine, yet still the best houseboy in the world. The trip in Spain was a delightful comedy with several scenes, enlivened by the alguazils of Cordoba, the brigands of the Sierra Morena, by Petra, Anne and Carmen, the dancers of Seville. From the picaresque adventures that marked the crossing of Spain from Madrid to Cadiz, the friends kept two remembrances of extreme happiness—the evening and the night spent in huts made of branches in the heart of the Sierra Morena with the gentlemen of the mountain; and the ball at Seville, heavy with sensual effluvia; the women dancers who teased with the motion of their legs, their breasts, their arms, eyes, mouths, their hips, who pranced, beat with their feet, approached each man and retreated only to come back closer again. Men's friendships, women's desire—that for Alexandre was happiness.

On November 18, 1846, in the harbor of Cadiz, between the azure of the sky and the azure of the sea, the sloop of war, *Le Véloce*, promised by de Salvandy, was waiting for the travelers. The trip ended, the mission began, to sing the praises of the conquest of Algeria and the heroic courage of its soldiers so that settlers and industrialists would rush there. On Sunday, November twenty-second, Alexandre touched Africa near Tangier. He jousted for a target with the first Arab he met on his path, bow-legged, with a hooded burnoose and a rifle five-feet long. He felt the Moroccan's hatred and the disdain for the European invader. But the marvelous bazaar in Tangier, the fishing and the hunting quickly erased this first impression. At Gibraltar they found Alexandre fils who had been lost in the amorous delights of Cordoba. The sloop again cut the waves of the Mediterranean, escorted by a train of sea gulls. They went rapidly through Tetouan to reach Mellila quicker. There they expected to pick up some prisoners returned against a ransom after many years of captivity. But impatient to be again in Algiers, the prisoners had not waited for *Le Véloce* but had left aboard a felluca. The travelers were rejoined at Djema-R'Azouat, where they embraced, banqueted, and paid their homage at the tomb of the hero of Sidi-Brahim, Captain Geraux. Alexandre voluptuously breathed the epic perfume that emanated from that miserable military camp. Religiously, he collected stories about the battles. When he arrived in Algiers on the twenty-ninth, Alexandre was disappointed; General Bugeaud was absent for some fifteen days. Alexandre decided to continue the trip toward Tunisia on board *Le Véloce*, which the commandant had put entirely at his disposal. After a detour to Bizerte, Alexandre arrived off Tunis on December 4, 1846.

He peacefully invaded the Regence of Tunis during the absence of the Bey, who was paying an official visit in France. The caravan settled into the heart of the Casbah. Then Alexandre was everywhere at the same time: with Sheikh Medine who was rendering justice, at the Bardo where he was received by the Bey; at Carthage where he visited the very Louis-Philippish tomb of Saint-Louis. He admired its interior, sculpted in Arabic style by an artist called Younis who at that time was working on the tomb of the Bey. Alexandre admired everything so highly that he imagined a Moorish room in his palace at Port-Marly. He had to have Younis do it and he explained to the Bey in justification of this fancy:

> You have him make your tomb; I want him to make a room for me. Your room is for habitation after your death; you are, of course, less in a hurry and therefore it is up to you to give me my turn first.

Le Véloce went back to sea. It anchored off El Djem so that Alexandre could admire the great Roman arena in the moonlight. At Bone, they made an excursion to Hippone. At La Stora, the caravan left for Constantine, where they were received by Général Bedeau. On his return to La Stora, Alexandre found a gift left for him during his absence, a ferocious vulture that he had to whip with a riding stick to get it to the ship. Then, white Algiers, where Général Bugeaud was passing through:

Ah! Ah! It's you, Monsieur, who commandeered my ship, dammit! Don't feel embarrassed, it only has two hundred twenty horsepower for your promenades!

Monsieur le Maréchal, I figured out with the captain that I had cost the government from my departure from Cadiz, 11,000 francs in coal and food. Walter Scott, during his trip to Italy, cost the English Admiralty 130,000 francs. That makes 119,000 francs that the French government still owes me.

Bugeaud accepted this whimsical defense and invited Alexandre to the investiture of the Sheikh El-Mokrani. Couscous, feasts, balls, and the dream unreeled. On January third, Alexandre and his troop, increased by Younis and his young son, Mohammed, embarked on *L'Orénoque*. A few breast strokes from this ship, *Le Véloce* was anchored. The crew was on the bridge, in the shrouds, and in the crow's nests, waving handkerchiefs and hats. Alexandre, immobile, fixed his eyes as long as possible on these officers and these sailors who found it fitting to give pleasure to a poet.

On the evening of January 4, 1847, *L'Orénoque* landed at Toulon after a thirty-nine-hour passage. Alexandre's heart was heavy as it was each time he set foot again in France. Why?

In France there waited small enemies and long hatreds. As soon as he has crossed the border of France, the poet is really only a ghost who witnesses the judgment of the future. France means the contemporary competitors, that is to say, envy.

(*Le Véloce*)

Alexandre was right to be fearful, for he had abandoned everything when he left. During his absence his theater had been rebaptized because the name of a prince should not be associated with a theatrical speculation. Hippolyte Hostein had proposed the new name, Le Théâtre-Historique. "It's excellent," Dumas confirmed. He had neglected the *Mémoires d'un Médecin, Joseph Balsamo*. Girardin was furious, his subscribers complained. Storms gathered.

Alexandre immediately rushed to the Boulevards to marvel at the facade of his theater, whose program he explained:

It will embody in stone my immutable thinking. The building is supported by antique art, tragedy and comedy, which is to say by Aeschylus and Aristophanes. These two primordial geniuses uphold Shakespeare, Corneille, Molière, Racine, Calderon, Goethe, and Schiller. In the middle of the facade, Ophelia and Hamlet, Faust and Marguerite represent Christian art while the two lower caryatids represent antique art. And the genius of the human spirit, with its finger raised, points out heaven to man." (*De Paris à Cadix*, I)

The paint was drying. Séchan, Diéterlé and Desplechin were putting the last brush strokes to Apollo's chariot which sumptuously decorated the ceiling. The company had assembled to welcome back the chief from his Mediterranean peregrinations. Alexandre embraced Mélingue, Rouvière, Bignon, Lacressionnière. With emotion, he again met Beatrix Person. And so what did it matter that Girardin and Véron had joined together in a legal suit to make him live up to the March 26, 1845 contract? Actually, he had promised them a total of nine volumes of novels. And what did he deliver? *La Dame de Monsoreau*, four volumes and thirty-one chapters of *Balsamo*, abandoned since September 4, 1846. These gentlemen were angered. It was their right. Alexandre decided to defend himself. The litigation went to court on January 30, 1847 as a prelude to the opening of the Théâtre-Historique. For publicity, Dumas always knew how to create an event; the public was no dupe. "All eyes in the Court were looking for Monsieur Dumas. The audience was disappointed. Wouldn't he come?"

That afternoon at twelve-thirty, the Tribunal opened wide its doors. There he was, slightly fatter. He saluted the public with an imperial gesture. Murmurs at first, then a brouhaha, jokes, then a sudden silence. The President gave the accused the right to speak:

Gentlemen, I thank you for having agreed that I can present my own defense because the affair that brings me before you is not a question of interest but is a kind of duel of honor. I regret not seeing here Messieurs de Girardin and Véron because, in this duel, I will be obligated to shoot in the air [Laughter].

And Dumas embarked on an ocean of figures; the society audience felt slightly seasick:

It remains for me to give 30,000 lines of *Monte-Cristo* (*Journal des Débats*), 36,000 lines of *Bragelonne* (*Le Siècle*), etc. In total 175,000 lines. I had two years to write these volumes at a rate of 80,000 lines per year. I challenge MM. of the Académie to create as much. Even though there are forty of them . . . [Laughter].

Last August, M. Véron came to beg of me something I refused at first because I had no time; then I finally accepted under the condition that I would write these volumes by the agreed time on sheets numbered and paragraphed by him so that he would not imagine that I was giving him any old piece pulled out of a drawer.

As for M. de Girardin, I have given him a novel entitled *Fabien*. But he has told me that it is very much inferior to my last work. So I threw *Fabien* into the fire. It will never be seen again.

I was told that, as an infringement to my engagements, I have delivered to *La Mode* a novel entitled *Elisabeth*. This novel could not have been written by me. I have always had a deep antipathy for that name, Elisabeth. I have composed twenty-seven dramas; I have written a multitude of novels but in them you will not find, not even once, the name Elisabeth. Here are the circumstances in which I left Paris for Spain and Africa: I had written 158,000 lines in eighteen months. I was cruelly tired. My health was affected. The doctor declared that I was afflicted with a neurosis. He suggested the distraction of traveling. . . . It was therefore a case of major necessity that interrupted the fulfilling of my contract. . . .

No one can be asked to do the impossible, not even Alexandre Dumas. During the next hearing he was represented by an attorney. The King's Prosecutor came to moderate conclusions—by judgment of February nineteenth, Alexandre was fined six thousand francs for damages and interest and was ordered to deliver eight volumes to Girardin and six volumes to Véron.

Dumas had let the King's justice do its work. He was entirely involved in his theater where he was now staging *La Reine Margot*.

He ordered decor and costumes, commanded the last work to be done and, in the evening, rehearsed Beatrix Person again and again. The young actress was quaking: it was her real debut and she was cast in the role of Catherine de Medici, which demanded that she hide her charming youth under artificial wrinkles, her popular vivacity under the gravity becoming a political queen.

On February eleventh, the play was roughly polished, the scenic effects already tested, when someone rushed to the proscenium, waving a galley proof of a page of the *Moniteur*. "Read," he cried to Dumas: "Stormy session at the Chambre des Députés." M. de Castellane had confronted the government:

> I hear that a contractor of serials has been charged with a mission to explore Algeria. A ship of the royal navy has been sent to Cadiz to take this Monsieur aboard. Am I not allowed to say that this was a breach of respect for the flag? I recall that this ship had previously been outfitted to receive the King.

Embarrassed, the Minister of the Navy mumbled that it was a misunderstanding, that the ship had stopped in Cadiz for service and it took on board the person M. de Castellane mentioned. "Why say the person," roared a deputy, "why not say the Marquis de la Pailleterie?" The minister, interrupted, mumbled some more.

Great tumult in the hemicycle. "Is it true," fulminated Léon de Malleville, Deputy for the Périgord, "that a minister said Dumas will reveal Algeria to Messieurs les Députés who do not know it?" The target of this outburst, de Salvandy, faced the attack courageously.

But Alexandre had reached the boiling point. He took up a pen, some paper and wrote a haughty reply to the newspapers:

> The *man* who boarded Le Véloce is a man who never says more than what is—moreover, he had no need to say anything since the fact was mentioned on his passport and his passport, issued by the Ministry of Foreign Affairs and signed by Guizot, was in the hands of the Captain.
>
> As for this extraordinary mission, what were the conditions in which he carried it out? By leaving his most important business, by losing three and one-half months of his time and by adding twenty thousand francs of his own money to the

ten thousand that M. the Minister of Public Instruction had allotted him.

As for *Le Véloce*, that, it is said, I appropriated by surprise, actually it had been perfectly well arranged beforehand to send it for me at Cadiz by M. le Maréchal Bugeaud who had orders to fetch me and the persons who accompanied me, *either at Cadiz or at any other point on the coast where I would be and where* Le Véloce *had to seek me out.*

Another sheet of paper, a flash of the épée to wipe out the public insult:

The office of Deputy has its own privileges; the Tribune has its rights, but to all privileges and to all rights there are limits. These limits, you have exceeded with regard to me. I have the honor to ask you reparations. (to Léon de Malleville)

Another sheet again, to Victor Hugo, the glorious friend, the Peer of France:

We have all been insulted at the Chamber; we were told that the French flag loses its dignity when it shelters Letters. This cannot be ignored. I ask satisfaction tomorrow from M. Malleville, my son from M. Lacrosse, Maquet from M. de Castellane.

Would you serve me as a second . . . ? (February 11, 1847)

It is probable that de Salvandy intervened to stop a scandal that the sensitive Government feared above all. His self-esteem wounded, Alexandre was sweetly bandaged by Delphine de Girardin:

It is such a man that they dare to call a 'Monsieur,' avoiding to pronounce his name. But a Monsieur, as M. de Castellane pronounced it, is an unknown, someone who had never written a good book. Certainly M. Dumas is much less a Marquis than M. de Castellane; but M. de Castellane is much more a (plain) Monsieur than Alexandre Dumas. (from the Vicomte de Launay's *Chroniques Parisiennes*, *La Presse*)

A scratch with a claw was worth a slash of an épée. But there was little to be displeased about in these parliamentary turbulences. These rough debates, these haughty protestations reproduced in all the newspapers served as so much free advertisement. Scandal pays! It could almost be believed that all the participants had played their parts to better orchestrate the opening of the Théâtre-Historique.

On the evening of February nineteenth a long line formed in front of the theater. Luckily the winter was mild and pleasant. Some vendors of hot bouillon offered their wares; they were soon followed by merchants of straw. People bargained, spread the straw and sprawled on the fresh litter, under the stars. At midnight a baker passed to offer the first batches from his oven. At daylight, the next day, a street singer settled himself before the newly glued poster; on the spur of the moment he had composed a song, quickly printed and distributed to celebrate the event. When the theater doors opened, the public was sucked inside, admiring, exclaiming. At six-thirty, however, when the curtain rose, some loges were still desperately empty for fear of asphyxiation or of rheumatism, so ran the rumor because the ventilation and the heating were not quite adjusted. The public also feared a play that ran so long that it rolled well into Sunday morning. The sumptuous decor and the authenticity of the costumes silenced the reproaches that could have been made against a heap of crimes, treasons, poisonings, gallantry without love, libertinage without passion. Dumas and Maquet had cut a popular drama out of the same stuff they used for their serials. More than one delicate spectator had silently left his loge to restore himself in a nearby café with stoves kept burning all night.

At three in the morning, without food for nine hours, exhausted, tired out by the theatrical shocks invented by Dumas, the public found enough strength to applaud, led by the young Duc de Montpensier who was initiating his young Spanish bride into the inimitable thrills of a premiere in Paris.

The future appeared magnificent. Dumas devoted himself wholly to the theater, to *his* theater. In a letter to Maquet, February 23, 1847, he defined his relationships with Hostein, the director, and with Maquet, his collaborator:

I intend to claim those hundred francs (rights on the tickets) for any performance given at the Théâtre-Historique, whoever the author might be. In fact, according to my agreement with Hostein, an agreement which confers on me literary and moral control over the works played at the Théâtre-Historique, I would have to research, find, read and direct, if necessary, and even correct or rewrite each play—thus it would give me, as collaborator's renumeration so to speak, the most legitimate right to collect the hundred francs as stipulated in the agreement. . . .

Therefore, you can consider your own right of forty francs as author's tickets, applicable daily and to all kinds of performances.

As the theater closed very seldom, except on the eve of new plays, this arrangement was a gold mine for Dumas, who could expect an income of 150,000 francs per year.

As an artistic director, he expounded his program in the first chapter of his Spanish *Impressions de voyage*, which appeared fragmentarily in *La Presse*, beginning on March twelfth:

Our theater . . . would be more rightly called Théâtre-Européen. While we lack those great masters Corneille, Racine, and Molière, now buried in their royal tomb on the Rue de Richelieu (the Comédie-Française had a monopoly on the repertory of these classic writers), we will have those powerful men of genius named Shakespeare, Calderon, Goethe, and Schiller. . . .

Already the Théâtre-Européen was an act of gratitude for Shakespeare, Schiller, and Goethe, who had taught a new dramatic expression to the generation of 1830. Dumas had to open his theater with a new play, but he kept in reserve two masterpieces of the European repertory: *Hamlet*, written in collaboration with Paul Meurice, that he had vainly offered to the Comédie-Française, and *Intrigue et Amour* by Schiller. The Théâtre-Historique glorified the great ancestors but wanted also to vaunt the sacred generation of 1830; Victor Hugo, with the revival of *Marie Tudor* and *Lucrèce Borgia* (August and October 1848); Alfred de Vigny, of whom Dumas had requested his *Othello* and the revival of his *Chatterton* (April 28, 1847); Alfred de Musset, with the creation of *Le Chandelier* (August 10, 1848); Honoré de Balzac, who was finally able to impose himself on the theater with *La Marâtre* (May 25, 1848), and again, mostly, and always Dumas, himself, who revived the works that had catapulted him to glory. The Théâtre-Historique gave a lot of revivals. Its master kept in his heart an incurable nostalgia for the fraternal friendships of 1830. Twenty years after . . . could the Mousquetaires find each other again, tie again the knots that once united them so strongly? They had aged: Athos-Hugo was a Peer of France; Porthos-Balzac had married into the aristocracy; Aramis-de Vigny had retired into his ivory tower; d'Artagnan-Dumas alone was still battling, although some believed that his exploits began to smell a bit of the enterprising innkeeper. Could they be galvanized into acting together again? Nothing irremediable had happened, but the public was looking elsewhere. Deprived of revolutions and riots, it enjoyed the violence of melodrama and the wonders of great spectacles. Dumas, who could sense so well the desires of his public, flowed with the current of his time. All he did was target the naive exclamations of his audience. His stage became the visual realization of his serials. Besides the adaptation of his great successes—*Le Chevalier de Maison-Rouge* (August 3, 1847), *Monte-Cristo* (February 3, 1848), *La Jeunesse des mousquetaires* (February 17, 1849), *Le Chevalier d'Harmental* (July 26, 1849), *La Guerre des femmes* (October 1st, 1849)—Dumas called on Paul Féval and showed *Les Mystères de Londres* and *Les Puritains d'Écosse* and also Bouchardy's indestructible melodrama, *Lazare le pâtre*. The public was in command and Dumas had to mold his first project to the wishes of the greatest number. Romanticists already belonged to history, and their sons, still in their twenties, produced small plays, such as Jules Verne's *Les Pailles rompues* and Alexandre fils', *Atala*. Dumas had to wait, and to endure he invented the theater of the spectacular.

It was an echo of his own life. Torn from his real self by too much celebrity, Alexandre could find himself again only through an inextinguishable nostalgia. More and more Alexandre's book of rich hours contained black pages.

On July 6, 1848, the Duc de Montpensier gave a feast at Vincennes. Under tents and an immense marquee, where the princesses gathered, there was dancing. Alexandre walked along the main allée, lighted with colored glass, under trees decorated with Chinese lanterns. With his son's help, he forced his way through the crowd.

He had copiously filled his plate at the various buffets. Tired-eyed dancers, half asleep, still had the strength to look at the fireworks until the first glimmer of dawn. A beautiful feast, but why this tinge of sadness? The good Gautier was glum, and the crowd, lined up to see the guests pass, bedecked in their embroidered clothes, had thrown spiteful words, booed Boulanger and Achard, spat in Tony Johannot's carriage. Clouds of hatred were in the air around this magnificence: "When the masses look at the wealthy with such eyes, it is not thoughts they have in their minds, it is issues," said Victor Hugo.

Alexandre had passed in the middle of this double row, had felt this anger against young people who had done nothing except be born well. He, the poor child from Villers-Cotterêts, the former hard-working office boy, understood this revolt against injustice. But he had crossed over the barrier now. He was the friend of princes, proprietor of a theater, and each line coming from his pen was worth three francs. Rich? All proclaimed it, especially this monumental folly on the Marly heights, now invaded by upholsterers and furniture merchants. On the first floor, the Bey of Tunis' stucco artist traced innumerable arabesques in plaster. Even at the Villa Medicis, Alexandre hurried the decorations and furnishings. In his cashmere drawing room he would display his arms: rifles, a carbine rifle, épées, Arab sabres, hunting knives, five daggers and yatagans, Arab masses, a Catalan knife; in his Persian drawing room there was a desk made of tortoiseshell and bronze marquetry, game tables in ebony, gondola chairs. Where would he put Barye's group sculpture, a gift from the Duc d'Orléans? His paintings by Delacroix? His Decamps? His Bonhommé?

On July 25, 1847, Alexandre had his house-warming party. The date had not been left to chance—it was the day before the master had begun his forty-sixth year. Six hundred friends or would-be friends overflowed into the garden, into the rooms, admired the beautiful statues by Auguste Préault, James Pradier and Antonin Moine, then pounced upon the food that had been ordered from the Pavillon Henri IV at Saint-Germain-en-Laye. Perfume smoked from incense burners. Alexandre was everywhere, radiant and triumphant, loaded with decorations, medals and a heavy gold chain crossing his vest. He talked, narrated, exclaimed, kissed all the pretty women who passed, warmly shook the hands of all the men.

On that day, he loved all life which responded to his own elation.

Michel, the gardener, closed the heavy garden gates which bore the monogram "AD." From the porch, Alexandre faced the valley, looked at the first reflections of the twilight on the quiet Seine. His son put his arm around his shoulder and murmured, "It is beautiful!" "It was beautiful," replied the father.

V

Revolution, Late, Too Late

On the boulevards, the Théâtre-Historique provided a lavish income: *La Reine Margot* lasted until the end of May. Of course, *L'Ecole des familles*, a drama in verse by Adolphe Dumas, whom Alexandre had defended at the Comédie-Française, had been a flash in the pan, but Dumas and Maquet had great hopes for *Le Chevalier de Maison-Rouge*, and rightly so. Twelve revolutionary scenes, an intersection of the district Saint-Jacques at night, an apartment, a garden with a greenhouse and a pavilion, the court of the Temple, a section of the Temple, the Conciergerie, the room of the revolutionary tribunal, a bank of the river under the bridge at Notre-Dame, the room of the dead at the Conciergerie: nine different sets, thirty actors, crowds of extras, and a chant:

> We, friends, who far from the battles
> Succumb in obscurity,
> Let us at least dedicate our funeral
> To France and her liberty;
> To die for our fatherland,
> Is the most beautiful destiny
> The most worthy of envy.

which, during that summer of scandals, announced the future revolution. The people suffered from unemployment, the destitute multiplied. "Down with the thieves; down with the assassins!" was the general cry when it was heard that the Minister of Public Works had trafficked in some obscure concessions in salt mines; that the Director of Army Supply Stores had speculated on the grain market with state money; that the King's aide-de-camp gambled and cheated; that the Prince d'Eckmuhl had knifed his mistress; that the Duc de Choiseul-Praslin had killed the mother of his several children so that he could marry their governess. The ruling classes had dirty and bloody hands. The bourgeoisie was worried, for the discontent did not reach only to ministries. It went as high as the King who clung desperately to his policy of inaction. Old age had diminished the fine politician of 1830 who, upheld by the stiff Guizot, refused reforms that most of the clear-sighted people demanded. It was time to open the windows and appeal to the true country. Banquets were organized in the British fashion by the dynasty of the left: feasts for notables—cold turkey and suckling pig at Rouen—which ended with a toast to the Institutions of July.

Alexandre wrote the chant for the coming revolution; the people joined in the chorus. But he was so distant now from the feelings of the people. Perhaps to get old was to allow one's individuality to petrify. While the premiere of *Le Chevalier de Maison-Rouge* had been postponed ten times because of scenery difficulties, it at last triumphed, reaching its hundredth performance on November eleventh, and Alexandre amused himself in his Château Monte-Cristo. He organized magnetism seances to test this new "dramatic means" that he had tried out in *Les Mémoires d'un medecin*, which appeared again in *La Presse* on September 3, 1847, after a year's interruption. His readers had accused him of charlatanism or of imbecility when he was actually looking for a personal conviction.

On September fifth, M. Marcillet and his somnambulist were at Monte-Cristo. They were touched by the poor Paul Benzoin-Water who was dying from typhoid fever. On the second floor, in the Persian drawing room, the blindfolded somnambulist had played cards and had read a closed book and some folded letters whose handwriting he had recognized; he had even predicted that the poor Paul would be in great danger and die on Tuesday. Paul died on Monday, September thirteenth. In spite of this slight imprecision,

Alexandre was convinced, especially when on a Sunday, either the third or tenth of October, during M. Marcillet's absence and with only his own strength of will, Alexandre had succeeded in putting his black manservant Alexis to sleep, who, as if bowled over by a ball, had fallen back on a couch. The guests held their breaths. Alexis did his tricks with cards, took the audience on a visit of Tunis, and guessed who had given a blessed medal to the charming Louise Pradier. This last stroke belonged to nothing less than the miraculous, as the lovers of the unfaithful Louise were innumerable.

Were these magnetism seances, similarly Mesmer's tub on the eve of the Great 1789 Revolution, only social games in which charlatanism and credulity played the most important part? Alexandre's attitude was of an unusual gravity. He confessed to the Abbé Villette, "I would like to demonstrate what you preach so well, the immortality [of the soul]." It must be remembered that during the tragic night of Général Dumas' death, Alexandre had awakened with a start at the precise moment when his father expired. And later, when Mme. Dumas died, Alexandre had desperately waited for a sign from beyond. Death was always the winner; Alexandre, a man of little faith, asked God for reassurance. After his mother, the Duc d'Orléans, Charles Nodier, Victor Letellier. Whose turn would it be tomorrow? Today it was Frédéric Soulié, his first collaborator, the rival and forever the friend. Frédéric died on September 23, 1847. On the edge of his open grave, Alexandre cried. This big, laughing devil was the most sensitive of men.

A little of life leaves us each time we lose a friend; we must therefore clutch it, keep some shreds of it. Dumas chose a large blue sheet of paper and wrote, "I was born at Villers-Cotterêts, a small town in the département of Aisne . . ." His *Mémoires* were begun at the very moment when he triumphed, when all Paris sought invitations to the Château Monte-Cristo, when the success of the Théâtre-Historique paid his princely expenses so well. Who was the slave who reminded Caesar that he was a mortal? During that autumn of 1847, precisely on October eighteenth, Alexandre wrote those first lines at his summer pavilion at the Villa Medicis, a theatrical replica on his island of the Château d'If. Michel showed the garden to visitors who came with a note, scrawled by the master: "Have them visit Monte-Cristo." Beatrix Person, "the little cat," was there learning a new role and also the little Marie, already sixteen, who had to leave Ida and then her boarding school. She renewed her chagrin while writing to the person dearest to her, to Ida:

> The life I have here is intolerable. I was hurt in my heart when I saw that Papa was not ashamed to put his hand into that of a woman of loose life.

Alexandre mused on his past while the present pressed down upon him. The political reform campaign was in full swing. He wrote to Odilon Barrot, in *Les Débats*, on December 2, 1847:

> I am in bed, horribly sick with a grippe which took hold of my head and chest; convey my regrets to your reformists; tell them in my name that in my heart I am with you. I was supposed to toast the press, that is to say, the writers who were fighting in 1830 and who fight again in 1847 for the popular principle of reform. I am toasting you from here; be my echo there.

If Alexandre had taken sides, it was by duty, the ardent obligation that *Les Trois Glorieuses* imposed on their veterans. His enthusiasm had departed with his youth, but convictions remained. The Republican spirit revived after being forgotten for some ten years. In December, Alexandre was elected Commandant of the National Guard of Saint-Germain-en-Laye and was ready to play an important role in the events he guessed were coming. On February 22, 1848, it rained torrents. Before subscribers could meet for yet another banquet, students and workers had cried, "Down with Guizot! Long live the Republic!" They built barricades. "I have nothing to fear . . . I am needed," claimed Louis-Philippe that very afternoon. On the twenty-fourth, army and rioters hunkered down on their respective positions. The National Guard seemed to sacrifice its fear of the Socialists in exchange for its hatred of Guizot. Could the army fire on the National Guard? "No," answered Louis-Philippe who demoted Guizot and replaced him with Molé. A ministerial crisis might thus be settled but the workers were not satisfied by such a simple reshuffling; they persisted in demanding a republic. The troops fired on a parade of demonstrators. The corpses were piled upon a cart. A funeral procession formed, lugubriously lighted by torches, it crossed the Saint-Martin and Saint-Denis districts to reach the City Hall of the third district at three in the morning. No longer merely a ministerial crisis, the regime itself was in question. History was marching behind the sixteen cadavers who bounced along the pavements of Paris.

As Commandant of the National Guard of Saint-Germain-en-Laye, Alexandre was in the center of the melee. He organized a march against the Ministry of Foreign Affairs, seat of the already defeated enemy, Guizot. Very early, Alexandre had felt his solidarity with the revolt of the people. On the twenty-second he was working as usual on *Joseph Balsamo* or on *Le Vicomte de Bragelonne*, when the crowd's roar reached him. He then wrote to Maquet:

> Were you able to work in the middle of all the tumult? I am also writing to Hostein to advise him not to play this evening. It seems to me that it would be an insult to the public grief.

He had also confided to Hostein, "The Prince protects us, it is true, but our real protector is the people. Within three days there will still be a great people and there won't be any small princes."

On February twenty-fourth, he foresaw the continuation of the barricades, the Tuileries invaded, the disorganization of Louis-Philippe, the merry dance of Presidents of Counsel, each one lasting no more than an hour. Too late, always too late. Around noon, the King abdicated in favor of his grandson, then fled to Saint-Cloud. The Tuileries was invaded and some people caught pillaging were shot. What the bourgeoisie began, the people of Paris would finish. The Duchesse d'Orléans was now at the Chambre des Députés. Her two sons, the Comte de Paris and the Comte de Chartres, were quietly seated at her side. Would it be a regency or a republic? The deputies hesitated until insurgents burst into the hall. Then fear gave birth to the Republic, a temporary government was named. No more little princes, even if they were sons of the dear Duke! Alexandre's heart was torn apart. All his convictions were for the Republic, all his sympathy for the Regency, but since the people had decided, he resigned himself to their decision.

Dumas was lost in the general commotion. He walked the streets, he went to City Hall, seat of the temporary government. He escorted his friend Lamartine everywhere and applauded the latter's speech on February twenty-fifth: "The tricolor flag, citizens, went around the world with the Republic and the Empire with your liberty and your glory while the red flag has only been dragged in the blood of the people around the Champs-de-Mars." As a writer himself, Dumas felt honored by the choice of a people who put a poet at their head. Had the time of the prophets come? Would poets lay down their wreaths and flowers to finally lord it over the Republic, as Plato had imagined? In the night that fell on the illuminated boulevards, Alexandre was ready.

He became a born-again politician; his past ambitions, his disappointed expectations revived. He could recognize himself in this temporary government which, in a sixty-hour session, had ratified and bolstered just about everything and had abolished the death sentence for political actions. He belonged! He was one of them as he wrote to his battalion of the National Guard, to which he had been "the first to announce the great revolution which has just happened in the Capital." He was at one with these men who, during a solemn ceremony, proclaimed the Republic at the foot of the column of July 1830. Alexandre marched with a great crowd of students, workers, and National Guardsmen from City Hall to the Bastille arm in arm, with François Arago dressed in black clothes and a tricolor scarf and, in his lapel, the red rosette that all the members of the government were wearing. In spite of the enthusiasm around them, Dumas and Arago remembered their previous revolution: *Les Trois Glorieuses*, the massacres at the Saint-Merri Cloister and all those men—the most courageous, the most determined—who did not live to see the twenty-seventh of February; nor hear Arago proclaim with a strong voice that "the people of Paris seem to have dropped a maleficent royalty into the most scornful oblivion and have become preoccupied with the basic interests of the people, with the immortal principles which will become for us the moral law of politics and of humanity." Men took off their hats, flags were lowered, drums beat the salute and a resounding "Long live the Republic" broke out. Alexandre trembled.

Would he remain a spectator in the unfolding political drama or an actor? Insipid question! An actor, of course. In 1831 he had felt certain he would become a deputy; the same certitude returned quickly and he said it publicly to Girardin in *La Presse* on February twenty-ninth:

Beginning today, there are two men within the writer: the politician must complete the poet.

Is it not a beautiful thing, tell me, to see the powerful hands of the geniuses of France stretched above our heads, protecting France, challenging Europe and waving to the eyes of the world this holy maxim, 'All for one; one for all.' And so, as if I had been able to divine these events, in *Balsamo*, I had prepared for you a book in which the revolution of 1789 was to appear in its entirety.

Not that I make myself the indiscriminate flatterer of this revolution. The poet does not flatter either people or kings; he says the truth to everyone, but while the people listen, the kings plug their ears.

Yes, what we are seeing is beautiful; what we are seeing is great because we see a Republic and until today we had seen only revolutions. Pray God to guard us who are his eldest sons, who are the saviors of his world.

The pathos echoed the time. The old republican sentiment came from his father. There remained the friendship of princes, and Alexandre refused to be unfaithful. It was an honorable feeling that he proclaimed in *La Presse* on March fourth and seventh. He protested to the Duc de Montpensier that he would "never forget that, during three years outside of all political sentiments and in opposition to the desires of the King, the Duke had consented to treat him almost as a friend":

When you were living at the Tuileries I boasted of it; today, now that you have left France, I claim it.

On March 6, 1848, Alexandre crossed the court of the Louvre. He stopped when he saw an empty pedestal; the statue of Ferdinand d'Orléans, his dear Duke, had been toppled. Was it the people who had committed this injustice? No, it was the Governor of the Louvre. Alexandre raised his voice. He called on artists, poets and historians who would declare that "this statue must be put back on its base, for it had been raised for the prince, the artist, the great and enlightened soul who had returned to heaven even as the noble and kind heart had returned to earth":

The Republic of 1848 is strong enough, believe me, to consecrate this sublime anomaly, a prince who remains standing on his pedestal before a royal house falling from the heights of its throne. (*La Presse*, March 7)

The athlete trained himself for the fight, hoping for only one trophy: the tricolor scarf of representatives of the people. He was armed with his immense popularity; he built yet another journal: *Le Mois, a monthly and political digest of events, day by day, hour by hour—entirely written by A. Dumas.* The title seemed to announce a simple role of recorder, but could he limit himself to that? Not now. "It is time for each honest citizen to carry, written on his forehead, what he thinks of public matters; so be it, we have a forehead wide enough and a heart honest enough; our forehead does not hide one word of what is happening in our hearts." In his heart, in March 1848, was a unique and devouring desire: to leave his metier as a prophet—some would have said as a "histrionic actor"— to become recognized as a guide. For him readers were not enough; he wanted voters.

He multiplied the proclamations, the manifestos of good faith; he called on the workers of Paris and reminded them that without counting six years of education, four years as a notary and seven years as a bureaucrat, he had worked ten hours a day for twenty years, or 73,000 hours; that during those twenty years he had composed four hundred volumes and thirty-five dramas; that, after a simple calculation, he could affirm that "dramas and books have provided the work of two thousand one hundred sixty persons, without counting the Belgian copiers and the foreign translators." Let the workers bring their votes to the worker! "With the love of a brother and the humility of a Christian," he saluted the priests of Paris and assured them that, if among all modern writers, there is one who had defended the spirit, proclaimed the immortality of the soul, and extolled the Christian religion, it was certainly he, Alexandre Dumas, who believed "spiritual food as necessary as material food." Let Messieurs the Pastors lead their flocks to vote for their brother! Should Paris fail, the Lord of Monte-Cristo could put his hopes on his department of Seine-et-Oise. On Tuesday, March twenty-eighth, the streets of Saint-Germain were ready for action. The temporary authorities and the clergy went in a procession up the hill toward Versailles. The doors of Monte-Cristo were wide open. Grave and solemn, Alexandre took the lead and they all went to a poplar that Michel, not without grumbling, had uprooted the day before: the Tree of Liberty. The parish priest blessed the tree and the convoy retreated the same way, to the Theater Square where a large hole had been dug. The tree was abundantly watered with words. Alexandre came forward with a strong voice:

Citizens, it is the third time in 50 years that we plant a tree like this one. The first time was in 1789; it represented Liberty; the second time was in 1830; it represented Equality; the third time is 1848 and the tree represents altogether Liberty, Equality, and Fraternity. Citizens, you have planted the symbol; now, it remains to you, to make it real. Do not forget that liberty is like a tree; it is by its roots that it grows again.

He cried, "Long live the Republic!" The crowd shouted back its echo. He was taken to the club of the workers whose enthusiasm had corresponded to his, and by acclamation he was named their honorary president. That evening he was certain of his election. Even a heckling at the club from a very well-dressed gentleman— "Monsieur, if you are not a bastard, your father was one"—did not shake his confidence.

On the walls were posted his professions of faith which could be summed up in five formulas: no more royalty; no more privileges; no more substitutes for military service; remuneration for work done; and liberty, equality, fraternity for all.

Resolutely to the left, this program was close to that of Louis Blanc, who started the national workshops. But it was dangerous to be on the left in Seine-et-Oise, a deeply rural department. For Alexandre, the results of the April twenty-third elections were not just bad, they were catastrophic. When the figures for each district were known, Alexandre had a right to be desperate: the central office had not even taken the trouble to post them.

Amid general indifference, the dream had collapsed. Alexandre was sent back to the boulevards, to the footlights. *Monte-Cristo,* a drama played in two long evenings on the second and third of February 1848, was the last theatrical event during the July Monarchy. The revolution which filled the streets emptied the theaters, the true social barometers. Hostein chose to close the Théâtre-Historique and to take his company on a tour to England, an expedition which brought only disappointment. What good would it be to present new plays, condemned in advance to failure? Dumas did not take the chance, and let Hostein convince Balzac to show *La Marâtre*, an intimate drama. It "flopped," on May 25, 1848.

On May fifteenth, during a march that was intended to be peaceful, Paris was caught up by fear, a fear of the red specter. Alexandre veered toward the right. On May 20, 1848 he wrote to Alexandre Bixio:

> Do you believe in a man who, in 1832, wrote to Louis-Philippe, 'Sire, you have still fifteen to eighteen years to reign.' Who, in 1834, wrote to Bonaparte [Louis], 'Prince, you will come back to France only through universal suffrage . . .' Believe this man when he tells you—if you do not throw your socialist army into Italy, if you do not unleash it to devour that monarchist carrion called Austria, you are done for—and we are too.

The party of the Right triumphed in the subsequent elections— Hugo was elected in Paris, as was Louis-Napoléon Bonaparte in the departments of Sarthe and Yonne. Dumas applauded and was indignant that some people tried to invalidate Bonaparte's election. He was a good loser, for he had just been defeated by this same Louis Bonaparte in Yonne: 14,989 votes against 3,458. It was better to be nephew of an emperor than the son of a nobody, even if you were a great writer. But Louis-Napoléon chose Paris and left the other departments vacant. Backed by a local newspaper, Alexandre began a new campaign:

> I do not let myself easily be intimidated when I am on the platform. I have no political ambition, since any post I could get would cost me instead of bringing me money. No, I only have this intimate conviction that wherever I go, I bring with me a certain light which is in me. . . . I recognize no superiority, except that of intelligence. With this in mind, I yield before two men: Lamartine and Hugo. (in the *Tonnerois*, June 10, 1848)

He began his campaign, dividing his life between writing for income (he had just started *Le Collier de la Reine* which he expected to give to *L'Evénement*, Hugo's sons' newspaper), and his political chores.

By carriage he traveled through the department of Yonne from seven in the morning to ten in the evening, banqueting, shaking thousands of hands, astonishing the notables with his endless fantasies. Amusing, indeed, but who needed an amusing representative? In Paris, the national workshops had been discontinued. Seventeen to twenty-five-year-old workmen had to enlist in the Army. Paris again threw up the barricades; the workers became the masters of Paris. The republican legalists were heartbroken and tried to parley. "Ah, Monsieur Arago, you never were hungry," replied a worker. In the past, Alexandre had almost been hungry, but it was not enough. He approved the forces of order when they named Cavignac as head of the executive. But he deplored the thousands of dead, those who were shot, those who were exiled "in this colossal fight, so formidable and so heroic on both sides." He reported the events in *Le Mois* and his objectivity as a witness could not always resist his compassion. The republic, believing it could save itself, was massacring its proletarian class. The enthusiasm of the first hours had passed. It became difficult to dream still of an ideal republic "having, for all those who would recognize its laws, some of the majesty of a queen, mixed with the affection of a mother; a republic which would appeal to the love of her first born, all the men whose powerful arms had given her strength, all the great minds who made her glory, all the high intelligence which had made her prosperity." This in spite of the three thousand corpses lying in the cemeteries of Paris and of the six thousand citizens deported to the penitentiary of Cayenne and to Algiers, "in the name of fraternity". Alexandre still wanted to believe it, but he rejected the men who had almost sunk the ship of the Republic and he placed his hopes on the crowned head of the providential man of the hour, Bonaparte.

The revolutionary of February, who implicitly recognized the right to work—an extreme advance of socialism—seemed to adopt an ideological palinode which could not be explained were the economic situation not at stake. Business, in general, was ailing; the business of Dumas in particular was sinking fast. The Théâtre-Historique survived only by accumulating debts and, of course, could not supply Dumas with his daily sixty francs. On January twenty-fifth he had to make a fictitious sale of his furniture at Monte-

Carlo to a straw man in order to avoid garnishment and he had to consider doing the same with his buildings. The order that Dumas wanted was an order that filled up theaters. It did not bother him if the order took the face of Louis-Bonaparte. After all, was he not—since his visit to Arenenberg fifteen years ago—on good terms with the Bonaparte family? Had Alexandre not visited him in prison at Ham? The family was not ungrateful, as Alexandre related to Émile de Girardin on November 8, 1848:

My dear Émile,
Not only is King Jerôme not running for office, but he is backing me.
Now you can say that he denies any candidacy and that he will, with joy, see mine succeed.
Those are his very words this morning.
Back me strongly and you will see me at work.

But neither a king's support, nor Girardin's, could do anything. Once more Alexandre was hopelessly defeated. From his campaign in his department, he would keep only some good friends and hunting companions. From that time he had made himself the incense bearer of Louis-Napoléon who, after the vote for the Constitution on November 4, 1848, presented himself as President-elect to the voters of universal suffrage.

Actually, Louis-Napoléon was only a matrix, albeit a vague one, in which Dumas and some others believed they could cast their political dreams. The Bonapartist pretender was triumphantly elected on December tenth. On the eighteenth, Dumas tried out a role of political advisor and preached a nationwide reconciliation, a dynastic syncretism within the Republic which did not even exclude the revolutionary hydra! Let the banishment of the Comte de Chambord be lifted, let the Princes d'Orléans take back their offices, let Lamartine become Vice-President of the Republic, let Général Cavaignac be made Marshal of France! Dumas was composing a political serial! It was time that he returned to the planks of the stage, far from the counselors of political power.

The Théâtre-Historique had to be saved from bankruptcy. On October 14, 1848, *Catilina*, a "Roman" drama which put the avatars of the Republic on the stage, here and now, had a handsome success. But Hostein was weary of Dumas' exigencies and wanted to get rid of the draconian contract that tied them together. As Dumas wrote to Maquet in October of 1848,

> M. Hostein thought: I will wear Dumas out by using small and great means. Dumas will withdraw for the sake of peace, dispossessed of all his rights to the theater he had built and . . . it will all be for me.

The ship leaked and Hostein, the rat, wanted to leave it. Dumas tried to bail it out. He had sold his horses and given his three monkeys to the Botanical Gardens. Toward repayment of his debts, he gave his vulture, Jugurtha, to a restaurant owner; and finally, for fear of those other vultures, the bailiffs, he had made a fictitious sale on March 22, 1848 of Monte-Cristo to a straw man for thirty thousand francs. In the Office of Mortgages, the registration of claims multiplied: ninety-three! An ocean of debts! Notable among them was that of "Mme. Marguerite Josephine Ferrand [Ida], living by rights with her husband and residing in fact at Florence, separated as to her estate from her husband by judgment of the First Chamber of the Tribunal of Seine on February 10, 1848." Ida claimed a sum of 147,608 francs and seventy-four centimes—her dowry and the interest on her dowry.

The revolutionary storm had knocked Alexandre down. The director of his theater wanted to throw him out; he now lived in a house that no longer was his. What did remain? Only his popularity could still bring in money. *La Jeunesse des mousquetaires* was revived with great success: eighty-nine performances from February seventeenth to June 30, 1849. *Le Collier de la reine* enchanted the subscribers to *La Presse*, but it was not enough. But in this year of 1849, Alexandre felt himself closer to the dead than to the living. On May 7, 1849, he wrote to the Duc de Montpensier: "Instead of going to look for reality in life, we look for the dream in death."

Still a guest at the banquet of life, happiness became scarce and more and more often gave way to the veiled figure of Melancholy. It was facing Alexandre when he wrote to Véron, as a preface for *Mille-et-un fantômes*:

> I go on like everyone else; I, I am movement. Please God guard me from preaching immobility! Immobility is death. But I go on like one of those men of whom Dante spoke,

whose feet walk ahead, it is true, but whose head is turned backward toward their heels.

And what I most seek, what I regret above all, what my retrospective glance searches for in the past is the society which is passing, which evaporates, which disappears.

(*Le Constitutionnel*, May 2, 1849)

The dead were summoned on the threshold of the supernatural stories he took pleasure in telling, as endlessly as Scheherazade, to delay the scythe which, when his turn would come, would mow him down. The protective dead who, through the prestige of his writing, might resurrect, for an instant, for the length of the tale: Charles Nodier and the habitués of the Arsenal, the Villenave family in the small, humid house at Rue Vaugirard:

For twenty years so many events, as an always rising tide, have stolen away from the men of our generation the re- membrances of their youth, so that it is no longer with the memory that we must remember—memory has its twilight in which distant recollections are lost—but with the heart.

(*Le Testament de M. de Chauvelin*)

Like tarot cards, the inverted images pointed to death. The rev- olution had passed, its movement had slowed down and with it the illusion it secreted. Alexandre, at last, perceived that he was mortal.

But one must pretend and try to forget what one has learned. A king was crowned in Holland—an artist, who admired Dumas' work and told him so. On May 9, 1849, Alexandre embarked for Amsterdam "to attend, in all probability, the last coronation to take place in Europe." He was accompanied by his son. There was the pleasure of the trip, the need to breathe different air. And, above all, to forget. From Antwerp they descended the Escaut River, imagining they were skirting the landscapes of Hobbema or Paul Potter. On May eleventh, from a balcony on the Keisergratz in Amsterdam, Alexandre saw the great cortège of musicians, the cavalry, the mixed gathering of carriages and people. How many such royal or popular entrances had he seen already? Finally came the King, blond, bearded, with blue eyes; his face expressed great kindness and firmness. Alexandre bowed and it seemed that the King returned his salute. "Yes, it was you that he distinguished, you his poet," someone confirmed later to Alexandre. The poet beamed, he whom neither the people nor the princes of his country had recognized. The Queen, gracious and melancholic, received him three times during the two days he spent in Amsterdam. Such ephemeral happiness had to be grasped quickly.

The rehearsals for the *Testament de César* had begun at the Comédie-Française, a drama by Jules Lacroix, or rather mounted under the name of Lacroix, as it was Dumas who had perfected a rough sketch of his collaborator. But his contract with the Théâtre-Historique imposed anonymity. When he returned from Amsterdam Alexandre went to the Comédie every day. On May twentieth, at 11:30, an employee of the theater asked for him, "Mme. Dorval sent for you; she is dying and does not want to die without seeing you again." Alexandre stifled a cry and rushed to the Rue de Varennes. He had not even known that Marie Dorval was sick. Since the death of her grandson Georges on May 16, 1848, she sat on her folding chair in front of the child's grave, reading him the Bible, humming songs for him, deranged with love. When Alexandre came to her bedroom, Marie made an effort to smile and hold out her arms. How distant the passion of Rouen and Bordeaux! How far the days of delight! "Ah, it is you; I knew that you would come." Alexandre buried his head, crying into the sheets. Marie's daughter and son-in-law left the room. "You are not going to die," Alexandre mumbled. Marie put her hand on her former lover's hair:

Oh, my Alexandre, you know that since the death of my little Georges I was just waiting for a pretext. The pretext has come and, as you see, I have not let it get away.
—Oh! my God, my God! my God! Are you very sure that you are going to die?
—Look at me.
—I do not find you as much changed as you say.
(*La Dernière année de Marie Dorval*)

Pious lie! Marie implored Alexandre: she did not want a common grave; she wanted to be reunited with her little Georges. She had no money since she could not act anymore. Alexandre would take care of everything, as he indicated with a nod because words stuck in his throat. Marie again placed her already-cold lips on his forehead. When the family came back, Marie put her hand on her son-in-law René's head. He had supported her during her interminable agony. They believed they heard her say, "René, sublime!" And then Marie Dorval was no more.

Alexandre bustled about to keep his word. What were six hundred francs a year ago? Nothing. But today he was ruined. By scraping all his drawers he succeeded in finding two hundred francs, a pittance. He knocked at the door of the Minister de Falloux who gave him one hundred francs from his personal funds. Victor Hugo begged two hundred francs from the Minister of the Interior. To round out the sum, Alexandre pawned his beautiful decoration of the Nisham. Marie could be buried. At her grave, Alexandre was urged to speak. He stepped forward and opened his mouth, sobs choked him; he could only bend down, break a flower from a wreath and press it on his lips.

Adèle was dead. The aging Antony wept.

VI

Disasters

The king was naked and now without any delusion of his power. Death was stronger, and even the march of events became foreign to him. Like an exhausted Cassandra, Alexandre foresaw but could not change the course of things to come. "The principle has already derailed and the man is very close to failing," he said of the Republic which rallied to conservatism after the spring 1849 elections, and of its President, the fluctuating and alarming Bonaparte. *Le Mois* had sadly ended its career with its February first, 1850 issue, preceded by *La France nouvelle*, of which Alexandre had been named chief editor (from the first to the thirtieth of June, 1848). In the euphoria of the revolution's victory, one might have believed the press could do anything. But the multiplication of newspapers hit a financial wall; the subscribers, overstuffed with preaching, went back to their previous reading habits. Most of the ephemeral political sheets were addressed to people who could not read. Dumas now wrote only in other sheets, especially in Girardin's *La Presse*, but also in *L'Événement* of the brothers Hugo (*Le Trou de l'enfer, Dieu dispose*).

Could the Théâtre-Historique be revived? After the success of *Le Chevalier d'Harmental* during the summer of 1849 (forty-six performances, in spite of a bad season) and the decent run of *La Guerre des femmes*, Dumas gave one of his better dramas, *Le Comte*

Hermann. On November 22, 1849, Melingue, Laferrière, and Béatrix Person enjoyed a last triumph at the Théâtre-Historique. The Prince-President attended one performance. "Where was M. Dumas?" noted *Le Corsaire* and Dumas replied on November twenty-fifth to its director:

> M. Dumas was in a very solitary corner from which he deplored altogether the instability of human things and the prompt and easy forgetfulness of men. M. Dumas didn't take part in the reception for the President. As is his custom on the days of first performances, M. Dumas had reserved the two loges of M. le Duc de Montpensier, to avoid the chagrin of seeing another prince in those loges.

This Republic, this President were not his, and his divorce from them was proclaimed openly in public. He resigned himself to it. Had he become an Orléanist? Indeed, he missed the Regency and the exquisite urbanity of the Duc de Montpensier. But mostly he missed his own performance during his ascending march under Louis-Philippe. But under Louis-Napoléon, never. Alexandre was now alone, pulled apart by a detestable present and that past in which he looked for his reflection. He had broken off with the forgetful Hostein, replaced in December by Max de Revel who very quickly showed himself to be a crook. The last lights of the Théâtre-Historique still threw a gleam on the Boulevards. Max de Revel was dismissed by the actors and gave his position as Director to M. le Comte d'Olon, a naif who put his small inheritance into the venture. Still, *Urbain Grandier, Pauline* and Jules Verne's comedy *Les Pailles rompues* were performed but the public had deserted. Dumas tried everything, begging the Prefect of Police not to be too strict with vendors who resold seats "because we have been obliged, in order to survive through the summer, to make an arrangement for author tickets issued by the Théâtre-Historique" (June 14, 1850). Comte d'Olon's thirty thousand francs were sucked into the salaries of the grumbling actors. This temporary administrator very soon passed the dreadful honor of directing the theater to a very second-class actor, Doligny, who owed this promotion to the role of Thompson he had once created in *Richard Darlington.* Dumas pulled the strings. Doligny was, as d'Olon had been, one of his puppets. He paid the actors day by day:

"Open this drawer and, if there is any money in it, take half of it," he said once to Boutin who complained.

It was summer, the dead season, and Merle, the cashier, lamented before his empty cash box. Some new plays, always adapted from Dumas' novels, were put together with the hope of stirring up some interest: *La Chasse au chastre* and *Les Frères corses*. Nothing worked. Doligny could not get the security money and the license he needed and chose to retire. A new Dumas' puppet called Guerville, a dramatic author, flanked by Vivien David, his legal chief, also tried, but for lack of money the transaction failed again. Unpaid, the actors revolted and decided to saw off the branch on which, for three years, they had perched snugly: they refused to play after the October sixteenth performance. *Lazare le Pâtre* and *Pauline* had been announced for the seventeenth and the eighteenth but each time had to be cancelled. Finally in November, to top their stupid ignominy, four of the actors drafted a demand for declaration of bankruptcy against d'Olon and Doligny to the Tribunal of Commerce of the Seine. Alexandre, indignant, chewed on his chagrin. Who were these actors who set the terrible judicial machine in motion? In the course of the preliminary investigations, the evidence established that Alexandre participated in the direction of the theater and that he was one of the directors, if not the only one. He could not hide any more behind his straw men; his fate was now gambled in court.

With a last legal document, Dumas gave notice that he was retiring from the theater and pretended to be free of all engagements he had contracted with the real estate company. But it was too late. At the Tribunal, it was one hearing after another. On December 6, 1850, the artists' attorney demanded that Dumas share the judgment of a declaration of bankruptcy asked against d'Olon and Doligny. Dumas' defense lawyer fought step by step, but on December twentieth, the verdict fell like the guillotine's blade.

Dumas and his proxy, Doligny, in the capacity of co-directors and administrators-in-fact of the Théâtre-Historique, were declared to be bankrupt. A judge and a syndic were named while the creditors pushed and shoved at the Court's door. Dumas did not accept the judgment and went on to an appeal. Meanwhile he asked for a stay in reporting the declaration of bankruptcy. This was followed by a creditors' appeal. They pretended that d'Olon should share the responsibility of Dumas and Doligny.

Everything was menacing and in suspense. The closing of the Théâtre-Historique and the financial disaster scared away the usual sycophants of the successful. Maquet himself—the loyal Maquet— complained. Dumas summed up the situation for him:

> I am engaged to write with you three plays per year. The first year we did *La Reine Margot* and *Les Girondins* (*Le Chevalier de Maison-Rouge*). They were sufficient for the year. It is not my fault; it is our fault.

> 1847: a glorious year during which only two creations—if *Hamlet* which was a revival was not included—attracted an always renewing flow of enthusiastic spectators each evening.

> During the second year we did *Catilina, Monte-Cristo*. They were sufficient for the second year and you, yourself, had agreed that you should stop because Hostein had ceased to pay.

> 1848: the revolution interrupted the progress of *Monte-Cristo* by keeping the spectators in the streets. Hostein did not pay the one hundred francs due each evening.

> During the third year we did *Les Mousquetaires, d'Harmental, La Guerre des femmes*. During this third year only, and after Hostein's demand, I have used my backlog and did *Le Comte Hermann* which I offered to you twice in collaboration.

> 1849: a return to order after the presidential elections, and also, the return of hope. But after the half-failure of *La Guerre des femmes*, Maquet had tired of so much working and not receiving his share of money that his illustrious collaborator, burdened with debts, could not always guarantee him.

> This year again we produced *Urbain Grandier*—and since you have, quite rightly, ceased working for two months, I have told you: 'You see a play in *Chicot* (*La Dame de Monsoreau*), I don't; if you can pull out a play from the novel. . . .
> Today you tell me that I work in collaboration. How many times, my friend, have I told you to read *Pauline*: why should

I try to make a play without decor and without my name out of *Le Corricolo* (*La Chasse au Chastre*)? To pay you the small arrears you mentioned to me, dear friend. How could I pay you if I didn't use all possible means? Now I have a third in *Les Lansquenets*. I do not know how much it will make. I have a third in *Pauline*, which did not ask me any work of execution or any work of production. I have half of a play at the Vaudeville. And what did I say to Dulong [the dramatist's agent]? 'We will put all that to the account of Maquet.'

1850: The Théâtre-Historique agonized. Maquet sulked in his tent. Dumas lived on expedients, getting into rather dubious theatrical enterprises: he turned over his novels *Pauline* and *Les Frères Corses* to Grange and Montépin and took part in *Chevaliers du Lansquenets*, performed at the Ambigu-Comique on May 4, 1850. Was all this the end of a collaboration? Dumas was in despair. He looked on collaboration with anyone but Maquet as impossible. That small penknife slit in their contract made a large breach; nothing important would again come from their joint pens.

A bright spell lightened the dark sky when he attempted a last effort to save the Théâtre-Historique. Dumas thought he would change his *Fille du régent*, a five-act comedy, played before at the Théâtre-Français, into a twelve-scene drama for Melingue. He looked for an actress, young and poetic, for the role of Hélène. His old friend, Mlle. George, who survived by giving lessons, recommended one of her pupils, Isabelle Constant. When this child appeared, blond, pink and white, and looked with lovely blue and thoughtful eyes at the old master, he was immediately seduced. At last he had found Ophelia, the Juliet he had sought so long. He engaged her. Béatrix Person, the current favorite sultana, was on a tour. Alexandre, who was to join her later, wrote to her on August second:

My good pussycat,
I have not enough money to leave at one o'clock. I won't have any until this evening and will leave at eleven. *La Chasse au Chastre* went perfectly well. Nonetheless we must take immediate measures.
I hope you know your part.

What part? Hélène's of course, that he was having Isabelle rehearse. Born at Excideuil on February 22, 1835, she was fifteen-and-a-half-years old. Instead of playing Romeo at forty-eight, Alexandre assigned himself the role of Pygmalion. Isabelle had remarkable diction, but also a frail constitution and she was timid. How would she stand up to the passion of her aging lover? How would she resist the tempest that Béatrix would let loose when, upon her return from the tour, she discovered herself replaced on the stage as well as in bed? Béatrix sued for breach of contract, showing Alexandre's letter dated from the beginning of September:

You are free to do whatever you would like. Only you understand that it would be disagreeable to see each other—at rehearsal. Give up your role: your salary will be paid, if you play or if you do not play.

It was Alexandre's special talent to dismiss whatever did not please him. What could the actress do against the all-powerful master of the theater? She had to withdraw. On September 23, 1850, Isabelle was the sweet and fragile Hélène with Melingue, who multiplied himself by playing three roles alternatively. It was an honorable success for Isabelle, but it was not enough to cure the Théâtre-Historique. Isabelle, whom Alexandre already called "Zirza," acted in the play only fifteen times. Love erased the gap of years. Alexandre was still young, still happy, even if this love was threatened:

I loved a child. . . . How had she loved me in spite of the immense disproportion of age? How had she given herself to me, in spite of her chastity? It was a mystery, of which I took advantage, without trying to analyze it closely. But such a bliss could not last. One day, symptoms of illness appeared. . . . I ran to my physician. . . . He took her pulse; he examined her; he made her breathe and listened to her inhale and exhale. He wrote a prescription—ordered her to take every morning a spoon of cod liver oil and half a glass of donkey's milk. This she finished in the evening as she was not strong enough to take the entire portion. . . . His last words were: 'Treat her with care, my friend; she is a flower that can be killed as well by the cold as by the heat and especially by love.'

The big Alexandre transformed himself into a nurse and rented 96 Boulevard Beaumarchais, "a pretty apartment facing south." From the police he obtained the right to decorate the windows with flowers, thanks to an exterior construction. He padded this nest like a goldfinch, with wadding and sateen, and so that he need not leave Isabelle day or night, took two rooms for himself on the same landing. In spite of his care, Isabelle weakened, seeming to wilt toward the earth. The lover and his fragile mistress took sweet, sad walks. Isabelle would stop after fifty steps, lean back to breathe better, and look for a bench. In the spring of 1851, on a bench of the Botanical Garden, a man, some fifty years old, read to a languid fifteen-year-old child—doubtless his daughter—Aeschylus, Sophocles, Corneille, Molière, Shakespeare, Schiller. The pale sun warmed the sick woman. He told her, "Let us suppose that a first-class theater wanted to play all the masterpieces of world literature. You could be—not only because of your physical beauty which gives you the appearance of an English vignette, but because of your talent—the Juliet of Shakespeare, the Gretchen of Goethe, the Louise of Schiller, the Laura of Petrarch, the Beatrice of Dante, the Isabelle of Dumas." Isabelle smiled in a dream . . . this was glory, certainly, but one had to live to enjoy it. She tried.

The failure of his theater, the approaching break with Maquet, his new love . . . events hurried past him in this year of 1850. And yet, when the financial and sentimental crisis was at its peak, in August of 1850, Alexandre traveled. Or rather fled. On the morning of August seventeenth his servant put the newspapers on the night table. Distractedly, Alexandre opened them: "This morning, August twenty-sixth, the news came from London of Louis-Philippe's death which occurred at his temporary residence at Claremont where he was with his family." Once again death robbed Alexandre of a span of his remembrances. The preceding week, on August twenty-first, he had held the pall at Balzac's funeral along with Sainte-Beuve and Victor Hugo. He had again been asked to say a few words, but he was not touched enough. His eyes were dry. He did not like Balzac as a person but only admired his talent.

Alexandre did not like King Louis-Philippe, neither his character nor his political ideas. The King, however, had opened his office to him, had given him bread—very dry bread, indeed, sometimes well soaked with tears—but bread nonetheless.

Alexandre did not hesitate. At seven-thirty he took the train for

Calais. The next day, at ten in the morning, he was in London. He took upon himself to go to Claremont. He stopped the carriage at the park gates and walked to the château. The generals, aides-de-camp, and officers he met pretended not to know him. Dumas knew them very well. He signed the open register in the vestibule and then he returned to London. He understood he was undesirable; others did not understand why, with his republican opinions, he would come to the King's funeral. The princes were finally . . . princes. He had come as a pilgrim to honor a great misfortune. He was sent away like a tourist. However, he was received by Lord and Lady Holland in their sumptuous house where they had been hosts to the greatest of the English painters and writers. Then he rediscovered the emotions of his youth intact, visiting Newstead Abbey where his dear Byron had grown up, loved, suffered, and the small church at Hucknell which contained his tomb. He wanted to render his homage to the body of a king and it was over the ashes of a great poet that he bowed. He went to the exhibition at Liverpool, then back to Paris after this English intermission.

For France and for Alexandre, the year 1851 was a period of anxious uncertainty. Eighteen-fifty-two would bring the Republic's return to power, the real, social Republic, yet the Bonapartist party was spreading out, led by the President, Louis Napoléon, who had his name acclaimed in the provinces.

France held its breath. Alexandre held his breath and balance, resting himself, as if having reached the summit of a mountain; he discovered the downward slope of the past and that of the future from which he turned away his eyes. He spun a cocoon around his past. It was then that he set about writing his *Mémoires* which he had desultorily resumed in 1850. With the prestige of writing, life began again. He was again that small, diabolical newborn child who walked on the tips of his toes. The almost fifty-year-old man forgot the weight of years that crushed him, the glaring debts and that suit which threatened. He worked in his apartment, Rue Beaumarchais, in which he had piled up some incomplete sets of books he used for historical collections he gave to Cadot: *Louis XV, Louis XVI, Le Drame de quatre-vingt-treize.* Across the landing, in her nest of a room, Isabelle was in pain. She had coughing spells, but sometimes seemed to regain some of her strength. She was able to play the part of France in *La Barrière de Clichy*, the military drama that Dumas had cut out from a pattern sketched by Marco-Saint-

Hilaire, that bard of the Empire. It was the role of a daughter who consoled her old father. Like a mirror the theater reflected the author's image: aging, bankrupt, fallen from his position in the literary world but consoled by this young girl, almost a child. So, Dumas was writing military dramas, historical collections. Had he put aside novels? Not quite yet. After *Le Collier de la reine*, Dumas and Maquet went back to their series on the Revolution with a new novel entitled *Ange Pitou*. But the reactionary government re-established some previous taxes, fearing the serials by such writers as Eugène Sue, George Sand, and Alexandre Dumas, carriers of progressive messages. Thus restricted, the newspapers were compelled to curtail the publication of the romantic serials to three days a week and to fall back on memoirs and historical testimonies. Even *La Presse*, as powerful as it was, could buy only a few serials. Girardin was reported as having written to Dumas:

> I desire *Ange Pitou* to be in a half-volume instead of six volumes; in ten chapters instead of one hundred. Fix that as you want, and cut, if you don't want me to cut.

Slack demand hurt the obsolete collaboration with Maquet. What good was it to produce something when there were no takers? Alone, Dumas finished *Ange Pitou*. Ange Pitou was a bit of himself, of Villers-Cotterêts, of the surrounding villages. The novel was grafted on the *Mémoires* and gradually Dumas passed from one to the other. Ange Pitou, a child from Villers-Cotterêts who captured the Bastille, the poor, uneducated and kind child, was an alter ego he had created with a backdrop of the Revolution. The collaboration with Maquet, however, sighed its swan song with a beautiful novel which took place in the time of Louis XV. *Olympe de Clèves* which appeared in *Le Siècle* beginning on October 16, 1851, explored the back stages of provincial theaters and of the Comédie-Française of the time.

Eighteen fifty-one: bookstores stagnated while hoping for a return of business, and theaters hesitated after the reestablishment of censorship. Only the hagiography of Napoléon still sold well. Alexandre's project for a *Bragelonne* with Maquet for the Ambigu-Comique theater, a benefit performance for Rachel, failed sadly.

Rachel was tired, the booksellers were short of money, the newspapers were drying up. They all rejected Dumas as the rind of a fruit from which all the juice had been squeezed. Perhaps, during that spring of 1851, Dumas was not far from agreeing. If he still lived, it was mostly through his son. Alexandre fils had a violent passion for the "Lady of Pearls," the beautiful, capricious Lydie Nesselrode, who wore sets of pearls, sapphires or rubies depending on the color of her clothes: white, blue, or red. One night, the "sultan," the son, took his father into one of those elegant furnished apartments that were generally rented to foreigners. Lying on a small settee of straw-yellow damask, Lydie was hardly covered with an embroidered chiffon negligé, which permitted one to see that she did not wear a corset, with pink silk stockings and Kasan slippers. Untied, her beautiful black hair fell down to her knees. She had a triple strand of pearls around her neck, pearls around her arms, pearls in her hair. Alexandre père could not quite suppress a stir of desire. But the scandal of her blatant liaison with Alexandre fils had angered her husband, Dimitri Nesslerode, son of the Minister of Foreign Affairs for all the Russias, and had provoked the Tsar's express order for Lydie to return to Saint Petersburg. With a broken heart, she obeyed, and Alexandre fils, who had rifled all the money remaining in his father's drawers, followed her.

Alexandre père relived his past through the romantic adventures of his son who raced throughout Europe, from Brussels to Dresden, from Dresden to Breslau. The antique musketeer did not spare advice to his young Raoul de Bragelonne of a son:

> You are right to stay; things being where they are they must be pushed to their end—only be careful of the Russian police, brutal as the devil, which, in spite of the protection of our three Polish friends—or perhaps because of this protection— could bring you quickly back to the border.

Young Alexandre had stopped at the Russian-Polish border, at Myslowitz, after an order had been given that he be denied entry to Russian territory. His father wrote to him, sending news from Paris: duels, deaths, and on April 22, 1851, news from the performance of *La Barrière de Clichy*:

> It took place yesterday—an immense success in spite of a pyramid of mistakes by the chief stagehand who was fired at once. . . . Isabelle had in her small role a very nice success.

But the father was so poor, he could not send anything else. So that the trip not be a total loss, he urged Alexandre to learn German. Alexandre fils didn't even dream of improving his education. He was reading love letters. From Lydie? No, the eccentric Russian princess had gone out of his life when she crossed the Russian border. The letters which moved Alexandre fils were those which George Sand once sent to Chopin. Dead love reflected his dying love. Alexandre fils had piously unwrapped a carefully labeled bundle that Louise, Chopin's sister, had received after her brother's death and that she had to leave with a friend before entering Russia at Myslowitz, for fear that the rough hands of the Russian police would desecrate the remembrance. The sensitive desecrator, Alexandre fils, deciphered the words of love the ink of which had yellowed. When the breezes of spring made the pages flutter, he believed that he felt the breath of time. The son revealed his discovery to his father who hastened to inform yesterday's lover. On May 23, 1851, Dumas wrote to George Sand:

Allow me to send you a fragment of a letter from Alexandre who, at Myslowitz, found an opportunity to speak of you. Try to decipher his writing. Perhaps you will find yourself in the letters he mentions; by what he says it probably won't be very difficult.

The discovered letters reopened the wound that George believed was healed and Dumas commented on May 30, 1851:

Your letter has deeply saddened me. Why do you insist that your heart has aged and what is that affectation of yours that wants me to see it full of wrinkles? Not at all, your heart is the heart of Indiana, of Valentine, of Claudie and not that of Lélia. Your heart is young, your heart is kind, your heart is great and to prove it, as you can see plainly, it bleeds at the slightest wound.

Another July evening at Monte-Cristo, where the château had almost fallen asleep with its builder's ruin and had kept nothing of its splendor, except Michel, the gardener, Alexandre père was lying on the grass, admiring the sunset which fired the Seine. A young bearded man climbed the steep path and stopped twenty steps away.

It was Alexandre fils. The father jumped up, vigorously embraced his son and they sat on the grass. Alexandre fils talked; he was so bored at Myslowitz that he had let his beard and moustache grow for distraction. He told of the long wait for a letter, a word, a sign from the fickle Lydie. With the gesture of a conspirator, he showed a bundle of letters—George Sand's to Chopin. If he gave them to his father to read, it was under a seal of secrecy. The letters were sent back to George Sand who, in the sunset of her life, built a fire in the hearth of Nohant and burned them.

While waiting for a foreseeable catastrophe, Dumas worked mostly for the theater. In Maquet's company he attempted to exploit the vein of their previous romantic triumphs. There was *Le Comte de Morcef*, third part of *Monte-Cristo* (Ambigu-Comique, April 1, 1851) and *Villefort*, fourth part (same theater, May 8, 1851). There was *Planchet et Cie*, an adaptation of *Bragelonne*. In the autumn, when he was opening the hunting season at Mormant, he invited Maquet to compose with him the plan for a new drama, *Le Vampire*. Again a return to the past, to the year 1823 when, freshly arrived from Villers-Cotterêts, he had marveled at the frenzied melodrama. This warmed-up dish, now slightly rancid, offered nothing to Alexandre, except a role made to the fragile Isabelle's measurements, short and poetic, that of the fairy Melusine who appeared in the fifth scene, with time only for a monologue in verse.

Alexandre had finished with his childhood when he gave the two first parts of his *Mémoires*, which were not subjected to the stamp tax, to Cadot who sold them back to Girardin. Soon Alexandre would begin the narration of *his* revolution.

The fateful hour had rung: on November 19, 1850, the appeal to the actors' suit began before the Second Chamber. To begin, Dumas' attorney recalled the marvelous prosperity of the Théâtre-Historique:

Ninety-three performances of *La Reine Margot* produced 275,110 francs; one hundred fifty-six performances of *Le Chevalier de Maison Rouge* produced 353,036 francs; one hundred twenty-three performances of *Monte-Cristo* brought 141,758 francs; and finally, ninety-one performances of the *Mousquetaires* raised the sum of 172,792 francs, in total 982,696 francs. Certainly, here was the prosperity under which the position of the artists was very bright. Therefore Dumas was not the tyrant of the Théâtre-Historique; he had been its benefactor. The contracts he had made with the various directors of the theater assured him only a part of the profits. A certain general responsibility could be conceived if M. Dumas had cut the lion's share for himself, if he had drained the resources of the theater for his profit. It is very certain, on the contrary, however, that the theater had lived off him.

But the counsel for the defense knew that he had to fight against a legend that could discredit his client before the judges: "How with such profits," he exclaimed, "can M. Dumas not be rich? What is this disorder; what is this prodigality that dried up the sources of such a prosperity?"

About some men as well-known as M. Dumas there exists a quantity of preconceived ideas and rash judgments; people who have never seen him go repeating everywhere that he lives with the exaggeration of an ill-conceived luxury. Details are given, thousands of more-or-less genuine anecdotes are told and these flighty conversations finally take on reality to society.

M. Dumas is not avaricious; he is generous; he does not bargain with his friends when they need him. He likes the luxury suitable to his great position, but he has never stepped beyond the limits that separate appropriate expense from foolish prodigality. After 1848 he suffered enormous losses. Several publishers who had paid him with notes defaulted and he has been forced into considerable refunds. M. Dumas' true passion is work. What I admire in him are the qualities of mind, the manifestations of his thinking, and also his strength for work. He works incessantly; he works always. In the morning, the day, the evening, his imagination, always ready, pours out these thousands of treasures that make up his work.

Then the attorney traced Dumas' long Way of the Cross from the last months of the Théâtre-Historique up to the litigation in Court by those four poor, deluded hams. He offered a letter, signed by twenty-four actors of the same theater who showed surprise that Dumas could be considered as anything but an author. Was this letter entirely spontaneous? Dumas might well have solicited it.

With the large sleeve of his legal gown, the attorney swept away the documents, pointed out the contradictions of the accusation, and the incoherences of the declarations into bankruptcy. Then he charged into his peroration:

> M. Dumas has written much and his work has reached an immense popularity. One must give him justice; his literary goal has always been honest and moral; he has never looked for his heros in the lower depths of society; he has never poeticized vice or crime or tried to make them interesting. He has never given in to those dramatic excesses that reveal the decadence of mores and of literature. Choose at random. What is *Les Mousquetaires*, if not a picture of history largely and strongly drawn? What is *Monte-Cristo*, if not the power of man ascending to the marvelous for the punishment of the wicked of this earth? Therefore M. Dumas, his head held high, marches along the path of literature. The public follows him with respect and curiosity. . . . This bankruptcy has not corresponded to the public feeling. It is already long ago that first performance of *Henri III* was given. It was a solemn evening, an evening when a prince of royal blood, standing, and bare headed, saluted the destiny of the young writer.

This appeal to the judges' morality and Orléanism made little impression on the lawyer for the treacherous artists. He attacked Dumas before General Attorney Metzinger himself, and finished him off in his summation:

> M. Alexandre Dumas has not been able to resign himself to the collapse of an enterprise on which he had founded his hopes for success and fortune. He has exhausted his efforts and his resources to keep this theater alive and thus it is that, perhaps without being conscious of it, the author has turned himself into a gambler, a producer of public spectacles, thereby, assuming the qualification of a tradesman for which he must today suffer the consequences.

Dumas waited for a miracle after the eight-day postponement of the judgment. And it was a coup d'état that surprised him. During the night between the first and second of December, there was the usual Monday reception at the Elysée Palace. The Prince-President was in a mood, while only a few hundred meters away, under the orders of Morny, Minister of the Interior, generals of the army began their sinister work of arresting some Montagnard and three Orléanist deputies. The dissolution of the Legislative Assembly was posted on walls as well as that of the State Counsel. The Second Republic was no longer alive. The deputies who attempted to resist were imprisoned. A handful of republicans tried to stir up the workers; a few barricades were built sporadically but the army rapidly engulfed the barricaders.

Where was Dumas while the Republic was slaughtered? He wandered along the streets as he liked to do in time of riots and revolutions. He soon understood that the dice were loaded, that the game was lost in advance. One could die for honor's sake, as did Baudin, but what good did it do? So, die Republic, but long live republicans! As testimony of Alexandre as the rebels' savior, there remains only one letter from Dumas to Bocage, December 3, 1851:

Today at six o'clock 25,000 francs have been promised to the person who arrests or kills Hugo.

You know where he is. Under no circumstance must he go out.

Order reigned in Paris. Hugo had hidden, then escaped to Brussels under an assumed name. His friend Alexandre followed, pursued by the judgment of December eleventh, a judgment confirming the one of the previous year.

The heroes of romanticism buried themselves in exile.

PART
VI

To Escape, To Escape,
To Escape!

I

Exile

On December tenth, the day before the court judgment, Alexandre had his passport stamped with a visa. He knew in advance that he could be condemned and he wanted to avoid arrest; he had to run away. It was a night of freezing rain. On the quay of the terminus of the northern railway, his servant, Alexis, fussed over the meager luggage that had been hastily packed. The train was leaving at seven o'clock. Alexandre fils embraced his father, comforted him: "It was only one suit lost; it will be settled; you will come back soon."

When they arrived in Brussels the next day, Alexandre gave the driver the name of the Hôtel de l'Europe, at the corner of the Place Royale. His son left him then, the literary future of Alexandre fils was at stake in Paris, where the rehearsals for *La Dame aux camélias* were beginning at the Vaudeville theater. The play had escaped the claws of the censor, thanks to the Duc de Morny.

Alexandre père was never alone for long, and did not have to be alone in the Brussels of 1852, which had accepted the French outlaws of May fifteenth and now received those of December second. Some 400 to 800 of the 7,000 expatriates from the coup d'état were, or would be, authorized, to live in Belgium. The exiles met in the galleries of the Passage Saint-Hubert. They were easy to recognize by the nervousness of their movements, the virulence of their remarks. Distressing news bulletins followed one after the other. The plebiscite of December twentieth and twenty-first had ratified the coup d'état by a majority. The event had been solemnized with a *Te Deum* at Notre Dame. On the official buildings the *Liberté, Égalité, Fraternité* were scratched out to be replaced by eagles. The re-establishment of the Empire was near. Sixty-six politicians were banned from French territory.

Paris was silent, but the cabarets of Brussels were filled with chatter. Alexandre avoided mixing with the pale and feverish outlaws. He could cite his life-long republicanism but, if he were in Brussels, it was not because of his politics but because of a bankruptcy. For him Brussels was only a place where he could redeem himself, and this could happen only through his work. At his table, in the Hôtel de l'Europe, in shirtsleeves, without a tie, "mind racing behind a quiet face," he smiled before his large blue sheet of paper. Upon his arrival he had contacted his old friends, Méline and Hen, booksellers in Brussels who, with their copies, spread French literature all over Europe. Together they set up a business publishing in Brussels an edition of Dumas' *Mémoires*, the only true one since the serialization printed in *La Presse* beginning December sixteenth, 1851. They "were so severely mutilated by the censor that they were unrecognizable, even to the author's eyes." Dumas decried the censorship even before the censors had sharpened their scissors. It was in part a bluff for publicity, in part a political maneuver. To pose as a victim of Bonaparte's censure was to belong to the group of the outlaws.

In Paris, the faithful secretary Edmond Viellot, ex-employee of a surveyor who owed his good or bad fortune to the fact that he could imitate the master's handwriting and have it mistaken for the real one, sent the roughs of the *Mémoires* that Alexandre corrected rapidly before giving them to Méline. Sometimes parts of it disappeared during these manipulations. Lapses were showing: Dumas stormed, protested, alerted his son; he cursed the thoughtlessness and the lack of care of the Parisians who left him in financial need. The Director of the Ambigu-Comique, who had planned to revive the old *Napoléon Bonaparte*, had just refused him an advance of one thousand francs. A *Napoléon* at this time could have been taken for a favor toward the regime. "I don't give a damn about what could be said," replied Dumas to his son, "just try to squeeze a one-thousand franc advance out of him" (January 17, 1852). The refusal of the Ambigu-Comique spurred his political conscience. He claimed he would loathe allowing the theater to stage a play that could seem a flattery. In his frantic quest for money, however, Dumas was prepared for a few small betrayals in spite of his desire to join the group of refugees.

In this most provincial atmosphere of Brussels, Alexandre lived modestly, almost in penury. The strict minimum: coal to fight the rough Brabant winter, a lamp to light the night work of the writer, postage for letters to keep alive the complex network of his business. During this time Alexis, with nothing better to do, got drunk on faro, the local beer.

To fulfill his contract with Cadot, Alexandre intended to finish his revolutionary tetralogy in Brussels: *La Comtesse de Charny* would follow the unfortunate *Ange Pitou*, shortened to avoid the tax stamp longer works required. But to write it, Dumas needed *Histoire de la révolution* by his dear Michelet. He hunted for it in all the Brussels bookstores and could not find a single copy. What could he do? Hen came to his rescue. A Flemish writer, Henrik Conscience, had written a short charming rural novel, *Le Conscrit*. Dumas could develop these "some hundred pages" into a five-volume novel which could rival *La Mare au diable* of George Sand. Dumas did not know Dutch and could not read Conscience's novel. It did not matter because there was in Brussels a poet, André van Hasselt, a great admirer of the romantics, who had a knowledge of almost all the European languages. He would take great pleasure in translating for Dumas, who therefore wrote to Conscience to get his permission to use some details from his book. "The author and the book are entirely at your disposal," was the response, and Dumas actually threw himself into the Dutch novel. As a homage to the Flemish writer, he entitled his own book *Conscience l'innocent*. He borrowed not just a few details but the whole plot, simply moving it in space and time to the Villers-Cotterêts of his youth.

Dumas wrote very fast—a volume every ten days—and sent each one at once to *Le Pays*, whose publisher said he was "enchanted." With this new success, Alexandre regained his relish at structuring still more success. He left the Hôtel de l'Europe for a house that he decorated luxuriously. After the performance of *La Dame aux camélias*, his son could come there and father and son would again find the joy of living together.

La Dame aux camélias had its premiere on February 2, 1852. It was a triumph, and from one day to the next it brought the son the glory that the father had known with *Henri III et sa cour.* Was Dumas père proud of it? "Enchanted. Receive all my embraces," he wrote, rather drily. Then, later, on the third or fourth of February:

> You must . . . settle the business of your manuscript and put one over on Porcher. Wrangle the most money you can from him and come [to Brussels], seeing that we are at low tide.

His son was feasted, recognized at last, and Dumas thought only of the manna that was falling from the theater's galleries. He was "sick and without a sou," but most important, he felt that his son was escaping him. This success meant an emancipation, making his son an adult by breaking off the financial ties that had bound him to his father. Their relationship began to reverse. The son became the father of his father, the protector; he asked for accounts and succeeded where his father failed. He would become rich, an academician, perfectly integrated in the society of his time.

If the theater robbed him of a son, for the time being it gave him back a little financial ease. Paul Meurice had created a play from *Ascanio,* an old novel he had written with Dumas in 1843.

Dumas, who had no part creating this drama, which was accepted by the Théâtre Porte-Saint-Martin on March eleventh, nonetheless puffed up his pretensions:

> Mme. Person will not act in any play of which I wrote a line and I do not believe I wrote more than one line of *Ascanio,* since I do not want to give roles to people who have made me bankrupt. Isabelle, for whom Colombe seems to be written, will play Colombe. If you do not want to engage her by the year, let her be engaged by the performance, fifteen francs a day like the circus; it will certainly not ruin you.
>
> See that I am sent a role, or rather a manuscript, at once, by return post, and within five or six days she will be in Paris, knowing the role.
>
> I beg of you to change nothing of these conditions and also to ask Meurice to use only his name; he will get my share of the author's rights with his own and will give it directly to you, without anything being put into writing.

The stratagem was clear. The trustee of the bankruptcy could not touch the eventual profits. The direction of the Théâtre Porte-Saint-Martin was reluctant; Béatrix Person was cast as the Duchesse d'Étampes. There was also a resistance to get involved in the financial schemes of Dumas, who was attempting a show of strength. Dumas wrote to Antenor Joly:

I make positive opposition to the performing of my drama, for whose staging one thing only was forgotten—to consult me.

The theater director gave up. *Benvenuto Cellini*—the title Meurice had given to his adaptation—was not a drama any more, but a business. The play was performed on April 1, 1852, to unanimous applause. The critics pressed around Alexandre who had come back expressly from Brussels. He had been able to obtain a safe conduct from the Tribunal of Commerce on March 22, 1852 which permitted him to tramp again the pavement of Paris. He had admired the tender Isabelle in her role of Colombe and again found his ex-"Little Pussy Cat," Béatrix Person, on the stage. He was happy again. Even if the play was not the vein of gold he had hoped for, it was, at least, financial security for a few months.

With a great present success came a great future literary project as Dumas dreamed of completing Conscience, which represented the triumph of Good with a fantastic counterpart, an illustration of the triumph of Evil whose hero would be the Wandering Jew. On March 16, 1852, he wrote to Antenor Joly:

What would you say of an immense novel in eight volumes in *Le Pays* which would begin with Jesus Christ and would end with the last man in creation, giving five different novels, one taking place under Nero, one under Charlemagne, one under Charles IX, one under Napoléon, one in the future? I intend to write this novel, entirely composed in my head, for a review, since the serial cuts interrupt too much. By making the serials much longer, we will get the same result. . . .

The principal heros are the Wandering Jew, Jesus Christ, Cleopatra, the Fates, Prometheus, Nero, Poppea, Narcissus, Octavia, Charlemagne, Roland, Vitikind, Velleda, Pope Gregory VII, King Charles IX, Catherine de Medici, the Cardinal de Lorraine, Napoléon, Marie-Louise, Talleyrand, the Messiah, and the Angel of the Calix.

This could appear crazy to you, but ask Alexandre [fils], who knows the work from beginning to end, what he thinks.

The "monster novel," as Joly immediately called it, had the ambition of being a universal epic which unreeled before a passive and immortal witness, the Wandering Jew. Dumas wanted to develop in it his conception of history, which he had fixed once and for all in *Gaule et France*. He wanted to show, behind the sound and the fury, the finger of Providence pointing toward more civilization and more freedom.

But in Dumas' correspondence, the great affair of this spring of 1852 was his installation in Brussels, Boulevard Waterloo, in a house he rented from M. Meuus. He had ordered the remodeling, which was now dragging from lack of money, but he was already thinking of the interior decoration. From Paris he had received the flotsam from the wreckage of Château Monte-Cristo: the big vases and the sculpture group by Barye, a gift of the Duc d'Orléans, his Mousquetaire desk, two candelabra from Pompeii, a bronze chandelier, a small mirror, and, most important, his Delacroix and Decamps. He only left his worktable to watch the decoration progress.

Finally, on April tenth, Dumas could give his housewarming party. What did the guests discover? A two-story house rich in appearance with a porte-cochère and a balcony. In the corridor there were divans on the right and left, a staircase hidden by drapes, a greenhouse in the back; in the great drawing room the walls had been hung with a garnet-red cloth and gold nails which served as a background to a bric-a-brac collection of statues topped by a Venus de Milo perched on a tall, carved chest. It was not easy to thread one's way through the prie-dieu, sideboards, Algerian divans, oak armchairs, and enormous porcelain vases. Close to the ceiling hung small escutcheons in relief, with the arms of the principal contemporary poets: Chateaubriand, Lamartine, Victor Hugo, Charles Nodier, and, of course, the master of the house. The azure-blue ceiling was strewn with golden stars. Up the staircase covered with a thick rug was a bathroom wainscotted with marble; on the left, there was a small drawing room with drapes made of white cashmere shawls. Its walls disappeared under precious paintings: *Hamlet in the Cemetery*, *Tasso in the Hospital for the Insane*, a Decamps painting. Then there was a bedroom decorated with Persian cloth, lighted by one opal lamp. Farther on was a small green-and-gold boudoir with a divan of cherry-red silk. Finally, on the top of the house, drapes covered the entrance into the attic, a mansard room fitted out as a work room.

Alexandre was preparing his theater-in-exile. Each decoration corresponded to characters and scenes projected from his dramatic imagination. The mansard workroom was ruled by Noël Parfait; Alexandre had lodged this ex-agent, banished from French territory, at the Hôtel de l'Europe where they had lived "half-brothers, half-friends." Then he had made of him his right-hand man, his copyist, proofreader, secretary, and steward. In the studio at Boulevard Waterloo, he sat at a table before the door of the master's workroom, bent over his desk where he read, wrote, and collated. When Alexandre was stricken by a sudden sleep, Parfait put his pen down, relieved, and sighed, "A five-minute stop." His intelligence, his gift for management could not limit him to simple employment as a copyist. He took the finances of the Dumas household in his hand: He was order incarnate in the den of disorder; he tolerated prodigality but only within limits; he frequently scowled at Dumas who called him *"Jamais-Content"* [Never-Pleased]. He looked askance at the servants with their white ties setting the tables for fine suppers in the greenhouse; he attempted to keep the account books balanced by making money with the author's past work. Laughingly, Dumas grumbled for he had never been so rich or so poor at the same time. But Dumas cursed his jailor with tenderness. Very soon the virtuous Mme. Parfait and her young Léonie could join their husband and father in the mansard. Virtue lodged beneath the roof beams while license ran riot on every other floor.

The installation of Parfait in the household at Boulevard Waterloo was much more than the presence of an individual or of a family, it was the visible presence of the Republic. Dumas' house now became the meeting place of republicans, an oasis of luxury and sociability. It was frequented by all the expatriates, those who had been assigned a residence in Brussels or those who, from Namur, Antwerp, Gand, or Spa, arranged for an escapade now and then in Brussels. Dumas opened his arms wide; he compromised, sometimes, with his principles but never with his heart. The salon and the table were open. When their nostalgia for France became too strong, they found the comfort of a kind heart. When money was short, Alexandre opened a drawer or called on Parfait. But the guest Alexandre always expected, his dear Victor Hugo, came only too rarely.

Alexandre and Victor again had found one another in the provincial calm of Brussels, yet Victor had chosen austerity and visited Juliette Drouet only after nightfall. Charles, his son, had also arrived and he loved feasts and pleasure and enjoyed the mixed company at the Boulevard Waterloo. Victor eventually followed him and finally agreed to Alexandre's wish to introduce the biography of his brother-in-literary-arms into his own *Mémoires*. Hugo talked, Alexandre took notes from dictation. Sweet hours they were, by the light of the opal lamp, as the past unreeled, the voices sometimes trembled, the eyes teared when they recalled the past and the friends now lying under the earth. Victor, in spite of his apparent stiffness, was sometimes overcome by the same emotion that Alexandre incessantly expressed.

The studio in the attic, the large and the small salons where refugees argued interminably! There were more corners in the house: the boudoir, for example, with its cherry divan where, in turn, one by one, passed the lovers, the women of an hour, the semi-official mistresses. There was Isabelle, who between performances of two plays made expeditions to Brussels. There was also Marguerite-Veronique Guidi (née Garreau), a lover and creditor who haunted the days and mostly the nights of Dumas after 1848. Alexandre owed her money and, therefore, love. Mme. Guidi also insisted on participating in the literary enterprise, in dealing with booksellers, the theater directors, with the trustee in charge of the bankruptcy. Alexandre fils sometimes complained about the influence of this invading mistress. His father rebuked him:

See here, I have had mistresses; you have known all of them—with all of them you began by being on good terms and you ended on bad terms. I still have your letter in which you told me that Mme. Guidi was a charming woman and there was no inconvenience in her coming to see me.

There were also those women who resurfaced from the past, such as Louise Pradier, and Nathalie, the actress of the Comédie-Française on a tour in Brussels who, as Alexandre wrote to his son

on April 20, 1852, "does not make a sou and is bored to death."
There were also unexpected visitors:

Now you are rich enough to buy and send me—after trying
it on a pretty brunette, about twenty to twenty-five, whom I
believe you have at your disposal—a summer hat, fifty to seventy francs. Do not hesitate going ten francs more. I have slept
with a very beautiful girl who does not want to accept anything
more than a summer hat, either light yellow straw or simply
white. (to Alexandre fils, April 1852)

At fifty, as at thirty, Alexandre continued to drift. He did not
run after an improbable happiness any more. He conquered his
confusion by repeating incessantly the same gestures of love.

There was also at 73 Boulevard Waterloo another secret place,
a young girl's apartment. Marie Dumas, rather against her father's
advice, had come to him on the first of May. Very embarrassed by
what went on upstairs, Alexandre rented her the small adjoining
house and had it attached to the main house. Marie learned to know
the dark troop of refugees. She was the only woman in the middle
of all those exiled men deprived of their usual companions. Thus
Marie became a sexual focus for them, though, for her father, she
was still the image of chastity.

The well-ordered play was cast. Scenes followed one after another, ranging from the tragic to buffoonery, scenes of political
conspiracies, scenes of amorous farce; grave scenes, too, of friendship. The principal hero was not on the stage for long periods of
time; he was absent more and more often when business called him
to Paris. But he was in Brussels when Victor Hugo—asked to leave
the city—bade goodbye to the outlaws. Alexandre followed Hugo
to Antwerp where he had been named president of a banquet in
honor of the man who had to run away. Émile Deschanel had spoken
in praise of Dumas:

I propose a toast to our writer, the one who has best known
how to make money from French wit and to give it an imprint
that makes it travel throughout the world.

The next day, a long procession of refugees accompanied Hugo
to the quay. After much speech making, Hugo embarked. When
the ship stood off some distance from the pier, women waved their

handkerchiefs. A beating rain could not disperse the crowd in which Hugo could identify Alexandre's white vest: "Alexandre Dumas had been kind and charming up to the last minute. He wanted to be the last one to kiss me. I cannot say how much this effusion touched me," Hugo wrote to his wife, Adèle, from London.

Suddenly Brussels without Victor Hugo seemed empty. Alexandre escaped again. He had a ready pretext: the monster-novel *Isaac Laquedem* was to begin with a long walk along the Appian Way. Alexandre had to see Rome once more. Either on the fourth or on the fifth of August, he left Brussels.

Despite his promise to Marie to travel with her to Turin, Dumas traveled in the company of Mme. Guidi until Baden before descending to Italy where he intended to sign a lease with the bookseller Perrin for *La Maison de Savoie*. In spite of the letter he received from Turin, dated September 5, 1857, Parfait was worried:

> I consigned all the books of our beloved Victor, in such a way that it would make his holy word bear fruit. After supper we gathered in a room and there I read the important passages of *Napoléon-le-Petit*. Everybody was surprised, enchanted, carried away! Following this reading, there were so many requests for more that I left my last volume in Lyon, the second capital of the Empire.

Parfait approved of this anti-Bonapartist propaganda activity but he regretted this expensive trip which could break down the delicate financial balance he tried to maintain. Marie, too, had received a letter, supposedly sent from Chambéry on August 22, 1852:

> Do I need to tell you that I regret, my dear love, that I am very much lonely . . . we will take some other trip together to console me for this one. Thank Bouquié for me; he had not come to meet me at Cologne and he made me take the longest way so that we could travel together on a trip he would never have made and which I have made three times. Besides, if he had kept his promise, he would have spoiled my understanding of humankind, he would have made it good.

In fact he was not lonely since in the carriage he had held Isabelle at his side. He skipped the expected stops at Chambéry and Turin, the quicker to reach Rome via Genoa. He built up a fiction to deceive Marie. If he was in Rome, he claimed, it was because *Le Pays* had printed in its August thirtieth issue a letter that alleged that he was in Rome.

This was anything but true. Rome (or rather the rediscovery of this city through the surprised eyes of Isabelle) had always been the goal of his trip. She was blooming under the warm Roman sun, resting while her lover visited the recent diggings out on the Appian Way under the direction of Visconti and the Chevalier Canina. Explained to Marie and to Parfait as a business trip, it was above all a sentimental escapade which was also a topographical recollec- tion of Rome, a necessity for the novel he planned.

Long faces greeted him when, about the first of October, he returned to 73 Boulevard Waterloo. He lied again, locked himself in his workroom and finally confessed so he could go back sooner to his innumerable projects. Now *Isaac Laquedem* possessed him. "The capital work of his life, this powerful epic which will follow through the ages the symbolic legend of Isaac Laquedem" (*Le Pays*, August 30, 1852).

Dumas spent his nights writing while Parfait made several copies. On the fifth of October, he sent the first part of the book to *Le Constitutionnel* which Millaud, owner of *Le Pays*, had just bought. By letter, Dumas outlined his ambition:

What I would desire from you is that you explain to your readers that I am giving them a book which has no precedent, in any literature; a book which needs, as all books containing a great thought, to be read entirely before being judged. The value of the book is mostly in the immense ensemble formed by six novels in the middle of six different civilizations, tied together by the same subject, pursuing the same idea. . . . All that I can affirm, during this twenty-year period of gestation in my mind, is that the book has so come to maturity that I have now only to pick up the fruit of the tree of my imagination. Therefore, you will not have to wait; I do not compose any- more, I dictate to myself.

Alexandre might dictate, but religious orders were watching. On January 15, 1853, *Le Constitutionnel* warned its readers that "a feeling of propriety determined its resolution to discontinue the appearance of all the parts of M. Dumas' novel that referred to the history of Jesus Christ."

L'Univers, Union Catholique, was scandalized:

> to see an author clothe the Son of God, the truth itself, with the attributes of a character of novel; but what offends the most in this infamous profanation which M. Dumas believes he is authorized to make, is not so much the scandal, the impiety, the sacrilege that it fosters, as is the author's stupidity, the idiotic satisfaction he manifests and the candor with which he defiles eternal truth.

What *L'Univers* denounces is this mixture of sacred and profane which defiles Christ and makes him merely a superior man, a vulgar Balsamo whose magnetic influence acts on weaker beings. The humanization of Christ leads to fraternization of God and men and to the leveling of hierarchies. The leveling spirit of the revolution is at work again.

Conclusion: the Prince must act to make us forget he ever was a President.

Dumas had hastily come back to Paris, to rally his friends, the closest to power in the government.

He believed he could get away with the suppression of just two segments of the serial. Eternal optimism! The censor slashed fifteen segments. It was not censorship any more, but assassination. Dumas resigned himself to a gross mending of his work with big stitches that joined one part to the preceding one. But it was useless; more mutilations were demanded. *Isaac Laquedem* stopped abruptly and Dumas never returned to it again. "Alexandre Dumas waited for the proper time to continue his work but, as is well known, death came to surprise him during the war in 1870 and the important work he had conceived was unfortunately left unfinished," concluded the Levy edition of his work. An editor's fable. It was not the political power or the surrounding bigotry which condemned *Isaac Laquedem*, the cause was deeper: it was the lack of interest among the readers of *Le Constitutionnel*. They expected to be entertained, while Dumas offered them a meditation on universal history. Something was broken that had lasted ten years—the complicity between an author and his readers. The death sentence against *Isaac Laquedem* hit deeper than the novel itself. Dumas would write novels again, but for the most part they came from the workshop, hacked out with awkward collaborators whose original sins Dumas could not repair.

Now Alexandre lived either in Brussels or in Paris. In between, he lived on the Paris-Brussels or Brussels-Paris trains. The proceeding called "Affirmation of Debts" opened on June 12, 1852 and closed on April 18, 1853 with a process of registration of debtors' claims. One hundred fifty-three creditors were counted. The ways for an honorable settlement were open. In Paris as well as in Brussels, Alexandre, who hated unpleasantness and tears, tried to organize a coexistence between his daughter and his official and unofficial mistresses. His sense of theater, of entrances and exits, was sometimes masterly, but the comedy of life does not permit rehearsals, and the talent of the stage director was often at fault. In December 1852 he wrote to his daughter, Marie: "I ran away from Mme. Guidi's following a tearful scene—Let her go to the devil. . . ."

And to Alexandre fils:

Isabelle will go to see you tomorrow evening and I will go to meet her. At what time? I don't know but I will go. Not a word to Isabelle about my trip the day before yesterday. And try not to have your friends talk about it.

To Marie, at the end of March 1853:

Since I have arrived [in Paris] I have been a nurse and a worker. . . . My coat will come to you, to your great surprise— it is because I faked leaving tonight and Isabelle, who cannot go out, sent my coat that I had forgotten at her place—it was given to a gentleman who was leaving, too—and this gentleman, vainly having looked for me in the cars of the train, will give you this object this morning.

The sad Isabelle was so sick that Alexandre feared for her life. The dance steps of farce were mixed with tearful scenes—the young girl, death, and the old lover.

To Marie for Easter 1853:

I went to Isabelle's last evening. I knew she was sick. I found her very sick. It is a setback from which she will recover this time but a third time she will not be so fortunate.

I found her with fifteen leeches on her side and a physician who preferred to burn her with the "infernal stone" rather than to stop the bleeding with Boquery water. They had just put a mustard plaster on her back. I spent the night in an armchair. She did not cease to toss and complain. Alas! She is so young, poor girl; she will have great difficulty in dying. This morning she was worn out as are all the people with this unfortunate disease; she spoke of a white dress that she will have made in the spring. Then she said her Easter mass in bed. She seemed to be a figure of wax. If you had been there, my dear heart, you would have made a beautiful drawing of her, all full of feeling.

Alexandre passed from Rue de Laval where Isabelle rested, a little calmer, to No. 1, Rue d'Enghien where Mme. Guidi expected him. He found her "a little better." But, as he added to Marie, "You know what better means for her: remission in a chronic illness."

By confiding to his daughter, by calling upon her pity for his unfortunate mistresses, both consumptive, Alexandre tried to make Marie his accomplice. Marie, however, was resisting, encouraged by yet another mistress, Mlle. Anna, who could very well have been Anna Bauer, the woman from Baden to whom Dumas gave an illegitimate child in 1851.

Isabelle was expected in Brussels. Alexandre proposed schemes so that the sentimental comedy did not turn into heavy drama and wrote to Marie in April of 1853: 　　　　　　　　　　　　　．

I fear so much to upset you that I went upstairs to tell you— and then I did not dare to tell you—that, in spite of all I have done to prevent the trip, Isabelle will arrive this evening.

What shall I do, my child? I am sad because, these past four or five days, I sensed that as soon as she felt better she would rush back here. For nothing in the world would I want you to sulk like you did during her last trip. I love you so, my dear child, that your face is my gaiety or my sadness. Be courageous and do not hurt me during the three or four days she will be here.

Alexandre feigned false departures, false returns. He put Viellot, in Paris, in charge of monitoring his mistresses' traffic and asked that Marie retouch the decor in Brussels: "I will return with Mme. Guidi; if Isabelle's portrait has been put back in my room, have it removed."

Alexandre had never known the art of breaking off, letting time end liaisons which, often born from passing desires, burdened him with bonds that he did not know how to untie and that made him an eternal prisoner of his amorous fantasies.

The innumerable round-trips between Paris and Brussels permitted him to renew his relationships with theater directors. His financial settlement made possible the sharing of profits between Dumas and his creditors. Dumas could return to the theater, but his imagination had dried up. He threw himself into adaptations, seconded by his "usual translator," Max de Goritz. A fine name for a poor devil who, one morning in January 1853, came to 73 Boulevard Waterloo, claiming to be a noble Hungarian pursued by the Austrian police, an outlaw without a sou. Alexandre felt sorry for him—all the more because the so-called Mme. de Goritz was pretty. With a pale face, decorated with an ash-blond moustache, de Mayer, alias Max de Goritz, haunted the house from then on. Dumas hired the pseudo-count to translate for him plays by German authors: Iffland, Kotzebue, *Les Forestiers*, *La Femme sans amour*, *La Conscience*, *Le Marbrier*, *La Veillée allemande*, a theatrical sheaf which they would thresh much later because, in the meantime, Dumas gave himself wholly to his return to the most prestigious of theaters, the Comédie-Française. Arsène Houssaye, administrator of the theater since April 27, 1850, was Alexandre's friend. Dumas had taken advantage of one of his sojourns in Paris when he brought Marie to study painting under the tutelage of Louis Boulanger. He had contracted with the Comédie for a five-act comedy to be delivered during the second half of July: *Louis XIV et sa cour*. More than twenty years later, the new title recalled his first triumph, *Henri III et sa cour*, and heralded the ambition of a renaissance.

Parfait wrote to his brother that on August 8, 1853, after his first act was finished, Dumas went,

to write the second and third, guess where? . . . At Compiègne! Useless to tell you that he had arranged a rendez-vous with one of the many loose women with whom he ruins himself.

Alexandre stayed at the hotel of his old friend, Vuillemot (who later would give him many recipes from his cookbook): *Hôtel de la cloche et de la bouteille.* He gave himself up to writing and to love.

Then Brussels again, where he reworked the third act that did not please Houssaye, and then finished the play.

Again Brussels to Paris and Zirza-Isabelle's kisses and the emotion brought about by the imminent reading of the play, a reading which took place the afternoon of August 30, 1853. The play was accepted unanimously. "Splendid reading," proclaimed Alexandre to Marie and he went back to Brussels, his heart filled with hope.

But he had not taken into account the perennial intrigues of the actors and actresses. He had certainly not considered the spite of newspapers which noted that "a part of the money intended as bonuses to authors as an incentive premium or proof of satisfaction has just been given to such recognized authors as Émile Augier and Alexandre Dumas." Dumas was enraged. Did he need an incentive premium? "I am not one of those who need to be encouraged; I am one of those who are remunerated. Neither a minister nor the Théâtre has to give me approval. I have never worked for any minister and it has been ten years since I have worked for the Théâtre-Français," he replied arrogantly. Dumas also did not count on the censorship of Napoléon III, who was then nicknamed "Badinguet," to whom the play had been shown on October eighth. Sinister rumors spread: the play had been stopped.

According to the report from the censors, "it was feared that its subject contained allusions to the Emperor's marriage and that the whole play could be taken as a critique of that great event which was still echoing throughout France and Europe."

On October eighteenth, Parfait wrote again to his brother:

Once informed, Dumas left for Paris immediately. For two days he has maneuvered to get the interdiction lifted. But when he saw that all his efforts would be useless, he made a great decision and wrote the following letter to Houssaye:
"My dear director,
I arrive in Brussels after being notified by the theater that the *Jeunesse de Louis XIV* was stopped by censors. Today is Tuesday; I ask you for a reading next Monday. I will read you five acts. I do not know yet what they will be for the news

took me by surprise. But these five acts will be called *La Jeunesse de Louis XV*. I will manage so that the decor you ordered can be used; I have been assured that the sets are ready. It goes without saying that there won't be in *La Jeunesse de Louis XV* a single line or situation from *La Jeunesse de Louis XIV* which will remain intact and yours in case it will, some day, please the censors to return this work to you. If I should be ready before Monday, I will be honored to advise you."

Before an assembled and incredulous press, Dumas carried off the announcement of his literary tour de force. "The play is finished; do not worry," he wrote to Marie and to Parfait to reassure them. Act I was started on Tuesday, October eleventh at seven in the morning and finished the next day at two-thirty. Act II was completed on Thursday. Act III was finished on Friday the fourteenth at six in the evening. Act IV, begun Saturday at midnight, was finished the same day at nine in the morning. Dumas gave himself an hour of rest and then began Act V at ten and, and at a quarter to noon, inscribed "End" to the work. The promise had been kept; Dumas could read the play before the committee two days before the deadline he had imposed upon himself. The play was completed in about one hundred hours and received on Saturday, October fifteenth, all white balls, with acclamations, with amazement. Success intoxicates like champagne and in this state of excitement, everything seemed possible. Dumas asked for the privilege of opening a theater.

He created a newspaper. He began to live again as if nothing had happened, as if, returning from exile, he had again found a throne misplaced in an unfortunate accident.

II

The Return of *Le Mousquetaire*

"**G**irardin has received the semi-official notice to postpone publication of the *Mémoires*," Noël Parfait wrote to his brother on December 23, 1853:

Dumas, furious, became excited. Much had been said about his literary tour de force and this clamor about him had already intoxicated him. He had believed he could terrify his enemies in high or low places by publishing a newspaper in which he would have his words printed constantly. He found I don't know who as a money lender and *Le Mousquetaire* was created! *Le Mousquetaire!* Now, I ask you . . . on this past November twentieth, this sheet appeared. It didn't terrify anyone; no one seemed to take notice of it and it will remain, if it remains at all, merely as the most incredible monument to egotism and personality! It is not even a curiosity; it simply makes people shrug their shoulders, that's all. *Les Mémoires* which make up the principal part since politics are now excluded—the newspaper is purely literary—are no more than an indigestible collection of stale backstage anecdotes and quotations placed without order, plan, or purpose, entirely at random. Truly, those who, like myself, love Dumas sincerely can only be very distressed to see him mess up his talent and compromise his literary reputation.

Now, all this does not prevent the house of Brussels from running as before, a bit lamely, but still running. Dumas has, if we can believe him, no intention of abandoning it. The fact is that he could not do it today unless he refunded his landlord and his creditors (which would take an amount of twelve to fifteen thousand francs) or sank again into a new bankruptcy.

You will tell me that it is absurd to go start a newspaper in Paris, live there in a furnished hotel and keep at the same time a substantial household in Brussels; but it is precisely because it makes no common sense that he does it. Now, I patiently wait for the disaster. It won't be long in coming; I'm very certain of that. *Le Mousquetaire* will collapse and Dumas will come back to Brussels. Only he will come back after having increased the amount of his debt that, thanks to my persistence over two years, I succeeded in diminishing. He knows it very well himself for he said recently to Barthelemy, "If I had had Noël with me for the past five years, I would now have fifty-thousand francs set aside."

Parfait played the Cassandra of 73 Boulevard Waterloo, deserted by its master who sent bulletins to the subalterns in Brussels. Alexandre announced to Victor Hugo on November 5, 1853:

You know that my *Mémoires* have been stopped but as it cannot be admitted openly, it was done by pressure on Girardin and Girardin wrote to me that he cannot continue them. I am going to publish a newspaper to put my enemies up against the wall, we will see then whether they can stop the *Mémoires*.

The prospectus for the journal was already written. Dumas had a fictitious interlocutor ask a question: "Why do you start a newspaper?" To which he replied that he was tired of being successfully attacked by his enemies and badly defended by his friends in other publishers' newspapers, that he had still forty or fifty volumes of *Mémoires* to publish which became more and more compromising as they came nearer to the present time, especially because he intended to take on his critics. The specimen issue came out on November twelfth. The newspaper offices were located in the square court of the famous restaurant La Maison d'Or, No. 1, Rue

Lafitte, in the wing that faced the restaurant, across from a fencing master. The premises consisted of a small room where the cashier was supposed to work, a cubicle where unsold copies were thrown at random, a very small room for the editorial staff, into which, in spite of the notice "Entrance forbidden to the public," all the Bohemians of literary Paris soon marched.

Alexandre towered above the tumult of the main floor from his small apartment rented on the third floor:

> Imagine a sort of office looking almost ascetic. No decorations. Not a painting or a statuette. A small pinewood table with the simplest of red coverings. On this table, an inkwell, pens, blue paper. Here and there, three caned chairs: this was the extent of the furnishings. The only apparent luxury was a sort of small Etruscan vase in which bathed either a rose, a sweet-william, or a branch of lilac, the last vestige of some recently completed idyll. Dressed lightly, even in winter, with pants covering his feet, bare-headed, his arms bare, moving constantly his enormous frizzy head, the illustrious mulatto, bent over his sheets of paper like an ox over his furrow, spent all his hours throwing black ink on blue paper with the nib of his pen; and he said, he finally found a bitter sensuality in this exercise of a galley slave. (Ph. Audebrand, *A. Dumas à la maison d'or*)

Le Mousquetaire, journal de M. Alexandre Dumas, had to furnish daily to its readers seventy thousand alphabetical characters. In spite of the young collaborators with whom he knew how to surround himself, Dumas provided the essential copy. Philibert Audebrand, historiographer of the newspaper, made an almost exhaustive list of the aides Dumas recruited: Joseph Méry, a friend for twenty years, sixty and straight as an arrow, and the discreet Gérard de Nerval, his mind drowned in the shadows of insanity, who gave to the newspaper *El Desdichado* and *La Pandora*.

Who else? Alexandre fils, of course, who, as a well-known writer, hesitated to entrust his prose to this shoddy newspaper, Octave Feuillet, and Paul Bocage, nephew of the creator of *Antony*, whom Dumas especially liked. A squadron of talents in action in the main floor offices shouted, argued, joked until a Moldavian Boyar who occupied the second floor began to wonder whether someone was being slaughtered or a woman was suffering the pangs of childbirth. The administration was left to chance. How did the subscriber, regularly each day at the hour of his absinthe aperitif, receive his copy? A miracle! No fixed salaries and yet the employees were punctual. No money and yet there was a cashier, Michel, the ex-gardener of Monte-Cristo whom Dumas had chosen for the very excellent reason that Michel could neither read nor do figures. In spite of everything, *Le Mousquetaire* pleased the public of the Boulevards and its circulation reached ten thousand copies. Had Parfait been wrong? But the Cassandras are always right. The request for the privilege of having a theater was not granted: neither *La Jeunesse de Louis XV* nor *La Jeunesse de Louis XIV* could escape the censors' claws. Its immorality, its impropriety in mixing a man of the Church (Cardinal Fleury) with bedroom intrigue was criticized. Dumas wanted to try again and proposed a third *Jeunesse*: *La Jeunesse de Lauzun*. Burnt once too often, Arsène Houssaye did not accept.

There remained only *Le Mousquetaire*, a purely literary newspaper. Alexandre called the romantic musketeers to his rescue. On December 20, 1853, Lamartine replied: "You ask my opinion of your newspaper. I have opinions about human things; I have none about miracles. You are superhuman. My opinion of you is an exclamation mark. There have been studies to determine the nature of perpetual motion. You have created perpetual astonishment!" On December twentieth, Michelet told him, "With my mind I visualize your fights of all kinds; I am so impressed by your indomitable talent which bends and bends again before so many absurd obstacles, and not less by your heroic perseverance."

At the beginning of January 1854, Alexandre had in hand a note from Victor Hugo: "I read your newspaper. You are giving us back Voltaire, a supreme comfort for the humiliated and silent France." Alexandre hesitated; he would have liked to publish this note but that could endanger the only thing that remained to him—acceptance on the soil of his own country. He committed the small cowardice of not publishing it, but atoned by showing it to everyone he met and by printing, as often as he could, the name of Hugo, the famous outlaw, by reciting everywhere verses from Hugo's *Les Châtiment*. He even was so bold as to offer a copy of the book to Princesse Mathilde and Prince Napoléon, cousin of the tyrant-emperor.

Alexandre became daring—he defamed the pale Caesar of the Tuileries:

> Irony of ironies! This stranger that the people acclaimed as if he were the nephew of the Man of Destiny had been disowned at his birth by King Louis; there is not a drop of Bonaparte blood in his veins. All the chancelleries know that he is the son of Hortense Beauharnais and of Admiral Woerhuel. We stoop before a Dutchman!

He could not find a worse insult than "He is a damned Dutchman!" Less than nothing! But his hatred for the Emperor did not include the Emperor's family. He continued to call on Princesse Mathilde and Prince Napoléon, his friends from Florence. It did not enter his mind to disavow them. Thanks to Mathilde, he obtained the Legion of Honor for Van Hasselt. Thanks to Napoléon, he obtained prizes for a lottery benefitting the expatriates. Inconsistency? "Dumas sees the Jéromes often—he adores all that glitters—even if it is not gold," wrote Hetzel to Hugo. A logic of feelings established an order that had nothing to do with political parties. Dumas loved Victor Hugo but he loved Mathilde and Napoléon just as much. Where was the crime? Was he less of a republican for it?

His life was now punctuated by the newspaper that had to be delivered to subscribers every evening. He was the musketeer who threw himself into a violent attack on Buloz to avenge the injustice of that Director of *La Revue des deux mondes* who had praised or destroyed one by one the works of the greatest of the literary greats of the time: Hugo, George Sand, Delacroix, Clésinger, and attempted to assassinate them through his own critic-drudges.

If *Le Mousquetaire* indulged now and then in spite, it preferred philanthropy. Skimming through the paper, one could believe one was reading *Le Moniteur* of good deeds and of virtues. Was Abbé Moret attempting to save the disadvantaged children from misery and loneliness? Alexandre alerted all Paris, opened an appeal and knocked at all doors. The house of Notre-Dame-des-Sept-Douleurs was founded. A certain young actor was threatened with induction into the army? A deferment was obtained. Artists' graves were falling into ruin? The paper called on the public conscience—a grave for Marie Dorval, a grave for Frédéric Soulié, a grave for Balzac. But Balzac's widow refused to hear of it, not wanting her husband's name used in an operation that she considered highly commercialized. She even summoned Dumas before the Tribunal on May 3, 1854. The judge settled the case in Solomon's tradition: he granted the widow the simple grave, Dumas a monument. But in spite of all his efforts, benefit performances and subscriptions, Dumas was never able to erect for his late rival the marble memorial that Clésinger would have created.

Alexandre visited cemeteries and at each step he stumbled on the grave of someone he loved. Death had triumphed, although he, still strong, fought to survive, to extend his time of glory. The young people who surrounded him at the Maison d'Or and his young mistress kept him under the delusion that neither age nor death could have dominion over him. The chaos that followed him everywhere left little time for reflection. Anecdote masked actual history. In February of 1854, *Le Mousquetaire* was in a great commotion. The usual translator, Max de Goritz, was wanted by the police of Vienna. Alexandre was called to the Prefecture of Police where he was shown a formidable record: the so-called Count Max de Goritz was in fact a German Jew. Mayer was his real name. He lived with a woman who claimed to be the child of one of the men who pretended to be the last Dauphin, Louis XVII. He was an adventurer of the most dangerous kind; his talent ran from simple theft to burglary, "if necessary, . . . assassination." Alexandre was dumbfounded. He admitted to the police that "Goritz had run away." But the police of the Empire did not take long to find and arrest the pseudo-count.

At Brussels, Parfait was in despair. The master had abandoned 73 Boulevard Waterloo and had left Marie there alone. No money, although an effort was made to have the Théâtre Vaudeville of Brussels play *La Jeunesse de Louis XIV*. The army of process servers reappeared.

Dumas promised money; he promised *Les Mohicans de Paris* which, if sold to the United States and to England, could save his household from destitution. *Les Mohicans*, the longest of Dumas' novels, nineteen volumes, more than a million words, was a complex of intrigues which permitted the author to run through all classes of society, choosing exceptional characters: ex-officers of the Empire, the Duc de Reichstadt, Inspector Jackal, informers, convicts, students, and artists. There was much borrowed from Eugène Sue's *Mystères de Paris* in this novel and much of Paul Bocage, a favorite disciple of Dumas, who liked to call him the Maestro. This book first appeared in *Le Mousquetaire* on May 24, 1854 and would continue to 1859, passing from *Le Mousquetaire* to Dumas' next newspaper, *Monte-Cristo*.

Without Parfait to watch the cash register of assets and liabilities, Alexandre survived with expedients and substitutes. He called constantly on his savior, Hirschler, who had disentangled the skein of business after the bankruptcy settlement. Hirschler always rushed in to help, took some "louis" from his pocket for Alexandre to distribute like a prince to the collaborators of the newspaper who needed money the most. "A 'louis' for Gabrielle," the pretty young woman who between 1836 and 1840 had driven Alexandre and Roger de Beauvoir crazy. She had gained an almost monstrous weight; she was short of breath but had kept her aristocratic manners. She signed "Comtesse Dash" to apocryphal memoires and to historic novels and "Marie Michon" to her gossip column in *Le Mousquetaire*. Hirschler was everywhere, dealing with editors and journalists, debating with theater people. "He is making a fortune behind your back," insinuated malicious or perhaps exceptionally lucid acquaintances. "I know it very well, and am very pleased that it happens," Alexandre invariably retorted. "Remember that this same man picked me up twice from failure." For the most part, this zealous and admiring steward assured an almost material quietness that permitted Alexandre to chase his whimsies. He had found a small townhouse at 77 Rue d'Amsterdam, that he furnished with cast-offs from 73 Boulevard Waterloo. He argued with the directors of the Comédie-Française, the Vaudeville, and the Odéon, to whom Dumas had given plays that year.

Romulus, at the Français, came out from the author's bottom drawer. It was a light comedy in one act, taken from a novel by Auguste Lafontaine, written by Paul Bocage and Octave Feuillet for the Théâtre-Historique, then revised by Dumas before it was accepted by the Comédie-Française on October 9, 1851. On January 13, 1854, Alexandre was in Arsène Houssaye's loge. He was beaming, he laughed uproariously. From an orchestra seat, a peevish, lugubrious spectator asked him why he laughed. "Eh! by God, don't you see that I am laughing in your place?" Everyone in the audience applauded the author's witticism.

Le Marbrier, shown at the Vaudeville on May 22, 1854, was the product of many writers: de Goritz had translated one of Kotzebue's plays intended as a vehicle for Bocage the actor; the actor and his nephew had smoothed the translation; Brunswick composed a first version; Dumas then rewrote the whole play. It was not so much the play, but the actor for whom it was written, Bocage, the immortal Antony, now aged, worn out, still acting in the style of 1830. Dumas, on bad terms with the director of the theater who had changed the cast, did not attend the premiere, but instead sent his servant to represent him. The latter, after each act, brought home news from the battlefront. "Great success," he announced, but the critics did not agree.

La Conscience, five acts and six scenes, pulled out from the Iffland's trilogy, was played at the Odéon. Then *Le Crime par ambition,* long ago translated by Goritz, caused a flutter around the Latin Quarter. It was said that at the general rehearsal Laferrière was superb in the role of Edouard Rihberg. For lack of money, the students could only walk up and down the arcades of the Odéon; they could not go in, yet they inhaled the scent of glory even before knowing the fate of the play. A carriage stopped along the sidewalk, and a very tall man, a kind of giant, advanced under the arcades. Someone cried, "Long live Dumas," and a chorus echoed, "Long live Dumas." Dumas stood, filled with emotion: "I am very touched, my children, very touched. But what are you doing here? Instead of acclaiming me in the street, go applaud my play inside." Not a sou! Alexandre had known that himself; he opened wide the door leading into the theater. "Theater should be free for the young," he said. "Ah! If I were rich! Come in, my children." They crossed the dark corridors following the steps of the glorious guide; they could perceive the rustle of the audience, some shreds of light; they passed by the ticket-checker. "Give these young men good seats. I am paying today," said Dumas. He left to take his place in his loge with some friends. The play? The young men did not pay attention; they watched, still dazzled by the author in his loge. They sought a look from him, each wanting to believe the author's smile was for him alone. When the curtain fell, the applause made the theater shake. Then they were back on the pavement on that November night, lonely and still trembling.

In spite of success the author did not feel as intoxicated as in the past. He thought of the dead, of the exiled, of Victor Hugo to whom he dedicated *La Conscience:*

Receive it as the mark of a friendship that survived exile and that will, I hope, survive death.
I believe, in the immortality of the soul.

A lassitude for living sometimes overcame him. *Le Mousquetaire* was ailing, and its first collaborators, tired of never being paid for their writing, had deserted in a group. With the help of Millaud, Villemessant attempted to take over the name and the title of Editor-in-Chief. Dumas wrote him a refusal in November of 1854:

All my life I have dreamed of having my newspaper, all mine: I have it at last and the least it can bring me is a million per year. I have not yet touched a sou for my articles; at forty sous for each article, that makes two hundred thousand francs I have earned since the creation of *Le Mousquetaire*, an amount that I leave quietly in the cash box, to get in a month five thousand at once. Under such conditions, I need neither money nor a director; *Le Mousquetaire* is a business made of gold and I intend to exploit it all alone.

Eighteen fifty-five. On January twenty-sixth, a friend came into the theater at the end of the matinee and reported a great tragedy: the poor Gérard de Nerval had been found hanged, at dawn, in the Rue de la Vieille-Lanterne. He had spent the night in that infamous street in a house of ill repute and in the morning he was found hanging from the bar of a window, the tie of a kitchen apron around his neck. Alexandre took a carriage and went to the street and up the balustrade to the top of the staircase. A tame crow cawed as it clung to the bannister; it belonged to a locksmith whose workshop threw sparks through the door. Alexandre climbed up—at the top of the last three steps, a window, dark, with iron bars. It was from the cross bar . . . Alexandre closed his eyes, overcome by images of happiness: Gérard at Jehan du Seigneur's, Impasse du Doyenné; Gérard with him entering Mannheim; Gérard tenderly in love with Ida, Rue de Rivoli. Today Gérard was stretched upon a slab in the morgue. Alexandre wanted to take possession of his dead friend. He decided to take a collection for "a flagstone of black marble," on which verses by Méry would be engraved. A poet's tomb, a king's epitaph. But Théophile Gautier and Arsène Houssaye insisted that he leave to jealous friends the sad joy of paying for the stone. On Tuesday, January thirtieth, at noon, Gérard's body was taken to Notre Dame. Over the font, a gloved hand offered Alexandre the holy water. He looked fixedly at the veiled silhouette behind a pillar and seemed to recognize a perfume. He thought of it constantly on the way to Père-Lachaise cemetery and remembered it as the perfume that came from the letters he regularly received with a donation for the charities sponsored by *Le Mousquetaire*: a fine and aristocratic handwriting, a monogram, "E.M.," surmounted with a crown: Emma Mannoury-Lacour.

Emma wanted to see Alexandre again. When she took off her heavy winter coat and sat on a couch, she seemed to be thirty or thirty-two (she was born on October 4, 1832). She was rather tall with a thin, supple waist, dark azure eyes which at first seemed black; she had long blond hair, falling in English ringlets, teeth small and white, and her lips, touched with red, made her complexion even paler. Something in her revealed fatigue or pain. A woman tired of fighting an illness of body or of spirit. Emma blushed under Alexandre's persistent look. She stammered her admiration for the great writer who, to encourage her, was holding her hand. He immediately felt a great sympathy, he wanted to know everything about her. Little by little, she dared to confide: yes, she was unhappy. Married twice, twice badly. The first time was with a school teacher from Vire. But it could hardly be called a marriage. Emma blushed even more, while the libertine smiled. Separated from her first husband, she had remarried, four years ago, with Louis-Anatole Mannoury-Lacour, a landowner from Monts in Normandy. Attorneys had arranged the marriage. The finances matched, but the bodies . . . a woman married twice and still a virgin! She had given herself up to poetry and wrote charming, melancholic verses.

Emma returned several times to Rue d'Amsterdam; she had won Marie over with compliments on her work. She resisted a little, then she gave herself awkwardly and passionately. She had not lied. Alexandre, vainglorious for having made her discover the pleasures of love, once more made promises. It was not an adventure, but the last love of a life in which there had been so many. He kept his word; he left *Le Mousquetaire* and rushed to Caen to join his new mistress at Emma's family house, 17 Rue des Vieilles-Carrières-Saint-Julien. On May 6, 1855, he wrote to Marie:

It's working out. Emma, can you understand such a crazy woman, threw herself on my neck in front of everybody. Here I am obliged to kill A[natolle]. We are leaving together for a village called Harcourt and we will come back only tomorrow morning.

Near Thury-Harcourt, at the end of a beautiful lane of trees behind a wrought iron gate, Alexandre discovered the small château of Monts, a modern building with an Empire pediment and the straight, gloomy lines of early nineteenth-century architecture. Holding Emma's arm, they took long walks in the immense park. Buds announced the end of winter. In spring, Marie was invited as a lightning rod to protect Alexandre's and Emma's liaison by giving it the appearance of an anodyne friendship. Emma became pregnant and Marie indignant. Alexandre wrote to her on April 19, 1855:

I do not see the matter from quite the same point of view as you, who examine it from the point of view of sentiment. I will examine it from the social and, above all, the human point of view.

Everyone is primarily responsible for his or her faults and even for infirmities with no right to expect support from others. If an accident or a deformation has made such and such man impotent—it is up to him himself to bear all the consequences of it and face everything that comes with it. If a woman is guilty of a fault, if she forgets what is considered her duty, it is up to her to atone for this weakness through strength as one atones for a crime by repenting; but the woman with her fault, no more than the man with impotency, has no right to ask a third person to carry the weight of her personal fault or her own misfortune. Before the child was created, I offered these objections; they have been weighed and resolved with these words: For my child, I will have the strength to say what needs to be said and to take everything through to a good end. It was following this determination that the being, who does not yet breathe and who is condemned in advance, was conceived. Nothing is easier in the world than denying birth to a baby to whom, now that it is on its way, a social class is refused.

Children of adultery cannot be recognized either by the father or by the mother; this one will be doubly adulterous. In what condition would he arrive with a mother in such a state of health—this is her own opinion—that she could die from one moment to the next.

With a father already old, who, when asking for fifteen more years of life, reveals himself almost exigent; at fourteen, the child could find himself without money, lost in the midst of the world.

If it is a girl, if she is pretty, she will have the recourse to ask for a number at the police and to become a ten-franc courtesan. If it is a boy, he will play the role of Antony until he perhaps plays the role of Lacenaire.

In such case, it's better to destroy—but, after all, it's better not to create.

I would be offended if under the affected pretenses of a ridiculous sensitivity such a decision was taken—it would hurt all my ideas about the unjust and the just; it would rob me of a part of my respect and, I am greatly afraid, with a part of my respect—all my love.

M. A[natolle] is impotent, too bad for him.

Mme. M[annoury-Lacourt] had been weak, too bad for her. But no one would dare say "too bad" for the one who will see the light of day as a result of this impotence and this weakness.

Each one of us risked something in the deed committed. Mme. M. risked a suit for separation and she was so well resigned to it that she was going to send me a copy of her marriage contract which she didn't do. As for myself, I risked a slash of an épée or a shot of a pistol and I remain ready to risk that still.

Had he broken off with Isabelle? No, for on May second, at the Païva's, the insipid Païva, he took with him his "damsell." Delacroix met him there in the midst of a crowd of young men with and without beards, forty-year-old juvenile leads, barons, German dukes, and journalists. Alexandre triumphed in this shady salon where he dined each week. He was consulted about everything, particularly on the talents of the cook, but this mediocre society rapidly bored him; usually, he yawned and fell asleep.

On May twenty-second, Alexandre dined with Delacroix. They

then took a cab to fetch Isabelle, "the little one he protected," to go and see a tragedy and an Italian comedy. The young cavaliers of the romantic revolution had really aged. But Alexandre protested: Didn't he still live like a young man? Lowering his voice, he boasted: he still had mistresses; he even tired them out. His relation with the little one—he motioned to Isabelle—was an exception for she was dying of consumption. He saw her every day, but mostly as a father who provided her with material security and relaxation. "Happy man!" murmured Delacroix. Not aged, indeed, but alone, terribly alone in spite of the tumult surrounding him, in spite of his two children, who ceaselessly preached at him.

And his work? He was tired of writing day and night without respite and of never having a sou: "I leave two novels half finished . . . I will go, I will travel, and I will see upon my return if a Hercules has come to finish my two imperfect enterprises." He wished to leave *Les Mohicans de Paris* and *La Comtesse de Charny* to run away, away from the large cemetery that Paris had become: "The men of our generation have already almost as many friends lying under the earth as remain with them: Soumet, Soulié, Balzac, d'Orsay, Gérard de Nerval."

And soon Delphine de Girardin. *Le Mousquetaire* was framed with a large black border. More than a friend, a brother, a defender: "In her salon we spent many good, many sweet and also many joyous moments which flew by so quickly that midnight, one, two in the morning had come and we were still talking of saying our prayers for the Angelus. Charming spirit who made those hours so rapid and so light" (*Le Mousquetaire*, July 3, 1853).

The hours lengthen like shadows when the sun sets. His best hope lay in the compensation he expected from "a suit that should assure his future, something like 800,000 francs to begin, not counting the rest," as Dumas had confided to Delacroix. A suit against the newspaper *Le Siècle* and its publishers, Michel Lévy brothers.

He dreamed of fortune and enduring love with Emma who languished in her Normandy. Alexandre trusted her with letters he had sent to Isabelle, letters from a father as much as from a lover, melancholic letters:

You make me live again the most charming days of my youth. Do not be surprised, therefore, if, my heart having returned to its twenty-fifth year, my pen is also of the same age. I love you, my dear angel. Alas, there are only two real loves in a life: the first one, which dies—the last one, from which one dies. I love you, unfortunately, with this last love.

Among Aglaé Tellier, Isabelle, and now Emma, how many charming bodies had given themselves, for love, for the desire of a position, for gain? Remembering them could not cheer him in his solitude, the bitter solitude, more bitter yet when his own children betrayed him. Parfait wrote to his brother Charles on August 28, 1855:

It's now two months since he had to separate from his daughter and to separate violently, after frightening scenes. She had played atrocious tricks on him, unbelievable and wanton, for no reason, since her father treated her with unequalled kindness, a kindness that could even be called a weakness. And God knows how she exploited him when I was not there to restrain her a little. But you understand that it is not her foolish prodigalities that brought on the break. Dumas would not have become angry for so small a thing and I speak of it only because her need to spend money and to gratify all her whims would have prevented her from doing anything that could have caused trouble with her father. I will not tell you what happened, first because it would be much too long and then because there are details that I really would not dare to write. No one knows what has happened to this young person since Dumas threw her out of his home. . . . I do know what she made me endure for two-and-a-half years. We had again become good friends since we kept a distance from one another but it is not her fault if I have remained on good terms with her father. Moreover, Dumas knew this and lately said to Barthelemy, "When I think that because of this miserable creature I was twenty times at the point of breaking off with Parfait, the best and the most devoted of my friends."

But was she so guilty, this child of chance, torn away from her mother and brought up by her father's mistress, then thrown into the perennial anarchy that Alexandre stirred up around him? Alexandre sighed: His daughter paid the bill for his own licentiousness.

Sometimes a telegram would call him, "I am at Le Hâvre. Come. Emma." A room opening upon the sea at the Hôtel d'Angleterre was a bright interval for the scarcely graying . . . good-natured giant, and the frail woman. But one morning the appeal became a summons, and Alexandre wrote to Mme. Porcher in the autumn of 1855:

> I must leave for Caen tonight. The person you know is having a miscarriage with her husband at her bedside and not able to cry.

Alexandre borrowed money so he could protect Emma and her secret. But had Anatole not already guessed?

Alexandre was exhausted, a stranger in his own country: "My most beautiful flowers to my best friends; my body is in Paris, but my heart is in Brussels or in Jersey," he had written in an open letter to Pascal Duprat (*La Libre Recherche*, first issue).

To Parfait and Hugo, he wrote on November 15, 1855:

> Today, the nineteenth, I am called before the Imperial Prosecutor for having said—My body is in Paris but my heart is in Brussels and in Jersey.
>
> At last—I have waited for that a long time.
>
> Do you understand that, my dear Noël, do you understand that, my dear Victor?
>
> Prosecuted for a mark of sympathy for some outlaws. . . .
> I have a good mind to become naturalized as a Belgian.

He felt almost pleased for this small persecution from the imperial jailer which bound him even more to the other exiles, which linked him with the old days when he still was someone, when he still wrote. Now he was just a compiler, deprived of invention. *Le Lièvre de mon Grandpère* was, however, a charming story. But it was a story by Cherville Gaspard de Pekow, Marquis de Cherville, ex-lieutenant of the Hunt, whose love for an actress, Emma Daveney, had driven him to become the head of the Vaudeville theater of Brussels. Today, without a sou, he had proposed a few stories to Hetzel and Parfait, like him, both natives of Chartres. Unpublishable. However, from their ore a good writer could extract some gold nuggets. They had thought of Léon Gozlan, but the deal did not go through. "Why not Dumas?" suggested Parfait. Dumas seized the opportunity; necessity has its iron demands.

Parfait and Hetzel had invented for Dumas his latest collaborator, a weak and whimpering creature. Rightly modest, he had neither the rectitude, nor the talent, however second-class, of Maquet. Dumas' worst novels would originate with him. To make money, he would loan his name to whomever asked to give an added value to words falling from another's pen. It was not collaboration any more, it was deception. Dumas signed and signed: *Madame du Deffand* and *La Dame de volupté* by the good Gabrielle, Comtesse Dash, "published by Alexandre Dumas," claimed the title page; *Les Mémoires d'un jeune cadet*, a translation of *Adventures of a Younger Son* by Edward John Tralawney, done by "Victor Perceval," pseudonym of a young woman, Marie de Fernand, born at Bagnères-de-Bigorre, who had imagined that the shortest way to literary success passed through the bed of a famous writer. He signed *Le Pélerinage de Hadji-Abd-el-Hamid-Bey* that he put together from notes of Du Couret, more a fabulist than a traveler. Did Dumas ever write the work attributed to him, or that he attributed to himself? Rarely. He was, however, indignant that his paternity for *L'Orestie* could be doubted. A tragedy in three acts and in verse imitating the classic style, *L'Orestie* opened at the Théâtre Porte-Saint-Martin on January 5, 1856. In *Le Mousquetaire*, he issued a challenge to whoever could prove that in this tragedy, one verse, one single verse was not his. The challenge could be a confession about several of his other works. *L'Orestie* was quickly produced but with difficulties. Alexandre wrote to his son in December of 1855:

> Send me at once 200 or 300 francs if you have them with you—I must buy material and have costumes made for the old men who seem to come out of the Temple's [shelter]. *Credit was refused to Fournier*, he confessed to me last evening.

With a director and an author without a cent, the fate of the play remained in suspense, as happened on the eve of each premiere. Once more, on January 5, 1856, Alexandre turned to his distant friend, Victor Hugo:

Within two hours *L'Orestie* will be played. I have a moment of rest, the only one in six weeks. I take advantage of it to write to you before my battle.

I have received everything, my friend—that pebble that I would not exchange for gold, unless that gold could save the life of a man—the drawings that I forwarded,—everything, except the announced portrait . . . —Is it not a portrait in profile? It is very beautiful although it saddened me very much. You seemed thinner, but still strong. There was in the temples and the chin that sublime will of the great exiles—My God! When will this life of work to which I am condemned permit me to go to see you? What a day of joy when I will embrace you, my friend, you of whom I think eternally, you whom I love and admire a little more with each pulse of my heart.

What about *Les Contemplations?* I am expecting them as a ray of light, as an inspiration. Why didn't they come while I was making *L'Orestie?* They would have sustained me in my labor—which, feather for you, is a rock for me. Thus, at each applause, my dear Victor, I will send you half of it; the boos will be for myself alone.

Applause, mostly. "A beautiful success," wrote Marcelle Desbordes to her husband. The actors went backstage and pulled Alexandre to the front center of the stage so that he received the audience's applause. A success which rang like an echo of other distant triumphs. The play was dedicated to the people, those people, led on a leash, whom Dumas, Hugo, Sand, Michelet would guide with their writing, out of the land of bondage where they were reduced to the role of helots. To educate the people, to preach to them, to make them stronger and better!

Alexandre had his reward with a letter from Victor Hugo, dated Hauteville-House, January twenty-second:

Here is, dear Dumas, the hardly-smiling portrait which had not reached you. This severe face turns toward Little Bonap with indignation, toward *L'Orestie* with admiration. I applaud you from the depth of my tumult of winds and waves. You are making an uproar and I hear it. I often interrupt my day-dreaming to cry, 'Bravo, ocean, and bravo, Dumas.'

The receipt of this letter was an instant of pure happiness as was the marriage of Marie, who returned to the paternal fold. She was marrying a very young man, Pierre-Auguste-Olinde-Petel, son of a physician of Chateauroux, hardly twenty years old. A poet, he had sent flittering verses to *Le Mousquetaire*. Alexandre took this young, awkward man under his protection, introduced him to Rue d'Amsterdam. Marie had fallen in love with him, although at times his behavior had seemed almost strange. Alexandre, the father of the bride, fretted but took care of everything, even the witnesses:

My daughter will be married on the twenty-eighth of this month. She is writing to you, my dear Victor, to request that you become her witness by proxy with Lamartine. We see each other often, never without speaking of you. In fact, you are one of my heart's need, my dear Victor, and I speak of you, I, your young friend, as an indiscreet young lover speaks of his mistress. It is one of the beautiful and great mysteries of nature; it is one of the sweet mercies of God that men, who can separate bodies, have no power over the hearts of men. . . . Marie expects a letter from you in which you will tell her that through the mediation of Boulanger, you agree to be her witness. It will be her title of nobility.

He handled the marriage contract: "Only one of Marie's jewels is valuable. It cost nine thousand francs (it is called *the Monte-Cristo jewel*). Put three thousand francs for furniture. Clothes and trousseau, two thousand" (to Morin, end of April). The actual document was signed May 4, 1856, the day before the marriage at the notary's office. Alexandre multiplied the number of the announcements.

He arranged for tickets to Lyon for "the children's purse is that of two young newlyweds." After the nuptial benediction had been expedited, Marie and her young husband left for Italy. Alexandre felt lonely. He opened Victor Hugo's *Les Contemplations*: "It is splendid, marvelous, extraordinary. Never had arms stretched so far, never had hands been raised so high. God be blessed for suffering, since He permits anguish to send forth such cries."

Alexandre was at Isabelle's bedside; she was still frail, but saved. He wrote to Victor Hugo, April twenty-fourth:

I had at my home, since yesterday, a poor twenty-year-old mother who had just lost her child the day before; she cried for the Lord's mercy; she had not been able to weep, even when seeing the father cry; she did not doubt; she did not complain; she did not curse; only the tears that could not come out fell back on her heart and choked her.

I, who was nothing more than a friend, I raised my arms to the Lord and asked him for help.

Paul Meurice came in with your two books; I understood that she would be saved. I took the books from Paul's hands; I ran to her; I knelt, telling her, 'Mother, I bring to you the only consolation for mothers who have lost their child; I bring you tears.' I opened at random, I should say providentially. I fell on *Le Revenant* and I read. At the tenth verse, she cried.

You have known this mother, my dear Victor, she told you goodbye at Brussels. And you have loved her as you love all that is beautiful, all that is good.

He closed the book, squeezed Isabelle's thin and burning hand. He had to continue living. On July twenty-first, he left Paris with Paul Bocage to travel again the road to Varennes which had decided the fate of France. It was a trip of a few days to research and check out the accredited historians. Later on, in December, he went to Bourg-en-Bresse to visit localities for *Les Compagnons de Jéhu* and study the documents relating to the prosecution of his characters. Little by little he abandoned *Le Mousquetaire* to his collaborator, Xavier de Montepin. Without the master's signature the newspaper had no real existence, the subscribers did not renew. Dumas detached himself from a newspaper that did not give him an income.

At Monts, Emma, far from her lover, dreamed, cried, and wrote. She attempted to join her Alexandre with poetry. Alexandre had promised that her beautiful verses—which Verlaine would never forget—would be published. Moreover, he offered to join his own poems with hers in an anthology. Under the name of Emma Mannoury-Lacour, under the title *Solitudes*, it was a joint work of the two lovers. It was born as if the dead child of the previous year had been resurrected.

At the beginning of 1857 only love illuminated a life that was drowning in the shadows of evening.

III

The Flame in the Wind

Dumas had once claimed: "I will go around the Mediterranean; I will travel the whole circle. I will write the history of the antique world, which is nothing less than the history of civilization.

It remained for him to achieve this undertaking, to see Venice, Illyria, the Ionian Islands, Greece, Constantinople, the shores of Asia Minor, of Syria, Egypt, Cirenaica, Tripoli. Names of cities made him dream: Byzantium, Appolonia, Corfu, Cyrrha, Delphi, Cerigo, Pergamum, Samos, Tyre, Jerusalem, Alexandria. He had to have a boat that did not draw more than a meter and a half, so he could get into all the ports of the Greek archipelago and land in all the coves of the Asiatic coast: four men, an apprentice, and a cabin-boy as crew, a captain in command. As for himself, Alexandre asked only a library and a bed. The itinerary was already traced. How could he find the treasure in which he would have only to dip his hands to draw out the means for this great trip? By creating another newspaper, *Le Monte-Cristo*, a weekly filled with novels, history, trips, and poetry, published and edited by Alexandre Dumas alone. Delavier the bookseller would take care of managing the business.

Le Monte-Cristo was a letter sent by Dumas to all his friends, known or unknown, week after week, a ship's log that the biographer had to consult before beginning his narration. On the evening of March 27, 1857, Alexandre left Paris for London. Lord Palmerston's minority government had dissolved the Parliament and convoked the electors for the beginning of April. Alexandre convinced Girardin that he was exactly the very special envoy *La Presse* needed.

Hardly out of the train, Alexandre rushed to Westminister to attend the election of Lionel Rothschild, a winner at the last elections who had not been able to take the post because of the religious oath demanded of representatives. Then he went to Southwark where Admiral Napier's election was debated among hooting, brouhaha, and bravos. But the picturesque reality was far from equal to his own description in *Richard Darlington*. Still, he conscientiously reported the stakes and themes of the electoral campaign. His two first reports to *La Presse* were published on the twenty-ninth and the thirtieth of March, both dated from the Saturday of his arrival in London. The next day, seated on the stenographers' bench, he was present for the proclamation of the City results. Rothschild was elected, a triumph for the liberty of conscience.

On Wednesday, he commented on the meaning of the elections and on Thursday he went to the provinces, to Brentford in Middlesex. Then, even before the results were known, he disappeared, but not before prophesying, "The majority won by Lord Palmerston is, at this time, in true danger. Within three months, this majority to which he belongs, will have either compelled him to gallop on the way of progress or will have run him over" (*La Presse*, April fourth).

But where was Alexandre? A letter to Girardin, April 2, 1857, informed, "I am leaving tomorrow for Guernsey. I will be in London Monday evening."

When the boat approached the jetty at Guernsey, it was almost five years since, on the quay in Antwerp, Victor Hugo and Alexandre Dumas had left each other after a long embrace. His throat choked up, tears in his eyes, Alexandre recognized his friend's silhouette on the pier of Saint-Pierre-Port, a statue beaten by the wind of exile. In the excitement of disembarking, they clasped each other— exclamations, smiles and happiness burst out on this fourth of April, 1857. Alexandre somehow managed to settle into Hauteville House, where construction was still being done. Together in the drawing room overlooking the shore, they became drunk with talk. They recalled the *Courrier du Figaro*, in which appeared a vile attack against Victor Hugo, signed "Suzanne," who was no other than the actress Augustine Rohan. Alexandre did not beat around the bush. On March 5, 1857, he wrote to the Director of the Théâtre-Français, "I have for M. Victor Hugo such a friendship, such an admiration that I desire that the person who attacked him in his exile never act in my plays any more." The press reproduced the letter. Victor had thanked him, "Great hearts are like great stars. Their light and their heat is inside them; you do not need compliments, you don't even need thanks, but *I* need to tell you that I love you more every day, not because you are one of the shining lights of my century, but because you are also one of its consolations" (March 8, 1857). They perhaps alluded to the litigation Maquet had begun for recognition of co-authorship in the novels written in collaboration. Alexandre and Victor inextricably mixed the remembrances of the past with the present, the golden age and the iron age. "Visits such as his . . . seemed like a window briskly opened on France, through which came air and sun." On April sixth, Victor was back in his night of exile, and Alexandre had returned to his penitentiary.

In London, no letters from Girardin requesting other articles were waiting for him. Dumas rushed to Paris where he was ready to launch his newspaper. The first issue came out on Thursday, April twenty-third; at the head of the page was a reproduction of an engraving: Edmond Dantes, hero of the novel *Monte-Cristo*, after his escape from Château d'If. Then *A Talk with My Readers*, the continuation of *Les Mohicans de Paris*, the first chapters of *Harold ou le dernier des rois saxons*, translated by Dumas (in fact it was by Victor Perceval) and the first chapters of *Octave August*, and finally, the correspondence and various news. If it did not bring the expected triumph, the weekly publication was quite successful with ten thousand copies sold. In his *Monte-Cristo*, Alexandre, casual and debonair, went back each Thursday to the chat interrupted the preceding week. He mentioned the five things that impressed him the most during his trip to London: a musket under a shed, a Scotsman on a stage, a judge in a café, a merchant in a store, a rooster under a cage. He also related his preceding winter trip to Bourg-en-Bresse, where he went to research his novel *Les Compagnons de Jéhu.*

The warp of the weekly *Monte-Cristo* was slacker than that of *Le Mousquetaire*. That year Alexandre made more small trips. He returned to England (May twenty-fifth to thirtieth); a nabob invited him for the Epsom Derby and he immediately accepted. He visited

Madame Tussaud's Wax Museum in which was found the alleged guillotine used on Louis XVI, walked around Hyde Park, was saddened by the French prostitutes at Cremorne, swallowed the dust on the road to Epsom, wondered at the Crystal Palace and the Exposition of Manchester. All this from Tuesday to Saturday, so he could avoid the dull English Sunday during which the roosters were shut under cages to prevent improprieties. On July twenty-fifth, he was at Auxerre with friends of 1848 and joined them in the torchlight parade. In August, he was at his friend Vuillemot's in Compiègne. In Pierrefonds, at his instigation, Ruggieri illuminated the ruins with sumptuous fireworks. In September he could only look on while his friends hunted, for his right knee would not bend. Was old age approaching? Alexandre wanted to ignore it.

One September morning, his servant introduced into his workroom a charming young woman, twenty-three, radiating whiteness, with blue eyes, light brown hair, magnificent teeth—Lilla von Bulyovski, a Hungarian actress. She asked Alexandre to be her cicerone in Paris. Alexandre did not offer the least resistance and gave her letters of recommendation, invited her for dinner two or three times a week, and introduced her to the theaters. When she was ready to leave, money spent and curiosity gone, Alexandre decided to follow her, although she had not conceded any favor. Soon they were in Brussels, where Marie Pleyel gave a concert for them alone; then they sailed down the Rhine from Cologne to Mainz, living in an intimacy lacking only actual possession. Imperfect happiness, enchanting remembrances. Each time he traveled, Alexandre met with vanished faces which appeared throughout the scenery he passed. Death reaped with wider strokes . . . that summer Musset; then Béranger; after Béranger, Eugène Sue. The *Monte-Cristo* recorded these names, dead figures who once were friends.

The evening of September twenty-fourth, Alexandre left Lilla in the care of the great tragédienne, Sophie Schroeder, who had agreed to coach her. A kiss on the forehead. Then he found himself alone in Mannheim, alone in Paris where he went back to work on novels—*Le Meneur de Loups, Black, Les Louves de Machecoul*—the story lines of which had been cut out by Cherville. After ten years, Alexandre was back to the same formula he used with Maquet. "Dig hard," he implored. But Cherville was not the indefatigable worker that Maquet was. He wrote to Hetzel:

I am working, not enough for my liking. I get into a bad mood against myself when I have not done anything, but I have not yet the kind of energy that nails a man to a table. It might still come.

Without boasting, what makes me hope, that is, if the beginning interested you and continues to satisfy you, is that I have not yet gotten down to serious work, . . . what I have done up to now is more the result of a sort of loafing rather than a labor worthy of the name.

Dumas suggested, begged, commanded, pestered, promised, as he wrote to Cherville in August, 1857:

Finish your novel quickly, as you say.
If there is anything to change, I will change it.
Send me your *'conte fantastique'* and your hunting novel [*Le Chasseur de sauvagines*] as soon as it is done.
You know that when passing through my hands, the monument doubles, triples, quadruples.

Cherville invented, Dumas executed, but not always; alone he began *Ainsi soit-il* which was definitively rebaptized *Madame de Chamblay*. The spring of his novel gushed from his very own life. It was a transposition of his liaison with Emma Mannoury-Lacour. As for the theater, almost nothing: a comedy in one act, *L'Invitation à la valse*, the first scenes of which had been written in London on a gloomy Sunday. It was performed at the Gymnase on August third. It was "made for my dear little child, Isabelle, to whom the manuscript belongs" (April 10, 1857).

The year 1858 began sadly as a telegram brought the news of the death of the great tragédienne, Rachel, on January third at Le Cannet. On Monday, January eleventh, Alexandre cut through the crowd waiting for the funeral procession on the Place Royale. Even the trees were loaded with clusters of people. When the carriage started out, pulled by six horses richly covered with trappings of gold and silver, Alexandre took the silver tassel that was handed to him. A continuous and deep line of people stood from the Place Royale to the Père-Lachaise cemetery which was already crowded.

Workers in smocks came to shake hands with Alexandre, "For you and for Victor Hugo."

But even as exile and death seemed to be overpowering, life brought some joys. On January sixteenth, the Gymnase performed *Le Fils naturel*, a dramatic comedy in five acts. The author? Alexandre Dumas fils who, after *La Dame aux camélias*, shared his father's glory and was flying from one success to another. In his loge Dumas père received the acclamations intended for his son as if they were for himself. Another of life's burdens, that suit which Maquet had imposed upon him, reached a judgment on February 3, 1858. The judgment gave Maquet 25 percent of the author's rights for the eighteen novels on which he had collaborated but refused him all proprietary rights.

At the beginning of March, Alexandre was in Marseille where the stars of the theater had asked him for a play. He had immediately jumped on a train to offer an adaptation of *Jane Eyre*. "Already played at Brussels, signed by two young Belgians," accused an actress who had not been included in the cast. This did not put off Dumas, who proposed to read the following Thursday a drama, *Les Gardes forestiers*, that he would have to write in the meantime; his friend, Berthaud, offered him his country house, La Blancarde. He claimed the play was done in five days, and it was performed with success fifteen days later on March 23, 1858. A big lie, indeed, intended for the readers of *Monte-Cristo* who loved tours de force! Actually, Dumas gave the Grand Théâtre a twenty-year-old play, translated in 1853 by Goritz. Yet the lie was a half-truth; Dumas wrote a play at La Blancarde in two days, a one-act comedy, *L'Honneur est satisfait*, which was played at the Gymnase in June. Feasted at Marseille, happy for his glory, the rays of which shone to the provinces, he wrote to his son to take care of Isabelle so she would not be able to rejoin him. Then he carried his escapade even further:

[Edmond] About is here—we will probably spend the holy week in Rome. Why don't you come? (April 1858)

Dumas was in Rome? Not at all, he was in Saint Petersburg! A young couple, Russian aristocrats, Count and Countess Koucheleff-Besborodko, traveling to discover Europe, had stopped in Paris at the Hôtel des Trois Empereurs, followed there by an innumerable retinue of attendants: an Italian maestro, a writer, a physician, maid servants, and most important a spiritualist, Daniel Douglas-Home, who since his childhood possessed the gift of clairvoyance and the power of evoking spirits. The Count and the Countess attracted Alexandre, who was charmed by the beauty and the grace of his hosts, the lively talks in their salon, the continuous activity around them. Some days before the couple's departure, the Countess invited Alexandre, "Come with us to Saint Petersburg." But how, in five days, could he get ready for such a trip? And if he went to Russia, he would not stay in Saint Petersburg. He would want to see Moscow, Nidjni, Kazan, Astrakhan, Sebastopol. "Marvelous," responded the Countess, "I have an estate in Koralowo, near Moscow; the Count has a property at Nidjni, steppes at Kazan, fisheries on the Caspian Sea, a country house at Paschatka." Alexandre had a fit of giddiness! He stepped to the balcony above the Place du Palais-Royal and tried to think. Surely the trip he intended to take in Greece, Syria, and Egypt was being arranged, but it would take five months for the shipbuilder at Le Hâvre to build the schooner. And in the meantime, why not? All the more that an event of unforeseeable consequences was approaching: the emancipation of the serfs on the Imperial estates. Alexandre responded to the Countess: "Very well, I will leave with you." Douglas-Home, who was going to Saint Petersburg to marry the sister of the Countess, embraced Alexandre. It was settled, Alexandre would be his witness.

Russia! Alexandre fils was rather surprised for he was the one who chose his mistresses among Russian women. After the lady with the pearls, it was Nadeja Naryschikine, "a green-eyed siren." Moynet, painter and decorator, was flabbergasted. Dumas so insisted that Moynet accompany him as his illustrator that Moynet finally accepted. Five days to pack, to put things in order.

Before going to the train station where mountains of luggage discouraged the employees of the Gare du Nord, Alexandre clasped tightly the dear little child, Isabelle. As the train slowly left, Alexandre abandoned two novels in the process of being published (*Ainsi soit-il* and *Les Mohicans de Paris*). But he had promised the readers of *Monte-Cristo* that his letters from Russia would be for them. From week to week they could follow their narrator's peregrinations through Russia. On June eighteenth, he wrote from Berlin; on the nineteenth from Stettin, where he embarked on the *Wladimir* for Saint Petersburg where, after a transfer to Kronstadt, he arrived on June twenty-fourth. He was settled in a sumptuous apartment in the Villa Besborodko, whose park had a circumference of three miles. Two thousand serfs, the moujiks, moved around quietly, and Alexandre told one of them, "Well! You are free now." And the man answered, "Your Excellency, it is what they say." The serfs did not know what freedom was. How could they believe in it? Saint Petersburg and the whole of Russia were only a large facade that hid the barbarian, the primitive, the oriental.

Alexandre was enchanted by the white nights on the banks of the Neva, pearl gray, iridescent as opal. With the novelist Gregorovitch as a guide, he discovered the "modern" city and its ugly green roofs. He rediscovered the beautiful black eyes, the beautiful shoulders of Jenny Falcon, sister of the great diva, Cornélie Falcon, whom he had known as a child in 1822. An actress with expectations, she had followed the mirage of an engagement in Saint Petersburg where the Count Dimitri Naryschikine fell in love with her. For fifteen years she gave the prettiest balls in the capital. She decided that Alexandre should come to celebrate her birthday and should go with her and her lover to their villa at Petrosky Parek. Alexandre had never known how to resist beautiful eyes. The pleasure of love—"I have sinned," Jenny confessed later—the happiness of discovering a country savage, passionate, and violent, did not make him forget his readers.

I work like a convict to finish the newspaper two months in advance or to double the serials in case of need. I always will keep in advance. . . . (to Van Loo, June 30, 1858)

No time to write to his friends, but his readers were satisfied with impressions from his travels, long digressions on history, poetry, Russian mores. They discovered Russian literature through translations of novels that Dumas proposed to them. He used the Russian domain as he had, some years before with Goritz's help, exploited the German. There were letters to his intimate friends from Moscow where he was a guest of Naryschikine and of Jenny, nothing from Nidjni. At Kazan on the Volga, however, for an instant he felt the need to take a break from the whirlwind pace of his trip and on October 9, 1858 he wrote to Van Loo:

I am writing you from the capital of the Tatars. I am some three thousand miles from you. Are you hunting? I hunt, myself. I have killed hares that are becoming white because of the winter; I always hesitate to shoot them because they seem to be cats. And there are white partridges which look like pigeons but there are heath cocks which are magnificent game. The ducks and snipes are here by the thousands. In twelve days I will be in the Caucasus and we will hunt bear and wild boar. I am going to write a note to Delavier at the same time I write to you. I am accomplishing a real tour de force writing as I do while I travel.

My boat trips proved to me that a boat twelve-feet wide and sixty-five-feet long will be sufficient for my trip to Greece. This will decrease the price of the boat by some twelve thousand francs.

Alexandre wrote not only to Van Loo, the adroit woodcarver and the woodworking artist of the Faubourg Saint-Antoine, to whom was reserved the honor of laying out the interior of the future boat. On the same day he wrote to Emma:

My dear love,

I arrive from the Ural Mountains where I met neither post-man nor post office. I wrote to you twice after Moscow but from miserable villages where directors of the moujik post do not read and who allow the letters to be taken by whoever wants them. When I asked him if my letter would reach you, he answered—as Montaigne says, "What do I know?" and Rabelais, "Perhaps!" or the equivalent.

I am at Kazan on the Volga. Without being very civilized, the Tatars seem to belong to the category of men that I had left for some time to become surrounded by a species half-ape, half-bear—not described by Buffon. I am looking for a boat, a craft, a bark that could take me to Astrakan; those whom I ask shake their head: they are afraid to be caught by the ice.

On August eighth, I was on the battlefield of the Moskowa; the potatoes had frozen that morning. Pretty country! Now, my love, I will hasten to go to Tiflis; I hope to find there a letter from you, only one letter during all the time I was in Moscow; it was very little. It is true that you have nothing to do except fear, suffer, and cry, poor dear creature of the Good God!

You would not believe this, my darling, but except for the days when I was with you these past four years, days of joy are very rare in my life, the only good time I spent was in this solitude that I just made for myself either in these large pine forests, without limits, where I hunt heath cock, or on the immense Volga, inhabited by birds, as one of those seas where no one has ever ventured. Beside you, no one loves me in the world, no one thinks of me, no one worries about me. I feel very lonely, very forgotten by everybody, so well that I enjoy, or almost enjoy, the happiness of being dead without having the displeasure of being buried—I am a day ghost rather than a night specter. If our life cannot be settled for next year, I will leave again and live again the same way.

I am rejuvenated ten years in strength and I could almost say in face. I adopted a kind of Circasian costume which fits me very well and is very practical. Whenever I do not wear it, I am in my dear black velvet dressing gown, and in shirts of Caucasus silk, red or yellow.

It's a good thing, this liberty to do whatever one wants, to wear whatever one wants, to go wherever one wants. For the rest, as soon as I am back in civilized country, I enter into another kind of perpetual triumph which would be another person's joy and pride and which is my torture. A great pleasure, however, was waiting me at Nidjni; I found there again the hero and heroine of my novel, *Maître d'Armes*, who were pardoned by Emperor Alexandre after thirty-three years in Siberia! Judge how they received me.

I leave Kazan on the first of October on the Russian calendar [October twelfth at home] and I descend the Volga. I just found a boat; I stop five or six days at Astrakhan. I sail down to the Caspian Sea to Baku where I will see the fire worshippers. From there I go to Tiflis, where I take an expedition in the Caucasus with the Prince Bariatinsky.

Then I embark on the Black Sea and I come back on the Danube. I will be in Paris around November twenty-fifth. You understand that my greatest joy would be to see you immediately. I will let you know as soon as I arrive and if there is a possibility, I will get off from the Strasbourg train to take the one to Le Hâvre. (October 8/10, 1858)

The Volga froze behind his boat. He reached Astrakhan where his host put the most beautiful house in the town at his disposal. The civilian Governor gave him the honors of the city. In luxury and calm he again read the notebook in which he had thrown some descriptive, historical and picturesque remarks, a notebook that a fervent admirer, Basile Davidoff, had given him in Moscow. He looked over maps of the Russian Empire and summed up for his son the trip he had just finished:

Your letter reaches me at Astrakhan! Lockroy said that one does not come back from Astrakhan. For an instant I believed that Lockroy was the prophet's prophet. For a while I believed I was trapped here for all the winter. But be reassured, I am taking the road again tomorrow. Do you want to have an idea of the trip I made? Take a map of Russia—it is worth the trouble.

. . . From Kalaisine to Ouglich—see Mérimée's *Le Faux Démétrius*—following me on the river to Kastrama—from Kastrama to Nidjni-Novgorod, the fair of fairs where there is a town made of six thousand shops and a bordello with four thousand girls. All is done on a grand scale, as you see. From Nidjni, where I rediscovered Anenkov and Louise, the two heros of *Le Maître d'armes*, back to Russia after thirty years in Siberia. Incidently, tell this to Grisier [the fencing master] and add that we have spoken often of him. From Nidjni [I went] to Kazan where I found one of his pupils, Colonel Hahn, passing through the Tchouvaches—a people you never heard of, but one of whose shirts I am bringing you as a sample. From Kazan, still descending the Volga [I went] to Kameschin. At Kameschin, pay attention, I went to the Kirghis. Look on the map for a lake or rather for three lakes: Lake Elston. I camped there, in the middle of the steppes and ate— with a charming man, M. Becklemicheff, ataman of the Astrakhan Cossacks, a mutton from the sea-salted marshes, to which those of Normandy cannot be compared; they served us the tail separately; it weighted fourteen pounds. . . .

Once at Astrakhan I hunted a little along the Caspian where wild geese, ducks, pelicans and sea lions abound as petrel and frogs do on the Seine. When I returned, I found an invitation from Prince Tumaine. He is a kind of Kalmouk king who has fifty thousand horses, thirty thousand camels, and ten million sheep plus a charming eighteen-year-old wife who has slanted eyes, teeth like pearls, and who speaks Kalmouk only. She brought in marriage to her husband who already had ten thousand of them, one thousand five hundred tents with all the people who were in them.

This dear prince who, besides his fifty thousand horses, his thirty thousand camels, ten million sheep and eleven thousand five hundred tents, has two hundred seventy priests, some who play cymbals, others clarinets, others sea conches, and still others trumpets which are twelve feet long. First in the Prince's pagoda, they played a Lamaika Buddhist *Te Deum* which had the enormous merit of being short. Five minutes more and I would have returned to you having lost one of my five senses. After the *Te Deum* he gave us, I must say, a very good lunch whose *pièce de résistance* was a haunch of horse. If you see Geoffroy Saint-Hilaire, tell him that I accept his advice and that compared to horsemeat, beef is merely veal. I say veal because I believe that veal is the meat you despise the most.

After the lunch, we had a race of five hundred horses mounted by young Kalmouks of both sexes. It was a race in which there participated four of the ladies-in-waiting of the Princess who herself rides a horse well enough to match Daure and Boucher [horse-masters in Paris]. A thirteen-year-old boy won the prize which was a young horse and a calico dressing gown. After all that we had a race with sixty horses mounted without saddle by Kalmouks between twenty and twenty-five years old, one more ugly than the next. Let's pretend that it was a prize for ugliness instead of a prize for racing: the Prince would have had to crown them all.

And then we crossed the Volga, which, facing the palace of Prince Tumaine, is hardly a mile wide, and went to see a herd of four thousand wild horses. The Prince excused himself for not being able to show me more of them—informed of my arrival only the day before, it was all he could assemble during the night.

Then began a marvelous show: the chase of those wild horses with lassoes. Mounted bareback by Kalmouks, they carried their riders into the Volga, struggling in the water, rolling in the sand, kicking, biting, neighing: ten, twenty, fifty of them; it was a storm of riders that must be seen to get the idea. We crossed the Volga again and saw the hunting of swans with falcons. This, with the clothing of the Princess and her ladies-in-waiting, had a medieval air which would have enchanted you, as much a partisan of the modern as you are.

After that we sat at a table. We began with a potage of colt in which there lacked only a crow to match our suppers at Sainte-Assise [the country house of Dumas fils in Seine-et-Marne]; The rest, except for a horse's head in "mock turtle" soup, was borrowed from bourgeois cuisine.

At the same time, three hundred Kalmouks ate in the courtyard: a horse, raw and hashed with onion, two cows and ten roasted sheep. I have not seen the wedding feast of Ganache but I do not regret it now that I have seen Prince Tumaine's banquets. Would you believe that I ate some raw, hashed horse meat with small onions and that I found it delicious. I could not say as much of the mare's milk brandy. Ugh! We went to bed late—in the evening we had tea under the tent of the Princess. We will have tea in my garden, under a tent exactly the same. As I was the hero of the feast, they came to dress me in a coat, fur-lined with black mutton. Two Kalmouks with all the strength of their arms, buckled me with a silver belt which gave me a waist like Anna's. Last, they put in my hand a whip with which Prince Tumaine kills a wolf with one blow by striking it on the nose. You will see all that. I will loan it to you to astonish Rusconi, if Rusconi is not dead.

We went to bed. Ah! This is the great question! You know that since I am in Russia I have not seen the tail of a mattress. A bed, as such, is a completely unknown piece of furniture that I found only the days, or rather the nights, when I slept with French people.

But there were bedrooms with perfect floors and after some time, one finds that some floors do not lack elasticity. I prefer those made of pine in spite of the slightly playful idea they recall.

The next day they brought us in our bedrooms a large cup of camel's milk. I swallowed it, praying to Buddha. Confidentially, I will tell you that Buddha is a false god and if he had his altar in the open air, I would have paid him back in his own money.

Finally, after lunch, I took my leave of Prince Tumaine by rubbing my nose against his own, which is the Kalmouk way to say, 'Yours for life.' Also, I took leave from the Princess by improvising a few verses.

All this was received with smiles which did not need to come from Paris, I assure you, to have their own value.

And, finally, as said King Dagobert to his dog, there is no company so good that one does not eventually have to leave it. I had to leave the Kalmouk Prince, the Kalmouk Princess, the Kalmouk sister, the Kalmouk ladies-in-waiting. I wanted to rub my nose with that of the Princess but was warned that this politeness was done between men only. I regretted that.

In her park at Monts, already russet with autumn, Emma folded back the letter she then hid in her bodice. She sighed, dried her wet eyes—her Alexandre, her lover, so lonely, so melancholic, always the same; November was not far and soon she would go to the Hôtel d'Angleterre at Le Hâvre.

Alexandre fils closed his atlas still laughing rather drily. His father, that big kid, was always the same with his thirst for life intact and so amusing that one could not be severe with him. He read his father's letter of November 16, 1858:

My dear child, here I am at Derbend, on the Caspian Sea. We have, as you can see by looking on the map, crossed a part of the Daguestan, that is to say, passed over Shamyl territory. There were difficulties: The day before yesterday we left in a ditch fifteen Circasian corpses who had killed three of our Tatars and wounded eight.

You cannot have any idea of the ease with which one becomes familiar with danger. Definitely, there is no merit in being brave; it is only a habit.

We leave tomorrow for Baku where are the fire worshippers,

then for Sumaka where are the bayaderes, then Tiflis where is our friend, Baron Finaud; from there I come back by Mount Ararat and Constantinople. I rather think that I will postpone Sebastopol until a next trip.

I will be with you most probably to wish you a good year.

Not so fast, Alexandre, you will welcome in 1859 at Tiflis, at the home of your friend, Baron Finaud, in the heart of the Caucasus. That day, again, Dumas wrote to his son:

Good day, friend. Happy new year, good health, all the most tender and the most paternal wishes are yours from my heart. I love you.

Sometime between January thirtieth and February fifth I will embrace you if I can cross the snows of Souram.

I leave Monday for Mount Ararat.

Try to see Dennery; tell him that I bring back a Circasian novel in which there is, I believe, the makings of a beautiful drama.

It would be rather novel, it seems to me, a Tatar hero and Tcherkess heroine, staged by a man who has screwed a Tcherkess and shot a rifle with Tatars.

The son's finger ran on the map, along the blue of the Black Sea. Alexandre père had left Russia; he saw Constantinople, where he received a sum of 650 francs from M. Baudouy by promising to refund it within eight days after he had returned to Paris (February 23, 1859). The tracing finger crossed the Bosphorus, the Sea of Marmara, stopped on one of the Cyclades, Syra or Syros, fatherland of old Eumeus. Why Syros? Because the best boat builders work there. Alexandre père and Nicolas Paghida signed a contract on February twenty-eighth:

M. Nicolas Paghida agrees to deliver to M. Alexandre Dumas, within fifty days from today, a ship in the shape of a clipper, sixty-two French feet long by fifteen wide and nine feet deep inside, from keel to deck, all rigged, pegged with copper, with two anchors and two small boats, one for four oarsmen, for the agreed upon price of seventeen thousand francs.

Already, all around Paris rumors about his passing through Athens, his arrival at Marseille, his return to Paris. Everybody talked about Vasili, the frightening Georgian he had brought back with him as a servant, who was a sensation at the races and who, when he entered the ball at the Opéra on March thirty-first, stopped dead the great cotillion which was dancing at full speed. Alexandre had taken a bath, opened his trunks, and displayed around him all the objects, arms, material, knickknacks that he pulled out one by one. The remembrances came out as from an uncorked bottle: the adventurous life; great, infinite spaces, the sumptuous hospitality, the irresistible popularity. And Paris, once more, the venom of the tabloids, the rapacity of the booksellers, the dishonesty of theater directors. The grind, the daily and nightly toil, again and again. To leave yet again. At the time of the toasts at Vuillemot's, where a meal for forty guests had been prepared to salute his return, the good Méry rose with less ease than usual. Alexandre was not listening—already he had pulled up the gangplank. Before him the Mediterranean unrolled its treasures.

IV
An Odyssey in 1860

What was the graying Ulysses's dream? To rediscover his Penelope in an improbable Ithaca?

Alexandre's Penelope was dead: Ida had died on March 11, 1858, at Genoa in the arms of her dear Prince de Villafranca. Alexandre, always so quick with tears, had dry eyes when he said to Alphonse Karr who brought him the news: "Mme. Dumas came to Paris a year ago and had her one-hundred-twenty-thousand franc dowry paid back. I have her receipt."

To live near his Telemachus? Alexandre fils, tender and respectful, of course had his own life to live and, anxious about the literary and social position he had acquired, often scolded his old father, who would not rein in his eccentricities.

Did the old Ulysses still desire the Circes, the enchantresses who, with his consent, ruled his life? He still did, but now with a kind of disillusioned lassitude. He still loved Emma, his poor Emma who was coughing more and more and hastily hid her handkerchief spotted with blood. With a paternal tenderness, he still loved the little Isabelle, but at his age love could no longer make his entire world.

The old Ulysses dreamed of the tireless rocking of a schooner on the Mediterranean waves between sky and water.

He dreamed, but he had to return to his chains to earn the means to inhabit the dream. Cherville roughed out some more bad novels that Dumas attempted, sometimes unsuccessfully, to mend: *Le Médecin de Java, Le Père la ruine, La Marquise d'Escoman*. Cherville worked slowly, always looking for the next sou. Literature and finances were inextricably mixed. Alexandre wrote him in 1859:

> I could send you only three "louis" having only two hundred francs. Try to send me one or two chapters tomorrow—Wednesday—so that I can pull out, if possible, four hundred or five hundred francs for the fifteen. Send me at least the end of the chapter "Where François Guichard . . . shot at the prince and got a snipe."
>
> (Chapter from *Père la ruine*)

For *La Marquise d'Escoman*, collaboration turned out to be difficult. Alexandre asked Parfait to send him one of Cherville's books, *Les Mémoires d'un trop brave garçon*, in which "there is his love affair with a provincial society woman."

Cherville owed eighteen hundred francs to Hetzel, whose loan was secured by the *Mémoires*. Dumas agreed to take the eighteen hundred francs out of his account. He received the manuscript. Cherville wrote—slowly, too slowly:

> I have received your ten pages today, Sunday, only. You put sugar in your ink; the pages are so stuck together that they tear when separated. Remember that I need twice as much as that for what I want to send to *Le Siècle*.

Beginning April 13, 1860, *La Marquise d'Escoman* would appear in *Le Constitutionnel*.

Cherville, the poor horse who stumbled at each obstacle, could not haul Dumas' carriage all by himself. Dumas called on Benedict Revoil, who translated *A Lion Hunter in South Africa* by R. Gordon-Cumming under the title *La Vie au désert*. He also called on Du Couret, with whom Michel Lévy would deal; "He will use my name, will buy the property and recognize by personal letter that the property (*L'Arabie heureuse*) will revert to me at the end of five years." (to Parfait, December 4, 1859). He called on Dr. Felix Maynard for notes from which he wrote *Voyage aux terres antipodiques*, published by *La Presse* (*Les Baleiniers*). Finally he called on Victor Perceval, who translated *Stories of a Detective* by C. Water (*Mémoires d'un Policeman*). The nature of this collaboration may have been more than literary. Victor Perceval was the pen name of Marie de Fernand who gave birth that year to a little girl who was named Alexandrine. An admirer's tribute? Or an attribution of paternity?

This heterogeneous collection of collaborators—a down-at-the-heels nobleman, an unhappy bohemian, a pseudo-explorer, and ex-whaling boat physician, a young girl from a good family who had lost her virtue—could surprise, even shock. However, the truth must be considered. Dumas had discarded literature, he had nothing to prove any more. He wanted money to re-enact Ulysses' voyages. He was chasing a dream and did not care that his assemblyline production was scorned. Thanks to almost thirty years of work, he had made his name. He now used it.

After his return from Russia, Alexandre took back possession of his space. He found Marie near her young husband at Châteauroux. She was not really happy. Olinde showed signs of mental disorder; she forgot these problems by painting angels, seraphims, thrones. Alexandre went to take the cure at Pierrefonds. He rented "on the side of the river Marne a small house with an immense garden," at Varenne-Saint-Maur. Sometimes he sat near the water and contemplated the slow-moving current or a cart that crossed on the ferry from one side to the other. Then he went back to the house. Cherville, who had settled there, or Fernande (Marie de Fernand) compiled sheets upon sheets.

A light went out, the sweet Marceline Desbordes-Valmore, on July 23, 1859, the last "glimmer from the old days we remember, that the generaton following us has not even known." (*Le Monte-Cristo*, July 28, 1859). Suffering from water on the knee, Alexandre could not attend the funeral of his very old friend. He was in a black mood. He expected his boat, which had left Syra on June fourth. At last a telegram informed him that the *Monte-Cristo*, as the clipper was christened, had entered the port of Marseille. From there it would go by way of canals to Paris where Van Loo would fit it out.

Soon Alexandre was in Marseille in the midst of sailors coming from the four corners of the world. His two-master was alongside the wharf with its five Greek sailors and its captain, Apostoli Podimatas, all at the orders of Dumas. The next day they sailed to the Château d'If but canal travel was out of the question. The *Monte-Cristo* drew too much water. It would have to travel along the Midi Canal, around Cape Finistère, and then up the Seine where artists in Paris waited to decorate it. Bad news again! The *Monte-Cristo* could not pass the locks at Pont d'Agde; the sailors who wanted to go back to Milo and Hypsara debarked and planned to return at the end of February when the boat would be completely fitted out.

From Marseille, Alexandre could have heard the cannon roar from the direction of the Alps. The Piedmontese prime minister Cavour did not want Italy to remain a simple geographic space; he wanted a nation. The war of Piedmont against Austria was to return Italy to itself, proclaimed Napoléon III, who took the side of Piedmont. Victories at Turbigo, at Magenta, a bloody slaughter at Solferino, were followed by a truce, then the preliminary peace treaty agreed upon at Villafranca September 12, 1859. France had obtained Lombardy and gave it to the King of Sardinia in exchange for Nice and the Savoie. After this give-and-take, the cannons fell silent. Cavour, betrayed, tendered his resignation. Italy waited to be made into a nation. With adroit little insertions, *Le Monte-Cristo* brought its little stones to the building of Italian freedom, such as the portrait of Garibaldi which appeared June 30, 1859:

His voice, of an infinite sweetness, resembles a chant. Under the ordinary conditions of life, he is rather more distracted than attentive and seems more a man of calculation than of imagination. But pronounce before him the words 'independence' and 'Italy' and he wakes up as a volcano and throws his flame and spills his lava.

(A. Dumas, *Montevideo ou une nouvelle Troie*)

Another political event, unconditional amnesty for all political exiles on August 16, 1859, transformed the life of Dumas, who was very tired of his suits against Michel Lévy—who, on his side wanted to bring them to an end as well. Alexandre did not have to look long for the man he needed to hasten the arrangement: Noël Parfait, when the amnesty gave back to him his country. Parfait wrote to his brother Charles on January 20, 1860:

Toward the beginning of December Dumas wrote me a long letter in which he unreeled a plan, a scheme which was supposed to secure my future in Paris. The letter boils down to this: There was a tentative reconciliation between the brothers Lévy and Dumas. After a long litigation, it is proposed to end all the current suits on the condition that the brothers Lévy buy for ten years the right to reprint, in quarto format at one franc, his complete works. Dumas would have ten centimes per reprinted volume and the brothers Lévy guaranteed they would pay him immediately *a minimum* of one hundred fifty thousand francs. This contract, the details of which I will spare you, should, if you listen to the Lévys, bring to Dumas in ten years no less than three or four hundred thousand francs. I was invited to go back to settle definitively the details with the brothers Lévy in the name of Dumas. My good and great friend added that, as he would have to take next spring a trip which would last not less than a year or eighteen months, he needed someone to watch over his interests during his long absence who was entirely devoted to him and this someone he found in me; that if I were willing to accept the mission he offered, that is to say watch over the reprinting of his work, authorize printing, stage the seven or eight plays that he will leave unfinished when he departs, receive all his author's rights from the Lévys, from the theater and the newspapers, I will receive for all that a percentage I would fix myself (I fixed it at 5 percent); that I would have during his absence use of his apartment in Paris, of his country house at Varenne-Saint-Hilaire, in the likely case that his son would not go to live there; so that if finally I agreed to this arrangement, it would be Dumas who would consider himself obligated to me.

The business with the brothers Lévy was briskly done: the contract was signed on December 20, 1859 and immediately represented 120,030 francs paid within twenty-four hours, twenty thousand francs on March 1, 1860 and nine thousand francs every four months thereafter, beginning July first.

Alexandre was rich. He left, chasing history which wore, that winter, the mask of Garibaldi. He was happy. The presence of Parfait near him in Paris guaranteed him slightly less disorder in his business, the Lévy contract financed his trip to Greece and the

Middle East, and on November thirtieth at the Gymnase his big son, Alexandre, had a success with *Le Père prodigue*.

Alexandre passed through Marseille where the *Monte-Cristo* was in dry dock to be lined with copper. Built at Syra, it was flying the Greek flag. As the Greek consul had threatened to take possession of the boat because Alexandre refused to pay indemnities to his idle sailors, a subterfuge was used: It would sail under the flag of Jerusalem, which could be obtained only in Florence. A boat trip to Livorno, a train from Livorno back to Florence—Sardinian now, and mourning its late Grand Duke.

A provisory license would be granted within fifteen days to the French consul in Livorno. While waiting for it, Alexandre had a great desire to meet Garibaldi. At Genoa he took the train for Turin. The thermometer registered below eight degrees Centigrade, and the snow reached as high as a man's waist. Garibaldi was staying at the Hôtel de l'Europe in a small room. Alexandre gave his name, and Garibaldi came at once. They drank coffee but were soon interrupted by a messenger from King Victor-Emmanuel. Garibaldi ran to the palace, came back, said he had to be in Milan the next day. He kept a serene face despite the King's order to dissolve the Society of the Armed Nation. Garibaldi vowed he would make his own war, and Alexandre would be part of it. When the time came, Garibaldi would let him know. On a piece of paper Alexandre wrote "I subscribe for twelve rifles. January 4, 1860." Courtesy was returned with courtesy. Garibaldi, in turn, took a pen and wrote, *"Raccommando ai miei amici l'illustro amico mio Alessandro Dumas, 4 gennaio 1860."* It was understood that they would see each other at Milan to write Garibaldi's *Mémoires* together after Dumas had seen Rome once more and discovered Venice. Alexandre was not alone; he had with him a young girl. He liked to celebrate his new loves in the "country where the orange trees bloom."

Yesterday, Isabelle; today, Émilie. Hardly twenty, frail and delicate, so delicate that Mama Cordier, her mother, had taken her out of the linen shop where she worked to put her to work at the Halles because the odor of the fish market was good for the chest. She liked to read and she dreamed of the theater. She had been introduced to Dumas before his trip to Russia. As always, he had promised his protection. But he had not forgotten the fresh face, the adolescent body of the young girl. She had gone to Rue d'Amsterdam and had stayed there. She had put her little hand into the enormous paw of Alexandre Dumas.

That night Venice had donned the coat of Scaramouche, a gondola glided on a mirror of ink. Venice, in mourning, in the sadness that succeeds despair, had seen for a moment the white sails of the French fleet before falling back under the Austrian boot. On January 12, 1860, the first day of Carnival, all theaters were closed. From the Rialto Bridge, Alexandre peeled off a poster that announced the closing, the announcement of the death of liberty. Only a puppet show was playing and Pulchinello harshly beat a victim who wore an Austrian policeman's hat.

Then Verona, the town of Juliet. Émilie's Romeo was graying and pot-bellied! Mantua—a villa on Lake Como where they met Garibaldi, limping from a recent accident with his horse. He agreed to dictate his *Mémoires*, but after two days Dumas stopped; Garibaldi seemed bored. "Here," said the hero, "I write my *Mémoires* at a time of discouragement; they go up to my return to Europe. We will continue later, since you promised me that everywhere I go you will come to join me."

In the evening at Milan, at a ball at the club of the nobility; in the corridor is a bowl full of gold and banknotes, contributions to the patriotic cause. In the room were six Venetian women, alone, dressed in black, who were repeating, "Do not forget weeping Venice." At Livorno the nationalization license for the *Monte-Cristo* had been refused. "Your Captain is Greek and Orthodox. Impossible. One of the first conditions required of a Captain navigating under the flag of Jerusalem is that he be a Catholic. Alexandre was dumbfounded, but seeing Rome again put him back in the saddle! He arranged for Émilie to visit the Appian Way; they watched the flow of the Tiber; they sat under the arcades of the Colosseum. He should write the history of Rome. Alexandre visited the French Ambassador, the Duc de Gramont, an old friend. The Duke had a yacht to sell. Built at Liverpool, made of mahogany and maple, it had cost 110,000 francs. He had just sold it for 36,000 francs. But the new owner, who had married in the meantime, had a wife who could not stand the sea and he wanted to sell the boat back. For a song! Alexandre rushed to Marseille to get rid of his own Greek barge and to buy the *Emma*, previously the schooner of the Duc de Gramont, formerly duc de Guiche, slender of prow, fine of body, elegant and aristocratic in her lines. Alexandre had fallen in love with the *Emma*—13,000 francs! He left the schooner in the hands of an architect who would again embellish it and went back to Paris where he bustled about anticipating the profits from his contract with the Lévys, looked for money for the poor, neglected Fernande [alias Victor Perceval], took another trip to Marseille to settle the fate of the *Monte-Cristo* and to choose another captain. A Breton replaced the Greek, a Captain Beaugrand with a smiling face, honest eyes, strong hands. A schooner, a captain, all was now ready to circle the Mediterranean.

On April twenty-seventh, Alexandre stopped at his friend Charpillon's at Saint-Bris (Yonne).

Charpillon was a solicitor. Alexandre left with him important papers to give to Alexandre fils in case of an accident. On the twenty-eighth, at four in the afternoon, Alexandre settled at the Hôtel du Louvre in Marseille. On the *Emma*, he found thousands of gifts sent by friends, known and unknown. The City of Marseille feasted the creator of Edmond Dantès; the Mayor invited him to dinner, offered him a title of bourgeoisie and concession for land in the Catalans. Alexandre beamed with pleasure. On May eighth, the ship was ready.

All Marseille was on the wharf on that Wednesday, May 9, 1860. The schooner unfurled all her flags. In small groups the passengers walked the gangplank to meet Captain Beaugrand, Podimatas, the pilot, and the crew: Pierre-François Bremmond from Cannes, the second-in-command, who could do everything; Louis Passerel, from Calvi; Fulairon Thibault, the apprentice; Schmaltz, the thirteen-year-old shipboy, son of an orchestra conductor. Then came Legray, the photographer who would record the notable moments of the trip, arm in arm with Edward Lockroy, a young painter, son of Lockroy, the actor who created the role of Monaldeschi. And there was Albanel, the young ship doctor, and Paul Parfait, son of the good, dear Noël. There was also a strange hermaphrodite who wore a fancy midshipman's uniform made of violet velvet with blue and gold shoulder knots, none other than Émilie Cordier, also known as "The Admiral." But where was the young Greek from Cappadocia, the translator who spoke Turkish and French as well as Greek and to whom Dumas gave the means for completing his education in France? And where was Vasili, the splendid Georgian servant whom Alexandre had fished out of Poti during the trip to Russia? Vasili knew how to kill a sheep and cook it as shashlik; he knew how to transform a pig into sausages; he could catch carp with a casting net: an indispensable servant to a traveling master. Trunks and baskets were lined up but someone was still missing, Cherville the collaborator.

At last, Alexandre appeared. At nine-thirty the anchor was hoisted and a tugboat pulled the schooner out of the port. The *Emma*, impeded in turn by a head wind and then by a dead calm, was dawdling. Sea sickness quickly reduced the dauntless travelers to wrecks. On May thirteenth, they had only reached the little port of Hyères and they steered for it to have dinner on the terrace of the Hôtel de l'Europe. The next day, they went down to eat a bouillabaisse at the invitation of an ex-banker from Marseille.

As the *Emma* glided on the water, Alexandre gazed into the immensity, dreamed, and summoned up a charming twilight such as only opium smokers could know. He savored the delights of idleness. On the fourteenth, they landed at Nice, rushed to Alphonse Karr's who had a farm and a shop, and ordered strawberries and eggs. On May fifteenth, they dined under the rose trees of Alphonse Karr's garden. Once they had drunk their champagne, sixty guests brought their glasses to Alexandre to engrave his monogram, "A.D." with a diamond the Princess Apraxin had removed from her finger. On May eighteenth, the *Emma* arrived at Genoa, which was filled with rumors. It was said that Garibaldi had debarked at Marsala and was marching toward Palermo. Alexandre asked for details on the preparation of Garibaldi's expedition which would decide the great question of popular or divine right. He wrote to Emma Mannoury-Lacour in May 1860:

My dear love—I arrive at Genoa. I receive your letter and I answer from Alexandria [Italy] where I had to go the very day of my arrival with a friend of Garibaldi. The latter tired of waiting for me and left to make war on his own account as he had said to the King of Sardinia when he resigned. I will stay five or six days in Genoa to write there these accursed *Mémoires* [*Mémoires de Garibaldi* translated from the original manuscript by Alexandre Dumas], which, half-done, are half translated already.

I don't know how to tell you where we will go when leaving Genoa. It is according to the turn that the Garibaldi affair will take, the newspapers have stupidly announced that I was going to join him in Sicily, so that here I am, personally at war with the King of Naples. Besides, be reassured; it is impossible to have a better vessel than the *Emma*. She is strong and an excellent sailor. Not only will I send you flowers, but all kinds of photographs to put in stereoscope from the Hyères islands, and at Karr's I have been greatly feasted.

We are nineteen on board. And I do not spend on passengers and crew together twenty francs per day. You have no idea of the saving I will have, once the first expenses are paid, by remaining on a ship.

Ah! darling, the day when we will be free, if you can stand the sea, you will see what life is like being absolutely one's master, far from all worries. It is a royal life. You have my sad hours and my gay hours, my dear child, since you live incessantly in the background of my thinking. And I do not live one hour that my heart and my mind do not turn to you.

(May 21, 1860)

The present time overran the past that Dumas tried to capture in the *Mémoires*. On Dumas' pages Garibaldi fought for the independence of Montevideo, while, on the Sicilian coasts, he was forging the unification of Italy. The present also cancelled the future. The sweet Emma—who had composed a second book of poems, *Les Asphodèles*, for which Dumas tried to get favorable reviews by Saint-Félix, Karr, and Deschanel—was dying in her house at Caen.

Contradictory news swirled over Genoa, blowing alternatively enthusiasm or despair. Alexandre could not wait any more, he had to leave for Palermo. He would steer toward the sound of the cannon. He had an account to settle with the King of Naples who had killed his father in the Taranto jails. On May thirty-first, at three o'clock, in spite of abominable weather, stormy sea and headwind, Alexandre gave the captain orders to run up the sails. On the evening of June fourth, they anchored off the north shore of Sardinia. Alexandre left his group of young people to scatter on the coast, shooting at random everything that moved. Then, at four in the evening on the fifth, he steered for Sicily, went farther than the Island of Caprera on which, like a modern Cincinnatus, Garibaldi

liked to retreat. The sea was calm. The navigators amused themselves in pulling on board a turtle that they tried to season and
make edible. On June eighth, at last, they could see the land off
Alcamo; Alexandre decided to go straight to Palermo. The next
day, at nine in the evening, seven shots of cannon. What did they
mean? Was it the beginning of a bombing or the last sigh of a battle
that would continue the next day? On June tenth, at dawn, they
could see the houses of Palermo, white in the early light. The
Sardinian flag waved on the fortresses. A small boat, loaded with
fruit, came alongside the *Emma*. Garibaldi was master of the city
since Pentecost. Alexandre jumped into the fruit boat. What of once
happy Palermo! Barricades, crumbling houses, monuments burned
and occupied by men in red shirts, brandishing rifles. Alexandre
felt thirty years younger; it was like 1830, another Bourbon was
thrown out. At the palace of the Senate, he fell into the arms of
Menotti, the son of Garibaldi, who took him through the ruins of
the streets. In front of the cathedral they met Garibaldi, who cried
with joy when he recognized Alexandre:

—'Dear Dumas, I missed you.'
—'So, as you can see, I am looking for you. My congratula-
tions, my dear general.'
—'It is not me that you must congratulate; it's these men!
What giants, my friend!'

Garibaldi—felt hat with a bullet hole, red shirt, gray pants and
a scarf knotted around the neck forming a hood—threw his arms
around Dumas and, clinging to each other thus, the dictator and
the writer crossed Palermo, a city trembling with its recovered
freedom. At the bend of a street, Alexandre believed he heard an
aria from *Norma* . . . and thought of Caroline . . . just twenty-five
years ago, in Palermo.

Alexandre settled at the royal palace, in the governor's quarters
that Garibaldi had put at his disposal. There was an immense
drawing room from which a dormitory could be improvised. The
balcony overlooked the square. Garibaldi, too, lodged in the royal
palace. Every morning two bands woke him up. Shrill volunteers
trained under the balcony, and streets and squares resembled a
huge field of poppies with red shirts everywhere. In Palermo, Alexandre especially noticed the freeing of prisoners who were loaded

with flowers. Each carriage showed a flag that the Sicilian women kissed with loving fervor. Before a convent, nuns clung to the bars and cried, "Long live Italy," and clapped their hands furiously. Alexandre appeared on his balcony and received a frenzied ovation. That glorious day, June 20, 1860, Palermitans rolled a formless object in the dust with their feet—the head of the statue of King Ferdinand, the poisoner of Général Dumas.

On June twenty-first, Alexandre left Palermo in two requisitioned carriages to follow a column of volunteer Piedmontese. They stopped at Villafrati in the house of the Marquis de San-Marco. From the terrace, paved with earthenware and trimmed with wild hollyhocks, he saw the undulating wheat fields, strewn with the troops' red shirts. Alexandre arrived at Agrigento and soon was back on the *Emma* which was to continue its trip toward Malta, Corfu, and the Orient. At Alicata, however, Alexandre felt a slight remorse. Shouldn't he witness to the very end this beautiful drama of a people's resurrection? He wrote to Garibaldi about July 6, 1860:

Friend,
I just crossed all the width of Sicily.
There's great enthusiasm everywhere but no arms!
Do you want me to look for some in France? I would choose them as a hunter. Answer General Delivery at Catania. If you tell me, 'Yes,' I will postpone my trip in Asia and I will do the rest of the campaign with you.

He also wrote to his son (July 6):

We are doing marvelous things here—which must make you laugh. As soon as I have settled at the palace of the King of Naples, I will write you to come join me.
Orders have already been given for refurnishing for me, in antique style, the house of the poet at Pompei. . . .
Palermo, Catania, Zelle, and Girgenti have followed the example of Marsala and made me a citizen of their towns. I am composing for you an escutcheon with two eagles supported by three Graces with the Château d'If at the chief. Are you pleased?
    You know that I love you. Write me a word at Athens; I

will be there in a month unless Garibaldi is in Naples. That
devil of a man is for the time being the strangest sight to look
at.

Alexandre spent only one-and-a-half days at Malta, time to fetch
letters and money, time to let disembark Legray, Lockroy, and the
physician, Albanel, who were splitting away from the group. They
wanted to continue the trip to the Orient. Forty hours later the
ship reached Catania, which offered Alexandre honorary citizen-
ship, music, and illuminations. Émile had now become Émilie
again; her dress better disguised her waist, which was swelling.
Alexandre was satisfied with his new paternity which proclaimed
the vigor of his old age. At Catania he received Garibaldi's answer,
"I await you, for your dear person and for the handsome offer of
guns" (July 13, 1860). The *Emma* unfurled her sails to cross the
channel. Off Milazzo they could hear the cannons booming. *Emma*
dropped her anchor. Alexandre went up on deck and followed the
battle with field glasses. After an hour's shooting, the Neapolitans,
forced back from house to house, retreated into the castle. Victory!
Alexandre debarked at nightfall in the middle of the final shooting.
Garibaldi was stretched under the porch of a church, on the flagstones, with his supper beside him, a piece of bread and a pitcher
of water. He was asleep.

On July twenty-second, Alexandre joined Garibaldi on the ship
Turkery; a 100,000-franc credit was opened to him for the purpose
of buying arms. "On your return, you should create a newspaper,"
Garibaldi added. About July 23, 1860, Alexandre wrote to his son:

My dear child, a coincidence of circumstances, too long to
explain to you but which, instead of being disagreeable, would
offer a profit of ten thousand francs, could bring me back from
one instant to another to Marseille. In such case, you would
be notified by telegraph and you would see me arrive; we
would leave again together which would be excellent. In fact,
I can praise myself for my two plays, can't I? [*L'Envers d'une
conspiration*, at the Vaudeville, June 4, 1860, and *Le Gentilhomme de la montagne*, Théâtre Porte-Saint-Martin, June 12,
1860]

On July twenty-ninth, Alexandre embarked on the *Pausilippe*, a steamboat of the Imperial Post, for Marseille. Émile or Émilie was with him; she had to go back to Paris to be delivered. At Naples, they discovered with stupefaction a city entirely won over to Garibaldi's cause, even the police. At Marseille Alexandre bought 1,000 rifles and 550 carbines for 91,000 francs and had them loaded directly on the ship. He boarded the *Pausilippe* again on Thursday, August ninth. At Naples he heard that a small troop had already crossed the channel to reconnoiter. At Messina there was a rumor that Garibaldi had been called back to Turin. A stratagem, Alexandre thought, and he gave the guns to Garibaldi's second in command. Alexandre walked in the Garibaldian camps which waited orders to cross the Straits of Messina. After twenty-five years, he saw once more the brave Captain Arena, beard and hair white of course, but happy. As was Alexandre himself.

Garibaldi was absent, and Alexandre left Messina on the evening of August sixteenth. He took on board the General's chaplain, Brother Jean. The *Emma* glided from port to port, pursuing epic adventures, as Alexandre wrote to Victor Hugo around July 25, 1860:

Dear Victor,
You love me too much not to want to know where I am and what I do. I am at Palermo, at Melaro, at Messina—everywhere an act of the great drama is played whose denouement will be the fall of the King of Naples, of the Pope, of the Emperor of Austria.
I am founding at Palermo a newspaper that you will soon receive.

The *Emma* had anchored in the Gulf of Salerno. Soon thirty Salernitans, guided by Brother Jean, boarded the schooner. Everyone drank to Garibaldi's health in the champagne glasses of the King of Naples, "borrowed" from the royal palace at Palermo. A rumor spread that Garibaldi was on board. Overloaded barks surrounded the ship, which was illuminated with Bengal lights and Roman candles. Alexandre offered a feast to the Salernitans. Garibaldi's troops had debarked in Calabria on the nights of the nineteenth to the twentieth, as Alexandre heard when he arrived in the Bay of Naples. He had made his men watch with loaded guns. The schooner had become a real enlisting office at a few cables' length from the royal chamber from which the little king, with his field glasses, looked toward a very dark future. His throne was not falling, it was collapsing.

On August twenty-third, Liborio Romano, Minister of the Interior for the constitutional regime named in-extremis by François II, had boarded the *Emma*, where Alexandre welcomed him as the official ambassador of Garibaldi. The Minister swore that he would fight for the constitutional cause as much as he could but, if the fight became impossible, he would take refuge on the *Emma*. The next day, Alexandre received the Minister's portrait with two lines: "Write below this portrait: *Portrait of a coward*, if I do not keep the promises I gave you last evening." The conduct of this second-hand plenipotentiary provoked the wrath of the King: "M. Dumas prevented General Scotti from giving assistance to my soldiers at the Basilicate; M. Dumas caused a revolution at Salerno; M. Dumas came into the port of Naples from which he issues proclamations to the city, distributes arms, gives out red shirts." The *Emma* was ordered to leave the bay and she sailed to meet Garibaldi on September second, and get away from the field of perpetual intrigues of which she was the center. On the fifth, off the village of Picciota, Alexandre distributed red shirts made on board to some twenty men who had come to get the news. They formed a troop with plans for an uprising in Cilento. Then with a soft northeast breeze, the *Emma* sailed toward Messina. On the morning of September eighth, Alexandre was told that Garibaldi had entered Messina. Anchor was hoisted at once and the rifles loaded aboard, but between Sicily and Calabria a storm rocked the schooner. Fortunately, on the twelfth, she was towed by a steamer and taken into the port of Naples. The next day Alexandre found Garibaldi again, lodged in a mansard. They embraced, weeping, "Here you are. Thank God, you have made me wait long enough," cried the dictator. For the first time he used the familiar "tu." On the fourteenth, by decree, Alexandre Dumas was named Director of Museums and Excavations. He was installed at the Chiatamone Palace from which, on September 15, 1860, he wrote to Van Loo:

A word in haste.
I am in Naples with Garibaldi. I live in a charming small palace on the shore. I have, and that is why I miss you, all the

hunting grounds of His Majesty, François II, at my disposal. But up to now, laziness has kept me from killing even one pheasant.

Good health, my friend. The newspapers will give you news of my politics.

Eighteen thirty was only a rough draft; 1860 was the final copy. The Bourbons were thrown out. The excitement of action, the friendship with an epic hero, a reward honoring his services: for Alexandre the breeze that came from Sorrento carried intoxicating perfumes.

V

Alessandro Dumas, Napolitano

Alexandre was in his city, Naples, the city of happiness and of feelings. He walked along its three much-frequented thoroughfares and its five hundred streets, through which no one ever walked. The time for epic adventures had ended; now it was time to manage. Mediocrity succeeded greatness. There was indignation that a foreigner had been named Director of Museums and Excavations, functions purely honorific. There were intrigues to discredit him to Garibaldi, and accusations that he had arranged to have himself fed at the expense of the municipality, that he organized orgies more suited for Capua than for Naples. There were suspicions that he had hunted twice on the royal hunting grounds and had carried away two carts of game. What was *not* said?

Dumas put discouragement behind him and harnessed himself to the tasks he had undertaken: to democratize Naples and Neapolitanize Paris. Once the war ended, he took off the uniform of war correspondent (his articles in *Le Siècle* were published in book format under the title *Les Garibaldiens*) to put on once again the peaceful clothes of journalist and historian. But in spite of the contract for 18,332 francs that Lévy had already paid, his cash register was empty. Dumas called on Garibaldi, who was pursuing the action north of Naples:

At Millazzo, I talked with you about founding a newspaper and at once, in your own handwriting, you gave me its title, *L'Indépendente*, and the epigraph which was to accompany that title.

In Naples you charged me by decree to write an archeological, historical, and picturesque piece entitled *Naples et ses Provinces* [decree of September 15, 1860].

As for the spirit of the newspaper, you know my principles, they are those which put a sword in your hand.

As for the work, you know my desire—it is to give it the lowest possible price to make it popular.

It is therefore important for me to decrease the expense that I intend to take upon myself alone, to be always, like my newspaper, independent.

Therefore, General, I come to ask you to have these two works printed at the National Printing for the length of their run.

This is what you offered me at Messina without giving to the National Printing anything but the paper.

I believe I am doing something useful for the cause to which I am devoted by asking you for this authorization.

For his historical work for which he would increase the number of photographs, lithographs, and wood-engravings, he asked the same day that a sum of four thousand francs be "assigned for travel expenses of four artists, two draftsmen, two engravers who would be appointed to open a school of drawing and wood-engraving in Naples" (to Garibaldi, September 22, 1860). But Garibaldi, very involved in the last battles of his campaign (Volturno and Caserta Vecchia on the first and second of October 1860), listened to the cannons and silenced the Muses. October 7, 1860, Alexandre complained:

What I am writing you is not very long. For mercy's sake, read it. When I tell you: *You forget me*, I am saying: *You forget you, yourself.*

All that I want to do is to help you.

As much as you are devoted to an idea, just so much I am devoted to you because your idea is the freedom of the world.

But the dictator Garibaldi and the danger of the revolution worried the Court at Turin which depended upon Napoléon III—"*Fate, ma fate presto* [Do it but do it quickly]," he is supposed to have said—to spread his army through Italy. It would occupy the Pontifical States. Garibaldi yielded; he would turn over his power to the King when the King arrived. Beside Garibaldi, the King made his official entrance into Naples on November seventh, and a plebiscite ratified the annexation of Southern Italy to the Kingdom of Piedmont. Garibaldi resigned: "When one has squeezed the juice to the last drop, one throws the orange rind into a corner," he admitted sadly. On the fifth, after refusing honors and gifts, he embarked on the *Washington* with all his baggage: a few small bags of coffee, a bag of dry vegetables, a few seeds, a case of macaroni and a packet of dried codfish. "So long, until we meet at Rome!" he cried to his volunteers gathered on the wharf. Alexandre was there, towering over the crowd with his frizzy mop of hair. "He is Cincinnatus!" Alexandre screamed. He felt cheated: from the first issues of *L'Indépendente* on October twelfth, he had fought against the tricks of Cavour, he had begged Garibaldi not to abandon Naples, not to abandon him, Alexandre. In vain, Garibaldi was floating toward Caprera. The red shirts were folded and put away.

Alexandre tried to amuse his great man:

My friend, I am sending you the schooner with which you could amuse yourself this next winter. She is equipped with all the gear needed for fishing. You won't have to be worried about anything. The crew have food and money for three months.

More Garibaldian than Garibaldi himself, *L'Indépendente* continued its fight. Private sadness added to public disgust. Emma died on November twenty-fifth at Caen. "I believe, although I would not swear to it, that three-quarters of my heart, if not my whole heart, died with her," he wrote later (*Le d'Artagnan*, June 11, 1868).

Naples was quiet. Alexandre hastened to Paris for Émilie had just given him a little girl on December 24, 1860 who was named Micaëlla-Clélie-Josepha-Élisabeth. The father heard of it on the first day of the year 1861 by a letter from his friend the Comtesse de Chambrillon, better known under the name of Céleste Mogador, a music-hall girl who had married the son of a good family. Alexandre, who had just become a grandfather, was jubilant. On January first, 1861, he wrote to Émilie Cordier:

> You knew, my dear Bébé, that I would prefer a girl. I am going to tell you why. I like Alexandre more than Marie. I hardly see Marie but once a year and I can see Alexandre as much as I like to. All the love I could have for Marie will be transferred to my dear little Micaëlla whom I see lying beside her little mother whom I forbid to get up and go out before I arrive. . . . I will fix everything to be in Paris around the twelfth [of January]. In spite of all my wishes, it would be impossible to be there before. If I tell you this, my dear love, believe the truth of it. In one hour my heart has enlarged to make place for my new love. . . .
>
> If during the first months you do not want to be separated from our child, we will rent a small house at Ischia, in the marvelous air and the prettiest island of Naples and then I will go spend with you two or three days of the week; finally count on me to love the child and the mother.

Dumas had abandoned the Committee of Elections in which he participated twice a week; he had left *L'Indépendente* to his collaborators. On his way he had met his son who was heading toward Naples to spend some time with his father.

Alexandre père had taken in his hands the little Micaëlla, no bigger than his thumb. Again he had reassured Émilie of her future. He made the rounds of newspaper publishers, theater directors, editors, but not with much success. Then he left again. He boarded ship at Marseille on Wednesday, February sixth. The next day he clasped in his arms the only real love of his life, his grown son, Alexandre. Dumas père closed his eyes in bliss. With the exuberance of a cicerone, he guided his son through the thousand beauties of Naples, his town. For the tenth time he repeated to him his epic adventures, and introduced him to the aristocratic and liberal circles he frequented. But Alexandre fils slept badly, had a small appetite and sometimes coughed. It was the son, already a bilious and catarrhic old man, who protested when his father launched into a business speculation, a factory for printing on glass that he had discussed with his publisher, Michel Lévy.

Probably because of this venture, his literary production stopped during that year. On May eighteenth, Dumas discontinued the publication of *L'Indépendente* which, only a few weeks before, he wanted to make "the newspaper of Italian unity, the symbol of the liberty of Rome, of Venice, of Hungary" (to Garibaldi, April 22, 1862). He had reconciled himself with Cavour who died on June sixth.

Alexandre fils, a bit less gloomy and in better health, returned gradually to Paris after a long stay at Nohant with his "maman," George Sand. His father wrote on August eleventh:

I am more worried than you about your health; there is the weakness of an infant hidden behind the cough of a thirty-year-old. My program, my dear child, is rather in the hands of God. I have put all the money I had, 12,000 francs, in the hands of the friends you know. With it they have opened a store for products of which I will have half. In opening they have been forced to create 12,000 francs more of debt. The store covers these at this time and in two months has already been able to pay 6,000 francs in profit. In the meantime, I am as always without a sou. I am so tired of Paris, my dear friend, that I will return there only when I will be sure to see only you and Marie. What to do there? How to live? Fighting fatigues me and in Paris one must fight.

Dumas' heart melted at Micaëlla's first babblings. He did not publish anything new that year. Through Parfait's acting as intermediary, Lévy merely published in book format old articles that had appeared in newspapers. Alexandre was overcome with a deep lassitude. Was old age like that? That vague sadness, that disgust for mankind. Was it really Alexandre Dumas who December 29, 1861 wrote to his son:

Maquet is a man with whom I cannot have any further relations. Maquet who, in trust was to have handed me the remainder, after keeping a third of *Hamlet* in which he never participated and two-thirds of *Mousquetaires* [the revival], has kept everything. To me, Maquet, is a thief.

Alexandre who never had a grudge, who had loved mankind too much, now had become somewhat misanthropic.

If he left Naples in January 1862, it was for family business. Marie, his daughter, had tired of her married life and decided to retreat to a convent. She had begun a suit before the Court of Chateauroux but it was dismissed. She had more luck before the Imperial Court. Back in his Neapolitan palace at Chiatamone, with the beautiful sun, facing a sea of azure, caressed by a sweet and perfumed breeze, Alexandre sometimes worked until two in the morning under his green oaks. He wrote, or rather he chatted with the readers of the *Monte-Cristo, the sole anthology of the unpublished work of Alexandre Dumas,* which its owner-manager Calvet had resurrected from its ashes. Alexandre chatted about Naples where people begged in summer while they stole in winter. In fact, the bell of Sant'Anna-del-Palazzo and the gilded fence of the fountain of the Geant had just been stolen. He talked of the Camorra, of bandits ancient and modern. He talked of the poverty and of the filth of Naples. He is still chatting with us:

What mostly strikes the foreigner who arrives at Naples is the horrible dirtiness of the streets; in not one of them is it possible to walk with patent-leather boots. After more than a year during which the Piedmontese policed it, they have not succeeded in organizing a corps of sweepers or in having the city cleaned.

In the busiest streets of Naples you will meet pigs which go around looking for their subsistence in the gutters. . . . And the pigs, it must be said, are not the most dirty users of the streets: At each step you meet a beggar who shows you his maimed arm, his sore face, his chest blistered with herpes. If you are in a carriage and your carriage stops in front of a store, your carriage is in one instant surrounded by a troop of beggars, calling on your pity with the most horrible exhibitions. If you give to one, you are lost; you have to give to all of them. . . . These beggars are like fleas, impossible to protect yourself or to chase them away! They climb on the footboard of your carriage; they come with you into cafés and shops; they wait for you crouched at the door of your hotel.

This was Naples, too, theft and plundering, idleness and the incapacity of the authorities, most particularly the police. An old inheritance from the Bourbons? Dumas brandished his whip: *L'Indépendente* began again its publication on May 15, 1862 and, in spite of the threats from the Bourbonians and from the Camorra, indiscriminately attacked all the ills that burdened Naples. The newspaper was conceived as a work of public health.

Alexandre had risen above his momentary discouragement. After abandoning it for two years, he worked again on *Ainsi soit-il*, the novel whose real heroine was Emma. He used the archives opened by the revolution to undertake a history of the Bourbons of Naples; he gave a definitive version of his correspondence relating to the epic of the *Mille* (*Une Odyssée en 1860*); he printed the first chapter of the *Volontaire de quatre-vingt-douze*. He worked again, he loved again. She was a songstress in her thirties, Fanny Gordoza, an "excellent soprano who recently sang with success at the San Carlo opera," he wrote to Jenny Falcon in October 1862. The revolutionary fever rose in him once again: "The insurrection in Albania, Thessalia, Epireus and Macedonia will take place at the end of March. First, they will throw out the Turks from fourteen provinces now in slavery; then they will push up to Constantinople, probably into the Bosphorus. If it happens, as I believe it will, it is at Constantinople that you will come to see me and not at Naples."

Oh yes, the Greco-Albanian junta, headed by Prince George Castriota Skanderberg, had called upon him:

The National Reform has not at its head a genius such as yours to lead the minds of the masses; it resembles an engine speeding along without a driver.

Dumas bit at the metamorphic bait. He put his schooner at the junta's disposal and recommended it to the gunsmiths of Paris. The revolution was marching on.

The spirit of the coming epic liberations filled him as he offered to send chronicles to Girardin in December of 1862:

If I put my signature on the articles, I could tell you nothing or I would be stabbed with a knife within fifteen days. Believe me, my friend, it is less for Naples and for Italy that I am ready to report to you, than it is for Greece and Albania where the Turkish issue will be decided.

I am in direct contact with the Albanian junta of Durazzo and with Prince Skanderberg who is going to do for Albania, and under my eyes, what Garibaldi has done for Italy. And I can, on this side, inform you not only about the Orient but about English politics which will not let go of the election of Prince Albert.

I am telling you very seriously and with great fear for the future of France that either we get into a war which will end by a battle of Zama or of Waterloo, or our influence will be completely lost in the Mediterranean. Nobody knows, except those who fight them and from whom it cannot be hidden, the truth about the politics, not of Lord Palmerston who is only a screen, but the politics of Sir William Gladstone, the great leader of the Greek Movement.

Girardin accepted—seventy-five francs per article, whatever its length. This money would keep Marie who, after her marriage disappointment, had retired to the Convent of the Ladies of the Assumption at Auteuil. Alexandre's letters from Naples, and even some signed by a copywriter of the newspaper (J. Mahias), followed one another in *La Presse*, beginning January fourth. Dumas continued his chats like the ones he did in the *Monte-Cristo*, which had not survived its eighty-second issue of October 10, 1862. Kidnapping, organization and the misdeeds of the Camorra and plundering—always the same themes which revealed the deep decay of the Neapolitan society. Could something really be done? Discouragement took over as he wrote to his son from Naples at the beginning of January 1863.

I am still held here for some time and when I say 'here,' I mean here or in Greece. I live without using the money of Paris. I abandon all that I earn and all my rights and I live here with what the newspaper gives me.

A day will come when I will step into your house and when I will tell you: after a turbulent life, the quiet life; after the storm, the port. That day will be a good day.

Naples had lost little by little all its magic. Alexandre knew now the vileness of the people, the perversity of the great, the fanaticism of the masses, everyone's irreligion and ignorance. Catholicism was only the cult of images, of madonnas, and of Saint-Gennaro, whom they one day insulted and threatened to drag to the torture rack and adored the next. No morals any more. It was not even dissoluteness coated with varnish, it was coarseness and cynicism without shame. For example, corrupt judges acquitted a lover who had assassinated a husband, money could buy murderers and false witnesses. Alexandre himself, swindled by his printer, had seen a long series of false witnesses, well-known for their shady activities in the neighborhood appearing before the Court which tried the thief. Moral impurity, bodily filth. It was said that only one glass of water was sufficient for the ablutions of Neapolitan ladies, even for the most richly adorned. *L'Indépendente* came into collision with century-old customs. A new Hercules would have been needed to cleanse these modern Augean stables.

During those first days of 1863, Naples was only a bridgehead for Albania and Prince Skanderberg. Alexandre had sent Prima, a young Sicilian, to London to deal with the Prince. Insurrection in Albania was expected to take place during the summer. Alexandre needed to contribute ten thousand francs, but in exchange he was offered the rank of General: "You have no desire to join the campaign in Albania. I have a post as my aide-de-Camp to offer you," he proposed to his son in March of 1863. A General, as was his father? Dumas père's first reaction was to accept but—from fear of ridicule—he resigned himself to be merely the superintendent of the military warehouses of the Christian Army of the Orient. His knowledge was rather short about the country he was supposed to free, so he ate up *L'Histoire de Skandeberg, ou Turcs et Chrétiens au XVème siècle* by Camille Paganel. He hustled to all the gunsmiths in preparation for the expedition.

One morning the Neapolitan police called upon Dumas. The pseudo-Prince Skanderberg was in reality a well-known offender and a crook, and he had disappeared with the funds. This con man had hoaxed Dumas and Garibaldi: "In a mess up to the shoulders! Like sots," added Alexandre with a sickly laugh about the adventure.

At this point, the only charm of Naples for Alexandre was simply that he was not in Paris. "My Paris is now more yours than mine," he confided March 30, 1863 to his son after the revival of *Don Juan de Marana*. This Paris where he was fleeced in spite of Alexandre fils' efforts to manage his father's business and his attempts to sell the adaptation of three of his father's novels for the theater: *Les Quarante-cinq*, *Joseph Balsamo*, and *Le Page du Duc de Savoie*. Marie, without authorization, took the money from the articles in *La Presse* and demanded, besides, one thousand francs to resume her suit for separation before the Imperial Court. And Fontaine was stealing openly:

> I see that I owe, on a promissory note, 3,500 francs to Fontaine. I never gave a promissory note to Fontaine but Fontaine imitates my writing well enough to have made out a note to himself signed with my name. What do you want? Nothing will surprise you any more when you are at this ripe age of 60 (to Alexandre fils, March 22, 1863)

Even before a transaction was completed, everyone fixed the amount each would get from it: it was Charpillon to whom six thousand francs was owed, who asked for an accounting; it was Bruslon who, from the arrears of the bankruptcy, had to get two hundred fifty francs every month: it even was Noël Parfait who asked eighty-six francs for the rent of a room in the house at La Varenne. It was also the Neapolitan spongers: "If some of the Italians who stop in Paris and bring you news from me try to borrow money from you, button your pocket and close your money-drawer," he recommended to his son on March 20, 1863. Finally, there was Girardin, changing like a weathercock, who too often skipped the Neapolitan correspondence, or the copy-chief at *La Presse* who found that Dumas definitely dwelled too much on the Camorra.

As disgusted as he was with Paris, Alexandre felt the need to go there to put his faltering affairs in order. In June he started on his way back to Paris but after he had greeted his friend Türr, who was Garibaldi's second in command, he had a whim to see Switzerland again, thirty years later. From Arona he crossed the Saint-Gothard in an excellent family coach. The situation demanded it. Émilie, or rather Émile, accompanied him, dressed in the charming costume of a young man. She called Alexandre "my dear papa," while a mischievous two-and-a-half-year-old girl called him simply "papa." Alexandre brushed aside all feeling of nostalgia. Was he even moved by the remembrance of Belle, companion of his 1832 trip, the mother of Marie? The speed of the trip did not invite sentimentality. Only one week to see again the Lake of the Quatre-Cantons, Lucerne, Lake Brienz, Interlaken, Lake of Thun, Bern, and the falls of the Rhine at Schaffhausen, all this to the rhythm of the railroad and the steamboats.

In the space of thirty years, Switzerland had invented the tourist industry. Dumas, a man always in a hurry, marveled at these convenient innovations. It was Swiss citizens whom he surprised:

> Sixty-one years old, and one could not give him more than fifty. When one sees his tall stature, his torso, his strongly built limbs, one wonders at first if it is indeed true that nature had lodged in this almost athletic body even more intelligence than matter; but from his lively and piercing look, his forehead from which thoughts seem to spring, the extreme mobility of his face and his clear, rapid and abundant speech, one soon perceives that one is in the presence of the author of *Antony* and of *Monte-Cristo*. (X. Stockmar, *A. Dumas à Berne*)

The carriage, the railway car, the boats ate up space. Alexandre let himself be rocked; he was making a plan for what, he estimated would be a six-volume novel, *La San Felice*, that he offered to Girardin at the end of June. He wrote to his son on July 3, 1863:

> I am leaving, and in leaving I give you an account of what I have done yesterday. I have contracted with *La Presse* for *La San Felice* for a cent a letter, 10,000 francs for a million letters. It is the same contract as Madame Sand's. I am very keen for being published again in a newspaper like *La Presse*.

Alexandre had taken the road to Naples in the company of the famous Dr. Ricord. At Lyons he met Marie who was returning alone from a trip to Jerusalem:

> Her husband becomes more and more insane and nasty. She— she spits enough blood to fill a basin. I had her examined by Ricord who told me, 'chest trouble.'

Naples was not the same any more. It was now inhabited by the characters of his future novel: La San Felice, a heroic and pure figure, Queen Caroline, the King Nasone, Lord Nelson, William and Lady Hamilton, Admiral Caracciolo, the republicans of the failed Republic, Cardinal Ruffo. Dumas had a beginner's impatience when he asked his son to read his work in progress:

Why, when you know with what impatience I expect your opinion of the first volume of *La San Felice*, as execrable as it might be, why don't you write to me? (to Alexandre fils, September 17, 1863)

Execrable? Of course, it was such a long time that Alexandre père had put his talent to the service of noble causes that he had forgotten literature. He was afraid of not being able to write any more. Again he wrote to his son in October 1863:

La Presse will begin its publication [December 11, 1863]. I had the copy done again. The volumes have now 300,000 letters instead of 200,000. There is a preface. Check the proof sheet of the hastily made preface. . . . If the publication is successful, have the other newspapers say a word about it, by Gautier in his column, etc. You understand that I must have a success.

A success to win Paris again, to re-enter the fight even "were I dead and tied to my horse like the Cid." It was a success. All of it seemed to Alexandre as most satisfactory or, as he put it, *"contentissime."* Rouy was enchanted, and Arsène Houssaye marveled at the reintegration of Dumas with his genius:

It has been six years that I have not done anything for newspapers or for the Théâtre-Français and during these six years, no work of high scope was created. I believe this one is serious; it is an evocation of an entire era, from the King to the bandit, from the Cardinal to the simple monk. And republican France will be above all of it, calm, loyal and poetic with the two characters of Championnet and of MacDonald.

I would like very much to create things of art. (to Houssaye, December of 1863)

Art before anything else, he wrote to his son in January of 1864:

Support me by speaking to me of *La San Felice*. With it, I simply have undertaken, as did Atlas, to carry a world but Atlas had an excuse: this world had been put on his back while I, I put it on my back myself.

Tell Gautier that I do for him, and for him alone, what I have never done for anybody. I recopy, so that he is satisfied with the style, so well that instead of earning three hundred francs a day, I earn only one hundred fifty. See of what amount he is my creditor at the end of three million letters. Also tell his two dear children that though I create style for their father, I create the picturesque and love for them.

Alexandre now organized his return to Paris as a renaissance: his Émilie and the little Micaëlla were waiting. He wanted a quiet family life with his grown-up children—Alexandre fils who had finally been able to marry his green-eyed siren [Nadeja Naryschikine], Marie, now free from the mad Olinde Petel—and, turbulent and charming, his little Micaëlla. A surprising family, but still a family. Of course, the desired calm could not come before the audit and settlement of the inextricable tangle of his finances. Alexandre insisted to Parfait in a letter of December 29, 1863:

I believe that at this hour it would be extremely easy to arrange my affairs: My debt to Lévy should be much decreased, that to Lefrançois *idem*.

There are two ways to arrange my affairs: to buy back the Guidi promissory note, the only one that weighs seriously upon me, and to make a deal with Bruslon—there are ways to arrange that. Find the sum which would permit us to buy back at half price or to abandon the whole thing on condition that all opposition would be lifted on half my income. In either case, I pray you not to breathe a word to Mme. Guidi; she is inclined to give her promissory note for 20,000 francs and God knows that I owe her that!

Parfait was reluctant. Things were not that simple, even with a touch of swindling. He tried, however, but he did not succeed. To be born again in Paris, Alexandre also counted immensely on the "good" Jew, Polydore Millaud, who had just created, at 112 Boulevard de Richelieu, *Le Petit journal* in which Alexandre had already begun again his philanthropic activities with a subscription for the creation of a library for the use of the Clichy debtor's prison. A newspaper, be it *Le Petit journal* or another, was the guarantee of a regular income.

Alexandre said goodby to his collaborators at *L'Indépendente* who would continue the work already started. For the last time he walked the via di Chaïja and the via Tolèd, glanced on the *Pausilippe* and the Italian sea. He was not losing all of Naples since he boarded ship with Fanny Gordoza, the diva with the fragile voice and the Vesuvian passions.

As the *Pausilippe* left in the bluish haze of those happy shores, Fanny squeezed the hand of her hero, her great man. She would be the Queen of Paris since he was its King returned from exile.

VI

The Fallen Oak

The train from Lyons arrived at the station at ten in the evening. Alexandre kissed his son, who was delighted yet uneasy about his return. "Let's go to Théophile Gautier at Neuilly," decided Dumas père. But it was late; the trip was trying, and Alexandre fils attempted to object. "Me? I am as fresh as a rose." Their cab stopped at Quai Voltaire in Neuilly. Alexandre made a racket before the dark windows. The good Théo's startled face peeked out. "We are all in bed," he grumbled. "Lazy! Am I in bed, me?" Théo shook himself out of his sleep and they gathered around tea and talked as they only talk in Paris. They talked of Naples, of *La San Felice*, of Dumas' ambition to take this hostile Paris once again, to reconquer it after a third expatriation: Florence, 1840; Brussels, 1851; Naples, 1860. Every ten years he had to get his strength back outside of France. As for the next time . . . they all fell silent, then they separated.

It was four in the morning. Alexandre trod the sidewalks of Paris with sensuous pleasure. Father and son went up the Avenue of Neuilly, the Avenue de la Grande-Armée. When they arrived at his son's place, Alexandre asked for a lamp. "A lamp? To do what?" "To light it. I will put myself to work." And Dumas, in the pale light of the early April morning, wrote a chapter of *La San Felice*.

Temporarily, he moved to the fifth floor at 112 Rue de Richelieu, in a furnished apartment overlooking the Boulevard. To work, he descended to the mezzanine, into the management office of *Le Petit journal* where his good friend, Polydore Millaud, had hired a new secretary, Benjamin Pifteau, a shabby and tenacious bureaucrat who shared the paycheck of his mistress, a girl in the chorus at the Opéra. *Le Petit journal* rejoiced in the return of the Master, who believed he would find his popularity intact on the Boulevards. He had been asked to carve a drama out of his *Les Mohicans de Paris*. Yet a shadow darkened this renewed happiness: Émilie threatened Alexandre with an alternative—either separation or marriage. Dumas chose separation and consoled himself in the arms of his volcanic Fanny Gordoza. Yet he wanted to recognize Bébé, their adorable four-year-old child, as his legitimate daughter. He wrote to Cordier on June 2, 1864:

Would you let me talk a moment with you who are a reasonable man?

I like Bébé very much and I would like to take advantage of being in Paris to recognize her and make of her my third child. But I will put three conditions that I hope you will find fair.

As long as Émilie is in Paris, Bébé will spend six months with her mother, six months with me.

If Émilie should leave Paris and go to a foreign country, Bébé will be given to me before her departure.

If Émilie lives with a person other than myself, I would take Bébé back and her mother would always have a right to see her.

I believe that I am reasonable in offering you these conditions and in asking that, in Émilie's absence, you talk with Maman Cordier. Bébé loves me very much and must not suffer from the necessities that separate us, Émilie and me. If these conditions are acceptable, notify two of your licensed friends and we will go to City Hall to add a filiation proceeding to the margin of Bébé's birth certificate.

Émilie did not want to hear of it. She knew that the Napoleonic Code gave the lion's share to the father. Had not Alexandre himself torn Marie away from her mother, the poor Belle Krelsamer? Alexandre would not be allowed to recognize Bébé who, however, was often seen at the Villa Catinat in Enghien. This villa, in the middle of a large park, near the lake, had been rented that spring. Alexandre turned the billiard room into his office. Besides *La San Felice*, he was adding the last strokes to his dramatization of *Les Mohicans de Paris* and had promised the librettos of two operas to Émile Perrin. He already had made a scenario for his novel *Acté*. In the villa, music was heard from every floor. Fanny tried to develop her thin stream of a voice under the direction of fee-hunting piano teachers, singing masters, and accompanists. She had been found a bit below par for acceptance at the Théâtre-Italien. Alexandre stood stoically under the cataracts of trills and roulades but took badly the continuous invasion of string pluckers. "I am a prey to music," he complained. A prey, too, to swindlers, spongers, parasites who, as soon as they had heard of his return and his moving to Enghien, trooped in. Alexandre paid for their cabs, prepared enormous risottos, left himself be submerged, tired but also enchanted by what he wanted to believe was popularity. Sometimes, surreptitiously, he left the Villa and the excesses of Fanny—who continuously hailed him with a resounding "Doumasse,"—to take refuge in the beautiful villa of Princesse Mathilde at Saint-Gratien or in the gothic-styled chateau of Émile de Girardin.

In July *Les Mohicans de Paris* was put into rehearsal and Alexandre came and went between Enghien and Paris. But the censors were watching: too many allusions to the political conditions of 1864. Forbidden! Alexandre took up his pen. On August 10, 1864, he wrote to Napoléon III:

Sire,
There were in 1830 and there are still today three men at the head of French literature.

These three men are: Victor Hugo, Lamartine, and myself. Victor Hugo is exiled. Lamartine is ruined.

I cannot be exiled as Hugo: nothing in my writing, in my life, or in my words can give cause for exile. But I can be ruined, as Lamartine and, in fact, I am being ruined.

I don't know what malevolence arouses censors against me. I have written and published twelve hundred volumes. It is not for me to write appreciations of them from the literary point of view. Translated in all languages, they went as far away as steam could carry them. Although I am the least deserving of the three, these volumes made me, in the five parts of the world, the most popular of the three, perhaps because one is a thinker, the other a dreamer, and I am, myself, only a popularizer.

Out of these twelve hundred volumes there is not one that could not be read by a worker of the republican Faubourg Saint-Antoine, or by a young girl from Faubourg Saint-Germain, the most chaste of our suburbs. And yet, Sire, to the eyes of censors, I am the most immoral man in existence. . . . Today, the censors stopped *Les Mohicans de Paris* which was to be played next Saturday. They will probably also stop, under more or less specious pretenses, *Olympe de Clèves* and *Joseph Balsamo* that I am writing at present.

The newspapers published the letter. Princesse Mathilde intervened with her cousin and the rehearsals resumed. One day when she unexpectedly went to see her lover, Fanny lifted a door curtain and collapsed on a bench, close to fainting after finding Dumas "in almost criminal conversation with a young actress." Alexandre readjusted his clothes. "Take this fool away. It seems that she has been fasting since yesterday and it hurts her to see others at table." The same evening, at the Villa Catinat, a few vases were hurled into the air, some chairs tossed upside down. Alexandre had outgrown the age of such passions.

Humbly, Cherville had again offered his services. Dumas agreed to rewrite his *Bourgeois de Paris*, rebaptized *Parisiens and provinciaux*, a previous project from before the Neapolitan epic. Now Cherville often took the road to Enghien. But there he found a society in decay. Where were the evenings at the Arsenal, when Marie sat at the piano, where were the chats with Hugo, Vigny, Lamartine? An extreme sadness constantly seeped in, in spite of the laughter, the exchanges of wit and pleasantries. They could not even be sad. Offenbach was hurling the Second Empire into a whirlwind of oblivion. Yet, to live, in spite of it all!

But as soon as the interest aroused by his return had subsided, Alexandre was wounded by the indifference which strikes all those who have the audacity to last too long. He left for Marseille in October. "I will stage *Les Mohicans*. Do you want to go there? I am going alone. But I must tell you that in all probability I will find some one down there," he announced to his son October 26,

1864. But could going to Marseille be called leaving? An American lawyer offered to publish one of his books in New York. Alexandre wrote to Nordhausen on October 8, 1864:

I always desired to take a trip to New York and what you offer me will give me the greatest pleasure. Only at New York one spends enormous sums of money. To go to New York, to leave my novels, to leave my dramas without a certitude [of a contract] becomes impossible for me.

He planned to make the trip within two months, once *La San Felice* and his two dramas (*Balsamo* and *Olympe de Clèves*) were finished. Would there be a place in the New York theater for a first-class soprano who had made her debut at the Théâtre-Italien, Fanny Gordoza? His correspondent guaranteed him the cooperation of the publisher, Harper's. Alexandre polished his plans for the trip. He would go as a tourist to New York, would take his novel—*Les Mémoires d'une favorite* (*Lady Hamilton*)—to Harper's, give lectures on Garibaldi and draft a picturesque history of the first five years of Lincoln's presidency, which he proposed to Nordhausen on November 29, 1864:

This book, translated into French and English, could throw a light on some facts that selfish interests would push back into the shadows. There is, for instance, in England a system of slanders against America which tends to make one believe that the North intended not so much the freedom of the Blacks as the oppression of the Whites. This is so true that in Paris I could not find one newspaper willing to open a subscription to help your sick and your wounded.

He would leave, he said, at the end of January on the ship *Washington*. Waiting for his discovery of America, Dumas settled on the first floor, 70 Rue Saint-Lazare, the site of the present Church of the Trinity. Marie had left her convent to live near her father. She devoted herself to her painting, sometimes clothed in very strange rags. Father and daughter would not leave one another again.

In December, in the auditorium of the Théâtre Folies-Parisiennes an unlucky impresario had organized a public exhibition of the works of Eugène Delacroix, who had died while Dumas was in

Naples. Alexandre gave a lecture on the life and work of the painter; the room was packed. Alexandre ascended the platform in white tie and tails to a triple salvo of applause, even more enthusiastic from the women's side. The lecture was a long return to the past, a slow walk in a cemetery. A first tear dropped, the emotion spread throughout the whole audience. At the end of the talk, hands stretched to thank, to console, to beg Alexandre to give his lecture once more. It was reproduced in *La Presse*.

In February, Alexandre escaped to Germany—the American project was postponed—and brought back for his four-year-old granddaughter, Colette, a doll "straight from Nüremberg, Mlle. Perrette." Then he returned to the last chapters of *La San Felice*. "Today 25 February 1865, at ten in the evening, I have finished the story begun 25 July 1863, the day of my birthday," he emphasized on the manuscript, as if he knew that that day, that hour, dated the death of a writer. Of course, more written words would come from his pen, *pro fame*, but Alexandre felt emptied and dispossessed. Nevertheless he had to take care of La Gordoza's career. It was in vain for her audition at the Opéra was a flop.

Alexandre returned to his wandering life. In April he was in Lyons, from where he sent a telegram of congratulations to Jules Janin for not having been elected to the Académie Française. Alexandre was in Lyons with the intention of giving another lecture on Delacroix. He needed money and on May 2, 1865, begged Michel Lévy:

I need 50,000 francs to clean up the whole situation: 15,000 for Mme. Guidi; 10,000 for other current debts; 6,000 to settle my daughter in her new lodging and the remaining for my personal needs. . . .

See to it, my dear Michel and put all possible haste to carry out this contract. . . . I will go to London and perhaps I will earn enough money there to liquidate [my debt] with the money I will get from this trip. If it is inadequate, I will decide to take the American trip and I will write the history of the Lincoln presidency.

I must take a great decision and you know that leaving France will not bother me much.

Money again and always. Would some come from this vast auditorium that had just been built in Rue de Lyon and was pompously named Grand-Théâtre Parisien? A popular theater in a popular neighborhood. With the money advanced by Polydore Millaud, he rented the hall in the name of his secretary, Darsonville. Its inaugural production would be *Les Gardes forestiers*, which has been such a success at Marseille in 1858. Alexandre had cast the roles with out-of-work actors. Every evening the rehearsals had to be interrupted each time a train started out or an engine whistled, for this strange auditorium had been built in the railroad arcades. A leaden sun warmed the city. Alexandre greeted the people of the neighborhood who acclaimed him; his popularity had found a refuge in those questionable parts of the city. Only the people were faithful to their heroes.

On that May 28, 1865, the heat was crushing. A crowd, however, had not hesitated to come to the suffocating theater. Victory! *"Les Forestiers* are truly an immense success," Alexandre informed his daughter. To Michel Lévy he wrote, "[It] takes the proportion of an immense success. Why shouldn't you print them separately for the provinces. Easy to play, they will be played everywhere." Money from it? None at all. Darsonville, whom Dumas had hired as director, had a strange conception of honesty, and Alexandre had to fire this unscrupulous man who did not pay the actors. As a compensation for the latter, Dumas organized a theatrical tour under his own direction. They went through Rouen, Soissons, Villers-Cotterêts. Posters blossomed on the walls of his birthplace: "Great dramatic solemnity. Extraordinary performance given once only by the artists of M. Alexandre Dumas," could be read by the children and grandchildren of those who had been Alexandre's playmates fifty years before. "M. Alexandre Dumas will attend the performance of his new play whose success has been so enthusiastic and so legitimate in Paris." All of Villers were grouped in front of the hotel where he was staying; many tried to see him through the windowpanes. There he was! With an apron and a toque! He stirred sauces, he basted the roast. The theater company would dine well that evening. As it happened at Soissons, as it happened at Laon, an ovation burst from streets that were generally so quiet. Alexandre was still a prophet in his own country. Was he delighted? August thirty-first he sent to his son a message of money and death:

With 100,000 francs cash we would see the end of indebtedness; 200,000 francs could take care of Doyen with the others. . . . Get busy with that: it means peace for the rest of my life.
Poor Villers-Cotterêts! All the people of my age are dead. It looks like a mouth that has lost three-quarters of its teeth.

He was at the end of his strength, but he still hoped to find, across this ocean of debt, a harbor of serenity. He was ready to do anything to survive, but not to forsake his friendships, and above all, not what was for him the capital friendship. Just after some Paris lectures had been cancelled, he wrote to the publisher of *La Presse*, on June 11, 1865:

[S]peaking of my friend Hugo 'I continue to hold my hand out to those whose change of opinion leads to misfortune and exile, but I refuse it to those whose change of opinion leads to fortune and honors.' I confess that, when I said these words, I believed I expressed a noble, moral axiom and did not proclaim a dangerous, political maxim.

Then, for default of France, foreign lands remain for me.

From his island, Hugo interrupted for a time his dialogue with immensity to turn toward his old friend. On June 16, 1865, he wrote to Dumas:

From you, no deed of valor surprises me and no deed of cowardice surprises me from those scoundrels. You are light; the Empire is night; it hates you, it's very simple; it wants to extinguish you, but that is less simple. It will lose its breath by doing it. The shadow it will spread on you will add to your radiance. In the end [the cancelation was a] glorious incident for you, and honorable for me. . . . I congratulate our old friendship.

Alexandre was willing to barter his small miseries against a great misfortune. He could only mimic exile by continually running away from Paris. In November he was in Vienna, then at Pesth with Marie. He came back through Prague where he stayed at the Hôtel de la Cour Anglaise on January fourth. He visited the palace of Wallenstein and immediately rushed away again. Even the trip itself did not bring him peace. With a supreme courtesy, he reflected to the world the image it was expecting from him. Edmond and Jules de Goncourt wrote in their *Journal*:

February 14, 1866. In the middle of our conversation comes Dumas père, white tie, white vest, enormous, sweating, puffing, wildly hilarious. He is arriving from Austria, Hungary, Bohemia . . . he speaks of Pesth where [his work] was played in Hungarian, of Vienna where the Emperor loaned him a room in his palace to give a lecture; he speaks of his novels, of his theater, of his plays that the Comédie-Française does not want to play, of his censored *Chevalier de Maison Rouge*, then of a theater license that he cannot obtain, then again of a restaurant he wants to open on the Champs-Elysées.

An enormous ego, an ego like the man himself, but overflowing with the good will of a child and sparkling with wit.

Alexandre settled with Marie at 79 Boulevard Malesherbes, near the Park Monceau. He tried to retrieve the furniture from his previous splendor which he had stored right and left, but he had no bed and he wrote to Van Loo on October 5, 1865:

The person who rented me the furniture for my bedroom is returning to Paris and taking it back. Therefore, I will find myself without bed and without chest of drawers. As for the bed, I would like it in peartree wood, blackened like ebony, of the simplest possible shape, looking like a sofa that could be used as such during the day. My monogram in gilded letters and a coat of arms on each post.

Marie was painting her *Salvador Mundi: Après la mort du Christ, les anges missionnaires*; her father wrote, or rather attempted to write. He had promised to Jules Moriac a novel for *Les Nouvelles*, which had just started publication again. The serial had begun on October 17, 1866, but as he was going along, the old writer became content with copying some seventeenth-century memoirs, and the serial was interrupted. Like the Maréchal de Soubise, Alexandre was no longer of an age to be happy. All his attempts failed, often miserably. Amédée de Jallais asked him to make a drama out of the novel, *Gabriel Lambert*. Dumas and his collaborator put themselves to work; the play came out well and was admirably cast. On the evening of the premiere, Alexandre paced along the corridors of the Ambigu theater, superb and confident: "I am sure of my play; this evening I scorn the critics!"

Alas, the critics did not appreciate being scorned. On Monday their columns let the old writer know it. In April he wrote to his "friends known or unknown, in France or in foreign countries." It was a question of opening a subscription for a renaissance of the Théâtre-Historique: "to applaud again what we have applauded before and so that our sons can applaud what their fathers applauded." The newspapers gave some publicity to this circular but the friends, the known as well as the unknown, did not follow with enthusiasm. Only two Polytechnique students gave him the amount of a collection made at their school. Touched, Alexandre warmly shook their hands. But he felt alone, more and more alone. "I only meet Alexandre [fils] at funerals; the next time, it perhaps will be mine," he used to say. For fifteen thousand francs he had sold Michel Lévy the rights for publication of his works in an illustrated edition.

On July 24, 1866, he celebrated his sixty-fourth birthday. He wrote a melancholic letter to a friend to which Marie added gently, "It is certainly not his sixty-four years that God sends him but his twenty-four!" Marie had just finished a novel, *Au Lit de mort*, at the request of her "dear papa," who has pestered her until she decided to write. Was genius hereditary? While Marie, alone, went again to Vienna, Dumas struggled to revive a newspaper, *Le Mousquetaire*. It was only a new name given to the *Nouvelles*, Noriac's newspaper, of which he was chief-editor since the spring of 1866. Polydore Millaud was probably behind these journalistic reincarnations. At first, it was encouraging: *Le Mousquetaire* did marvelously well but did not yet turn a profit. Another misleading hope: the publication of the newspaper had to be stopped in April 25, 1867. Alexandre was sinking, little by little, under the difficulty of living. His oldest friends were leaving him one by one. Each morning he dared not open the newspaper for fear of reading of a new disappearance. He had cried for Méry, he had cried for Roger de Beauvoir. Who was next? Himself?

He wrote to his dear Bébé, the little Micaëlla:

Not only do I, too, pray God evening and morning for you—but I think of you every instant of the day. I have a very sad heart that, having so little time to see you, I am not allowed to take advantage of that time. When I am dead, you will still have your mother for a long time but as for me, you won't have me any more.

Alexandre tried to divert his thoughts and shake off this sadness. In April, the photographer Liebert offered a surprising photo for sale: Alexandre in shirt sleeves, holding on his lap, snuggled against his vast chest, a superb young girl with long black hair, a magnificent body of which a close-fitting swimming suit revealed more than it concealed. The beautiful creature was American, a performing horsewoman at the Théâtre Gaité where she triumphed in *Les Pirates de la Savane*. Her name was Adah Isaacs Menken. She liked alcohol, poetry, poets, and publicity and was enchanted to walk on the arm of one of the celebrities of the world of letters. Paris was amused, Paris was roaring with laughter.

Alexandre fils was horror-stricken: "How distressed you must have been by those stories of photographs! But that's how it is. Age brings sad consequences to bohemian life. What a pity!" George Sand wrote to him. Superbly, the old writer and the young equestrienne ignored public opinion. "In spite of my advanced age, I've found a Marguerite for whom I play the role of your Armand Duval," replied Alexandre père to his son-father. Adah and Alexandre participated in all feasts, received in the apartment she had rented at the Chaussée-d'Antin, dined as lovers on the banks of the Seine. A few instants of happiness stolen from time that was becoming short: "If it is true that I have talent as it is true that I have love, both are yours," Alexandre murmured to her.

He seemed to sense, through this present time of feasts, operettas, universal exhibitions, a frightening sound of boots and cannon. He presented in serial format *Les Blancs et les bleus*, subtitled *Les Prussiens sur le Rhin* (*Le Mousquetaire*, January 13 to February 22, 1867) and *La Terreur prussienne* (*La Situation*). Prussia worried him; over there, in Bohemia, the Prussian army had routed Austrian troops at the battle of Sadowa, on July 3, 1866, then in July it had occupied Frankfurt. Prussia now formed a unified state from the Niemen to the Sarre. Indeed, Bismarck had to give up

Southern Germany under threat from Napoléon III. But for how long? Dumas was at Frankfurt where he inquired about the rapid campaign of 1866. He visited Gotha, Hanover, Berlin, the battle-fields of Langensalza where the King of Hanover had been forced to surrender, and Sadowa: "France, wake up; France remain your-self," Dumas cried in his two novels:

> On the road to progress, France is the symbolic leader of human reason; she is the column of smoke by day, the column of fire by night. Her politics can be summed up with two sentences: —never walk slow enough to stop Europe and never walk quickly enough to prevent the world from following her! (*La Terreur prussienne*).

The old Cassandra was sinking with his last wreckage, now and then enlightened by the rays of the great sun of 1830: *Hernani* was being revived. Alexandre praised this event and Victor Hugo wrote to him on June 7, 1867:

> My dear Dumas, you just wrote about *Hernani*, you the man of so many triumphs, a clever and eloquent page which re-minded me of our great wars of 1830 for the freedom of art. I have aged since that time and I passed from one fight to another one. In this second fight for the liberty of the people, I am only one of the defeated. But in the last fight, as in the first one, I have faith. It is sweet for me to know that you still love me a little after forty years. Your friend, Victor Hugo.

Antony was revived on October 4, 1867 at the Théâtre Cluny with Laferrière who played again the role of Antony. Alexandre wrote him:

> I confess to you that yesterday evening gave me back my faith I was beginning to lose. I feared that there was no more youth except within the old people. I am mistaken: I saw young people of eighteen applaud as if they had seen the seventeen changes of government I have seen. . . .
> Let's hope that there will now be, I would not say a di-rector—there is nothing now to expect from directors who make literature with fat oxen, lionesses in labor, and aquariums

where, a fine critique against the spectators, one sees oysters yawn—but a speculator who will understand that a country such as France, that a capital such as Paris does not renounce its supremacy of intelligence any more than that of its glory.

Ephemeral moments of light before sinking forever into the night. The rent for the Boulevard Malesherbes apartment had to be paid. Alexandre sold some furniture and dismissed almost all of his servants except Vasili, the faithful Georgian. The "women friends" of the old man, half actresses, half courtesans, ransacked the drawers of the desk: "If they could only leave me a poor twenty-franc coin," he complained. Mathilde Schoebel, his little "heather" he had known when she was a very young child, once found him lying on a sofa in his workroom, in pain.

You arrive just in time; I am sick; I need some herb tea and I call in vain . . . I believe I am left all alone. . . . And to think that I must go out to an evening party! . . . Be kind enough to look in the drawers of the chest and tell me if you see there some linen and a white tie.

Only a few nightgowns, not ironed, were there. Mathilde rushed to the neighborhood shops that were still open and looked for a very large evening shirt—which she finally found in the store aptly named "À la chemise d'Hercule"—with a white front strewn with red devils. Alexandre was above ridicule. What were a few unfortunate years at the end of a resplendent life and work to a spirit who had kept a formidable lucidity. To the architect Charles Garnier who had just unveiled the facade of the Opéra, Alexandre commented in a letter:

At last, Paris has its modern monument and I am very happy that it owes it to you, . . . without other help than your own talent. It is perfect. Let people talk, if they must. In any case, it won't be around me where there is unanimity. Only one thing slightly bothers the eye, and unhappily it is the only thing that you could not modify, it is the 'N' and the 'E' on the facade, whose spacing is a little brisk. It will be modified . . . by time.

Time would sweep away the hated Empire, but he, would he survive the Empire? He felt the weakness in all his body. He did not give up yet. The old fighter sometimes regained his courage. He had launched his last newspaper, the *d'Artagnan*, which came out on Tuesdays, Thursdays, and Saturdays, beginning February 4, 1868 and the *Théâtre-Journal* of which he was chief editor, little ephemeral newspapers which were only small change compared to the great enterprises of the past. "Remember just one thing; you are very rich and I am very poor," he wrote on April 30, 1868 to Maquet with whom he had coldly made up.

In June, Alexandre stayed at the Frascati house in Le Hâvre. The city was transformed into a great industrial and maritime exhibition. There were concerts, special performances, bull fights. Dumas, the poor mountebank, had come to make money with the remains of his glory. The provinces were less cruel than Paris. His lectures, or rather his familiar chats, still attracted a crowd. And this was true also at Caen, Cherbourg, or Dieppe, where he performed as well. He sent articles about the Exposition to the *Moniteur*, a serial on snakes to Villemessant, director of the *Grand Journal*, who soon interrupted the serial when he realized all Dumas did was recopy Buffon.

An old, white-haired man with a hypertrophied abdomen walked along the sea he had loved so much. He held a little eight-year-old girl by the hand: Alexandre and his daughter Micaëlla who lived with her mother at Le Hâvre. There was still some happiness for him, the babbling of this child, the summer sun on the water.

Adah had died in a painful agony from acute peritonitis in a small villa at Bougival.

Alexandre found a last artistic satisfaction when he returned to Paris. His drama, adapted from *Madame de Chamblay*, which had been overcome at the Théâtre Ventadour by the suffocating heat wave of June, was successfully revived at the Porte-Saint-Martin October 31, 1868. A sort of torpor weighed him down, his steps were heavy. He moved with difficulty and dozed in the middle of the day. His hand shook, and it was Leclerc, his secretary, or for a time, a chaste and timid young girl called according to the days, Saturnine, Aventurine, or Valentine, who copied under Dumas' dictation two new parts for *Les Blancs et bleus*, which he made into a five-act, eleven-scene drama which was played at Le Châtelet March 10, 1869. The last words of the play were "Long live the

Republic." For Alexandre, they were his last words on the stage. During a rehearsal the actor Taillade came to ask his directions for his role of Saint-Just. In the middle of the conversation Alexandre's eyes closed and he became suddenly silent. A sleep so deep was a portent of death.

Marie and Alexandre fils were worried. Their father tried to reassure them:

It is true my hand shakes but do not worry about this accident which is only momentary. Quite the contrary, it is the rest that has made it shaky.

What do you expect? It is so used to work that when it has felt me do it the injustice of dictating instead of writing myself, instead of remaining immobile it starts to tremble with anger.

As soon as I go back to writing seriously myself, it will take back seriously its majestic speed. (to Alexandre fils, May 1868)

They had a consultation with Dr. Piorry who recommended the seashore at Roscoff, where Alexandre Dumas composed his extensive *Dictionnaire de cuisine*, which was published after his death. He wrote to Marie in July 1869:

Nothing [is] funnier than our establishment. We are in a small village on the shore but we do not see the sea from which are fished what seem to be beautiful fish.

So that we do not die of hunger we are lodged at a baker's. But as he cooks only three times a week, his bread, even when it comes out of the oven, is hard enough to loosen our teeth. Since we are here, we have eaten meat once and it was bad. As for the rest, living in these conditions is very cheap; I have not yet gone out and I have not seen anything. I was in a hurry to send a volume which I will do tomorrow morning. . . .

Another Marie, the cook Alexandre had taken with him to give the last touch to his recipes, fumed when confronted with artichokes that were too tough, watery string beans and rancid butter. She could not take it any more and turned in her apron. All of Roscoff pitied this old, neglected man who had been such a great writer. He wrote again to Marie during the summer of 1869:

My dearest Minette,

Be a little reassured about our future; we will not die from hunger this time; the good souls of Roscoff have united and supply us with food. My barber goes fishing every night for us; yesterday he brought us a lobster and a sole; M. Corbière, an old friend of mine, has sent us small peas, large as bullets of a rifle; M. Drouet, the painter/sculptor, has sent mackerels and pigeons; the post office mistress sent us a bass and a red snapper. Finally we found ourselves on the point of opening a shop of eatable produce not long after we had thought we would croak from hunger.

Now as one cannot have everything at the same time, it is appetite that I miss; therefore I would like to have Goujon also put in the case of coffee that he is going to send me, a half-bottle of brandy, a half-bottle of absinthe to drink in pure water.

The winter was sinister. Sometimes Marie heard her father weep and complain. Distress was constant at Boulevard Malesherbes. Vassili ran to the municipal pawnshop to pledge a piece of jewelry or a knickknack or he went to Alexandre fils to ask for a few centimes. Alexandre was in physical and moral pain. He lived in a twilight state through which some flashes of brilliance passed. Invited by the gracious Pauline de Metternich to an evening reception at the Austrian Embassy, he could recover his old verve as the storyteller unreeling the intrigues of a novel of which he had not yet written the first line: *Création et rédemption.* Then he gave himself up once more to discouragement and bitterness:

My Cherville, We will not go again in the woods, not because the laurels are cut, but because I cannot walk any more, even in the midst of laurels.

You, who have still the seven-league boots of Puss-in-Boots fitted to the legs of the Marquis de Cherville, come to see me and we will talk of all known things and more besides.

He reread his own work. *Les Mousquetaires:* "It is good," he said to Alexandre fils. The *Monte-Cristo*? "It is not as good as *Les Mousquetaires.*" He worried for the future of his oeuvre: "It seems to me that I am at the summit of a monument which trembles, as if the foundations were sitting on sand," he said.

"Be in peace, the monument is well-built and the base is solid," replied his son, bringing a smile of almost childlike pleasure to his big lips. He went back to sleep.

At the beginning of spring, he was condemned to silence by a persistent abcess in his mouth. On the advice of his physician he gathered whatever money he could and traveled south. He visited Spain again and returned on August thirty-first. On the same date he wrote to Auguste Lafontaine:

I arrive . . . without a sou, as one always arrives. I find that Marie has left for Trouville. Do you want to give me one hundred francs to go and join her?

Alas! All my one-hundred-franc friends are dead; only you, happily, remain alive. Therefore I am obliged to call on you.

The war between Prussia and France had started badly. Marie had rushed back from Trouville. Her old father could hardly speak any more walled in by a horrible despair, he refused to accept the reality of the general political tragedy. On September fourth, he vaguely asked the cause of the turmoil in the streets of Paris. It was the proclamation of the Republic after the surrender at Sedan. He had closed his eyes; tears rolled down his cheeks. The republic! At that price! More a patriot than a republican, he felt his worn body collapsing. Paralysis immobilized him.

The Prussians began the siege of Paris. In an attempt to save the little life remaining to her father, Marie dragged him to a railroad car going in the direction of Dieppe and Puys where Alexandre fils had a summer house. "I come to die with you," the father said to the son who welcomed him. He was given the best room in the house, overlooking the sea. He revived a little at mealtimes then fell back into the same somnolence. He was dying by degrees. When the pale autumn sun was less timid, his armchair was pulled along the beach. His granddaughters, Colette and Janine, played about him picking up shells. Alexandre gave them good, fat kisses when they passed within reach of his lips. He was not unhappy any more; he accepted death. Through all his pores he absorbed the last moments of life. He was surrounded, pampered, loved. He had his children and grandchildren around him, young girls, too: Olga

Naryschikine, daughter of Nadeja, who looked like a Virgin of Perugia, came into the room when he was asleep. He heard a sound and opened his eyes. "Who is here?" he asked. "It is Olga," answered Marie who was watching over him.

"Let her come in!"

"Do you like Olga?"

"I hardly know her, but young girls bring light."

There was also Anouschka, the Russian chambermaid, who felt an infinite tenderness for this smiling, kind, and dying man who had to be helped like a child. "She finds you very beautiful," his son Alexandre told him. "Encourage her in this idea!" replied the man who had loved women too much. Reverently, his son took notes of the last words that slipped out of this body that was sinking into night. His wit was falling asleep but was not numbed. When he saw two gold "louis" on his bedside table, relics from the ten fortunes he had made and lost, he weighed them in his hand, and said, "Alexandre, everybody has said that I was prodigal; you yourself wrote a play about it. And so! Do you see how you were all mistaken? When I first landed in Paris I had two 'louis' in my pocket. Look . . . I still have them!"

France was settling into winter and into war. The Prussian troops were at the gates of Dieppe. On Monday, November twenty-eighth, in the middle of the afternoon, Alexandre asked to be put to bed. Now he was almost constantly asleep and during his rare awakenings he answered very clearly to the questions he was asked, always smiling. On Saturday, December third, he was between silence and indifference and woke up only once, to smile again. During the night between the fourth to the fifth, an apoplectic stroke was a prelude to death.

Marie had called the vicar of the parish of Saint-Jacques of Dieppe. The priest knelt at the foot of the bed with Marie and Nadeja; he recited the prayer for the dying. Then, before dispensing the last rites, he bent over Alexandre. He believed that he saw the eyelids flutter.

It was ten in the evening, the fifth of December 1870. Alexandre died without suffering. "He was the genius of life; he has not felt death," wrote George Sand.

Epilogue: The Last Judgment

The son had arranged to have his father's remains deposited temporarily in the cemetery that surrounded the small church of Neuville-les-Pollet, on December 8, 1870.

Once the war had ended, he had them carried to Villers-Cotterêts and buried in a grave dug beside Général Dumas and Marie-Louise Labouret, the parents he loved so much. A few friends came on April 16, 1872. "Less a mourning than a feast, less a burial than a resurrection," said the son. The day before the burial he had received a letter from one of his father's friends and he read it again in the carriage when he was leaving Villers-Cotterêts.

Paris, April 15, 1872

My dear colleague,

I read in the newspapers that tomorrow, April sixteenth, the funeral of Alexandre Dumas will take place at Villers-Cotterêts. I must stay with a sick child and I won't be able to go to Villers-Cotterêts. I deeply regret this.

But at least I want to be near you in my heart. I don't know whether I could have talked during this painful ceremony, as poignant emotions accumulate in my life and many graves open, one following the other before me. I would have tried to say a few words. Let me write to you what I would have liked to say. During this century, there was no more popular figure than Alexandre Dumas; his successes are better than successes, they are triumphs; they resound like a fanfare. The name of Alexandre Dumas is more than French, it is European; it is more than European, it is universal. His dramas have been played throughout the whole world; his novels have been translated into all languages. Alexandre Dumas is one of those men who can be called the sowers of civilization; he cleanses and improves the minds with some unknown, gay, and strong clarity. He fertilizes the soul, the mind, the intelligence; he creates a thirst for reading; he penetrates the human genius and sows seeds in it. What he seeds is the French idea. The French idea encompasses a quantity of humanity which produces progress wherever it penetrates. From this comes the immense popularity of men such as Alexandre Dumas. Alexandre Dumas seduces, fascinates, interests, amuses, teaches. From all his work, in such multiplicity, so varied, so vivid, so charming, so powerful, springs a kind of light which is France's very own.

All the most pathetic emotions of drama; all the ironies and all the depths of comedy, all the analysis of the novel, all the intuitions of history are in the surprising work built by this vast and agile architect. There is no darkness in this work, no mystery, no underground, no enigma, no dizziness; nothing of Dante, everything of Voltaire and of Molière; everywhere radiance, everywhere high noon, everywhere the sharpness of light. His qualities are varied and innumerable. For forty years this spirit spent itself like a prodigy. Nothing was lacking in him, neither the struggle which is duty, nor the victory which is happiness. This spirit was capable of all miracles, even to bequeath himself, even to survive himself. When he left, he had found a means to stay and you have it. Your renown continues his glory.

Your father and I, we were young together. I loved him and he loved me. Alexandre Dumas was no less tall in his heart than he was in spirit; he was a great and kind soul. I had not seen him since 1857. He had come to sit in my home of exile at Guernsey and we had set for ourselves an appointment in the future and in the fatherland, for September 1870;

the time has come; duty has changed for me; I had to return to France. Alas, the same wind blows opposite effects. As I was returning to Paris, Alexandre Dumas was just leaving it. I have not had his last handshake. Today I am not in his last cortège. But his soul sees mine. In a few days, I can probably do what I cannot do today. I will go, alone, to the field where he rests, and will return at his grave the visit he made to me in exile.

Dear colleague, son of my friend, I embrace you.

Victor Hugo.

Index